A people who know their minds
and can get real representatives to express them
are a self-governed people,
the practised masters of constitutional government.

WOODROW WILSON, 1908

W9-BHV-421

In Congress Assembled

In Congress Assembled

The Legislative Process in the National Government

by DANIEL M. BERMAN

Professor of Government and Public Administration
The American University

THE MACMILLAN COMPANY, NEW YORK
COLLIER-MACMILLAN LIMITED, LONDON

The Macmillan Company, New York
Collier-Macmillan Canada, Ltd., Toronto, Ontario

Printed in the United States of America

For Aline

Preface

Almost any institution of the American government could be analyzed in terms of the distance between the original conception behind its creation and the way in which it has actually functioned. Congress is no exception. It was established by the framers of the Constitution as the sole repository of the national legislative power, which, in turn, was to be strictly confined to a carefully delineated area. Its two chambers were to function on the basis of different principles—the Senate as a small and aristocratic assemblage of ambassadors from the states, and the House as a popular body. The Senate was expected to act as a brake on the more radical House, and both chambers together were to be counterbalanced by the Executive and Judicial Branches of the new government.

History has not dealt kindly with this plan. The President has come to play too prominent a part in the lawmaking process for anyone to contend seriously at the present time that all legislative power continues to be exercised by Congress. The specific enumeration of powers to which congressional actions were supposed to be limited is today of little more than historical interest, for development of the doctrine of implied powers has made Congress feel free to act in almost any field from which it is not specifically excluded by the Constitution. Moreover, it is not the Senate but the House that is a bulwark of conservatism; popular election of senators has helped convert the upper chamber into a body that bears little resemblance to the original conception. And the growth of organized interest groups that impinge on the governmental process at every point of decision has blurred the dividing line which was supposed to separate the Legislative and Executive Branches.

Today's Congress is thus an institution that is markedly different from the Congress of Washington's day. It is an institution that has developed values of its own, norms of conduct for its members, and rules of organization and procedure that often exercise a decisive influence on what it does. In another book, *A Bill Becomes a Law* (New York: The Macmillan Company, 1962), the author described Congress in terms of its actions on a particular item of legislation, the Civil Rights Act of 1960. The present work constitutes an effort to analyze the institution as a whole.

In studying the legislative process in the National Government, I have been aided immeasurably by my association with a number of organizations and individuals. First and foremost among the institutions is the American Political Science Association, whose Congressional Fellowship furnished an unparalleled opportunity to learn about Congress; on the expiration of the Fellowship, a period of service as a professional staff member of the Senate Subcommittee on Constitutional Rights made it possible to continue observing Congress at close range; and a subsequent appointment as academic director of the Washington Semester Program at The American University meant that the congressional process could be studied still further, in the company of challenging and stimulating students from colleges throughout the country.

Five friends participated so extensively in the preparation of the manuscript that in a sense they deserve to be acknowledged as co-authors. They are: Dr. Robert E. Goostree, professor of law and government, and Dr. Louis S. Loeb, assistant professor of government and public administration, both of The American University; Dr. Alan Rosenthal, assistant professor of political science at Hunter College; Dr. Nathan Smith, chairman of the Department of History and Political Science at Washington College; and Mr. Bernard L. Sperling, of Poughkeepsie, N. Y.

Individual chapters of the book were read by Mr. Philip S. Hughes, assistant director for legislative reference of the Bureau of the Budget, and by three of my colleagues at The American University: Professors Royce Hanson, Nathaniel S. Preston, and Richard G. Smolka. Dr. George B. Galloway, senior specialist in the Legislative Reference Service of the Library of Congress, was kind enough to comment on several chapters. Dr. Galloway's books and articles on the legislative process were of immeasurable assistance.

Gratitude is owed to three individuals who did much to facilitate the research: Mr. Samuel J. Archibald, staff director of the House Subcommittee on Foreign Operations and Government Information; Mr. Bernard Fensterwald, Jr., chief counsel of the Senate Subcommittee on Administrative Practice and Procedure; and Mr. William G. Phillips, staff director of the House Democratic Study Group. Mr. Robert K. Price and several of his fellow students at Pomona College supplied information that was of considerable value. Two editors at Macmillan, Mr. Robert J. Patterson and Mr. Joseph Falzone, were unfailingly helpful and cooperative. The assistance of Mrs. Patricia Q. Cloud and Miss Martha V. Short, is also acknowledged with thanks.

At every stage in the preparation of the manuscript, Mrs. Marylee Buchly demonstrated a combination of personal dedication and professional skill that leaves her without peer as a secretarial assistant. Dr. Edward McNall Burns provided from a distance the same kind of guidance and encouragement as when the author was his student at Rutgers University. The author's wife and his children, Stuart and Adriane, have suffered so much because of this book that they will probably feel a lifelong antipathy for Congress, for the author, or most likely for both.

One explanatory note: Although the term "congressmen" customarily refers to representatives rather than senators, it is used in this book in a broader sense, to encompass members of Congress generally.

Contents

1

Running for Congress

THE LIFE OF A CONGRESSMAN is hard. Give any senator or representative an opportunity, and he will describe in detail the hectic life he leads: the sixteen-hour day, the difficult decisions, the scramble to be in several places at once, the unrelenting pressures, the demands of constituents, and the almost constant need to campaign for re-election. No sane man, the congressman seems to be saying, would want this kind of job. Yet the congressman is sane, and the surest statement one can make about him is that he *does* want the job. Nothing, in fact, can strike such terror in his heart as the thought that some day the voters may return him to private life.

What makes a seat in the Senate or House so attractive? Why will the congressman fight tooth and nail to keep it, in spite of all the disadvantages he is so fond of describing? Why will his opponent fight just as hard to take it away from him?

There are probably almost as many explanations as there are congressional candidates. For some men, a seat in Congress is worth having because of the power that goes with it. The main inducement for others may be prestige, or the perquisites of office, or the opportunity to achieve national prominence. There might even be a completely unselfish motive: to help promote a program that one believes will serve the best interests of the country.

The motive or combination of motives had better be powerful. It will have to sustain a candidate's morale under extremely trying circumstances as he picks his way through the veritable jungle of obstacles that must be traversed if his aspiration is to be realized.

Winning the Nomination

The first problem faced by anyone with his eye on a seat in Congress is finding a way to secure his party's nomination. In a constituency where one's party has virtually no chance of winning, the nomination can often be had for the asking. Since ambitious men are understandably reluctant to go down to almost certain defeat, the nomination in such cases is more a cross to be borne than a prize to be coveted. The party is ordinarily so delighted to turn up someone who is willing to shoulder the burden that it will overlook the frequently eccentric motives impelling a man to enter a seemingly hopeless contest, and possibly volunteer to contribute something toward the costs of his campaign. It may even be willing to tolerate a professor of political science who wants to run for public office to learn something about the practical side of politics.

The situation will be very different in a constituency where the party stands a real chance of winning. The better that chance is, the fiercer the competition will be. A bitter contest, with no holds barred, can be expected if there is a lack of serious opposition (unless renomination is sought by an incumbent too firmly entrenched to be defeated).

The victor in such a contest is sometimes a party stalwart who has successfully claimed the nomination as a reward for past services. If the opposition party represents a real threat, however, faithful service alone will not weigh heavily in the scales. The party leaders will be more interested in the prospective nominee's potential for attracting support from voters able to make sizable campaign contributions and his ability to inspire a large turnout of party members on Election Day. Personality, speaking ability, a happy home life—all these will count. The factor that may mean the most, though, is the extent to which the name of the candidate is known, even before the campaign gets under way, to the voters who will be asked to support him. That is why an aspiring politician is inclined to consider nearly any publicity good publicity, short of being branded a felon. He is grateful for anything that keeps his name in the public consciousness.

Nothing serves this purpose better than to have held previous elective office. For one who is interested in a seat in the House of Representatives, almost any office will normally suffice to establish his name in the relatively small constituency—the congressional district—to which he must appeal. For a senatorial aspirant, on the other hand, a term in the House of Representatives or in a statewide office such as the governorship would be a logical stepping-stone. Service as mayor of a large city or as a member of the state legislature, too, may confer sufficient prominence.

No matter how much of a name a man has made for himself, however, the party will hardly ever yield to the temptation to give him a congressional or senatorial nomination if this means sidetracking an incumbent who is eager to serve another term. This is so partly because the individual who already occupies the office has proved himself to be a successful vote-getter. But there may be an even stronger factor at work. Chances are that the incumbent has been able to use his office as a base of operations from which to bestow favors on those from whom he will some day have to seek favors, and thus has put together at least a rudimentary political organization.

For this reason, a prudent politician will seldom challenge an incumbent in his quest for renomination. The only area in which this pattern is likely to be violated is a constituency that is completely safe for the party. The nomination in that case is such a valuable prize that a man may be unable to resist gambling against even the longest odds in order to win it.[1]

The head start that goes with incumbency is enjoyed not only by representatives and senators who have been elected to office in their own right, but also by senators appointed to fill vacancies created through death or resignation.[2] In 1962, Republican Governor Edwin L. Mechem of New Mexico showed how high a value is placed by some on even an appointive incumbency. Defeated in his bid for re-election as governor, Mechem took advantage of the situation created by the death of Democratic Senator Dennis Chavez. He promptly resigned his lame-duck governorship and was succeeded for the remaining month of his term by his lieutenant governor. Then, in accordance with a prior understanding, the new governor-for-a-month appointed Mechem to the Senate for the remaining two years of Chavez's term. In a similar development a few months later, the retiring Democratic governor of Oklahoma, J. Howard Edmondson, had himself appointed to the seat left vacant by the death of Senator Robert S. Kerr. Both

[1] See V. O. Key, Jr., *Politics, Parties, and Pressure Groups* (4th ed.; New York: Thomas Y. Crowell, 1958), pp. 483-84.

[2] It is only in the Senate that a vacancy may be filled through a gubernatorial appointment, and then not unless the state legislature has conferred such power on the governor. If it has, the appointee may serve until the next general election. At that time, the voters will choose a senator to serve out the unexpired term of the member whose seat has been left vacant. The situation is completely different when a vacancy arises in the House. The governor has the choice of either calling a special election or allowing the seat to remain vacant until the expiration of the two-year term. George B. Galloway, *The Legislative Process in Congress* (New York: Thomas Y. Crowell, 1959), p. 356.

Mechem and Edmondson hoped that two years in the Senate would make it easier for them to win election on their own in 1964.

Even though incumbency is a great advantage, it frequently happens that a House member is willing to give it up in order to become a candidate for the Senate. The prospect of serving in that chamber is alluring, for a senator is one man in a group of only 100, while the representative has all of 434 colleagues to compete with for prizes such as public attention, a role in debate, or a committee chairmanship. In addition, only a senator has a large staff—and a six-year term as well.

If adequate exposure in the constituency is almost always a *practical* prerequisite for obtaining a congressional or senatorial nomination, there are also some *formal* requirements for candidacy that must be satisfied. The Constitution[3] ordains that a representative must be at least twenty-five years old and a senator no younger than thirty.[4] The qualification regarding citizenship is also more stringent for the senator: he must have been a citizen of the United States for nine years, while only seven years suffice for members of the House.

In one respect, the constitutional requirement for membership in the two chambers is identical: both representatives and senators must be residents of the states that elect them. A representative need not live in his particular congressional district; residence anywhere in the state is sufficient. In actual practice, however, it is extremely rare for either the Demo-

[3] Article I, Sections 2 and 3.

[4] Congressmen, and more particularly senators, are almost always well above the minimum, but there have been exceptions. Edward M. Kennedy, a brother of the late President, was elected to the Senate at the age of exactly thirty. And in 1806 the Senate completely ignored the constitutional provision regarding the age of members and seated Henry Clay, although he had not yet reached his thirtieth birthday.

crats or Republicans to nominate for a House seat anyone who lives outside the boundaries of the district he wishes to represent. The underlying theory seems to be that a member of the House cannot know his district well enough to represent its interests unless he makes his home in it. There is, however, an argument on the other side: If several highly qualified members of the same political party live in a given district, the congressional ambitions of all but one must be frustrated, and the party (as well as the country) deprived of the services all the rest. Relatedly, it sometimes happens that in a particular constituency it is necessary for a party to scrape the bottom of the barrel to produce a candidate.

The rather strict residence requirement that tradition and the Constitution conspire to impose is in sharp contrast to the British practice. In England, where localism and sectionalism are nowhere nearly as strong as in the United States, there is no residence requirement whatever. The national party organization finds this to be an excellent arrangement, because it permits "safe" constituencies to be reserved for parliamentary leaders whose defeat would be calamitous to the party. By contrast, there have been cases in this country where even a Majority Leader of the Senate has lost his seat—and, of course, his position as Leader—merely because the voters in his home state became dissatisfied with him.[5]

[5] More than half a century ago, James Bryce sharply criticized the American practice. It leads to the election of inferior men, he said, for some parts of the country simply "do not grow statesmen." He also thought he perceived a connection between the residence requirement and the reluctance of many highly competent men to enter congressional politics. "A promising politician," he said, "may lose his seat in his own district through some fluctuation of opinion, or perhaps because he has offended the local wire-pullers by too much independence. Since he cannot find a seat elsewhere, he is stranded; his political life is closed, while other young men inclined to independence take warning from his fate." James Bryce, The American Commonwealth (New York: Macmillan, 1910), Vol. I, p. 195.

The decision as to who will receive a senatorial or congressional nomination may be made by either one of two methods: the direct primary election or the party convention. Primaries are used far more widely than conventions. From the point of view of an incumbent, however, the convention method is preferable. To assure himself of renomination under that system, he usually does not have to do anything more than maintain good relations with the party leaders. If, on the other hand, primaries are used, the man in office knows that at almost any time a fickle public may turn back his renomination bid. Party leaders, too, prefer conventions, for these can be controlled more readily than primaries.

Weakness of National Party

From the point of view of the national party, there is little difference between conventions and primaries. Whichever method is used, the party can expect to have little say in choosing candidates for the House or the Senate. Of course, in certain instances it may have such close ties with the local political leadership that it will be able to exert some influence on the selection of candidates, or well in advance of the campaign it might try to persuade a popular figure to offer himself as a candidate in a race that otherwise would almost certainly be lost. In the vast majority of cases, however, the national party will simply play no part in the nomination process.

Even a President seldom has anything to do with selecting candidates, although they may be planning to ride to victory on his coattails in the general election. When a President does involve himself, it is usually in behalf of a relative or a member of his official family. Otherwise, those trying to influence primary results have often burned their fingers in the process. Franklin D. Roosevelt was the most notable example. In 1938, he decided to play an active role in the

Democratic primary elections in order to purge congressmen blocking the New Deal program and assist those promoting it. In senatorial primary contests, for example, he endorsed the renomination of three Democratic incumbents and opposed the renomination of three others. But his efforts seem to have been counter-productive, if indeed they had any effect at all. Of the three senators he supported, one was defeated in the primary, and while the other two won their races it was generally agreed that the results would have been the same even if the President had not actively supported them. Far worse, all three senators whom Roosevelt opposed were renominated anyway. The President did succeed in purging a single member of the House, but he accomplished this only by abandoning the tactic of appealing publicly to the Democratic electorate and relying instead on a local Democratic boss to eliminate the undesirable congressman.[6] President Truman once managed to engineer the defeat of a Democratic representative, but the district involved was Mr. Truman's own. Presidents Eisenhower and Kennedy wisely, if modestly, proceeded on the assumption that what Roosevelt and Truman could accomplish only with great difficulty and in exceptional circumstances, they should not even attempt, except perhaps in subtle or covert ways.

Just as the national party will hardly ever involve itself in primary contests, it may be obliged to take a back seat in general elections as well. This is particularly true in "off-year" campaigns. In the absence of a presidential contest to bring to the fore at least some issues of national consequence, midterm congressional elections often turn largely on questions of strictly local significance. To the extent that voters are influenced by national considerations at all, they seem prone to punish candidates of the President's party, evidently

[6] Austin Ranney and Willmoore Kendall, *Democracy and the American Party System* (New York: Harcourt, 1956), pp. 287-89.

because of a generalized dissatisfaction with the state of the world and with the failure of the President to fulfill his campaign promises. Thus on only three occasions since 1874 has the party of the President gained congressional seats in an off-year.[7]

Although a midterm election is often a very serious problem for the President, the situation in an "on-year" election is generally somewhat different. With control of the White House at stake, there is a strong possibility that the victorious presidential candidate will find his party has also captured control of both houses of Congress. This phenomenon is sometimes referred to as the "coattail effect." What is meant is that congressional candidates are often swept into office merely because they run on the same party ticket as a popular presidential candidate.

It is by no means true, however, that a causal relationship always exists between the victory of a presidential candidate and that of his party's congressional candidates. Quite the reverse, when the triumph of a presidential nominee stems from his own personal popularity rather than from widespread public acceptance of his program, his party may well be unable to win control of Congress, coattails or no coattails. It happened just that way in 1956, when the voters enthusiastically picked Mr. Eisenhower, while at the same time turning thumbs-down on his party's congressional candidates.[8] Nor did the "coattail effect" operate in the next presidential

[7] President Woodrow Wilson stumbled badly in 1918 when he decided to intervene in the congressional elections despite the "hex." His efforts evidently served only to stimulate keen resentment. The Democrats were handed a crushing defeat, losing their majority in both chambers of Congress as the Republicans picked up 26 seats in the House and 6 in the Senate. See Tom Wicker, "Kennedy, Too, Hits the Campaign Trail," *The New York Times Magazine* (October 14, 1962), p. 24.

[8] The Democrats won a 33-seat majority in the House and a 2-seat margin in the Senate.

election, when a large number again split their tickets. Some who were influenced to vote for or against Mr. Kennedy because he was a Catholic, for example, did not permit that decision to affect the preferences they expressed in congressional contests, as the "coattail" analysts might have expected.[9]

Even when the party that has captured the White House also wins control of Congress, the President may discover that his troubles are only beginning. The reason is that not every representative or senator who wears the same party label as the President is willing to support the program of the President. Mr. Eisenhower, for example, learned during his eight years in the White House that a significant number of his fellow Republicans in Congress found his program too liberal for their liking. This type of problem is even more acute for a Democratic President, since the southerners in his party are almost always in basic disagreement with essential portions of his legislative program.

A Sense of Obligation

One reason for the existence of such situations is that the typical congressman feels little sense of obligation to his national party. The party has not, after all, been responsible for his victory at the polls. Moreover, as long as he retains the allegiance of his local constituency, the party cannot harm him seriously; often it can do nothing more effective than wail and gnash its teeth even if he chooses to oppose every element of its program. As a matter of fact, slavish adherence

[9] "[The] popular vote for lesser offices is a more party-determined vote than the vote for President." Philip E. Converse, Angus Campbell, Warren E. Miller, Donald E. Stokes, "Stability and Change in 1960: A Reinstating Election," *American Political Science Review*, LV (June 1961), p. 280. See also Malcolm Moos, *Politics, Presidents and Coattails* (Baltimore: Johns Hopkins Press, 1952).

to a party line, far from being a prescription for success at the polls, is often resented by constituents. Many people seem to prefer that their representative be an "independent" rather than a participant in "machine politics."[10]

In spite of these factors, President Kennedy decided in 1962 to make an effort to inculcate more of a sense of party loyalty in the Democratic members of Congress. During the formulation of his personal plans for the campaign, he adopted what his staff called a "strategy of concentration." This strategy sought to prevent the squandering of campaign resources in congressional districts where the triumphs of Democrats might be anything but triumphs for the Democratic Administration. There was to be no purge of party recalcitrants. The idea instead was to concentrate the resources that the President commanded—particularly his personal appearances—in congressional districts where they could be expected to enhance the prospects of his program.[11]

The results of the Kennedy experiment were awaited with keen interest. It was hoped that they might reveal whether the President could increase party unity through positive action designed to assist his friends, in place of the negative action that Mr. Roosevelt had resorted to in 1938, when he attempted to punish his enemies. The Kennedy experiment was later abandoned, however, because of the pre-election

[10] The appeal of the maverick is so great in certain states that it may be possible to build one's political career on a reputation for kicking over the traces. The electoral success of Wayne Morse (D., Ore.) and William Proxmire (D., Wis.) derives in no small measure from the reputations that the two senators enjoy as courageous individuals who refuse to bow to the dictates of party bosses. What seems to be reckless courage in attacking the congressional party leadership produces comfortable electoral dividends fairly reliably.

[11] Alan Rosenthal, "The Presidency and the Mid-term Congressional Campaign," paper presented at seminar of National Center for Education in Politics, Washington, September, 1962.

crisis over Cuba. Mr. Kennedy decided that it was desirable to refrain from further participation in a domestic political campaign at a time when people were looking to him more as President and Commander-in-Chief of the armed services than as the leader of the Democratic party. The question of whether a President can impose a form of party discipline through selective campaigning thus remains unanswered.

Advantages of an Incumbent

With or without the President's help, a congressional candidate's campaign for election is a grueling physical and mental ordeal. The incumbent who is running for re-election, however, can take solace from the fact that his opponent will have a much harder time of it than he will, for there are a number of highly significant advantages enjoyed by the man in office. These advantages are so great that one unsuccessful challenger declared flatly: "Elections are rigged in favor of the man who is already in."[12]

To begin with, a great deal of an incumbent's campaigning can be carried on at public expense. No one has yet devised a method of preventing a congressman from using the prerogatives of his office to further his personal political career, without at the same time impeding him in the performance of his public duties.

For example, Congress has by statute authorized its members to send letters and other communications through the mails without charge. The ostensible purpose behind the franking privilege is to make it possible for congressmen to carry on their official correspondence without worrying about

[12] James A. Michener, "What Every New Candidate Should Know," *The New York Times Magazine* (September 23, 1962), p. 23. The author of *Tales of the South Pacific* ran for Congress as a Democrat in a safe Republican constituency in Pennsylvania.

a fixed stamp allotment. It would, of course, be impossible to quarrel with the objective. The difficulty is that it is often hard to distinguish between the occasions when a congressman-candidate pursues the objectives of a congressman and the occasions when he pursues the objectives of a candidate.

Since the statute does forbid use of the frank to disseminate campaign material, a congressman who is running for re-election is certainly not free to circulate at the taxpayers' expense an outright appeal for votes. As long as he is careful not to mail out anything so blatant as that, however, he need hardly be inconvenienced, for there are many ways to circumvent the spirit of the law. One popular practice is to send a "report" to constituents to inform them of what the congressman has been doing and how he stands on the issues of the day. In producing such a "report," the member is relieved of a large part of the printing expense as well as the entire cost of mailing. The procedure is perfectly simple. To get a quasi-campaign item printed with what amounts to a public subsidy, he will merely ask that it be published in the daily *Congressional Record*. After it appears, he is entitled to order any number of reprints, and he has to pay only the costs of running them off. Because the public has already borne the heaviest expenses—those of type-setting and composition—the amount for which he will be billed is negligible. Even that relatively picayune expense, however, is often defrayed by a pressure group with an interest in circulating the material.

Congress does not keep a record of the total number of "reports" that are printed and mailed in any session. In a typical year, however, about 90 million pieces of mail go out in franked envelopes, and a periodical[13] that said "most" of these items are thinly veiled campaign documents was prob-

[13] *Progressive* (September 1962), p. 5.

ably not overstating the case. Moreover, a positive correlation exists between the number of "reports" that appear in the *Congressional Record* on a given day and the closeness of that day to the next general election.[14]

Since it is obvious that incumbent members benefit greatly in their campaigns from access to the frank, the suggestion has been made that the mailing costs of their opponents should be subsidized as well.[15] This proposal has never been given serious consideration. But even in the unlikely event that it should someday be adopted, the incumbent would still be ensconced firmly in the driver's seat as he campaigned for re-election.

For instance, he could continue to call on the members of his congressional staff for campaign assistance. During the months preceding an election, it is not uncommon for an incumbent to leave behind only a skeleton force in his congressional office to take care of routine matters, and transfer the bulk of his staff to his constituency. There its members write speeches, arrange meetings, issue press releases, and help put together a campaign organization, while the challenger and his backers have to pay in cold cash for all such services.

Staff members who join their principal on the field of battle are usually highly skilled persons. A senator's staff, for example, includes an administrative assistant, whose annual salary of approximately $18,000 is not very much lower than the senator's own ($22,500). That kind of money can normally attract a person who possesses unusual talent in the political

---

[14] It appears that "reports" in the *Congressional Record* are employed to affect the outcome of intraparty contests as well as general elections. One writer has found that they appear "with profusion . . . as the primaries approach." Key, *op. cit.*, p. 493, note 19.

[15] *Ibid.*, p. 549, note 25.

arts.[16] Serving under the assistant on most staffs is another professional who is an expert on legislative issues. There may also be a speech writer and a press relations man, not to mention stenographers and typists. In addition, a senior congressman has access to the services of the staff attached to any committee or subcommittee of which he is chairman.

The use of congressional aides in political campaigns gives a hollow ring to the claim that senators and representatives need larger and more highly paid staffs if they are to perform their legislative duties effectively. When congressmen are given authorization to hire additional staff members, they often look for individuals with political skills rather than technical skills. The result is that the personal ambitions of members are more effectively advanced than the legislative purposes of Congress. Even in years when no election campaign is on the horizon, a member may keep as many as half of his staff members in the constituency rather than in Washington, in order to build his political strength.[17]

Patronage and Other Bonuses

The congressman is often able to make and keep friends back home through the use of still another prerogative that is unavailable to his rival: distributing patronage jobs to his

[16] In the forefront of those who extol the virtues of the administrative assistants are the administrative assistants themselves. There is not much exaggeration in the claim that their idea of how to compliment a senator of unusual ability is to venture the opinion that he is almost good enough to be an administrative assistant.

[17] Staff employees who perform this function do their work customarily in an office that is provided without charge in a Federal building (usually a post office) in the congressman's constituency. In this office, which the member will use when he is back home, the staff will render a wide variety of services to prospective voters, trying in every way to make people feel that they have a congressman who is concerned with their needs and desires.

constituents. Not every member is in the enviable position of controlling patronage appointments. Few if any patronage rights, for example, belong to congressmen whose party is in a minority in their chamber, particularly if the party has failed to capture the presidency as well. By contrast, the member whose party has won the presidency and also holds a majority in his house of Congress is doubly blessed. The congressional party places a number of patronage positions at his disposal, and the White House will give the most serious consideration to his recommendations regarding Federal appointments in his constituency.

Of these two categories of patronage jobs, those whose distribution is controlled by the President are by far the more significant for members of the House and Senate. In the case of the House, the President will ordinarily defer to the wishes of a representative regarding nominations to postmasterships in his district, and where the Senate is concerned the prizes are even more valuable. A senator can be fairly certain that no major Federal job will go to anyone in his state whom he does not favor. More than that, he can almost always count on the fact that he will be invited to make a recommendation as each vacancy arises, and that his selection will hardly ever fail to win presidential approval.[18]

The other jobs that a congressman may distribute belong to him by virtue of the fact that his party has a majority in the house where he sits, regardless of whether it controls the White House. These are jobs in the Capitol itself, encompassing comparatively minor and unskilled positions such as those of elevator operator, doorkeeper, and member of the Capitol police force. They include also work in offices such as those of the Sergeant-at-Arms and the Secretary of the

[18] The closely related subject of "senatorial courtesy" is discussed in Ch. 13.

Senate, as well as assignments in the Capitol post offices, warehouses, telegraph offices, and folding rooms. Perhaps the quaintest jobs in this category are those of the congressional pages, whose function is to run errands for senators and representatives while they are in attendance on the floor.[19] Pages may be too young to vote or help out in a campaign, but their parents do not suffer from this disability, and for some of them the selection of a son as a congressional page is almost as highly valued as a nomination to Annapolis or West Point (which congressmen also control).

The majority party in each house has a special committee in charge of allocating patronage to individual congressmen. A senator can usually count on being given several positions to fill. In the House, the patronage committee of the majority party is supposed to divide up the available jobs among the state "delegations" in proportion to the number of seats the party has won in the various states, and within each state delegation the jobs are ostensibly distributed on the basis of seniority. But in practice the patronage committee—and especially its chairman—exercises a high degree of discretion. To be chairman of the patronage committee, therefore, is to be endowed with considerable power. A number of liberal Democrats in the House are frank enough to admit that for years they refrained from speaking out or voting against the House Committee on Un-American Activities partly because

[19] The pages are teen-age boys. Attired somberly during their working hours in blue suits, white shirts, black ties, black socks, and black shoes, they sit at the rear of the House and near the steps of the Senate rostrum, awaiting their assignments. Although their work is not arduous and provides nonmonetary rewards of a substantial sort, there is pecuniary compensation as well: the monthly pay is almost $400. Pages think this pay is grossly inadequate, however, and they may have a point. In order to complete their classes in a special page school before Congress convenes at noon, they are compelled to rise at 5:30 each morning.

its chairman, the late Congressman Francis E. Walter, was also chairman of the House Democratic Committee on Patronage.[20]

Some congressmen insist, with apparent sincerity, that they would like to see an end to the patronage system. As far back as 1926, one representative said that members should not be "burdened by office-seekers."[21] The late Senator Estes Kefauver (D., Tenn.) elaborated on this theme in more recent years. He considered patronage a detriment and a burden, for this reason:

> Handling patronage requires much time, always involves personalities, and inevitably leads to unpleasantness. The political support gained by dispensing positions on Capitol Hill is more than offset by the antagonism of the much larger number who apply and have to be turned down.[22]

Others, too, assert that "every patronage appointment results in one ingrate and ten enemies."[23] Yet a majority in both the House and Senate seem to believe that on balance the system does them more good than harm. It gives incumbents, after all, a head start with the voters, and for that a congressman is willing to put up with the king-sized headaches that the system sometimes inflicts.

The judicious use of patronage serves to endear an officeholder to a small, though sometimes highly significant, segment of his electorate. When the congressman who is a

[20] Walter was also chairman of the House Judiciary Subcommittee on Immigration, which screens the private immigration bills so important to individual congressmen.

[21] Robert Luce, *Congress: An Explanation* (Cambridge, Mass.: Harvard University Press, 1926), p. 90.

[22] Estes Kefauver and Jack Levin, *A 20th-Century Congress* (New York: Duell, 1947), p. 201.

[23] Joseph P. Harris, *The Advice and Consent of the Senate* (Berkeley: University of California Press, 1953), p. 393.

prospective candidate for re-election turns to the problem of how to appeal to his entire constituency, he has reason once again to appreciate his status as an incumbent. Right up to the moment when he officially declares his candidacy, radio and television stations back home will be happy to carry his weekly or bi-weekly "report to the people" without charge, on the theory that it is a public service to facilitate communications between a congressman and his constituents.[24] And the congressman does not have to worry about how to pay for the filming or taping of such a broadcast report, either, for Government-owned studios in the basement of the Capitol make their facilities available at bargain prices. The member may make use of these studios to produce regularly scheduled programs or for nothing more elaborate than brief film clips intended for use in television newscasts. Either way, he obtains on a subsidy basis a service for which his opponent must pay the full price. After the official campaign gets under way, this arrangement must come to an end. But the incumbent knows, and his opponent knows even better, that a congressman's campaign for re-election really begins on the very first day he takes office.

Private Bills

As if the incumbent did not already have a sufficient number of advantages, there are still other factors operating in his favor. One of these is the power he enjoys as a member of Congress to introduce private bills and thus win the gratitude of those who would be the beneficiaries of such legislation. Private bills are legislative measures providing relief for a

[24] If a station granted such free time during a campaign, it would obligate itself (under Section 315 of the Federal Communications Act) to make available "equal time" to all other candidates for the office, no matter how numerous they might be.

single individual or a small group. They are of a completely different order of magnitude than public bills, which may—such as in the case of income-tax legislation—affect virtually every family in the United States, or deal with vast groupings of individuals, such as workers, veterans, or women.

The largest number of private bills deal with immigration matters. Some of these constitute efforts to stave off the deportation of relatives or friends, while others are designed to authorize the immigration of such individuals. Both types of bills are reactions to the exceedingly restrictive provisions of the McCarran-Walter Act. That law, while facilitating deportations *from* the United States, made it all but impossible to bring individuals permanently *to* the United States from certain countries. It had this effect because it confirmed the "national origins" quota system, which particularly discriminates against individuals from the countries of Asia and southern and eastern Europe.[25] Were such individuals content to await their turn as regular quota immigrants, their turn would never come. As a consequence, their relatives in the United States often try to promote the enactment of private legislation to avoid the restrictions that otherwise stand in the way of permanent status.

Another broad category of private bills consists of claims against the Federal Government. Before 1946, the volume of this type of private legislation was even heavier than it is today. A pedestrian who was injured by a mail truck, or a sight-seer who fell and hurt himself in a Government building, had no right to sue the Government. Understandably, therefore, individuals in such predicaments lobbied for the passage

---

[25] Most of the countries that are given generous quotas have two traits in common: they enjoy such high standards of living and such stable political systems that few of their inhabitants have any desire to emigrate; and their people are predominantly of northern European stock.

of private bills. Appalled by the waste of legislative time that consideration of these relatively trivial measures entailed, a Joint Committee on the Organization of Congress recommended reform. Congress responded to the recommendation by passing the Tort Claims Act of 1946, allowing court suits to be brought in many kinds of cases that could previously be handled only through private legislation. The new law exempted several classes of cases from its provisions, however, and these exceptions have meant that a considerable number of claims bills must still be processed every year through the cumbersome machinery of Congress.

Members of the House get most of the requests to introduce private bills, since they are more accessible than senators. But far from considering this burden an onerous chore, most of them relish it as still another golden chance to earn the gratitude of their constituents.

The incumbent congressman is not without other such glittering opportunities. He can also attempt to keep constituents on his side by endeavoring to procure Federal funds for local purposes. And, too, he can curry favor with the voters by performing the "messenger boy" services that constituents seem to expect from their congressman: help in obtaining tickets to the Army-Navy game, information about whether a youth can be deferred from the draft, a phone call to procure reservations in a Washington hotel, or a place in the daily "special" White House tour for guests of congressmen.[26] In addition to all this, the incumbent can argue that the voters should return him to office because the constituency is better off with a congressman who is able to exercise some influence than if it were represented by a mere freshman. The

[26] A proposal to do away with this congressional tour provoked such roars of protest on Capitol Hill that it was hastily dropped at the order of President Kennedy.

voter, who cannot know when he may need the help of an influential congressman, may be willing to disregard the issues on which he differs with the incumbent and vote for him simply because, as one senator expressed it, he "has so much seniority on deposit in [congressional] vaults."[27]

The advantages which incumbency bestows are so great that it is difficult to exaggerate their importance. One congressional campaign strategist has estimated that incumbency is worth between 4 and 6 per cent of the total vote cast[28]—more than enough to make the difference between victory and defeat in many congressional contests. Still, it is a mistake to assume that the challenger does not stand a chance. In point of fact, virtually every election offers at least a few examples of incumbents, frequently with many years of service behind them, who are turned out by the voters for one reason or another.[29] The reason may be that the economic or ethnic composition of the constituency has changed, or that the congressman has failed to perform the personal services for people back home that voters seem to demand. It may be that the state legislature has established a new and carefully gerrymandered district. Or the congressman may simply have failed to discuss the issues that most concerned the voters—usually because he had lost touch with them.

The task of learning what constituents are really interested in is not a simple matter. To find out what voters think,

[27] Richard L. Neuberger, "A Senator's Case against Seniority," *The New York Times Magazine* (April 7, 1957), p. 15.

[28] Interview with Kenneth Harding, director, Democratic Congressional Campaign Committee, October 26, 1962.

[29] In the 1962 election, the casualties included three Republicans with considerable seniority: Alexander Wiley of Wisconsin, who had been in the Senate for 24 years; Homer E. Capehart of Indiana, who was completing 18 years of service in the Senate; and Walter H. Judd of Minnesota, who had occupied a seat in the House for 20 years.

candidates are turning increasingly to public opinion polls. In almost every state where there was a serious senatorial contest in 1962, at least one private poll was taken. Such polls, however, are extremely expensive to conduct. The cost in the average state exceeds $10,000. In a state the size of New York, it may be as much as $34,000.[30] That kind of money will buy a multistage poll that will enable a candidate to learn, at various points in the campaign, whether he is discussing the right issues in the right places, and whether his position on them is winning him support.

Although it is just as important for prospective members of the House to know their districts as it is for senatorial aspirants to know their states, it is frequently possible—except in a very large congressional district—for a sensitive politician to develop such a "feel" for what people are thinking that a professional poll would serve no useful purpose. For this reason, and for financial reasons as well, no more than one out of ten candidates for the House seem to have made use of polls in 1962.[31]

Sometimes an incumbent congressman will use his frank to poll his constituents regarding their opinions on subjects before Congress. Newspapers will occasionally cooperate by reprinting the questionnaires as a public service.[32] Such informal polls, conducted by the legislator himself, are designed primarily for publicity purposes: to keep the congressman's name before the voters. Because they are often worded so as to elicit predetermined responses ("Do you think we should continue to pour foreign aid money down the drain in countries that will surely go Communist anyway?"), their reliability as an index to community thinking is questionable at

[30] *The New York Times* (July 22, 1962), p. 45, col. 3 (city ed.).
[31] *Ibid.*, p. 28, col. 2.
[32] *Congressional Record* (June 4, 1962), p. A-4033 (daily ed.).

best. What they accomplish principally is to flatter the electorate by convincing voters that the congressman values their opinions. This kind of tactic seems to be an inevitable adjunct of electoral politics. Every effort is made by a campaigner to convince the voter that his opinions count and that he, as an individual, counts too.[33]

Even if campaigns are permeated with much amiable hypocrisy, however, they are by no means entirely lacking in value. The campaign that does little to educate the voter often does much to educate the candidate. There is no way to learn more about "the people"—their interests, their opinions, their prejudices—than by taking to the hustings.

[33] When a constituent asks his campaigning congressman, "You don't remember me, do you, Jim?" he usually gets an answer something like this: "Of course I do. I remember you very well." One student has written jocularly that many a congressman dreams of a retirement in which, when a constituent comes up to him and says, "You don't remember me, do you, Congressman?" he will be free to reply, "No, I don't, you son-of-a-bitch, and I don't give a damn either!" Donald R. Matthews, *U.S. Senators and Their World* (Chapel Hill: University of North Carolina Press, 1960), p. 69, note 1.

2

Campaign Costs and Voting Problems

THE COSTS OF CONDUCTING A CONGRESSIONAL CAMPAIGN are very high. As far back as 1952, Senator Paul Douglas (D., Ill.) estimated that a candidate had to be prepared to spend between $150,000 and $200,000 to make a serious race for the Senate in a populous state.[1] More recently, a colleague of Douglas, Frank Church (D., Ida.), told of Senate campaigns in which upward of a million dollars was spent by each side.[2]

One of the major items responsible for inflating campaign costs to such an incredible extent is the central role now played by television and radio. The total salary paid to a senator during his full six-year term may not be sufficient to cover the costs of the television time he will have to buy for a campaign in a large metropolitan state. Although a candidate for the House does not ordinarily have to reach a state-

[1] Austin Ranney and Willmoore Kendall, *Democracy and the American Party System* (New York: Harcourt, 1956), p. 365.

[2] Frank Church, "Campaign Money—How Much? From Whom?" *The New York Times Magazine* (August 26, 1962), p. 65.

wide audience, he, too, must sometimes reconcile himself to campaign costs exceeding by far the salary he will receive for his term.[3]

The new importance of television is not the only factor tending to make campaigns more expensive with every passing year. The steady increase in population is another cause. As the country's population grows, the costs of campaigning grow along with it, for the number of people in the average congressional district or state never stops increasing. In each new election there are more and more voters to be reached through newspaper advertisements, posters, and direct mailings, not to mention television and radio.[4] Many candidates are certain that much of what they spend has little effect on the outcome of the election. This realization, however, seldom results in any agonizing reappraisal of campaign budgets. James A. Farley, former chairman of the Democratic National Committee, once explained why this is so. "I know that half of what is spent is wasted," he said. "The only trouble is, I don't know which half."[5]

With expenses of campaigning continuing to skyrocket, the only factor that has tended even slightly in the opposite direction has been the relative brevity of recent campaigns. In the past, Congress was seldom in session after July 4, leaving four full months for unofficial and official campaigning. Of late, however, congressional sessions have grown steadily longer,

[3] William G. Phillips, "Congress: A Study in Political Realities," *American Federationist* (February, 1961), reprinted in *Congressional Record* (February 24, 1961), p. A-1214 (daily ed.).

[4] V. O. Key, Jr., *Politics, Parties, and Pressure Groups* (4th ed.; New York: Thomas Y. Crowell, 1958), pp. 538-40.

[5] Philip M. Stern, "The Money in Politics," *Progressive* (July 1962), p. 15. In 1960, more than $175 million was spent in all campaigns, including the presidential.

and campaigning time has been somewhat shortened.[6] The second session of the Eighty-seventh Congress, for example, did not end until October 13, 1962. For incumbents who remained in Washington until the bitter end, that left less than four weeks for the midterm congressional campaign. Still, the rising costs of reaching voters have been eating up the money saved as a result of shorter campaigns.

Who Gives?

There is general agreement that only a small proportion of the voters help to finance political campaigns.[7] All efforts to involve the rank and file have been unavailing; neither door-to-door solicitations nor return-mail appeals have met with very much success.[8] Most congressional candidates must therefore continue to depend for financial support on special interest groups and well-heeled individuals.

Some large contributions, of course, are the result of nothing more sinister than personal friendship, or the belief that a certain candidate shares the contributor's general viewpoint. But many are clearly intended to give the contributor access to the congressman, or to create a favorable atmosphere in which the two may discuss legislative matters.

The laws against bribery leave this area untouched. The late Senator Richard L. Neuberger (D., Ore.) could never understand why this should be so. He explained:

> If [my wife] Maurine or I ever would take $100 in cash behind the locked door of a hotel room to cast our vote for or against a specific legislative bill, we would be guilty of receiving a bribe.

[6] Doubtless one cause of the longer sessions is that Congress must deal with a legislative program that is becoming more voluminous and more complex every year, without an overhaul of its ancient machinery.

[7] David B. Truman, *The Governmental Process* (New York: Knopf, 1960), p. 308.

[8] Church, *op. cit.*, p. 16.

. . . but if, at the next election, we accept not $100 in cash but $1,000 in a check from the same donor, it is all perfectly legal, providing the check is made out to the Neuberger-for-Election Committee.[9]

Neuberger referred to the kind of situation he was describing as a "twilight zone" between bribery and legitimate campaign contributions.[10] The danger, of course, is that if a gift is large enough a congressman will hesitate to say no when the donor later seeks support for legislation to benefit the selfish interest he represents. Courage bordering on foolhardiness will be required to turn him away.

Some congressmen who do not possess such courage are nonetheless unhappy with the existing situation, for they do not relish bartering their independence for campaign contributions. They would be far more pleased if contributions came from a broad and representative segment of the electorate, for that way their fate would never be in the hands of a single man or group. In the absence of such an idyllic arrangement, however, even congressmen of conscience bow to what they look upon as cruel necessity.

Because of the widespread realization that large campaign contributions may introduce a serious element of corruption into the political system, legislation has been enacted to eliminate some of the grossest abuses. The law attempts to minimize the influence of money on politics by regulating both contributions and expenditures. It deals with contributions by placing a ceiling on the amount that any individual or group may give to a campaign fund, while at the same time outlawing contributions of any size from certain sources. And it makes an effort to regulate expenditures by prohibit-

[9] *Ibid.*, p. 67.
[10] Donald R. Matthews, *U.S. Senators and Their World* (Chapel Hill: University of North Carolina Press, 1960), pp. 72-73.

ing candidates from disbursing more than certain amounts. Factors exist, however, which prevent the regulation of either contributions or expenditures from being effective.

Ceilings on Contributions

Contributions were the subject of legislation adopted in 1940, in the form of amendments to the Hatch Act of the preceding year. Under the terms of the new legislation, which is still in effect, no individual may contribute more than $5,000 in any single year, either to a candidate running for election to a Federal office or to any committee campaigning for him.[11] The law, however, fairly cries out for circumvention. It does nothing, for example, to discourage a man of means from contributing the statutory maximum to each of several committees campaigning for the same congressional candidate. What is more, it permits every member of a family to contribute up to the legal ceiling. This has enabled families like the du Ponts and Rockefellers, which are no more bereft of issue than they are of funds, to make contributions in the hundreds of thousands of dollars.[12] To render the legal restrictions still more meaningless, the door is left open for an affluent individual to help shape the outcome of congressional elections throughout the country by contributing as much as $5,000 in every congressional district and state where there is a candidate he favors.

But apart from imposing a ceiling on individual contributions, the law also bars any contributions whatsoever from certain sources. Ever since 1907, it has been illegal for corporations to donate money in connection with Federal elec-

[11] Some states have imposed even more stringent restrictions of their own on congressional candidates. In Montana, for example, a senatorial candidate's expenditures are limited to $2250.

[12] Key, *op. cit.*, p. 562, note 49.

tions. Much the same prohibition was later extended to labor unions. The theory is that no one can claim to speak politically for all the stockholders of a corporation or all the members of a union.

Both corporations and unions have found it easy to circumvent the law. A corporation will place campaign workers on its payroll, or permit long-distance telephone charges and the expenses of television production to be billed to its account. It may lend a company plane to a candidate,[13] or print campaign literature for him. It does not even violate the law if it conducts a propaganda campaign to influence an election or if it assigns corporation personnel to campaign duty.[14]

Unions, too, have contrived to play an important part in elections while remaining in technical compliance with the law. Toward this end, for example, the Committee on Political Education (COPE) was created by the American Federation of Labor-Congress of Industrial Organizations.[15] For although the law prohibits a union from using its members' dues to make political contributions, it does not apply to an organization that depends on voluntary donations from union members. Despite the difficulty of building a sizable campaign war chest by soliciting individual contributions, COPE has been remarkably successful in keeping alive the influence of organized labor on congressional elections. Nor have the unions themselves had to remain entirely aloof from election campaigns, for a 1948 decision of the United States Supreme Court held that the law is not violated when a labor organization spends money to publish and distribute issues of a union

[13] Stern, *op. cit.*, p. 16.

[14] Key, *op. cit.*, p. 556.

[15] Prior to the formation of the merged labor federation, the AFL and CIO each maintained a campaign organization of its own.

newspaper containing endorsements of congressional candidates.[16] This ruling stimulated the extensive use of the labor press in campaigns. Unions are also free to publish and distribute the voting records of congressmen, and to conduct voter registration drives.[17]

Ceilings on Expenditures

Just as the legal restrictions on campaign *contributions* are filled with loopholes, statutory controls of campaign *expenditures* have also proved far from effective. It was in the Corrupt Practices Act of 1925 that Congress tried to impose limits on the amount of money a congressional candidate could spend. Whether his constituency was large or small, the candidate for a House seat could use no more than $5,000, and the expenditures of a senatorial candidate could not exceed $25,000, even in the most populous states. These ceilings are so much lower than the amounts candidates feel they must spend that they have been almost totally disregarded in practice.

As if cognizant of the unrealistic ceilings they were imposing, the framers of the Corrupt Practices Act almost invited resort to subterfuge, and candidates have been quick to accept the invitation. For example, the ceilings ordained in the statute apply only to money spent *by* the candidate, not to money spent *for* him. Accordingly, any number of individuals may each spend up to the maximum amount that is set by the Hatch Act for a candidate they support. The Act is subject to criticism also on the ground that its provisions do not

[16] United States v. CIO, 335 U. S. 106 (1948).

[17] Key, *op. cit.*, pp. 558-59. The law has been more successful in discouraging financial outlays from another quarter. Tight restrictions are enforced against campaign contributions by Federal employees, who are thus shielded from demands by the party in power that they help finance its campaign efforts.

apply to primary elections. This is a grave defect in the law. For in safe constituencies and one-party states, the primary election, not the general election, is the one that counts, and it is therefore only in the primary campaign that large sums of money are spent. In addition to these loopholes, the Act does not apply to certain types of expenditures, among them postage. Its restraining effect is indeed "purely illusory."[18]

In only one other way—imposition of a reporting requirement—does Federal law apply to campaign spending. Congressional candidates must file financial reports with the Clerk of the House or the Secretary of the Senate, and reports must also be submitted by political parties and committees that function in more than one state. The reports must contain information about every person who has given $100 or more to a congressional campaign: his name, his address, the amounts he contributed, and the dates on which he made the contributions. Under the reporting requirement it is obligatory to describe the use that is made of campaign money. Anyone to whom a payment of $10 or more has been made must be identified and the purpose of the payment must be stated.

No compelling reason exists, however, for anyone to take these requirements too seriously. Neither the Clerk of the House nor the Secretary of the Senate is authorized to investigate whether the information contained in reports is accurate. If one of them should happen to stumble across an infraction of the law, he is not even empowered to notify the Department of Justice or any other enforcement agency.

A depressing number of the reports have something of a make-believe quality about them. The law requires a candidate to disclose only money that he himself has received or spent, and funds that have gone through the hands of others "with his knowledge." Quick to take the cue, the typical

[18] *Ibid.*, pp. 560-61.

candidate professes to be totally in the dark about what others are doing for him. Neither is he compelled to relate what he, himself, is doing, if his activities are concerned with a primary rather than a general election.[19]

Recommended Legislation

The laws that are currently on the books, then, are totally inadequate to regulate the financing of congressional campaigns. Recognizing this, a Presidential Commission on Campaign Costs recommended in 1962 the enactment of entirely new legislation.[20] The members of the bipartisan commission[21] devoted much thought to the question of how to encourage large numbers of people to make political contributions and thus dilute the influence of the few large donors. They decided that this could best be done by holding out incentives to prospective contributors. For the poorest of them, the reward would be a tax credit: half of any contribution up to $10 could be deducted from the taxes owed to the Government. For anyone wishing to contribute a larger amount (more than $10 but less than $1,000), the incentive would also be attractive (though not so generous as the one available to the "little man"): the contribution could not be deducted from taxes owed but rather from the income that would be subject to taxation.

The Commission proposed that this tax-incentive program

[19] Herbert E. Alexander, "Money, Politics and Public Reporting" (Princeton, N. J.: Citizens' Research Foundation, 1960), p. 18. Some individual states have instituted more rigid regulation of congressional campaigning than the Federal law provides.

[20] "Financing Presidential Campaigns: Report of the President's Commission on Campaign Costs" (Washington, 1962). See also Jack W. Robinson, "Revision of Federal Law on Campaign Finances," *George Washington Law Review*, XXX (December 1961), p. 328.

[21] Headed by Dean Alexander Heard, now chancellor of Vanderbilt University. Heard is author of a significant study, *The Costs of Democracy* (Chapel Hill: The University of North Carolina Press, 1960).

should go into effect at once. After an eight-year trial period, it suggested, another and more far-reaching procedure should be considered: Federal matching grants for the first $10 of every political gift. The hope was that this program would increase the number of small contributions, while at the same time rewarding handsomely the party that successfully scoured the countryside for them.

So little did the Commission think of existing legal ceilings on campaign receipts and expenditures that it recommended repealing them in their entirety. On the theory that "publicity has a cleansing and policing power" which is more effective than rigid limitation, it favored establishment of a reporting system with teeth. Creation of a Central Registry of Election Finance would be a prerequisite, its members believed, if the job were to be done properly.

The recommendations of the Commission would obviously help to minimize the baleful influence that money continues to exercise on politics. The late President Kennedy said he was impressed by the report, and in both 1962 and 1963 he sent Congress legislation modelled after the proposals made by the Commission. If members of Congress were sensitive enough to the ethical issues raised by "twilight zone" contributions, they would have overcome the opposition of powerful pressure groups and enacted the presidential recommendations into law. Instead, the legislation was almost entirely ignored on Capitol Hill. The sad truth is that the majority of congressmen do not seem overconcerned with the moral implications of prevailing campaign practices. They continue to accept a situation which places a premium on the ability to persuade big contributors that they will receive fair value for what they invest.[22]

[22] Candidates obtain some financial support from campaign committees maintained by each of the two parties in both the House and Senate. See discussion in Ch. 9.

Voter Apathy

In spite of all the money, time, and effort that are expended to enlist support in political campaigns, tens of millions of Americans stay away from the polls on Election Day.[23] Nonvoting persists in the face of elaborate efforts to convince the qualified citizen that he should exercise his franchise. Before every election, he is admonished by the mass media that it is his civic duty to vote. He is nagged, wheedled, and cajoled. Appeals are made both to his patriotic impulses ("We are lucky to live in a country where free elections are held") and to his self-interest ("If you remain home, don't complain later about what Congress does"). Civic organizations vie with party workers in offering to transport him to the polls and even provide a baby-sitter if necessary. Still, people stay home in droves.

What accounts for the fact that so few Americans vote?[24] Undoubtedly one of the reasons is an almost complete sense of alienation on the part of some nonvoters, particularly among people of low economic, social, and educational status. Their feeling seems to be one of doubt that it is really possible for them to influence political developments. The professionals, the machine politicians, the "insiders"—*they* will make the decisions that count.

Yet there may be other reasons for what appears to be voter apathy. If a nonvoter lives in a one-party state or district, the

[23] Only about 49 per cent of people of voting age cast ballots in the off-year congressional election of 1962. The 1960 presidential election had produced a relatively high turnout: about 65 per cent. In other industrially advanced nations, the figure seldom falls below 80 per cent. Many nonvoters in the United States are women and young people. Richard M. Scammon, "Why One Third of Us Don't Vote," *The New York Times Magazine* (November 17, 1963), p. 36.

[24] See the report of the President's Commission on Registration and Voting Participation (Washington: Government Printing Office, 1963). The Commission was created by President Kennedy and later continued in existence by President Johnson.

explanation for his apparent apathy may be perfectly simple: he does not bother to cast his vote since he knows that it can make no difference. Even in a closely divided electoral unit, an inhibiting factor is sometimes at work. Regardless of the vigor with which the opposing candidates attack each other, an individual may very well come to the conclusion that for him not much is really at stake in their competition.

This may be a justifiable conclusion if insufficient effort has been made to apprise the electorate of the issues on which the candidates differ. It may also be defensible if such issues simply do not exist. One perceptive observer of Congress has noted that unless the country is willing to resort to compulsory voting, the "character and vigor of the party battle" will always remain the greatest incentive to voting,[25] for the opportunity to choose between Tweedledum and Tweedledee can hardly be expected to produce a large turnout on Election Day. In fact, when the ballot offers only such a choice, a perfectly intelligent "vote" is sometimes cast by the stay-at-home, whose abstention may signify disdain for a campaign turning on issues that are essentially trivial. Thus what appears on the surface to be voter apathy may really reflect a fairly sophisticated, albeit inarticulate, conclusion regarding the nature of the two-party system in the United States.

The Disfranchised

For a significant number of persons in the nonvoting group, the decision to abstain is made not *by* them but *for* them. Eight million of these could not vote in 1960 because they had not satisfied the residence requirements of their states. Some states provide that an individual cannot vote if he has

[25] Bertram M. Gross, *The Legislative Struggle: A Study in Social Combat* (New York: McGraw-Hill, 1953), p. 121. Cf. Anthony Downs, *An Economic Theory of Democracy* (New York: Harper, 1957), *passim.*

changed his residence within a few months of the election, even if he has done nothing more than to move from one address in the state to another.[26] He loses his right to help select his representative, his senator, and even his President because, as an angry journalist once put it, "he has not lived in one community long enough to be well acquainted with its candidates for sheriff and clerk of the county court."[27]

Another factor that prevents many people from voting is the requirement in some states that would-be voters must re-register periodically. The absence of a permanent registration system ideally serves the interests of a well-entrenched party organization, for such a "machine" benefits from low voter turnout. The party boss will see to it that those beholden to him register as often as necessary, along with their relatives and friends. Others, whose jobs do not depend on the results of the election, will be less inclined to put up with the nuisance of periodic registration. The result will be to make the vote controlled by the "machine" far more significant than if more people were registered.

Other reforms in addition to permanent registration have been suggested to encourage a larger number of persons to vote: more accessible polling places, longer voting hours,[28] simplified procedures for absentee balloting, and the more widespread use of the "short ballot" (in place of a ballot so

[26] When one has moved across state lines, it still does not seem sensible to deprive him of the right to vote in a presidential election. Yet such a result may follow automatically if the state to which he has come imposes a residence requirement.

[27] Volta Torrey, *You and Your Congress* (New York: Morrow, 1944), p. 9.

[28] If the polls are open for only part of the day, the man with fixed working hours may not have an opportunity to vote. The Federal Government and some private businesses as well solve the problem by giving their employees time off to cast their ballots.

cluttered with the names of candidates for minor offices that it is an ordeal to plow through).[29]

Even without these reforms, however, it cannot be denied that notable progress has been made in expanding the size of the American electorate. Conditions are far different than they were during the Colonial Period, when no women or slaves could vote, property qualifications were universal, and religious and racial restrictions were often imposed. Although the delegates to the Constitutional Convention did nothing to broaden the franchise, the obstacles to voting gradually began to disappear. First to go were the religious qualifications; property requirements held on somewhat more tenaciously, but were almost wiped out by the Jacksonian revolution of 1828; and in 1920, the Nineteenth Amendment gave the vote to women.

Democracy?

Racial disfranchisement, however, still remains to mock the nation's democratic pretensions. In the South, only 25 per cent of all eligible Negroes are registered, as against 60 per cent of eligible whites. There are 261 counties in which not even 15 per cent of the adult Negroes are registered.[30] In half of Mississippi's counties, fewer than 1 per cent of the Negroes can vote, and in those Alabama counties where Negroes outnumber whites the proportion is only 4 per cent.[31]

Disfranchisement of the Negro survives though it was

[29] Gross, *op. cit.*, p. 120. Use of the "short ballot" means that only relatively few offices are filled through popular election. The remaining positions are held by appointees.

[30] *Congressional Quarterly Weekly Report* (July 5, 1963), p. 1086.

[31] Social and economic factors may be responsible in part. See Donald R. Matthews and James W. Prothro, "Social and Economic Factors and Negro Voter Registration in the South," *American Political Science Review*, XLVII (March 1963), p. 24.

supposed to end with the ratification of the Fifteenth Amendment. That Amendment, which was written into the Constitution in 1870, provided: "The right of citizens of the United States to vote shall not be denied or abridged by the United States or by any State on account of race, color, or previous condition of servitude." The last section of the Amendment gave Congress power to enforce this prohibition through legislation. During the Reconstruction Period, Congress did just that. The legislation it enacted and the occupation of the South by Federal troops made it possible for Negroes to vote in great numbers for a time. But after the troops were withdrawn, Southern whites succeeded in reimposing disfranchisement through the threat and actual use of violence. In the 1890's, legal techniques were developed to make such violence superfluous. These included the "white primary," the poll tax, and the literacy test.

Of these three potent devices of Negro disfranchisement, two have ceased to be problems. The "white primary" died as the result of a series of Supreme Court decisions made between 1927 and 1953.[32] The poll tax, which the Court declined to invalidate,[33] remained on the books in only five states[34] when Congress proposed what would become the Twenty-fourth Amendment to eliminate it as a requirement in Federal elections. Only the literacy test has retained its vitality.

The literacy test has survived challenges made under both the Fourteenth and Fifteenth Amendments. Section 2 of the Fourteenth Amendment provides for the punishment of any

[32] Nixon v. Herndon, 273 U. S. 536 (1927); Nixon v. Condon, 286 U. S. 73 (1932); Smith v. Allwright, 321 U. S. 649 (1944); and Terry v. Adams, 345 U. S. 461 (1953).

[33] Breedlove v. Suttles, 302 U. S. 277 (1937).

[34] Alabama, Arkansas, Mississippi, Texas, and Virginia.

state that denies the suffrage "to any . . . male inhabitants . . . twenty-one years of age and citizens of the United States . . . except for participation in rebellion or other crime." As punishment for the use of any additional criteria (necessarily including literacy tests and even residence requirements), the Amendment says that the offending state shall have its representation in the House "reduced in the proportion which the number of . . . male citizens [who are improperly disfranchised] shall bear to the whole number of male citizens twenty-one years of age in such State." Congress unquestionably has the power to give life to this provision, but it has always declined to do so. All efforts to involve the Judiciary have been similarly futile.[35]

In 1915, the Supreme Court held that a literacy test does violate the Fifteenth Amendment when whites are effectively exempted by means of a "grandfather clause."[36] Where there is no such clause, however, the courts have refused to strike down literacy requirements, as long as they are impartially administered and also contain sufficiently precise criteria.[37] Congressional legislation, of course, could minimize the disfranchisement resulting from literacy tests. In 1962, the Kennedy Administration accepted a suggestion by the United

[35] E.g., Saunders v. Wilkins, 152 F. 2d 235 (1945) and Dennis v. United States, 171 F. 2d 986 (1948). For a suggestion as to how Section 2 of the Fourteenth Amendment could be enforced, see Thomas I. Emerson and Arthur E. Bonfield, "Forgotten Remedy for the Voteless Negro," *Nation* (January 21, 1961), p. 55, and Bonfield, "The Right to Vote and Judicial Enforcement of Section Two of the Fourteenth Amendment," *Cornell Law Quarterly,* XLVI (Fall 1960), p. 108.

[36] Guinn v. United States, 238 U. S. 347 (1915). Under a "grandfather clause," the state would not impose the literacy requirement on any person whose lineal ancestors had been able to vote in 1866, a date preceding ratification of the Fifteenth Amendment.

[37] Most recently, literacy tests have been sustained in Lassiter v. Northhampton City Board of Elections, 360 U. S. 45 (1959).

States Commission on Civil Rights and urged Congress to enact a law providing that anyone who has completed six grades of school be considered literate for the purpose of voting in a Federal election. Mr. Kennedy though, did not press hard for enactment of this legislation, and a token Southern filibuster was enough to block the bill in the Senate.[38] The partial disfranchisement of the Negro thus remains the most serious barrier to the achievement of universal suffrage.[39]

[38] Filibusters are discussed in Ch. 10.

[39] Aside from voting qualifications already mentioned, states generally exclude from the suffrage persons who have been convicted of major crimes or adjudged insane. Key, *op. cit.*, pp. 669-70. In addition, all states require that voters be United States citizens, although there is nothing in the Constitution compelling such an arrangement. Forty-six of the states permit only those who are at least twenty-one years old to vote. The remaining four states have a lower minimum age: Hawaii (twenty), Alaska (nineteen), and Georgia and Kentucky (eighteen). George B. Galloway, *History of the House of Representatives* (New York: Thomas Y. Crowell, 1961), p. 30.

3

Relationship Between Congressmen and Constituents

SOME VOTERS SHOW AN INTEREST IN POLITICS only during election campaigns. When no contest for office is in progress, they find it easy to put politics out of their minds. Others, however, have a lively and continuing concern with public questions, and between elections make a conscious effort to keep up with political developments. Regarding Congress, they are naturally interested in two questions: what role their representatives are playing, and what the institution as a whole is doing.

For information on Congress—and on government and politics in general—most people must lean heavily, if not exclusively, on television, radio, and the newspapers. It is ironic that the media which reach the largest number of people—television and radio—cover Congress so inadequately. The five-minute radio newscast, into which three or four commercials must often be jammed, does not provide the ideal forum for explaining the intricacies of the legislative process. Nor is the conscientious voter much enlightened by television news programs, with their tendency to exaggerate the importance of items for which pictures are available. To make the frustration complete, programs presenting interviews with congressmen are often conducted by newsmen more inclined to debate than to probe. Newton N. Minow, former chairman of the Federal Communications Commission, once referred to television as a vast wasteland. His remark is certainly applicable to news coverage in general and coverage of Congress in particular.

Newspaper Coverage

With radio and television doing little to satisfy a thirst for knowledge about Congress, voters must turn for systematic coverage to the newspapers. There are, of course, newspapers and newspapers. *The New York Times,* for example, reports on Congress extensively, and from a national rather than a local point of view. In a real sense the *Times* is a national newspaper; its decision to begin publishing a Western edition in 1962 signified its own modest assumption of that status.[1] In its coverage of Congress, the *Times* makes only minimal concessions to the fact that in name it is a New York paper. Its operating premise seems to be that its readers are a sophisticated lot, interested in everything Congress may be doing, not merely in actions that will have a direct effect on New York. Although the *Times* is in a class by itself in the thoroughness of its political coverage, there are other major newspapers—such as the *Milwaukee Journal* and *St. Louis Post-Dispatch*—that make some effort to avoid parochialism. A world of difference separates such newspapers (and those published in Washington) from most others, which either use their Capitol Hill reporters to provide news of exclusively local interest or else have no Washington correspondents at all.

Almost inevitably, the Capitol reporter for a newspaper or regional chain that pays attention only to matters of specifi-

[1] Early in 1964, economic considerations compelled the *Times* to give up publication of a Western edition.

cally local concern tends to develop an intimate relationship with the congressmen whose activities he must cover. Such a reporter, in the process of cultivating his sources, sometimes becomes their captive. His dependence on local representatives is so great and his association with them so close that he sometimes acts more like a public relations man than a reporter. From the news stories he turns out, the reader will hear much about what fine and obliging fellows his representatives in Washington are, but next to nothing about the things they are actually doing in Congress.

Since this type of reporter is expected to concern himself only with congressional news that has some local angle, his paper, like the ones with no Washington correspondent at all, must depend for general coverage of Congress on the major wire services, the Associated Press and United Press International. But the reporters for the wire services, too, are inclined to adopt an uncritical attitude toward their sources. To do their work with the necessary speed, they must be in almost constant contact with the congressional leaders, for it is the leaders who know best what can be expected to happen in the halls of Congress. The stories filed by wire-service reporters will thus be heavily influenced by the party heads. The "news" on a particular day will usually be what the leaders want the public to think is important. The congressional leadership finds this an extremely congenial state of affairs. Both the Speaker of the House and the Majority Leader of the Senate encourage its continuation by taking time from their busy schedules to meet at least once a day with the wire-service representatives.[2]

Some rank-and-file members of Congress are openly resentful of the press attention lavished on the leadership. The late

[2] Douglass Cater, *The Fourth Branch of Government* (Boston: Houghton Mifflin, 1959), p. 52. Other reporters, too, may attend these meetings.

Representative Clem Miller (D., Calif.), for example, lamented the fact that headline treatment is so frequently accorded to the pronouncements of the leaders and so seldom to the content of congressional debates or to the views of individual members. The result, he said, is that even those constituents who are most civic-minded "do not generally know what their congressman is doing, nor do they have a chance to find out."[3]

All the News?

Although the *New York Times* publishes far more news about Congress than the papers depending solely on the wire services, its coverage, too, is permeated with leadership attitudes. Because the *Times* has such influential readers, its reporters are often used by committee chairmen and party leaders as conduits of self-serving material. *Times* reporters, as a matter of fact, are in the forefront of those members of the press corps who start to think like congressmen instead of newsmen. This process has long been evident in the Senate, where reporters—as one scholar has put it—"tend to become socialized into the Senate folkways and to develop a sympathetic understanding of the senators' plight." [4] To the extent

[3] Clem Miller, *Member of the House,* ed. John W. Baker (New York: Scribner, 1962), pp. 58-59. There is, however, no necessity for a newspaper to rely exclusively on the wire services for news of the local congressmen. For a reasonable fee, it can subscribe to a service called *Congressional Quarterly,* which provides prompt information about how senators and representatives vote and about the precise nature of the issues involved. *Congressional Quarterly* also tries to keep members of Congress honest and hard-working by compiling statistics enabling one to judge, for example, how often a member who claims he "supported the President all the way" actually did so, and by keeping track of members who are absent when roll call votes are taken.

[4] Donald R. Matthews, *U. S. Senators and Their World* (Chapel Hill: University of North Carolina Press, 1960), p. 214. Matthews considers it more than coincidence that "probably the most rhapsodic book ever written about the Senate was produced by the chief congressional cor-

that they choose to cover the news this way, *Times* reporters delegate to those who hold power in Congress the right to determine what is newsworthy in legislative matters. The result is that even the reader who is willing to wade through thousands of words of copy may end up with nothing more than a carefully manufactured version of congressional news.[5]

Some of the major problems regarding press coverage of Washington can probably be attributed to the fact that reporters, being human, are inclined to do things the easy way, especially when they are assigned by their editors to a "beat" which is too vast for anyone to cover thoroughly. Although some of them, as a matter of principle, never use a press release from a congressional office, many more are grateful for a "hand-out," simply because it saves them work.[6] Such reporters may even try to cover complex committee hearings without any effort to prepare for them in advance.

---

respondent of *The New York Times*." The reference is to *Citadel*, by William S. White (New York: Harper, 1957). Matthews calls this book "an embarrassingly public love affair." *Ibid.*, p. 214, note 25. The House has only recently acquired a hagiographer, in the person of Neil Mac-Neil, a reporter for *Time Magazine*. See MacNeil, *Forge of Democracy: The House of Representatives* (New York: David McKay, 1963), *passim*.

[5] Coverage of foreign news by the *Times* seems to reflect this same tendency to gravitate to officialdom. The reader is often expected to view the world as diplomats want him to view it. "It is believed here in Washington" normally means that the Administration wants people to believe something or other. Similarly, an expression such as "it can be stated on the highest authority" usually means, if it appears under a Paris dateline, for example, that the French government wants to convince Americans of something, not—as some might infer—that a *Times* reporter has been given access to ultimate truth.

[6] "The Washington press corps is so dependent upon this prefabricated material (which most of them gladly make their own) that extemporaneous speeches, the give-and-take of debate, and the flow of committee questioning of witnesses are seldom adequately covered in newspaper accounts of Senate proceedings." Matthews, *op. cit.*, p. 208.

Secrecy in Congress

But the most conscientious reporter covering Congress, as well as the conscientious reader who wants to understand it, faces a major obstacle. In several respects, congressional procedures make it difficult, if not impossible, to learn what Congress is doing. For example, a great deal of important congressional business is transacted in secrecy. It is a truism that the really important decisions are more often made in committee than on the floor. Yet committees customarily meet in closed session when they vote. A committee may seal the fate of a bill by declining to report it out, but it does not have to disclose the vote by which its decision was reached or the positions adopted by individual members. In similar fashion, it may drastically alter the character of a bill by approving major revisions. Since the "marking up" sessions during which amendments are voted upon are closed to both press and public,[7] constituents have no way of determining what part their congressmen chose to play during committee consideration of important measures.

By no means do committees use "executive sessions" only for the purpose of voting on legislation. Frequently the public and press are barred at a far earlier stage of the proceedings, when witnesses are offering testimony. Nor is such secrecy resorted to only by committees concerned with sensitive subjects (like military policy and foreign affairs)[8] or when testi-

[7] Senator Kefauver wanted to make it mandatory for committees to publish all votes on pending legislation and amendments. Estes Kefauver and Jack Levin, *A 20th-Century Congress* (New York: Duell, 1947), p. 140.

[8] Although the Armed Services Committee often conducts hearings in executive session, it normally releases transcripts of the proceedings after representatives of the Department of Defense have had an opportunity to censor them.

mony can be expected to contain charges against particular individuals.[9] In fact, some of the committees that are most attached to secrecy neither deal with classified information nor have the problem of how to handle defamatory testimony. Examples include the House Ways and Means Committee, which scrutinizes tax legislation, and the House Appropriations Committee, which handles spending bills.[10] All told, committees hold about one-third of their meetings behind closed doors.

The contents of an executive session seldom remain secret for very long. It is customary that after such a meeting congressmen are besieged by reporters, and it is almost as customary for at least some of the participants to communicate their versions of what took place at the "secret" meeting. But these versions are too tendentious and unreliable to be of much use to the citizen in quest of enlightenment.

"Strategic Obfuscation"

Executive sessions of committees are not the only way in which significant information on Congress is kept from the voter. By transacting some of its most important business while sitting as a Committee of the Whole, the House avoids the necessity of using the roll call votes that the Constitution prescribes under certain circumstances when the House itself is in session.[11] The absence of roll call votes makes it safe for a congressman to do in secret what he would not dare in the open. If his constituents strongly favor a bill that he opposes, he can vote for a crippling amendment, secure in the knowl-

[9] In such cases, the committee may prefer to hear the witness first in executive session and then again in public session, after inviting whoever has been denounced to attend and testify.

[10] House Appropriations and almost all its subcommittees always meet in secret. See Ch. 12.

[11] The Committee of the Whole is described in Ch. 10.

edge that this vote, like all others in the Committee of the Whole, is unrecorded. Later, when the Committee of the Whole rises and the House itself takes a roll call vote on the entire bill, he can vote in favor of the legislation and even, as one congressman has put it, "proclaim . . . affection for [its] terms. . . ."[12] In addition, conference committees, which iron out House-Senate differences on legislation and thus usually put bills into final form, always meet in secret.[13]

The sheer complexity of congressional procedure, too, makes it easy for any member to delude his constituents about the side he is really on in the fight over a particular bill.[14] He may, for instance, speak passionately for a measure in public, while at the same time privately asking the chairman of the House Rules Committee to keep it from even getting to the floor. If the chairman obliges him, the congressman will, of course, issue a public statement denouncing "the irresponsible action of this dictatorial committee in bottling up a bill that is vital to the welfare of the Nation." The denunciation will help the congressman in his constituency while doing the chairman of the Rules Committee no harm in his own.[15] The situation is still as Woodrow Wilson described it in 1883: "Every suspected culprit may shift the responsibility upon his fellows. . . . How is the schoolmaster, the Nation, to know which boy needs the whipping?"[16]

[12] Miller, *op. cit.*, p. 48.

[13] See discussion in Ch. 11.

[14] "The questions that come up for decision may involve complex amendments, rejecting a bill or amendment by indirect means, or the reconsideration of whatever action has been taken earlier. By emphasizing procedural complications, the emergence of clear-cut issues or readily evident indications [of] where each voting member really stands are circumvented." Bertram M. Gross, *The Legislative Struggle: A Study in Social Combat* (New York: McGraw-Hill, 1953), p. 352.

[15] See discussion in Ch. 8.

[16] Woodrow Wilson, *Congressional Government* (New York: Meridian, 1959), pp. 185-86 (written in 1883).

Yet, contrary to what might be expected, the devices for congressional concealment and deception are not universally condemned. A former director of the Legislative Reference Service of the Library of Congress[17] defends the use of "strategic obfuscation." He has explained his position in this way:

> The member who eagerly takes a stand on every issue in accordance with what he believes to be the public interest unfortunately may not survive the next election. Far too many in the electorate feel so intensely on some one issue that a member's total record is ignored. If a member can block action on such an issue by some means other than a direct vote, the nation is more likely to have his services beyond the end of his first term, and he believes that this fact vindicates the necessary "strategic obfuscation."[18]

This defense rests on the questionable assumption that the devices for concealment and deception are used only by congressmen whose overriding concern is to serve the public interest. Quite to the contrary, "strategic obfuscation" is frequently employed by members who are covertly the creatures of special interest groups. Moreover, to defend the use of subterfuge by congressmen is to risk elevating cowardice to the status of a national principle. The congressman who really is upholding the public interest should be a man of courage, eager to bring his case to the people. If he fails to convert them to his point of view, he will at least retain his self-respect, whether he retains his seat in Congress or not.[19]

With most congressmen honestly convinced that their de-

[17] Ernest S. Griffith, in *Congress: Its Contemporary Role* (New York: New York University Press, 1961).

[18] *Ibid.*, p. 162.

[19] See John F. Kennedy, *Profiles in Courage* (New York: Harper, 1961), *passim* (first published in 1955).

feat at the polls would be a national disaster, however,[20] it does no good to point out that a masquerade is inappropriate in the Congress of the United States. "Strategic obfuscation" continues to allow members of the National Legislature to appear in false face before the people they purport to represent.

Public Opinion

The theory of representation on which the practice of "strategic obfuscation" supposedly rests is often attributed to the brilliant eighteenth-century English conservative, Edmund Burke. The philosophy of Burke did, indeed, contain significant elements of elitism. It was assumed, for example, that a member of Parliament possessed a keener intelligence than the ordinary voter, and that he was therefore duty-bound to exercise his own independent judgment in helping make national policy. When Burke ran as a candidate for a seat in Parliament, he heaped scorn on his opponent for promising to be guided by the instructions of the voters and to consider himself subservient to their will, not superior to it. Burke said he would make no such promise. Quite the reverse, he insisted on a representative's right to ignore the views of his constituency. In his opinion, a legislator should not even try to represent the selfish interests of those electing him to office, but rather the general interests of the nation at large. The man chosen by the voters of Bristol, he said, is after all "not a member for Bristol; he is a member of Parliament."[21]

But the very candor with which Burke advised the voters

---

[20] "It is a pretty poor congressman who cannot convince himself that the best interests of the Republic depend on his re-election." Denis W. Brogan, *An Introduction to American Politics* (London: Hamish Hamilton, 1954), p. 350.

[21] Quoted in George B. Galloway, *History of the House of Representatives* (New York: Thomas Y. Crowell, 1961), p. 209.

that he would feel free to ignore them places him in a completely different category than those who disregard the popular will while pretending to follow it religiously. In both England and the United States, the philosophical debate has raged for a long time as to whether a representative should emulate the Burkian model, or whether he should act the part of an ambassador, faithfully reflecting the views of those who have commissioned him. But throughout the course of this long argument, no one has thought until recently of defending a policy by which the representative claims to be acting according to one theory while really acting according to the other. John Stuart Mill, for example, inclined toward Burke's view, but he insisted that the voters were "entitled to a full knowledge of the political opinions and sentiments of the candidate. . . ."[22] In our own day, the late President Kennedy, while serving in the Senate, wrote a book about the congressmen of the past for whom he felt the greatest admiration, and in every case the quality that distinguished them was not the skillful use of "strategic obfuscation," but rather "political courage in the face of constituents' pressures. . . ."[23]

If Burke's followers have strayed far from his principles, the advocates of the alternative approach—that a representative should do the bidding of his constituents—have found it extremely difficult to translate their theory into practice. More than half a century ago, Lord Bryce put his finger on the problem: "The obvious weakness of government by opinion is the difficulty of ascertaining it. . . . Like other valuable articles, genuine opinion is surrounded by counterfeit."[24] John F.

[22] John Stuart Mill, *Representative Government,* in Robert W. Hutchins, ed., *Great Books of the Western World* (Chicago: Encyclopaedia Britannica, 1952), Vol. XLIII, p. 405 (first published in 1860).

[23] Kennedy, *op. cit.,* p. xxi.

[24] James Bryce, *The American Commonwealth* (New York: Macmillan, 1910), Vol. II, p. 357.

Kennedy, as a senator, offered testimony in support of Bryce's observation:

> In Washington I frequently find myself believing that forty or fifty letters, six visits from professional politicians and lobbyists, and three editorials in Massachusetts newspapers constitute public opinion on a given issue. Yet in truth I rarely know how the great majority of the voters feel. . . .[25]

Abraham Lincoln formulated his policy on this question while still a member of the Illinois State Legislature. He promised to be governed by the will of his constituents "on all subjects upon which I have the means of knowing what their will is. . . ." On all other subjects, he said, "I shall do what my own judgment teaches me will best advance their interests."[26]

Although there was no unanimity among the framers of the Constitution on an acceptable theory of representation,[27] there was a general desire to assure that a member of the House would be close to the people in order to understand them and represent them fairly.[28] That is why serious thought was given to the idea of annual elections, to prevent representatives from developing too great a spirit of independence. Even John Adams, who was distrustful of the common people, asserted his conviction that "where annual

[25] Kennedy, *op. cit.*, p. 18.

[26] Quoted in Galloway, *op. cit.*, p. 215.

[27] Those who felt that a representative should be the spokesman for his constituents included Benjamin Franklin, Thomas Jefferson, Thomas Paine, and James Wilson. On the other side were Alexander Hamilton and James Madison. *Ibid.*, p. 211.

[28] Senators, under the original constitutional provision, were not to be elected by the people but rather by the state legislatures. Article 1, Section 3. Popular election was not required until 1913, when the Seventeenth Amendment was ratified.

elections end, there slavery begins."[29] And the authors of the *Federalist* papers endorsed frequent elections because they wanted those who sat in the House to have "an immediate dependence on, and an intimate sympathy with, the people."[30]

The two-year term, which seemed too long to some delegates at the Constitutional Convention, has proved short enough in practice to keep representatives in a constant state of fear and trembling. Perpetually in a dither about how few days remain before the next election, they try hard between elections to maintain a cordial relationship with as many individual voters as possible. Senators, with their longer terms, have less reason to be afflicted steadily by the pangs of anxiety, but they, too, appreciate the importance of not permitting their continuing relationship with the voters to break down.

The Postman Cometh

Mail is one of the most important aspects of the continuing relationship between congressman and constituent. The deluge of letters that descends on Capitol Hill every morning almost defies description. On the average day, about 100,000 pieces of mail are processed in the Capitol post offices, with sixty employees needed to do the job. The typical member of Congress can expect at least 100 letters a day, and the senator from a heavily populated state is inundated, at the peak of the legislative season, by twenty times that number. If a congressman has a nationwide reputation, he may be bombarded by as many as 75,000 letters on a single issue. This is precisely what happened to Senator Paul Douglas of Illinois in 1962, when Congress was considering a bill to require the

[29] Quoted in Robert Luce, *Legislative Assemblies* (Boston: Houghton Mifflin, 1924), p. 110.

[30] Alexander Hamilton, John Jay, James Madison, *The Federalist* (New York: Modern Library, 1941), No. 52, p. 343.

withholding of taxes on dividends and interest. And Senator Hubert H. Humphrey (D. Minn.) says there are occasions when he is compelled to run a sort of miniature post office, with one person on his staff spending "all day long just opening the mail—not answering it—just opening it, just sorting it."[31] Every letter, of course, must be answered. As a consequence, processing the mail occupies more time than anything else in almost all congressional officies.[32]

There are not enough hours in the day for congressmen even to read all their mail, let alone answer it. In most offices, therefore, correspondence is handled almost entirely by staff members. An office that takes care of its mail with unsurpassed efficiency is that of Senator Philip A. Hart (D., Mich.). The senator himself sees no more than 50 letters a day of the 600 to 1,000 that are received. Most of these raise questions that require a personal decision, such as whether to accept a particular out-of-town speaking invitation. Where mail concerning legislative issues is involved, the senator participates only to the extent of helping to draw up form letters on the subjects of greatest interest to the residents of his state.[33] After a form letter is prepared, the rest is easy. A staff member makes the decision that a particular form would be an appropriate way to respond to a certain communication, an automatic typewriter prepares a copy that looks as if it were done personally,[34] a second machine affixes the senator's signature," and still other mechanical marvels fold the letter and stuff it into a franked envelope.

[31] *Congressional Record,* August 2, 1962, p. 14493 (daily edition).

[32] Among the handful of exceptions are the offices of southern congressmen. These offices receive relatively few letters, due perhaps to the region's low educational level and the large number of Negroes who are not permitted to vote and therefore may feel it is futile to write. Matthews, *op. cit.,* p. 220.

[33] Perhaps 175 such forms will be on file at any given time.

[34] The automatic typewriter can produce about 500 letters a day.

Sifting and Winnowing

Over half the communications that are received from constituents concern legislative subjects. Such mail often originates with pressure groups. Some of these "inspired" communications are easy to detect—the form letters and petitions, for instance. These will often be given short shrift, for congressional offices proceed on the assumption that signing a document written by someone else does not necessarily indicate that one really has strong feelings on a subject. But pressure groups are becoming ever more skillful at camouflaging the part they play in letter-writing campaigns. More than a quarter of a century ago it was already apparent to one observer that "a flood of letters may appear to a congressman to represent the demand of a popular majority when it is merely the propaganda of a well-organized minority."[35] In the intervening years, pressure groups have become increasingly adept at prompting their members to write "individual" letters that possess none of the earmarks of an organization-inspired communication. That is one reason congressmen do not leap to the conclusion that their mail always reflects constituency opinion.

There are other reasons why congressmen think a "letter count" can often be misleading. Certain classes of voters—retired older people, for example—obviously have more time to write than others. College graduates and men of means, too, are more likely to communicate with their congressman than the average citizen. Thus the opinions expressed in these quarters will seem to be more widely held than they really are. Some members also believe they must make allowances for the fact that people who are close to them and agree with

[35] Paul DeWitt Hasbrouck, *Party Government in the House of Representatives* (New York: Macmillan, 1927), p. 70.

their positions tend to write them more often than others, although there are congressmen whose impression is precisely the reverse.[36]

What types of constituent correspondence receive the most serious attention? Often the letters that count are from people who count—friends of the congressman, perhaps, or individuals whose opinion in the community carries great weight. A letter can also be effective if it contains information about how proposed legislation might affect the writer's own community, or his business, or his family.[37] Contrary to popular belief, a telegram carries little weight, because the congressman knows that sending one requires less of an effort than writing and mailing a letter.[38]

Although almost all congressmen admit that their mail is not a representative sampling of constituent opinion, none hold it so lightly in esteem that they fail to answer it promptly. Former Speaker of the House William B. Bankhead (D., Ala.) once said that the key to long tenure in Congress is close and prompt attention to the mail,[39] and no present-day member seems willing to subject this maxim to an empirical test by ignoring his mail and taking careful note of the consequences.

[36] The late Speaker Sam Rayburn once said:

> You'll find, if you'll look over your correspondence for about six months, that in all probability from 5 to 10 per cent of the people have written 90 per cent of the letters. The fellow that's back there and satisfied and things are going alright as far as he's concerned, you don't hear from him. It's the fellow that's discontented or unhappy about something.

[37] Kefauver and Levin, *op. cit.*, pp. 182-83. In a congressional office that makes extensive use of form letters, a communication will get extra attention if it deals with more than one issue and thus makes impossible the use of a form reply directed to only a single subject.

[38] Matthews, *op. cit.*, p. 223.

[39] Quoted in Kefauver and Levin, *op. cit.*, p. 172.

In addition to being prompt, congressional replies to constituent mail will almost invariably be polite and courteous, even to the point of obsequiousness. The congressman may seriously question the sanity of an individual who has written a particularly nasty diatribe, but his reply will contain firm assurances that before any decision is made "the most careful consideration" will be given to the opinions expressed. Only rarely does a congressman respond to his constituents with the candor regularly displayed by Senator Stephen M. Young (D., Ohio). Once Young received a letter asking sarcastically if the correspondent could emulate the wife of the late President Kennedy and have a horse imported to this country without cost. In reply, Young said that he wondered "why you need a horse when there is already one jackass at your address."[40]

Not all of a congressman's outgoing mail, of course, consists of responses to communications that have been received. Often a member wants so badly to place some material in his constituents' hands that he decides to send out a mass mailing. For this to be done even occasionally, a usable mailing list must be compiled and kept up to date. This places a heavy burden on the shoulders of the congressman's staff, but the results are believed to justify the investment.

For one blissful year, members of the House, who never stop worrying about their popularity, could blanket a state with literature without even using address lists. They had long ago been given the right to send unaddressed mail to rural areas, in order to make certain that all farmers received the bulletins published by the Department of Agriculture. The representatives conceived the idea of expanding the rural "junk mail" privilege to permit them to inundate ur-

[40] To another correspondent, whose letter contained a long string of denunciations, Young responded: "Dear Sir: What else is new? Sincerely yours, Stephen M. Young."

ban areas, too, with mail that would keep their names before the voters.

The Senate would not hear of this arrangement. Its members had no intention of placing the equivalent of statewide mailing lists in the hands of representatives who might develop senatorial ambitions.[41] To get around this roadblock, the House resorted to something of a ruse. In the closing hours of its 1961 session, it attached a "junk mail" amendment to an appropriations bill containing funds that were desperately needed by a number of executive departments and agencies. The House then proceeded to adjourn, and the Senate found itself on the horns of this dilemma: accept defeat on the mail issue or permit vital government programs to die for lack of funds. Senators sputtered and fumed, but there was no acceptable alternative to surrender. Surrender they did, and for one year House members had what they wanted.[42]

But the Senate did not forget the humiliation to which it had been subjected. In retaliation, it insisted during the very next congressional session that the House accept a new bill repealing the "junk mail" privilege, not only for cities but for rural areas, too. The House, beaten into submission by the adverse publicity to which it had exposed itself, capitulated. The following year, however, Senate conferees backed down and again gave the representatives what they wanted. The senators threw in the sponge after Congressman Tom Steed (D., Okla.), floor manager of the legislative appropria-

---

[41] *Washington Post,* August 3, 1962, p. A2, col. 2.

[42] Apparently the new privilege was used widely by incumbent representatives who were thrown into new districts as a result of the decennial reapportionment, which went into effect in 1962. *Ibid.,* February 16, 1962, p. A1, col. 5. Although senators, too, could make use of the privilege, few took advantage of the opportunity. They seemed to feel that sending "junk mail" to sophisticated city dwellers would succeed only in stirring up resentment.

tions bill, threatened to reveal the name of one of their colleagues who, he said, had two call girls on his payroll. For a time, the Senate as a whole balked at approving what its conferees had agreed to. Its rafters rang with denunciations of Congressman Steed, who went on boasting that he had "more spies and informers on [his] payroll than J. Edgar Hoover." But after getting the House to agree that the "junk mail" privilege would not apply outside the boundaries of a member's district, the Senate gave in.

"Errand Boy" Functions

A large number of communications that flow back and forth between congressmen and their constituents concern matters that do not have even the remotest connection with legislative issues. The congressman, for example, looks for occasions to felicitate his constituents on a happy event or to extend sympathy in case of adversity. His staff members comb the hometown newspapers to learn who has just been married, who has had a baby, and even who has died. The appropriate responses are sent: a note of congratulations to the newlyweds, a copy of *Infant Care* (the all-time best-seller of the Government Printing Office) to the proud parents, and a card of condolence to the bereaved.[43]

A significant portion of the congressman's non-legislative correspondence, however, is initiated by constituents. Some letters solicit the congressman's help in solving problems that have arisen in dealings with executive agencies; others are completely personal in character. What the congressman and his staff do in response to letters of this sort is referred to as "case work."

[43] Occasionally things get mixed up. A mother-to-be once requested a copy of *Infant Care*. What she received instead was another government publication, *The Wolves of Mount McKinley*.

Most congressmen seem to have an ambivalent attitude toward "case work." On the plus side, they take satisfaction from the opportunity to perform small services for constituents, because they are convinced that the rewards are great. A senatorial assistant has put it this way:

> When you get somebody $25 from the Social Security Administration, he talks to his friends and neighbors about it. After a while the story grows until you've singlehandedly obtained $2500 for a constituent who was on the brink of starvation.[44]

The kind of support that a congressman wins by performing "errand boy" functions is an asset of considerable value, because those constituents for whom he has done personal favors will probably remain in his camp no matter what positions he adopts on legislative issues.[45] On the positive side, too, the congressman who intercedes with an executive agency on behalf of a constituent has the feeling that he is helping to humanize a vast and otherwise impersonal institution. The theory is that each citizen is entitled to have a representative at the seat of a government that touches so many aspects of his daily life.[46]

But there in another side to the story. Not all "case work" involves the congressman in services of obvious value, such as learning why a desperately needed monthly retirement check is late or why the State Department has failed to act

[44] Matthews, *op. cit.*, p. 226.

[45] *Id.*

[46] Representative Henry S. Reuss (D., Wis.) has a plan to preserve such positive features of the congressman-constituent relationship while at the same time relieving members of a portion of the burden represented by "case work." He favors appointment in each house of an Administrative Counsel to help with the handling of constituent requests. The office would be modelled after the "ombudsman" device, which has operated in Sweden since 1809. See *Congressional Record,* February 11, 1963, pp. 2078-84 (daily edition).

on a passport application. For every such worthwhile mission, the congressman may be requested to perform a dozen others, such as locating a pair of hard-to-get tickets to the Army-Navy game, or quashing a parking ticket, or making a hotel reservation for a family planning to visit the Nation's Capital. The hapless congressman whose constituency is not far from Washington may even have to grin and bear it when voters mistrustful of the mails descend on him in person to make such requests.[47]

As is true of many aspects of his job, the amount of time a congressman must devote to the mail has increased steadily with the growth of population. Today the average member has about twelve times as many constituents as a man who served in the First Congress. Moreover, his intercession is sought on a much wider assortment of matters than before, because of the growing number of ways in which present-day government impinges on the lives of its citizens. Yet congressmen, although they complain about the letters, would have it no other way, for they feel that mail is of capital importance in maintaining good relations with their constituents.

Through other means, too, congressmen attempt to preserve good relations, on a continuing basis, with those whose votes they will need. There is no better way to do this than to spend time in their constituencies. It was partly to allow for this that the Legislative Reorganization Act of 1946 called for Congress to adjourn by the end of July, except in compelling circumstances. The exception almost immediately became the

---

[47] A congressman from a distant state gloried in the fact that he did not have to put up with such visitors and expressed sympathy for his less fortunate colleagues. "The poor bastards from nearby get them by the hundreds," he said. Matthews, *op. cit.*, pp. 79-80. But as transportation becomes more comfortable and less expensive, such smug comments may have to be revised. Griffith, *op. cit.*, p. 68.

rule, however, and today it is usually taken for granted that a session will not be concluded until the end of the summer at the very earliest. Members are thus faced with the need to pay frequent visits to their constituencies while Congress is still in session, if their political fences are to be kept properly mended.

Many congressmen from constituencies reasonably near Washington make it a habit to spend virtually every weekend in their home precincts. What is more, a considerable number have a way of starting these weekends early and ending them late, with the result that they stay for only three days a week—Tuesday, Wednesday, and Thursday—in Washington.[48] The days at home will probably furnish a member with opportunities to deliver a "nonpolitical" speech or two,[49] talk things over with constituents who drop by, and check on the vitality of his political organization. The congressman who lives far from Washington cannot return home as often as others because of the distance involved.[50] But he enjoys the same opportunity as his colleagues to keep in touch with his constituents by long-distance telephone. For the law does not speak in dollar terms about the amount of public money that may be spent on calls. Instead, each member is permitted a

[48] In many instances, the members of the "Tuesday-Thursday Club" are drawn to their home towns by other considerations as well as a desire to mix with the voters. A number of them, for example, are still active in their old law firms or businesses.

[49] Although congressmen are usually delighted to receive speaking invitations, Senator Kenneth B. Keating (R., N. Y.) read one such invitation with mixed emotions. The letter, inviting the senator to take part in a current events seminar, ended: "I hope you can come, Senator, because all of us would like to hear the dope from Washington." *The New York Times,* August 20, 1962, p. 8, col. 5 (city edition).

[50] Only three round trips may be taken each year at Government expense. Before 1963, the limit was two such trips between Washington and home.

certain *number* of free calls, regardless of their destination.[51] Congressmen from distant states also try to make up for the infrequency of their visits by publishing elaborate newsletters describing their activities and by maintaining full-time "district offices" back home.

Members of Congress have no doubt that the time they give to constituent relations is well spent. Stories abound of men who devoted their efforts to leadership positions or to the pursuit of national reputations and awoke one fine November morning to find that they were lame ducks because they had neglected the most important people—the voters back home.[52]

As they strive to maintain good relations with the voters and as they do their other work, too, congressmen receive extensive assistance from personal staffs that they are entitled to retain. An $18,000-a-year administrative assistant, for instance, relieves a senator of the burden of organizing and running his office, and serves as his alter ego in negotiating with other members and with the leaders of the party organization back home. The senator also has a highly paid legislative assistant

[51] Because of this arrangement, some congressmen choose to pay for their own long distance calls to points that are relatively nearby, in order to conserve their quota of free calls for those they make to stations far away.

[52] Lord Bryce wrote:

> An ambitious congressman is . . . forced to think day and night of his renomination, and to secure it not only by procuring, if he can, grants from the Federal Treasury for local purposes, and places for the relatives and friends of the local wire-pullers who control the nominating conventions, but also by sedulously "nursing" the constituency during the vacations.

He added, somewhat sourly: "No habit could more effectively discourage noble ambition or check the growth of a class of accomplished statesmen." Bryce, *op. cit.*, Vol. I, pp. 197-98.

to help him with his committee work, write his speeches on issues before Congress, and sit with him on occasion during Senate debates to keep him supplied with the facts and figures he may need.

The size of the additional staff with which the senator is provided depends on the population of his state. This system was established because of a realization that the burdens on a senator vary with the size of his electorate. Yet the Senate has not gone so far as to authorize twice as much staff assistance for a member from a state with 16 million people as for one from a state which is half that size. As a consequence, senators from the most populous states often discover that their allotment is far too meager, and if they are men of independent means they may dip into their own pockets to augment their staffs.

Since the average congressional district is considerably smaller than the average state, members of the House are not provided with anything like the kind of staff assistance that their senatorial colleagues get. The allowance of a representative will usually cover no more than three or four office employees.

Competent staffs have the virtue of freeing members of Congress from a great deal of onerous detail, but their very efficiency may at the same time keep legislators too far away from the flesh and sinew of legislative issues. If the congressman of today does not seem to measure up to the greats of the past, perhaps at least part of the explanation lies in the fact that he is too often spared the necessity of reading, writing, and even thinking. One of the main considerations that make large and efficient congressional staffs a mixed blessing is described in the following terms by two of the most perceptive critics of Congress:

It has happened time and again in recent years that an energetic staff man with an eye for influencing the future of the human race will convince a legislator of the importance of an idea. The legislator will give a hurried and often unconsidered green light, and the staff man will take off with the hounds: drafting bills, calling agencies in the legislator's name, pushing for hearings, writing committee reports which are signed but not always read by the elected representatives of the people, and generally making noises like a bird dog flushing a quail.[53]

It may be that the press of legislative work has helped make this situation inevitable, but the variety of non-legislative functions that congressmen find it advisable to assume is an even more important contributory factor.

Localism

Since congressmen assign such high priority to constituency relations, they are concerned with establishing a public legislative record that shows they serve local interests. They feel far less of a need to justify their votes in terms of the national interest. In contrast to a system of proportional representation, under which there would be no geographical constituencies, the American system of single-member constituencies (or, in the case of the Senate, dual-member constituencies) gives implicit constitutional sanction to a local basis of representation. Only naturally, therefore, "the pull toward things local is the most immediate and the most continuous influence to which the representative is exposed," as a leading authority has written.[54] And because the national party can exert so little influence on the re-election prospects of its members, a

[53] Stephen K. Bailey and Howard D. Samuel, *Congress at Work* (New York: Holt, Rinehart and Winston, 1952), p. 8.

[54] Fritz Morstein Marx, "Party Responsibility and Legislative Program," *Columbia Law Review*, L (March 1950), p. 284.

congressman seldom loses anything by "voting the district."[55] On the occasions when local considerations impel him to depart from the principles of his national party, chances are good that the leadership of that very party will be tolerant. In fact, it may decide that it would be wise to cultivate him, for he has demonstrated an instinct for self-preservation that should enable him to stay in Congress for many years and thus become a force to be reckoned with.[56] It is when a constituency does not care one way or another about an issue that its congressman will be most likely to vote as the party leadership would like him to.

The frequency with which the average congressman "votes the district" is by no means exclusively the product of carefully calculated self-interest. The congressman himself is usually so much a local product that it is second nature for him to think the way his district thinks. In more cases than not, the man has never left home. Although senators would rank higher than representatives on an index of cosmopolitanism, even they have seldom strayed far from their origins.[57]

[55] V. O. Key, Jr., *Public Opinion and American Democracy* (New York: Knopf, 1961), p. 487.

[56] William G. Phillips, "Congress: A Study in Political Realities," *American Federationist,* February 1961, reprinted in *Congressional Record,* February 24, 1961, p. A-1215 (daily edition).

[57] According to a study of the 86th Congress, 78 senators

> were raised in the states they represent, with the average senator now living but 22 miles from the town where he went to high school. . . . After college or law school, the senators returned to their home states and often to their home towns. . . .

Andrew Hacker, "Voice of Ninety Million Americans," *The New York Times Magazine,* March 4, 1962, p. 11. See also Hacker, "The Elected and the Anointed: Two American Elites," *American Political Science Review,* LV (September 1961), p. 539.

The congressman is in the happy position of one who is rewarded for doing what comes naturally.

Without doubt, a case can be made for congressional localism. As long as each constituency is shielded by its representative, none of the sectional and regional interests of the nation will be overlooked in the legislative process. In a country both vast and varied, this may surely be counted a blessing. Moreover, people tend to feel less alienated from government when they know that their problems—which are just as important to them as they are insignificant to the nation as a whole— are of vital concern to a member of Congress.

The localism that characterizes Congress contains nonetheless a vice that may outweigh these virtues: the danger that the country will never be able to solve problems national in scope until its legislators begin to think in national terms. Even before the ratification of the Constitution, James Madison displayed unhappiness over the likelihood that the national interest would be obscured. He prophesied gloomily that measures would "too often be decided according to their probable effect, not on the national prosperity and happiness, but on the prejudices, interests, and pursuits of the government and people of the individual states."[58] The national interest may be difficult to define, but critics of localism are certain that it is not simply the sum total of local interests or even an equitable compromise of regional differences.[59]

One example will suffice. Constituents will always be inclined to rejoice when a military installation is established in their area or a lucrative defense contract placed with some local industry, for the jobs that will be created will pump new life into the local economy. Fully cognizant of this fact, the typical member of Congress bends every effort to persuade

[58] Hamilton, Jay and Madison, *op. cit.*, No. 46, p. 307.
[59] Paul H. Appleby, *Big Democracy* (New York: Knopf, 1945), p. 134.

the Department of Defense that it should favor his constituency with a training base or two, or perhaps a missile contract. And when the Pentagon decides to let a new contract or establish a new base, it permits the local congressman—if he belongs to the party in power—to make the first public announcement, as if to imply that his efforts turned the trick.[60] Similarly, howls of anguish greet every announcement that a military base is to be closed or a defense contract dropped. Under such circumstances, does the national interest call for compromising the demands of the various constituencies for stimulants to their local economies? Or does it rather require that the demands be entirely ignored? The national interest in world peace and disarmament might better be served by closing existing military installations than by opening new ones, but this possibility will never be perceived if legislative policy continues to be formulated through the accommodation of local interests.

[60] One senator has protested bitterly against this practice. Senator John J. Williams (R., Del.) has expressed fear that "national or state political organizations [will] capitalize on the influence their candidates will have in Washington as an excuse to collect larger political contributions from these defense contractors." The senator related an incident in which the Kennedy Administration had wanted to do a favor for both senators of a state where a defense contract had been awarded and also for the representative of the particular district. He said:

> Three high-ranking officers were dispatched to the Capitol with a notification for each of the three members. To make sure that there was no partiality shown, the officers even synchronized their watches and by prearranged plan entered the offices of their designated congressional member on the exact minute.

The New York Times, June 18, 1963, p. 64, col. 1 (city edition).

4

The President in the Legislative Process

DURING AN AVERAGE SESSION OF CONGRESS, bills are introduced on subjects that grow more numerous and more varied with every passing year. These bills come from an incredibly wide variety of sources and combinations of sources. Some are the product of congressional investigations; the origin of others may be traced to a political party platform; still others are born in the minds of individual congressmen, or perhaps in the offices of interest groups with a stake in what Congress does. But the most important single source of legislation is none of these. That source is the Executive Branch.

In quantitative terms, legislation that originates with the President or with one of the executive agencies is not overly impressive. Of the total number of bills that Congress is asked to consider each year, perhaps no more than 5 per cent are Administration measures. But it is precisely to these few that Congress devotes most of its time, and it is these that constitute the majority of the public bills actually passed.

The overriding importance of the Executive Branch as an initiator of legislation is a relatively recent phenomenon.

True, the Constitution invited the President to participate in generating legislation by recommending "such Measures as he shall judge necessary and expedient" and by giving "from time to time . . . to the Congress Information of the State of the Union. . . ."[1] Yet virtually all the Presidents who preceded Theodore Roosevelt interpreted their power to originate legislation in far narrower terms than the constitutional wording would permit. Armed with the veto power, they were not apprehensive about allowing Congress a monopoly of legislative initiative. This situation has changed so radically, however, that a Washington newspaperman exaggerated only slightly when he said: "It is no longer the Congress that proposes and the President who vetoes legislation, but the other way around."[2]

The modern assumption of legislative initiative by the President applies to both the domestic area and the foreign and military fields. On matters touching international relations, Congress is least disposed to resent the President's paramount position. It grudgingly concedes that in a time of almost continuous crisis only the Executive possesses the expertise required for the formulation of a global American policy.[3] On exclusively domestic matters, it is less easy for Congress to accept a back seat. But here, too, Congress is ill-equipped to wrest the initiative from the Executive Branch. With today's society and its problems growing increasingly complex, only the President and the executive agencies seem able to develop programs that deal on an integrated basis with vast constellations of issues. Congress appears institutionally incapable of perceiving the interrelationships. For

[1] Article II, Section 3.
[2] James B. Reston, *The New York Times,* July 25, 1962, p. 32, col. 3 (late city edition).
[3] See Ch. 13.

while the committee system on which it relies has encouraged a helpful degree of specialization, there is no effective machinery for over-all coordination. Committees may know all there is to know about particular pieces of legislation, but Congress as a whole lacks a coherent view of how the proposals would fit into a general blueprint for domestic policy.[4] Furthermore, it is prevented by the cumbersomeness of its procedures from being able to act swiftly and decisively.

Because of such factors as these, Congress is willing to accept a subordinate position, especially during periods of emergency. In the first One Hundred Days of the New Deal, for instance, with the country paralyzed by the Great Depression, Congress converted itself into a rubber stamp to approve White House bills—one of them on the very same day it was introduced. A similar situation arose in 1941 with the Japanese attack on Pearl Harbor, when Congress unhesitatingly handed President Roosevelt war powers that were totally without precedent.[5]

Even when no acute emergency exists, the President and the massive Executive apparatus have had only token opposition to their assumption of the legislative initiative. The President's proposals have become, in effect, the congressional agenda. So encyclopedic is the typical legislative program emanating from the White House and so detailed are the recommendations it embodies that Congress usually has time to consider little else.

If both the perilous world situation and the increasing demands made on government have contributed to creating this condition, the political philosophies and personalities of

[4] See Sidney Hyman, "Inquiry into the 'Decline' of Congress," *The New York Times Magazine*, January 3, 1960, p. 39.

[5] Bertram M. Gross, *The Legislative Struggle: A Study in Social Combat* (New York: McGraw-Hill, 1953), p. 208.

several twentieth-century Presidents have also been factors. Theodore Roosevelt, for example, developed the argument that congressmen are often tools of special interests, while the President is the steward of all the people. This theory made it seem reasonable for Roosevelt to strive with great vigor to become "chief legislator," as well as Chief Executive. Wilson and Franklin D. Roosevelt chose to follow the trail that the earlier Roosevelt had blazed. Like him, they helped to engrave on the public consciousness the idea that a good President is a strong President—one who leads Congress instead of following it.

The President has no fewer than three separate occasions near the beginning of each congressional session in which to exercise leadership by outlining his legislative program and arguing for its enactment. Within a single month, he submits his State of the Union Message, Budget Message, and Economic Report.

State of the Union Message

Only in recent decades have Presidents revived the early practice of appearing in person before a joint session of Congress to present the State of the Union Message. Although George Washington and John Adams instituted this procedure, Thomas Jefferson promptly abandoned it, and the precedent he set of transmitting the message in writing was followed for more than a century. But in 1913 Woodrow Wilson decided that his message deserved a better fate than to be droned uncomprehendingly and incomprehensibly by congressional clerks. To give his State of the Union Message greater effect, Wilson went in person before Congress and converted what had long been a lacklustre ritual into a state occasion. Congress was put on notice that the new President planned to exercise leadership over its work.

Today it is taken for granted that the State of the Union Message is delivered in person and attended with appropriate pomp and circumstance. The Senate meets in its own chamber, and then its members troop to the larger House chamber, where seats in the front rows have been reserved for them. Members of the foreign diplomatic corps attend, as do the President's Cabinet officers and the Justices of the Supreme Court. As each contingent enters, its arrival is formally announced by the House Doorkeeper. Presiding over the joint session is the Speaker of the House, with the Vice President of the United States (as president of the Senate) seated at his right. (In the event that the Vice President has succeeded to the Presidency, his place is taken by the President Pro Tempore of the Senate.) When the moment which has been so dramatically prepared for finally arrives, the Doorkeeper summons his vocal strength, and bellows: "Mr. Speaker! The President of the United States!" The audience rises and applauds, and the President ascends the rostrum, where he shakes hands with the Speaker and the Vice President. The Speaker then gives him a formal introduction, the audience rises and applauds once more, and after it is again seated the President begins his address. In it he customarily takes stock of where the nation stands, and assesses the results achieved by past policies. He also looks to the future, making recommendations about the course that should now be charted. It is in this latter portion of his address that the President discloses to Congress at least the broad outlines of his legislative program, if not all the details. A great many of those details are supplied in the budget that the President submits later in the month and the message that accompanies it.[6]

[6] Other aspects of the program will emerge in a series of special messages, each devoted to a particular subject. And occasionally bills introduced in Congress with the President's sanction will speak for themselves.

Budget Message

When the budget goes to Congress, the press and public generally focus their attention on one issue above all others: whether or not it is balanced. But the document does far more than merely reveal the President's plans for expenditures in relation to anticipated revenues during the next fiscal year.[7] In actuality, it is the over-all program of the Administration, expressed in dollars. Its submission furnishes the occasion for the President to announce the appropriations he will request for programs already established by Congress, and to indicate the nature of any new programs he wants authorized.[8]

The President, of course, can only recommend; in the final analysis, it is Congress that determines the extent to which his recommendations will be followed. The mere formulation of his recommendations, however, involves a process both elaborate and complex. For in order to frame his recommendations, the President must pass judgment on all the individual budgetary requests made by the heads of the executive departments for programs they administer or want to administer. The President has the responsibility of considering these requests not merely in terms of whether they would be in the public interest but also with due regard for how they would fit into his total program.

In discharging this responsibility, the President is assisted by the most important of his staff agencies,[9] the Bureau of

[7] The fiscal year begins six months in advance of the calendar year. For example, Fiscal 1964 starts on July 1, 1963 and finishes on June 30, 1964.

[8] The difference between *authorization* and *appropriation* measures is explained in Ch. 12.

[9] "The Executive Office of the President" is the name given to the entire group of staff agencies: the Bureau of the Budget, the Council of

the Budget. The director of the Bureau is the only one of the top presidential appointees whose selection does not have to be confirmed by the Senate. In exempting him from the confirmation requirement, Congress has conceded that it is improper for an official with his responsibilities to be the servant of anyone but the President. The Budget Director has been referred to as the President's " 'no' man,"[10] for it is he, under power delegated by the Chief Executive, who must break the news to department heads that their requests are not in line with the program of the Administration.[11]

Central Clearance

Before 1921, the executive departments did not have to put up with central clearance of their budget requests. They would go directly to Congress with their proposals, knowing little and caring less about how much was being asked by other departments. The resulting chaos persuaded Congress to adopt a far-reaching reform.[12] The reform came into being

Economic Advisers, the National Security Council, the Office of Emergency Planning, the National Aeronautics and Space Council, the Office of Science and Technology, and the White House Office. Consistent with their importance to the President, these agencies are for the most part housed in the Executive Office Building, which is immediately adjacent to the White House, or in the White House itself.

[10] Hobart Rowen, "Washington's Unseen Powerhouse: David Bell and His Budgeteers," *Harper's Magazine*, July 1962, p. 46.

[11] To perform its function properly, the Bureau must know at least as much about what the President stands for as the President does himself. So conscientious are its efforts in this direction that while an election campaign is still in progress its Office of Legislative Reference will begin to compile records of the sometimes rash promises made by the presidential candidates. One of the two files is discarded after Election Day; the other is used to help prepare the incoming President's legislative program.

[12] Robert Ash Wallace, *Congressional Control of Federal Spending* (Detroit: Wayne State University Press, 1960), p. 18.

with passage of the Budget and Accounting Act of 1921. No longer were the agencies to be permitted to make their own individual decisions about how much money they would request from Congress. Now the President and the President alone would make appropriations requests on behalf of the Administration as a whole. It was to help him perform this task that the Bureau of the Budget was created by the 1921 law.[13]

But there was an easy way for executive departments to circumvent the intent of the Act. Although they were prohibited from going to Congress directly with requests for *appropriations,* there was nothing to prevent them from asking for new *legislation.* President Warren G. Harding, during whose administration the Budget and Accounting Act had been passed, succeeded in plugging this loophole with an order broadening the clearance function of the Bureau of the Budget. Under the order, not only appropriations requests but also legislative proposals that would involve the expenditure of funds had to be approved by the Bureau. Central clearance was carried still another step forward by President Franklin Roosevelt, who was the first to require that all legislative proposals, whether or not they entailed the expenditure of funds, be funneled through the Budget Bureau. Also during

[13] See Richard E. Neustadt, "Presidency and Legislation: The Growth of Central Clearance," *American Political Science Review,* XLVIII (September 1954), p. 641. Central clearance was not the only function assigned to the Bureau of the Budget. The Bureau was also given the responsibility of trying to save money for the Government by helping to improve accounting procedures, management policies, and inter-agency relations. The first Budget Director, General Charles G. Dawes, reportedly summed up these functions in the following words: "If Congress orders garbage dumped on the White House steps, it would be the Bureau's job to see that the largest amount got there at the least expense." Quoted in David O. Cook, "DOD Legislative Proposals and the Bureau of the Budget," *JAG Journal,* October 1959, p. 13.

the Roosevelt Administration, the Bureau was taken out of the Treasury Department and placed directly in the Executive Office of the President.

Under the elaborate system of central clearance that is now in effect, the budget submitted to Congress by the President takes almost a full year to produce. As early as March,[14] representatives of the Budget Bureau consult with the Secretary of the Treasury, the Council of Economic Advisers, and perhaps the President himself to begin developing the basic assumptions on which the budget to be submitted in January will be built. Once guidelines have been established, the Budget Director holds exploratory talks with the heads of the various departments to learn in general terms about the programs for which they want to request funds. It is not unusual for all the members of the President's Cabinet—as well as the heads of about eight other Federal agencies—to make personal calls on the Budget Director to argue their case.[15] Before the end of June, these discussions have usually produced enough information so that tentative budgetary ceilings for each agency can be established. Agencies are asked to respect these "planning figures" and to prepare detailed analyses of the costs of their proposed programs by the middle of September.

Submission by the various agencies of their analyses means that the preliminaries are out of the way and the main event can begin. During the fall months, the Bureau of the Budget holds hearings at which each agency must present detailed justifications of its budgetary requests. The hearings are conducted by examiners who are thoroughly conversant

[14] Ten months before the submission of the budget to Congress and sixteen months before the start of the fiscal year to which the budget applies.

[15] Rowen, *op. cit.*, p. 45.

with the respective agencies and their problems.[16] When the examiners finish their work, the Budget Director makes his own review, working out the most difficult policy questions in consultation with the President. Then, section by section, the completed budget is approved by the President. After that, only the Budget Message remains to be prepared.

The Budget Message and the State of the Union Message are two of the three formal communications that the President addresses to Congress in January of each year. The third is his Economic Report. This document, produced by his Council of Economic Advisers,[17] attempts to assess the state of the national economy and forecast trends that can be expected in purchasing power, employment, and production. It also may contain recommendations for Federal legislation to help achieve the goal of "maximum employment" set out in the Employment Act of 1946.

Causes of Executive Chaos

To make his influence most strongly felt in legislative matters, the President must continuously ride herd on two powerful institutions. The first is his own executive bureaucracy. The second is Congress. It is not easy to determine which one of the tasks is more difficult. For although the Bureau of the

[16] The examiners are badly outnumbered as they try to do their work, for more than one executive agency has several hundred specialists working on its budget. To make matters even worse, examiners have sometimes displayed an inclination to become partial to an agency they have dealt with for many years. Wallace, *op. cit.*, p. 20. This problem has been mitigated by the current practice of rotating examiners, a procedure which may diminish expertise but which certainly increases impartiality.

[17] The Council was created by the Employment Act of 1946. For a study of the forces behind the adoption of this statute, see Stephen K. Bailey, *Congress Makes a Law: The Story Behind the Employment Act of 1946* (New York: Columbia University Press, 1950).

Budget has tried hard to encourage the Executive Branch to speak with one voice, it is still far away from fully achieving its goal. The problem is not merely one of introducing efficient procedures to coordinate the activities of a gigantic organization. The real difficulty is that almost every individual executive department—and each of its subordinate divisions as well—can count on receiving powerful support from its "constituents": the congressmen and interest groups that share its legislative goals. Since these goals may be diametrically opposed to those of the President, the Chief Executive and the Bureau of the Budget confront an almost impossible task in trying to convert into reality a widespread myth: that the bureaucracy is the President's to command.

The average unit of the bureaucracy is far more deeply committed to its own particular program than to the program of the Administration as a whole. Accordingly, an agency whose pet project has been turned down by the Budget Bureau and the White House is seldom inclined to accept this verdict as final. If it has influential friends in Congress, it may be in an excellent position to challenge the President's decision.[18] Its prospects will be especially bright if its friends serve on a legislative or appropriations subcommittee that exercises jurisdiction over its programs. The bureau may then be able to take an appeal, so to speak, from the judgment of the White House. For although the Budget and Accounting Act prohibits units of the Executive Branch from requesting amounts in excess of the President's recommendations, this provision is easily circumvented by means of having sympathetic subcommittee members put on an elaborate show of dragging from the mouth of a "reluctant" departmental wit-

[18] David B. Truman, *The Governmental Process* (New York: Knopf, 1960), p. 430.

ness the amount that he had originally requested and that the Administration had later curtailed.[19]

Such collusion is probably unavoidable. Subcommittees and bureaus almost inevitably tend to think alike because usually both have established an intimate clientele relationship with the interest groups that dominate their sphere of activity. Much the same type of relationship may exist between a Cabinet-level department and a full committee. In an important respect, for example, the Department of Agriculture and the Agriculture Committee in each house are all spokesmen for agricultural interests. Neither Committee nor Department is always as dedicated to the branch of government of which it is a part as it is to the cause of agriculture. Much the same could be said about the Departments of Commerce, Labor, and Health, Education, and Welfare and the congressional committees with which they are associated. Given this fact of political life, even the most sophisticated techniques of administrative management will fail the President.

On occasions when there are differences between the aims of the executive agency and those of the congressional committee or subcommittee, the agency may still be able to achieve its ends by collaborating directly with its clientele interest groups. The agency is well advised to act discreetly, for Congress has a deeply ingrained institutional bias against "administrative lobbying."[20] Nonetheless, the agency usually

[19] J. Leiper Freeman, *The Political Process: Executive Bureau-Legislative Committee Relations* (New York: Random House, 1955), p. 17.

[20] Because of this bias, Congress has tried to hold the publicity activities of the agencies in check. It has forbidden the hiring of publicity experts, and has also prohibited governmental agencies from sending unsolicited literature through the mails under the frank. V. O. Key, Jr., *Politics, Parties, and Pressure Groups* (4th ed.; New York: Thomas Y. Crowell, 1958), pp. 754-55.

finds ways to assist the pressure group as it buttonholes members of Congress, attempts to organize constituent pressures against key congressmen, and rounds up witnesses to testify before the relevant congressional committee.

The Bureau of the Budget strives as best it can to counteract the fragmentation that always seems to threaten the Executive Branch. Under a presidential directive, every bill that originates in a department or agency must be filtered through the Bureau's Office of Legislative Reference[21] so that it can be determined whether the measure is consistent with the President's total program. When a bill originates in Congress rather than in the Executive Branch, the committee to which it is referred will, almost as a matter of course, ask the bureau involved for its views. The reply must be channeled through Legislative Reference before it is sent to the committee.

Procedures such as these, however, can have only a slight effect on the understandings that grow up between agencies and committees. They can, of course, have no effect at all on understandings that involve interest groups. This anarchic situation, which plays havoc with the classical theory of separation of powers, is especially intolerable to a President who is deeply concerned with the enactment of his legislative program. Franklin Roosevelt, one of the most programmatic presidents of the twentieth century, found one way out. To deal with dire emergencies, he often created entirely new agencies, such as the Works Progress Administration and the National Recovery Administration. Because they were new, he felt, these agencies would not be encumbered by loyalties that might sometimes prevent them from functioning as components of the Executive Branch.[22]

[21] Not to be confused with the Legislative Reference Service of the Library of Congress (dealt with in Ch. 7).

[22] This was one reason for the much criticized proliferation of "alphabet agencies" in the New Deal years.

President and Congress

The President faces a wholly new set of problems when he turns his attention to the question of how to get his legislative program through Congress. There are a variety of techniques that are available. He may try to stir up popular sentiment in the hope that the voters will bring pressure to bear upon Congress. He may work closely with the congressional leadership, presenting his ideas on tactics. Or he may prefer to deal directly with individual congressmen, instead of attempting to reach them indirectly through the electorate or through the leadership. If he inclines toward this technique, he will try to reap political advantage from every appointment he makes. He will allocate Federal funds and projects with careful regard for political considerations. He will communicate to key congressmen his keen personal interest in an item of legislation, perhaps mentioning directly the rewards and punishments he is in a position to bestow.

These are the techniques among which President Johnson can choose in his efforts to influence Congress. His predecessor, John F. Kennedy, favored a combination of direct pressure on individual members and cooperation with the congressional leadership. Franklin Roosevelt used his radio "Fireside Chats" to good advantage,[23] but with rare exceptions President Kennedy shied away from this technique. His televised press conferences did not furnish the occasion for the kind of advocacy at which Mr. Roosevelt was so expert. Liberals even criticized him for conveying the impression that he did not really care about what happened to his legislative proposals. They conceded that he sent eloquent messages to Congress. But when his legislative recommendations went down to defeat, they said, he always managed to perceive a silver

---

[23] Cf. Alan Rosenthal, "Could Kennedy Budge the Congress?" *New Republic,* May 4, 1963, p. 13.

lining in the cloud, thus suggesting that what he had requested was not really very important.[24] Instead of following in the Roosevelt tradition and trying to marshal public opinion in support of his programs, Mr. Kennedy generally preferred to play the part of the legislative technician, painstakingly attempting to carve out a majority in each house of Congress through approaches to individual members. He operated on a retail, rather than a wholesale, basis. He was a tactician rather than a strategist.

White House Liaison with Congress

In some congressional battles, Mr. Kennedy practiced his version of legislative liaison without even using any intermediaries. In 1961, for example, some obscure congressmen were flabbergasted when they received personal telephone calls from the President expressing his interest in the fight to expand the membership of the Rules Committee. Individual letters and invitations to White House chats were also used in the President's person-to-person approach to Congress. Most of his contacts with Congress, however, were through a special staff he had appointed in the White House Office.[25] This staff, headed by Lawrence F. O'Brien, could claim to be engaged in what was essentially a service function: doing

[24] The liberal *New Republic* made the point in these words:

> The President cannot have it both ways. He cannot say publicly in 1962 that the 87th Congress was a pretty good one and then expect outraged voters to give him something different in 1963. He cannot have "politics as usual" while hoping to "get America moving again."

February 2, 1963, p. 4.

[25] Only President Eisenhower before him chose to institutionalize congressional liaison in this manner. Presidents Roosevelt and Truman had been more informal in their procedures.

favors for congressmen. The favors, of course, were bestowed with an ulterior motive. Receipt of one of them made a congressman feel that he was beholden to the White House, and as O'Brien saw it such a sense of obligation was a type of promissory note. In time, the congressman would be expected to repay the debt.

The most intensive work done by the O'Brien staff was directed toward the passage of the relatively small number of bills that President Kennedy placed on his "must" list. In preparation for a struggle over one of these measures, a tabulation would be made of members who were sure to support the Administration's position and of those who were just as sure to oppose it. Members who fell into neither category— the undecided and the uncommitted—were the ones on whom the campaign would focus. The aim, of course, was to obtain sufficient support from this group to guarantee passage of the measure. Each member of the small White House staff would work on those of the "men in the middle" who were in the geographical group to which he was assigned.

The campaign to win a particular vote would often consist of nothing more than the presentation of reasoned arguments, accompanied perhaps by a statement that the President was keenly interested in the legislation and hoped the congressman would find it possible to cooperate. If the member was afraid that supporting the Administration would guarantee his defeat at the polls, the White House emissary would try to convince him that his fears were unfounded.[26] The congressman would be asked to indulge in more positive thinking and

[26] O'Brien's group believed that congressmen tend to overestimate the problems a particular vote is likely to create for them. One member of the group (Richard Donahue, April 25, 1962) once compared congressmen to hypersensitive baseball players. "They have the ears of a rabbit. Out of ten thousand cheers, they can pick out half-a-dozen boos."

consider the support an Administration vote could win for him instead of the opposition it might arouse.

When it was evident, however, that a member would really be courting defeat by voting with the Administration, the O'Brien contingent would ordinarily make no effort to convince the man that he should emulate the "profiles in courage" extolled by Mr. Kennedy in print. Among politicians there is an unwritten law that the party is not entitled to blood sacrifices unless crucial legislation can be passed in no other way. If those in charge of White House liaison expect a member of Congress to take a chance with his career when his vote is really needed they know that they had better not make the request too frequently.

Often O'Brien's men were able to reach a meeting of the minds with congressmen in an atmosphere of friendship and good will. Only when sweet reasonableness produced no results did they resort to threats and strong-arm methods. The most extreme sanction they could impose was to eliminate a congressman from consideration when patronage jobs were available and when favors were requested of the White House. A blacklisted member would be "dead" as far as the White House was concerned. He would find every office in the Executive Branch ignoring his requests for services, whether substantial or petty. For all practical purposes, he would no longer be recognized as a congressman of the President's party.

The threat of punishment did not have to be conveyed directly by O'Brien or one of his assistants, for during the Kennedy years the politically significant functions of the Executive Branch were coordinated to a remarkable degree.[27]

[27] O'Brien "trained Cabinet and agency liaison officers to alert him on their projects, problems—and potential vacancies." Edward P. Morgan, "O'Brien Presses on with the 'Four P's,' " *The New York Times Magazine,* March 25, 1962, p. 116. Periodically O'Brien summoned the liaison officers of appropriate departments and agencies to the White House for strategy conferences.

Instead of hearing from a White House staff member, a congressman might receive a telephone call from the Post Office Department or the Defense Department asking pointedly how he was planning to vote on, say, a farm bill. At once the member would recognize that the White House staff had enlisted the cooperation of two Government departments well known for the largesse they could bestow—or withhold.[28] Only minimal political sophistication was required to understand the message conveyed by the departments: if the congressman thought he might someday want a post office in his district or a defense contract to provide jobs for his constituents, he would do well to support the Administration position on agriculture.

Congressmen sometimes complained bitterly about the use of such bludgeoning tactics. O'Brien and the brash young men who worked for him were dubbed the "Irish Mafia." Stories abounded about the methods they employed, against Republicans as well as Democrats. A Republican congressman told the House that the Pentagon had asked a defense contractor to urge him to support the Administration's position on raising the debt limit. The implied threat, of course, was that contracts might otherwise be withdrawn, thus throwing residents of the constituency out of work.[29] Another representative was reportedly told that every military base in his district would be closed if he did not vote in a certain way.[30]

Even the most resentful congressmen, however, had a grudging admiration for O'Brien's efficiency. He and his cohorts maintained an exhaustive card index that provided up-to-date information about every member's needs, interests,

[28] Meg Greenfield, "Why Are You Calling Me, Son?" *Reporter,* August 16, 1962, p. 30.

[29] *Id.*

[30] *Congressional Record,* June 30, 1962, p. A-5727-28 (daily edition).

whims—and, of course, voting record.[31] The index enabled the O'Brien staff to apply indirect pressure on congressmen. A close personal friend, for example, might be persuaded to telephone a representative to offer advice about how he should vote on a pending amendment, or an old political crony might mention how happy he would be if a certain bill never emerged from committee. This kind of intercession often indicated that the card index had come through again.

Presidential Patronage

One of the most effective of the Kennedy Administration's levers was the judicious use of patronage. O'Brien's exact title, "Special Assistant to the President for Congressional Relations *and Personnel*" [emphasis added] was a candid admission of the extent to which the White House used patronage to obtain support in Congress. Presidents no longer control as many jobs as they once did, for creation of the Civil Service Commission in 1883 resulted in a drastic decline in the number of Federal offices that could be filled on a political basis. Nevertheless, potential patronage that was available to Mr. Kennedy when he became President in 1961 was hardly negligible: 36,000 jobs with an annual combined salary of about fifty million dollars.

The most coveted patronage controlled by the President

[31] O'Brien once spoke of the index in the following terms:

> We do maintain a card file which, of course, is a voting record that would normally be available to anyone. But we add to it intelligence relative to the member's position in the committee on a given matter, the attitude he may have expressed back home, for local consumption, on matters that may be helpful to us in the future.

Interview on Columbia Broadcasting System Television Network, August 26, 1962, printed in *Congressional Record,* August 28, 1962, p. 16764 (daily edition).

consists of Federal judgeships. Although every President pays lip service to the ideal of a nonpartisan judiciary, the temptation to use appointments to the bench as political prizes is seldom overcome. No Chief Executive in recent decades has appointed even 15 per cent of his judges from the ranks of the opposition party. Organizations such as the American Bar Association are critical of the extent to which partisan considerations dominate judicial nominations. Yet there is no indication that the prevailing practice has served to diminish the caliber of Federal judges or impair their independence. Qualified candidates, after all, are ordinarily available in both of the parties; a President, therefore, need not choose inferior judges even if he never looks for talent outside his own party. Nor is there any evidence that judges have been subservient to either the President or the party that placed them on the bench. The permanent tenure they enjoy encourages a spirit of complete independence from political pressures.

The life term helps make judgeships extremely valuable as patronage jobs. Not surprisingly, the majority party in Congress balks at creating new judgeships if the President who would fill them happens to belong to the other party. In 1960, for example, a Democratic Congress refused to authorize any new judgeships for President Eisenhower to fill, in spite of the universal recognition that congestion in the Federal courts had become intolerable. Moreover, that Congress even declined Eisenhower's offer to select Democrats to fill half of any new judicial positions. The Democrats in control preferred to gamble on winning the Presidency in 1960 and also retaining their congressional majority. That way they would be able to establish judgeships that could all be reserved for Democrats. The speculation was successful, and promptly after the election the Democratic Congress passed a bill creating seventy-five new judgeships. President Kennedy, as expected, proceeded to award more than 90 per cent of them to his fellow Democrats.[32]

Apart from judgeships, a wide variety of other desirable offices may be filled on the basis of patronage. United States attorneys, Federal marshals, postmasters, and customs collectors are patronage appointees. The President even has some patronage within the Legislative Branch—officials such as the Public Printer (who manages the Government Printing Office) and the Librarian of Congress. There are also some seats on the regulatory commissions.[33]

Yet the fact remains that patronage is not quite so important to a President today as it once was. Part of the reason is that an impressive number of jobs have been placed in the Classified Service, where they are distributed on the basis of merit rather than politics. Another factor is the increased availability of well-paying private employment. During the Depression, patronage could be used with far more telling effect. Franklin Roosevelt delayed filling many Federal jobs in 1933, with the comment, "We haven't got to patronage

[32] In a sense, the patronage represented by judicial appointments is of greater value to senators than to the President. For in accordance with the practice of "senatorial courtesy," the President clears each judicial nomination with the senior senator of his own party who represents the state in which the judge is to serve. If the senator disapproves, the President will ordinarily refrain from making the nomination. If he acts otherwise, the senator will declare the nominee "personally obnoxious" to him, and the Senate will refuse to grant confirmation. Often the President delegates to the senators the right to choose judicial nominees, and he merely places his stamp of approval on the selections. See Ch. 13.

[33] Typically, Congress strives to prevent the packing of the regulatory commissions by providing that neither political party shall be represented by more than a bare majority. Given the nature of the American party system, however, it is not hard for a President to find members of the other party who are in full agreement with his philosophy.

yet." His meaning was clear: there would have to be legislative results before executive spoils were handed out.[34]

Administrative Lobbying

The small White House staff dealing with congressional relations constitutes only a tiny fraction of the total number of personnel in the Executive Branch devoting themselves to "legislative liaison" (the polite term for administrative lobbying). Every department and agency has its own liaison officers, though technically all the work that is done in the bureaucracy to influence congressional action is illegal. The law flatly forbids both officers and employees of the Executive Branch to use appropriated funds for the purpose of lobbying.[35] This prohibition is violated on its face every time a letter is posted or a telegram is sent or a telephone call is made urging a member of Congress to support or oppose any legislation (unless, of course, there has been a congressional request for a statement of the Administration's position on a bill). When the law is flouted in a particularly flagrant manner, congressmen can be expected to kick up their heels. They did precisely that in 1962, lashing out at President Kennedy's Secretary of Health, Education, and Welfare, Anthony C. Celebrezze. They were angry because the department headed by Celebrezze had used $3562 of public funds to send congressmen telegrams soliciting support for a bill to aid colleges and universities.[36] But as long as liaison activities do not involve *direct* expenditures of public money, Congress will almost always look the other way. The Executive Branch has probably become too

[34] Andrew Hacker, "When the President Goes to the People," *The New York Times Magazine,* June 10, 1962, p. 62.

[35] 41 Stat. 68, 18 U. S. C. 1913.

[36] The ensuing uproar persuaded Celebrezze to issue what he described as "specific instructions that this procedure shall not be repeated." *The New York Times,* September 21, 1962, p. 1, col. 6, (city edition).

much a part of the legislative process for any other course to be followed.

In the best political style, departmental and agency liaison officials search diligently for ways they can be of service to congressmen, on the theory that expressions of gratitude will take the form of support for legislative requests. Each of the three armed services maintains liaison offices within the portals of Congress, in the Senate and House Office Buildings, to handle congressional inquiries with dispatch. The efficient liaison officer will overlook no opportunity to create a favorable impression. At times when his agency is not embroiled in any outstanding controversies, he may try to arrange consultations between the policy-makers for whom he works and selected members of Congress, "just so that we can get to understand each other's point of view." And when the time comes for testimony to be given before a congressional committee, he will see to it that his agency's witnesses are properly briefed as to both subject matter and manner of presentation.[37] The more skillfully such public relations devices are employed, the less of a need there will be for direct lobbying.

Techniques used in administrative lobbying are not significantly different from those employed by private pressure groups. The policy is generally to concentrate attention on congressmen in key positions, such as the members of the appropriate committees and the individual regarded by others in his state delegation as an expert on the subject.

[37] When such "little" things are ignored, the result may be exceedingly serious. As responsible a newspaper as *The New York Times* blamed some of the Kennedy Administration's problems with foreign policy legislation on faulty liaison: "Mail and telephone inquiries frequently are handled in an unsatisfactory manner. Spokesmen sent to the Hill to advise the members or to testify before committees often seem to be either inadequately or narrowly informed." June 16, 1962, p. 1, col. 2 (city edition).

When crucial decisions are to be made on the floor, administrative lobbying will often center on members whose votes are not yet committed. In 1962, for example, the Agency for International Development prepared for the use of its liaison staff a state-by-state breakdown of all House members, grouped into three categories: those who "can, on the basis of previous record, probably be considered as hopeless"; those who were "with us on basis of past record"; and those "whose records would indicate there is hope, but who cannot be considered as safe." The point, of course, was that the first two groups could be ignored; the emphasis would be on the 151 uncommitted members.

One way in which an agency may try to convert a neutral into an ally is by practicing "reverse lobbying." The "clients" (or customers) of the agency will be mobilized to apply pressure in the proper places. The Department of Commerce will find it easy to obtain the cooperation of business organizations; the Department of Labor will enlist the unions; and the Department of Agriculture will be assisted by the farmers' organizations.[38] A more indirect form of reverse lobbying is to release information that will result in favorable press headlines precisely at the time when an appropriation bill is scheduled to come up. The agency that seems to employ such techniques with the greatest finesse is the Federal Bureau of Investigation. A highly skilled public relations campaign has lionized FBI agents and established a veritable cult of personality around Director J. Edgar Hoover.[39] So impressed are

[38] In 1960, for example, the Treasury Department wanted to drum up support for establishment of what was to become the International Development Association. It persuaded the AFL-CIO and the Chamber of Commerce to back the proposal and testify before the relevant committees.

[39] The success of the FBI's relations with Congress has been attributed to "the many books and articles written about the exploits of the [FBI] agents, the continuous, favorable publicity accorded to Mr. J. Edgar

congressmen by Hoover and his well-timed exploits that they regularly approve an even larger appropriation for the FBI than the agency itself requests.[40]

In addition to the work done by subordinate liaison officials, it is usually necessary for agency heads and even departmental heads to devote a large percentage of their own working hours to legislative relations. Secretary of Defense Robert S. McNamara said once that in a single three-week period he testified for 66 hours before three committees. Dean G. Acheson estimates that as Secretary of State he spent about one full day out of every six working on congressional liaison.[41]

For all the time and effort expended by the Executive Branch on congressional relations, the results are often skimpy, in terms of promoting the basic legislative program of an activist administration. President Kennedy fared particularly badly. In view of this, it is surprising that he only seldom felt compelled to go to the voters directly, over the heads of their congressmen, on issues of special importance.

Hoover, and the speeches and writings of Mr. Hoover himself. . . . " J. Leiper Freeman, "The Bureaucracy in Pressure Politics," in Donald C. Blaisdell, ed., *Unofficial Government: Pressure Groups and Lobbies, Annals of the American Academy of Political and Social Science,* CCCXIX (1958), pp. 18-19.

[40] At the time when the membership of the Communist Party was relatively high, Hoover convinced congressmen that a large appropriation was necessary to cope with a menace of such proportions; when the ranks became depleted, he won congressmen over to the belief that the reduction of the party to its hard core made it more dangerous than ever.

[41] Acheson recalls that he appeared at 125 formal congressional committee meetings and had 89 additional informal meetings. The typical formal meeting consumed half a day, with preparation for it taking up another half day; an informal meeting customarily meant the sacrifice of about one-fourth of the day. Dean G. Acheson, *A Citizen Looks at Congress* (New York: Harper, 1957), p. 65.

A President can mold public opinion as no one else can. And it is patently true, as one political scientist has noted, that "Congress will act if it senses that pressure is building up back home in the constituencies. . . ."[42] Doubtless, no miracles would have ensued if Kennedy had chosen to emulate Roosevelt by appealing directly to the people. But the results would have been interesting to observe.

[42] Hacker, *op. cit.*, p. 62.

5

Influence of Pressure Groups

AT EVERY POINT IN THE LEGISLATIVE PROCESS, the presence of pressure groups and the lobbyists who represent them is easy to discern. Pressure groups influence executive agencies as they frame their legislative recommendations, and the President as he screens these recommendations. They help determine how congressional subcommittees will act and whether full committees will overturn their actions. They are in contact with congressional leaders when a decision must be made about whether to bring a bill to the floor, and in many cases they dictate what will happen if it gets there. After a bill has been enacted, they work on the appropriate officials of the bureaucracy to make sure it is administered in a manner favorable to them. Wherever decisions are made, there one will find the lobbyist and the pressure group for which he speaks.

The long list of "associations" appearing in the Washington telephone directory is at least a partial indication of how many pressure groups exist. An almost incredible total of more than one thousand associations can be found. There are associations representing railroads, soap and glycerin producers, and the missile and rocket industries. The registered bank holding companies have an association, and so do the sugar producers of Puerto Rico and the first-class mailers. There are associations of American universities, casualty and surety companies, oil pipelines, petroleum re-refiners, and even roll label manufacturers.

About 1100 registered lobbyists in Washington work for these associations and for other pressure groups. Perhaps the single most curious thing about today's lobbyists is that so few people in Washington seem to resent their presence, while so many defend ardently the role they fill. There was once a time when a single word in favor of lobbying would create the suspicion that its author had been paid a price for his utterance. The situation at present could not be more different. Today one hears only praise for the assistance that the lobbyist renders to Congress and the executive agencies, and for his help in preserving the constitutional right to petition government for redress of grievances. The existence of pressure groups, we are told, is essential to the survival of a pluralistic society, and is thus useful in repulsing the inroads of totalitarianism. Even the use of the term "pressure group" is frowned upon, on the ground that the term has pejorative connotations; the name "interest group" is preferred.[1]

Those who are most complacent about contemporary lobbying do not go so far as to deny that in the "bad old days" lobbying thoroughly deserved its unsavory reputation. They insist, however, that at least with respect to Congress the days when votes were exchanged for "party girls" and hundred-

---

[1] One who does not want to risk raising eyebrows in polite society will never use an adjective to modify the term "interest group." Never, for example, will he speak of a *"special* interest group," and certainly not of a *"selfish* interest group." An entire school of political scientists has come into existence to explain that there is no such thing as a "public interest" or "general interest" that is different from the sum total of private interests. See, e.g., Glendon Schubert, *The Public Interest* (Glencoe, Ill.: Free Press, 1961).

dollar bills are gone forever. They make much of the point that there is little similarity between the "new lobby" and the lobby of yesteryear. As one former congressman put it, the "practice of having legislators . . . embraced in the toils of the harlot is still in vogue at the seat of many state governments but has been practically abandoned in Washington, D. C."[2]

Occasionally, of course, something will happen to cast doubt on the theory that the "old lobby" is entirely extinct. In 1956, for example, Senator Francis Case (R., S. D.), who had not yet taken a position on a pending natural gas bill, made a dramatic announcement on the Senate floor: an oil company lobbyist had just attempted to give him $2500, supposedly to lubricate his re-election campaign.[3] Although the episode was greeted with loud public indignation, little attention was paid to the possibility that such brazen efforts were commonplace and that there was no reason to assume they were always unsuccessful. The general feeling seemed rather to be that all congressmen were as moral as Senator Case, who had exposed the bribery attempt, and that the Legislative Branch was therefore entirely immune from corruption.

[2] V. O. Key, Jr., *Politics, Parties, and Pressure Groups* (New York: Thomas Y. Crowell, 1958), p. 152, note 18 (4th edition), quoting *Congressional Record*, June 29, 1950, p. A-5076 (daily edition).

[3] Case declared that in the circumstances he would not vote at all on the bill. Other senators and representatives were not so squeamish, and the legislation passed. President Eisenhower, however, although he favored the bill, exercised his veto against it, on the express ground that faith in the democratic process would be undermined by the enactment of a measure promoted through such "arrogant lobbying." No effort was made in Congress to override the veto. Subsequent criminal prosecution led to the imposition of a $10,000 fine on the oil company (Superior) and also fines of $2,500 each on two of its agents. Edith T. Carper, "Lobbying and the Natural Gas Bill," in Edwin A. Bock and Alan K. Campbell, eds., *Case Studies in American Government* (Englewood Cliffs, N. J.: Prentice-Hall, 1962), pp. 217-21

The New Lobby

It is certain that no "new lobby" would ever have been involved in such an episode. The "new lobby," which prides itself on working in the open, takes pains to behave with complete propriety. Its techniques, however, are evidently just as effective as those that were used in former times. The very political scientist who originated the term "new lobby" had great respect for what these techniques could accomplish. Through their use, he said, the "new lobbyists" had made themselves "the 'third House of Congress,' the assistant rulers, the 'invisible government.' "[4]

What are the techniques through which the "new lobbyist" earns such tributes? One of the most common is the furnishing of research assistance. Perhaps he will compile materials that a congressman and his office will find helpful, or even write finished speeches to be used in committee, on the floor, or in public addresses. To a member who is sufficiently committed to the point of view he represents, the skilled lobbyist is in a position to render valuable assistance at nearly every stage of the legislative process. He may suggest certain questions to be asked at a committee hearing. On occasion, he may provide welcome advice on legislative tactics and help build up support for the member's aims among other interest groups and congressmen, as well as executive officials. He sometimes arranges for the appearance of witnesses at hearings, and even writes their statements. And it is not unusual for him to perform something of an intelligence function, briefing the congressman on precisely where things stand in the intricate maze of the congressional process.[5] His cooperation may be so extensive that for all practical purposes he is

[4] E. Pendleton Herring, *Group Representation before Congress* (Baltimore: The Johns Hopkins Press, 1929), p. 41.

[5] Donald R. Matthews, *U. S. Senators and Their World* (Chapel Hill: University of North Carolina Press, 1960), p. 183.

augmenting the congressman's staff with the facilities of his organization.

Such techniques are feasible, of course, only when the lobbyist is dealing with a congressman who is already sympathetic to his cause. How does a lobbyist attempt to influence others? A favorite method is to try to condition public opinion at the grass roots, in the constituencies of those members whose votes will be crucial. In 1962, for example, the Chamber of Commerce was interested in defeating President Kennedy's proposal that Congress authorize the establishment of a Department of Urban Affairs. The Chamber chose to concentrate all its efforts on two wavering members of the Rules Committee, whose votes would almost surely be decisive. A "task force" was sent into the congressional districts of these members. Its assignment was to arrange meetings, speak to people whom the congressmen respected, and work with the local "congressional action committees" of the Chamber to persuade the two representatives that they should help kill the bill.[6] In the same year, the Chamber used the identical method to help defeat another important bill—the one designed to expand the Social Security program by providing medical care for the aged. Again there was economy of effort. It was both cheaper and easier to work on the 25 members of the House Ways and Means Committee than it would have been to deal with the 437 members of the House[7]—and it was just as effective.[8] Woodrow Wilson testified that such a policy

[6] Both congressmen allowed themselves to be persuaded.

[7] The membership of the House had been permitted to rise temporarily to 437 in order to give seats immediately to representatives from the new states of Alaska and Hawaii. The reapportionment that went into effect in 1963 restored the number to 435.

[8] Subtlety was not the distinguishing characteristic of the printed materials circulated by the Chamber regarding "medicare." One brochure, in the shape of a medicine bottle, described the Administration program in the following purple terms:

of concentration was already widely used in the last century. The reason was precisely the same one that operates today:

It would be impracticable [for the lobbyist] to work up his schemes in the broad field of the whole House, but in the membership of a committee he finds manageable numbers. If he can gain the ear of the committee, or of any influential portion of it, he has practically gained the ear of the House itself. . . .[9]

The Influentials

It is far from rare for a pressure group to select an ex-congressman to be its chief lobbyist. Former Senate Majority Leader Scott Lucas (D., Ill.), who became a full-time "legislative representative" after he left Congress, makes no bones about the fact that his previous office is of considerable help in his present occupation. "I can see anybody in the Senate almost any time," he has said. "The Senate is a club and you're a member until you die, even if you get defeated for re-election."[10] In addition to Lucas, 13 other former senators and 69 former representatives have worked as lobbyists in recent years.[11]

But the pressure groups do not have to confine themselves to alumni of the Legislative Branch in their attempts to re-

---

. . . an election year elixir brewed by a nationally known team of political medicine-makers. Guaranteed to cure vote deficiencies and related ailments so prevalent during the month of November. Caution notice. Frequent and excessive use is habit-forming, tends to over-excite paternalistic glands, often deadens incentive nerves.

[9] Woodrow Wilson, *Congressional Government* (New York: Meridian, 1959), pp. 132-33 (written in 1883).

[10] *Congressional Record*, October 10, 1962, p. 21743 (daily edition). One of the privileges that a congressman-turned-lobbyist enjoys is the right to communicate directly with his former colleagues on the floor of the house in which he served.

[11] *Congressional Record*, October 10, 1962, p. 21743 (daily edition).

cruit influential lobbyists. Sometimes it is possible to persuade a former Cabinet officer that it is not beneath his dignity to become a lobbyist.[12] And "defense" industries have made a regular practice of retaining retired military officers, who may be able to influence their former Pentagon colleagues on legislation within the sphere of the Department of Defense.

In days gone by, one of the preferred methods used by pressure groups was to invite Congressmen to attend lavish parties that would often be highlights of the social season. Those who accepted would not have been amused by this limerick:

> There once was a lady from Kent
> Who said that she knew what it meant
> When men took her to dine,
> Bought her cocktails and wine.
> She knew what it meant—but she went.[13]

The influence of the "social lobby" has today become distinctly secondary, but it is by no means completely unimportant. In the words of a leading authority on pressure politics, entertainment still serves "to create a feeling of obligation on the part of the legislator toward individuals who have established sociable relations with him through entertaining him and his family." Although only the rare congressman will trade his vote for a night on the town, the social lobby remains "a means of reinforcing the preferences already held by various members of the legislative body."[14] In all likelihood, it was for the purpose of "reinforcing . . . preferences" that in

[12] Since 1955, for example, Mexican sugar interests in the United States have been represented by Oscar L. Chapman, Secretary of the Interior in the Truman Administration.

[13] Quoted in Don K. Price, *Government and Science* (New York: New York University Press, 1954), p. 87.

[14] David B. Truman, *The Governmental Process* (New York: Knopf, 1960), pp. 340-42.

1955 the Trujillo regime provided an expenses-paid trip to the Dominican Republic for members and staff assistants of the House Agriculture Committee only a few weeks before hearings were scheduled to begin on sugar legislation.[15]

The tactics that lobbyists employ are as varied as the causes they represent. Those who work for the American Medical Association persuade doctors in a particular congressional district to put pressure on a representative who may be leaning in the direction of "socialized medicine." The National Association for the Advancement of Colored People produces up-to-date voting records on all members of Congress, and sends its legislative representative throughout the country to circulate these tabulations and interpret them. The Chamber of Commerce maintains an extensive card catalogue, with a listing for each congressman and the names of members of the local Chamber who have his ear. Some highly effective work is done during election campaigns, when large sums of money may be spent on congressional races. The lesson for members of Congress is obvious: cooperation with the pressure group yields rich dividends, while the price of opposition is sure to be high.

Effectiveness of Lobbies

Are the techniques of the lobbyist effective? The late Senator Henry F. Ashhurst (D., Ariz.), after announcing that he had changed his mind on a certain bill before Congress, was asked by a reporter when he had seen the light. His reply was brief but to the point: "When did I see the light? I just felt the heat." A senator often finds it somewhat easier to with-

[15] The context of this situation is explored by Daniel M. Berman and Robert A. Heineman in "Lobbying by Foreign Governments on the Sugar Act Amendments of 1962," *Law and Contemporary Problems*, XXVIII. (Spring 1963).

stand the heat than a representative does. His state-wide constituency may be so varied that nothing really impels him to become a tool of any single pressure group. His maneuverability, in fact, may even enable him to engage in something of a bargaining process with the various groups that importune him.[16] If his state is large enough, the senator may even fit the cynic's definition of a statesman as "a politician held upright by pressures on all sides." By contrast, a member of the House finds himself in an incomparably more difficult situation. Because his constituency is relatively small, it will often be dominated by just a few interests—and the congressman will ignore the demands of those interests only if he is bent on political suicide, particularly if a coalition of lobbying organizations has been forged. It is not surprising, therefore, that the lobbyist wins more of his victories in the House than in the Senate.

Although lobbyists often succeed in persuading Congress to enact legislation they favor, they achieve results even more readily when the groups they represent want primarily to obstruct and delay legislation. A "defensive group" derives benefit from the sheer cumbersomeness of the legislative process in Congress. Its task is relatively easy, because there are so many junctures at which a negative decision will doom a bill.[17] While proponents of the legislation must win every match, the opposition requires only a single victory.

Lobbies do not find it difficult, therefore, to administer one defeat after another to Presidents who champion a positive legislative program. In the Eighty-seventh Congress, for example, the lobbies were far more successful than President Kennedy. The American Medical Association presided over the death of "medicare"; the American Farm Bureau Federa-

[16] Matthews, *op. cit.*, pp. 195-96.
[17] Truman, *op. cit.*, p. 354.

tion helped defeat the Administration farm bill; and the American Savings and Loan League could take credit for scuttling a plan requiring that taxes on interest and dividends be withheld at the source. The President's only major legislative victory—passage of the Trade Expansion Act—was achieved precisely because this time the powerful lobbies were on his side.[18]

One of the lobbying efforts in the Eighty-seventh Congress was so intensive that it stimulated a Senate investigation. That was the successful campaign by foreign sugar interests to expand or at least maintain the "country quota system," under which they could sell sugar in the United States at far above the world market price. Among other things, it was later revealed that some lobbyists had been retained on a contingent-fee basis: their pay depended on the size of the quotas they could extract from Congress. The danger, of course, was that the system of incentives might very well have tempted lobbyists to employ the most unscrupulous methods to increase the size of their employers' quotas. President Kennedy expressed displeasure at such an arrangement,[19] and the Senate Foreign Relations Committee promptly instituted a full-scale investigation into the "non-

[18] *The New York Times* gave this picture of the three-day period preceding the vote in the House:

> Singly and in groups, scores of lobbyists filled the corridors outside the House chamber to buttonhole members, or tramped through the two House Office Buildings to seek them out. The huge Capitol switchboard was alight from early morning until late afternoon.

June 30, 1962, p. 4, col. 4 (city edition).

[19] He told his press conference: "It's an unfortunate situation where men are paid large fees by foreign governments to secure quotas and where, in some cases, there are contingency fees. . . . " *Ibid.*, July 6, 1962, p. 8, col. 3 (city edition).

diplomatic activities of representatives of foreign governments."

When an attack is mounted against them, lobbyists for
foreign interests find themselves in an extremely vulnerable
position. Since their employers are not Americans, they cannot legitimately claim any right to influence the political
process of the United States. Domestic lobbies, however, have
no trouble justifying *their* existence. They make the point
that a pressure group is only an association of Americans
who share common interests and objectives. Originally, they
say, the members of a group may have joined together for
reasons having nothing to do with pressure politics; their
motivation may have been religious, cultural, or social. But
when a governmental activity reached into their sphere of
interest, they had every right to use their already-existing
organization to express their point of view.

The Case for Lobbies

A good case for the pressure system has been made by proponents of the "group theory" in politics. They argue that
governmental action is hardly ever the product of a debate
between opposing concepts of the public welfare; rather,
legislation commonly results from a struggle between pressure groups.[20] According to this analysis, men should not be
expected to act like dispassionate philosopher-kings, for whom
the highest good is the welfare of the community. It is rather
completely in accord with their nature that they should strive
to advance themselves and the groups with which they identify.[21]

Group theorists do not fear the existence of pressure or-

[20] Karl Schriftgiesser, *The Lobbyists: The Art and Business of Influencing Lawmakers* (Boston: Little, Brown, 1951), pp. 29-31.

[21] See, for example, No. 10 of *The Federalist Papers,* by James Madison.

ganizations. There might be danger, they say, if each individual in the country identified his interests with only one such group and if the various groups were thus engaged in a struggle for total power. The existing situation, as they see it, is very different. A man today is almost willy-nilly a member of many groups. As a worker, for example, he may belong to a trade union, but other interests may impel him also to join a church, an automobile club, a home-owners association, and possibly a political party. Thus no single group with which he is affiliated represents the totality of his interests. As a consequence, he will be unlikely to support any group in activities that extend beyond the limited purposes for which he joined it.

Some of those who advance this defense are not content to rebut charges against the pressure group system; they insist also on the affirmative values of the system. Because groups are instruments of pluralism, one defender of the system has said, they constitute "an especially American practical alternative to the program of communist centralism in ideology and government."[22] It is added by others that the influence of groups provides us with at least some of the virtues of functional representation, under which a congressman would directly represent an interest—such as industry, labor, professions—instead of a random collection of disparate individuals who happen to be living in the same geographical area.[23]

[22] Alfred de Grazia, "Nature and Prospects of Political Interest Groups," in Blaisdell, *op. cit.*, p. 113.

[23] Stuart Chase, *Democracy under Pressure: Special Interests vs. the Public Welfare* (New York: The Twentieth Century Fund, 1945), p. 9. Under a system of functional representation, the voter would not choose someone "to represent him as a man or as a citizen in all the aspects of citizenship, but only . . . to represent his view in relation to some particular purpose or group of purposes. . . . " Austin Ranney and Willmoore Kendall, *Democracy and the American Party System* (New York: Harcourt, 1956), p. 69, quoting G. D. H. Cole.

Implicit in any all-out defense of the pressure group system is the assumption that all interests in our society are fairly represented in it, and that thus unreasonable demands by any group will always run up against effective opposition. Such an assumption is not warranted, however, for an interest group that is not organized can make no headway against one that is organized, and an interest group without money cannot effectively oppose one that is affluent.

An expert on pressure groups has pointed out how one-sided will be the struggle between an organized group and an unorganized group: "The lobbyists for electrical utilities . . . are eternally on the job; the lobbyists for the consumers of this monopolistic service are ordinarily conspicuous by their absence."[24] The fact that consumers—and many other groups as well—are not organized is of critical significance, for it means that the system of pressure politics has no self-regulating mechanism to keep it fair, balanced, and equitable. Under such conditions, no invisible hand can possibly assure the existence of universal symmetry, or even of a tolerable equilibrium.

As might be expected, organization is found most frequently among groups with money. The poor man—whether for lack of time, lack of sophistication, or lack of group-consciousness—is not much of a joiner. And even when he does become a member of an organization, the resources of that group will normally be far too meager to support lobbying activities, especially on the national scene. Thus it is business groups that dominate the pressure system and give it what has been called an "upper-class bias."[25]

Just as the totality of pressure groups may not be represen-

[24] Key, *op. cit.*, p. 166.
[25] E. E. Schattschneider, *The Semisovereign People* (New York: Holt, Rinehart and Winston, 1960), pp. 30-32.

tative of the entire nation, many individual pressure groups are far from being representative of their own memberships. A lobbyist may try to give the impression that he speaks for the entire organization that has retained him, but often this claim cannot survive even the most superficial examination. Two questions will usually suffice: "What percentage of the membership generally attends the conventions that determine policy matters?" "When an issue arises during the period between conventions, who establishes policy?" The answers will customarily reveal that the "iron law of oligarchy"[26] is never more in evidence than in the formulation of a pressure group's policies. More often than not, the channels of communication betwen the membership and its "spokesmen" are, for all practical purposes, non-existent.

Regulation of Lobbying

It was not until 1946 that Congress chose to pass legislation to discourage lobbying abuses. Before that year, it had never moved to do more than conduct investigations of lobbying. During the Wilson Administration, a select committee produced sixty volumes of testimony on the lobbying tactics employed by the National Association of Manufacturers. Two decades later, a spectacular investigation was conducted by a special committee under the chairmanship of Senator (later Supreme Court Justice) Hugo L. Black (D., Ala.) into the unscrupulous efforts that lobbies had made to defeat legislation to regulate public utility holding companies.[27] But although both these investigations commanded much public

[26] Discerned by Robert Michels, in *Political Parties: A Sociological Study of the Oligarchical Tendencies of Modern Democracy* (Glencoe, Ill.: Free Press, 1949), originally published in English in 1915.

[27] One revelation by Black's committee was a particular sensation: companies that wanted to insulate themselves against regulation had inspired the sending of thousands of bogus telegrams to congressmen.

attention, neither resulted in any legislation. There might have been no legislation in 1946, either, had it not been for President Truman. As a senator, Mr. Truman had been chairman of a special war investigating committee, which had learned a great deal about the methods used by pressure groups. Upon becoming President, he took the lead in pressing Congress to eradicate what he considered to be a threat to its integrity. The result was the Federal Regulation of Lobbying Act, which was passed as part of the omnibus Legislative Reorganization Act.

The 1946 law rested on the premise that the dangers represented by lobbying could largely be eliminated by compelling the lobbies to operate under public scrutiny. Accordingly, the provisions of the Act were not punitive in character. Instead, they merely required both the lobbies and the lobbyists to place certain information about their activities on the public record.

What the lobbies were obliged to do was exceedingly simple. Each one was to keep detailed records of the contributions it received and the expenditures it made. These records were to form the basis of quarterly reports that were to be filed with the Clerk of the House of Representatives. Every report would list the names of any persons who had contributed $500 or more to the organization on a single occasion, along with the total amount that each had contributed during the entire calendar year. It would also contain information on expenditures: the identity of anyone who had been paid more than $10 by the lobby, and the purposes for which such expenditures had been made.

Registration and disclosure were the requirements imposed on the individual lobbyist who represented a pressure group. The registration would have to be accomplished before the lobbyist even began his work. In sworn statements filed with the Clerk of the House and the Secretary of the Senate, he would have to identify himself and his employer and answer questions about the duration of his employment, his salary, and his expense allowance. Once he had registered, he would be bound by only a single requirement. Every three months, he would have to file a sworn statement with information on certain matters: the receipts and expenditures that his work had entailed; the identity of those to whom he had paid money; the purposes of such payments; the names of publications in which he had "caused to be published" any articles or editorials; and the proposed legislation in which he was interested. The information furnished by the lobbyist, like that which was provided by his organization, would be brought to the attention of members of Congress through publication in the *Congressional Record*.[28]

Deficiencies in the Law

Several exemptions were included in the 1946 Act. The registration requirement would not affect a lobbyist whose activities consisted of nothing but appearances before congressional committees. Nor would it apply to public officials when they attempted in the course of their work to influence Congress. But a third exemption overshadowed the other two in importance. This one was implicit in the law's statement that the reporting requirement applied only to an organization "the *principal* purpose of which" was to affect legislation, or one that collected money "to be used *principally*" for legislative purposes [emphasis added]. This loophole enabled many organizations that were exerting a powerful effect on congressional legislation to escape the reporting requirement on the ground that their *principal* purpose had nothing to do with lobbying, since their efforts to

[28] Schriftgiesser, *op. cit.*, pp. 87ff.

influence legislation were merely incidental to other purposes. On this theory, an organization as powerful as the National Association of Manufacturers does not feel compelled to comply with the provisions of the Act.

The lobbying law has been subjected to other serious criticisms as well. It has been pointed out, for example, that its provisions do not affect attempts to influence officials of the Executive Branch, although these officials often enjoy considerable leeway in determining how a congressional program is to be carried out. And some critics have condemned the failure of the Act to cover efforts to influence congressional staff members.

Weak as the law was from the beginning, it was weakened still further in 1954 by a Supreme Court decision. The validity of the law had been challenged on the ground that the right to lobby is insulated from congressional action by the provisions of the First Amendment. A district court, impressed by the argument, ruled that the law was invalid because it abridged the freedoms of speech, assembly, and press. On appeal, the Supreme Court reversed this decision, but it saved the statute from unconstitutionality only by construing its provisions strictly. In an opinion by Chief Justice Earl Warren, it held that a person could be subject to the law's provisions only if he had tried to influence Congress by "direct communication with members of Congress."[29] According to the Court, indirect lobbying—such as attempts to stir up grass roots sentiment in order to generate pressure on Congress—could not constitutionally be regulated.

Whatever its legal merits, the Supreme Court decision was a grievous blow at the lobbying act, for indirect methods are often preferred by the pressure groups. In 1962, for instance, the American Medical Association spent $7 million to defeat

[29] United States v. Harriss, 347 U. S. 612, 623 (1954).

a "medicare" bill. Of that amount, no more than 3 per cent was used for "direct lobbying." Because of the Supreme Court decision, only that relatively insignificant portion of the money disbursed by AMA had to be accounted for.[30]

Little hope exists that the Supreme Court will ever change its mind about lobbying and the First Amendment. For the three Justices who dissented in the 1954 case—Hugo L. Black, William O. Douglas, and Robert H. Jackson—disagreed with the majority only because they would have gone further and declared the law to be a flat violation of the Constitution, instead of "saving" it by interpreting its provisions restrictively.

The law has turned out to be so weak that a responsible newspaperman has said it serves today only "to create the impression that lobbying is regulated, while, in fact, it is not."[31] As a consequence, demands have arisen from time to time for new congressional action. One expert on pressure groups wants the law amended to require a registered lobbyist to submit information about the size of his organization and the procedures by which policies are established. Such information would help congressmen determine the extent to which the lobbyist really represented those for whom he purported to speak.[32] A number of senators, headed by John L. McClellan (D., Ark.), have sponsored legislation to overcome the 1954 Supreme Court decision. They want to eradicate the distinction between direct and indirect lobbying and re-

[30] *Congressional Record,* October 12, 1962, p. 22040, quoting James McCartney, *Chicago Daily News,* October 11-12, 1962.

[31] *Id.*

[32] Belle Zeller, "The Regulation of Pressure Groups and Lobbyists," in Blaisdell, *op. cit.,* p. 98. The same writer has proposed two additional reforms: publicity should be given to expense accounts filed by lobbyists, and the law should be amended to cover those who try to influence the actions of executive departments and agencies. *Id.*

quire disclosure of both types of activity. To skirt the constitutional problem, McClellan would punish violations of the reporting requirements with civil instead of criminal penalties, for he believes that the Supreme Court might be more lenient with a statute containing no criminal sanctions.[33]

Encouraging Lobbies

But Congress shows no signs of being even remotely interested in strengthening the lobbying laws. Quite the opposite, it seems to have been so taken with the "new lobby" that it wants to encourage it to even more massive efforts. The most dramatic recent indication of a tendency to pamper lobbies came in 1962, when legislation was enacted allowing business concerns to deduct lobbying expenses from their taxable income. Under the new law, such expenses can be considered among the "ordinary and necessary" costs of carrying on a business, as long as they are incurred for the purpose of influencing legislation of direct interest to the taxpayer. Although the expenses of lobbying at the grass roots are not deductible, the costs of every conceivable type of direct lobbying are: appearances before committees, communications with members, and even personal contact with them. Moreover, the dues that are paid to organizations engaged in lobbying are now also deductible.

When the 1962 legislation was being considered, opponents centered their criticism on the point that the measure would make lobbies with a direct business and financial interest in legislation stronger than ever while doing nothing for the groups that really needed help—those trying to defend the general interest. Senator Proxmire of Wisconsin noted an ironic

[33] *Ibid.*, p. 94. Under the McClellan proposal also, regulation would be extended to lobbying in the Executive Branch, instead of being limited to lobbying in Congress.

contrast: a taxpayer would be allowed to deduct dues paid to the National Association of Manufacturers, since the NAM represented his particular selfish interest, but one of his neighbors who belonged to a disinterested church group or civic-minded organization could take no deduction, precisely *because* he had joined for unselfish motives. Senator Douglas of Illinois agreed with Proxmire. The new law, he said, would intensify and accentuate the lack of balance that already existed between "the great and concentrated power of special . . . interests" and the "diffused weakness of the general interest."[34] Douglas and Proxmire, however, were fighting a losing battle. Their colleagues overwhelmingly approved the tax deduction, (unanimously in the House, and with only 13 negative votes in the Senate), thus making lobbying by special interest groups more important than ever in the legislative process.

The Douglas-Proxmire attack on the 1962 measure directed public attention toward pressure groups of a special sort—those that do not function to protect the selfish interests of their members. Persons who join the American Civil Liberties Union, for example, do not generally anticipate that *their* right to speak will be threatened or that *they* will ever be defendants in criminal cases. Their motive in joining the organization is rather a belief that the maintenance of individual freedom furthers the public interest. Similarly, it has been observed that the members of the American League to Abolish Capital Punishment "obviously do not expect to be hanged;"[35] they form a pressure group simply because they oppose the death penalty on general principles that have nothing to do with self-interest. The formation of more such idealistic groups, each campaigning for what it be-

[34] *Congressional Record,* September 4, 1962, pp. 17403-04.
[35] Schattschneider, *op. cit.,* p. 26.

lieves to be the *common* interest, would be a step away from the prevailing situation, in which almost the only visible contenders in legislative politics are those who use the term "public interest" as nothing but a euphemism for what will benefit them.[36]

The average congressman, however, seems content with the prevailing situation. Pressure groups, after all, can often help him persuade his colleagues to support bills that he is promoting. So valuable is such assistance that senators and representatives often foster the creation of new pressure groups to help them get particular legislation through Congress.

[36] Some of the most powerful selfish-interest groups are small, but extremely influential on legislation of direct concern to them. It is therefore a mistake to ignore all but the large, national pressure groups when studying the factors that affect congressional action.

6

Committee Chairmen and Members

THE VOLUME OF LEGISLATION that the House and Senate are asked to consider gives the appearance of being truly staggering: in every Congress more than 20,000 bills are introduced. This statistic, however, has little meaning as an index of Congress' real work load. For an extremely high percentage of the bills are presented with no serious thought by their sponsors that they will—or even should—be enacted. The members just go through the motions, in order to satisfy constituents or local pressure groups that herculean efforts are being made to secure the passage of legislation they favor. Under these circumstances, it is not surprising that such a small proportion of the bills introduced in each session are even brought to the floor. The fate of the vast majority is to be ignored by the committees to which they are referred. Most of the remainder are abandoned at other points along the way. Only a minute percentage actually become law, and of these not more than a tiny handful possess general significance.

Without doubt, the standing committees—each one with

permanent jurisdiction over a particular class of legislation—are the principal instruments through which the process of elimination is carried out.[1] Because this is so, it is common practice for a bill to be framed in such a manner as to assure its referral to a friendly committee. In 1963, for example, the Kennedy Administration cast its civil rights bill on public accommodations in terms which virtually guaranteed that in the Senate it would be referred to the friendly Commerce Committee rather than the hostile Judiciary Committee.

The decision by the presiding officer to refer a bill to a particular committee is usually routine. This has been especially true since 1946, when the Legislative Reorganization Act narrowed the area of discretion by defining the jurisdiction of the various committees in fairly precise terms. Yet there are still occasions when discretion is available. In 1962, for instance, a serious question arose in the Senate over a bill that would authorize Federal courts to issue injunctions in certain cases against the use of literacy tests. The bill might have been referred to the Committee on Rules and Adminis-

---

[1] The Senate has 16 standing committees and the House has 20. A complete list follows:

Senate: Aeronautical and Space Sciences, Agriculture and Forestry, Appropriations, Armed Services, Banking and Currency, District of Columbia, Finance, Foreign Relations, Government Operations, Interior and Insular Affairs, Interstate and Foreign Commerce, Judiciary, Labor and Public Welfare, Post Office and Civil Service, Public Works, and Rules and Administration.

House: Agriculture, Appropriations, Armed Services, Banking and Currency, District of Columbia, Education and Labor, Foreign Affairs, Government Operations, House Administration, Interior and Insular Affairs, Interstate and Foreign Commerce, Judiciary, Merchant Marine and Fisheries, Post Office and Civil Service, Public Works, Rules, Science and Astronautics, Un-American Activities, Veterans' Affairs, and Ways and Means.

In addition, there are several special, or select, committees.

tration, which deals with legislation on voting, or to the Committee on the Judiciary, which has charge of legislation on the Federal courts. A majority on the Rules Committee would probably have favored the legislation, while the bill had more enemies than friends in Judiciary. It was to the Judiciary Committee, long known as a graveyard for civil rights, that the measure was finally sent. All such rulings on referral are made by the presiding officer, usually on the advice of the parliamentarian. Rulings may be overturned by a simple majority, but it is a rarity for this to happen.

Introducing a Bill

If a bill is to receive serious attention, it is important for it to be introduced by an influential congressman. The most desirable sponsor is the chairman of the committee to which it will probably be referred or of the subcommittee that will give it preliminary study. That way the measure is at least assured of a hearing. The committee chairman, assuming he belongs to the President's party, will customarily agree as a matter of courtesy to introduce any bill originating in the White House. In the event that he and the President are members of different parties, an Administration bill will probably be sponsored by the ranking *minority* member of the committee.[2] When the chairman or ranking minority member is not available as a sponsor of a bill, an effort will usually be made to prevail on another senior member of the committee or subcommittee to introduce it.

In cases where a congressman has prepared a bill only to placate a pressure group, however, he will certainly not try to impose on a senior colleague by asking him to act as sponsor. Instead, he will ordinarily offer the bill on his own. He

[2] Rank is determined by the length of a member's continuous service on the committee.

may even note that he is introducing it "by request," thus indicating that he does not necessarily agree with its provisions.

The formal procedure for introducing legislation is simple. The sponsor of a House bill merely writes his name on it and drops it in the "hopper" on the Clerk's desk. In the Senate, a sponsor must obtain recognition and then announce that he is offering a bill for introduction. Customarily the Senate reserves the first part of each daily session for the introduction of bills and the transaction of other routine business. This period is known as the Morning Hour—not too descriptive a title since it comes about in the afternoon and is two hours in duration.

Senate rules permit a group of members to join together as sponsors of a single bill, so that all of them can appear in a favorable light to an important pressure group. Multiple sponsorship, however, is sometimes used with quite another purpose in mind. When a significant percentage of the Senate's total membership—perhaps even an absolute majority—can be persuaded to sponsor a bill jointly, it is not quite so easy for the bill to be ignored in committee as it would be otherwise.

It is precisely because multiple sponsorship may serve as a device for applying pressure to a standing committee that the House does not recognize the practice. In view of its large membership, it is afraid that anarchy will ensue if the power of its committees is not guarded zealously. The House prohibition is often circumvented through the introduction of identical bills by several representatives. But in such a case each bill is printed separately and given its own number, so that the effect achieved in the Senate by listing a large number of members as sponsors of a single bill is largely lost. By insisting that each congressman's bill be set up in type individually even though it may be identical to fifty others, the House incurs large printing bills, but the leadership does not consider this an exorbitant price to pay for maintaining "regular procedures."

The morning after a bill has been introduced, copies are available in the congressional document rooms. One copy is delivered by a page to the chairman of the committee where the bill has been referred. What happens to the bill next depends in large measure on what that chairman decides to do.

Committee Chairmen

It is difficult to exaggerate the power of a committee chairman. Even on committees with comparatively democratic procedures, chairmen are generally able to exercise firm control, and what the committee does is seldom different from what the chairman wants it to do. Events have not served to outdate the description by Woodrow Wilson of those who command the committees: petty barons who "may at will exercise an almost despotic sway within their own shires, and may sometimes threaten to convulse even the realm itself. . . ."[3] Wilson went so far as to describe the American form of government as "government by the chairmen of the standing committees of Congress."[4]

The most awesome power of a chairman is his ability to

[3] Woodrow Wilson, *Congressional Government* (New York: Meridian, 1959), p. 76 (written in 1883). Baronial tendencies were certainly manifested by House Appropriations Committee Chairman Clarence Cannon (D., Mo.) in 1962 when he refused to speak on the telephone with the President of the United States. Mr. Kennedy had called about an impasse that had developed between Cannon's committee and the Senate Appropriations Committee. *Washington Post,* October 14, 1962, p. A4, col. 3.

[4] Wilson, *op. cit.*, p. 82.

prevent his committee from acting and thus prevent Congress from acting. The chairman of a committee that has no regular meeting day finds it particularly easy to block action. He need do nothing more than refuse to call a meeting. In the event that he does not wish to indulge in such heavy-handed tactics, he may accomplish the same results by scheduling a meeting for a time when he knows it will be impossible to obtain a quorum.[5]

Such obstructionist practices were supposed to end with the passage of the Legislative Reorganization Act of 1946. The Act provided that each committee, except the two Appropriations Committees, should "fix regular weekly, biweekly, or monthly meeting days for transaction of business. . . ." Most committees did bow to the requirement, but some others simply chose to ignore it. Even on committees which did institute fixed meeting days, members came to see that the 1946 law did not solve the problem by any means. For near the close of a congressional session, when time is short and the flow of legislative business heavy, extra committee meetings are necessary to deal with items on the agenda. The chairman, who alone has the power to call such extra meetings, is in a position to prevent consideration of legislation he opposes by simply failing to call the meetings.[6]

For members who want a particular bill released from captivity, the calling of a committee meeting is only the beginning of the battle. When a meeting does take place, the chairman is ordinarily the absolute master of the agenda, and he may be able to keep a bill that he opposes from ever being brought up. Moreover, he has the unlimited power of recognition. This means that he is perfectly free to impose silence on unfriendly members, giving the floor only to his cronies.

[5] Donald R. Matthews, *U. S. Senators and Their World* (Chapel Hill: University of North Carolina Press, 1960), pp. 159-60.
[6] *Ibid.*, p. 160.

The rules under which both the House and Senate function provide chairmen with still another device for obstruction. Under the rules, virtually none of the committees may meet while the parent body itself is in session.[7] In practice, the prohibition is ordinarily waived by unanimous consent whenever a committee requests. But if a chairman chooses to resort to obstructive tactics, he will see to it that a cooperative colleague on the floor registers an objection to any such request for special permission.[8] Through the use of this technique, hearings that could otherwise be completed in short order can be stretched out for weeks. And executive sessions, at which decisions are supposed to be made, can be turned into a farce through filibustering tactics. The chairman who desires to forestall action will simply give the floor to colleagues whose sympathy with his views is matched by their loquacity. They will keep talking until a bell rings to announce that the chamber is in session, at which point the chairman, in obedience to the rule, will adjourn the committee meeting.

Subcommittees

A number of committees have been moving, albeit slowly, away from the system under which a chairman operates "as a panjandrum of his little domain."[9] One aspect of this develop-

[7] This provision was adopted to free members for attendance on the floor. It has failed completely to accomplish that result. Early in 1964, the Senate voted to make the provision inapplicable during the Morning Hour.

[8] This is precisely what was done in the early stages of the 1963 battle over civil rights legislation. Southern senators succeeded in slowing down the Judiciary Committee, which was conducting civil rights hearings, by not allowing the committee to meet while the Senate was in session. As if to punish the entire Senate for even raising the subject of civil rights, they also refused for a while to allow other committees to meet at the same time as the Senate.

[9] Stewart L. Udall, "A Defense of the Seniority System," *The New York Times Magazine,* January 13, 1957, p. 17.

ment has been the establishment of subcommittees to take charge of the preliminary screening of legislation.

The creation of subcommittees has generally been resisted by committee chairmen, because such bodies almost inevitably become independent power centers. Those that represent the greatest problem to autocratic chairmen are the ones assigned specific jurisdiction over particular subjects, such as civil rights, or migratory labor, or anti-trust measures. Such subcommittees, and particularly their chairmen, frequently become authorities on the subjects with which they deal, and anything they say will probably command attention both among their colleagues and in the press. It is also often taken for granted that the chairman of the full committee will automatically refer to a specialized subcommittee any legislation within its jurisdiction. Because of this, the subcommittee may be able to thwart the committee chairman if he wants to bottle up a bill and not even permit hearings to be held on its merits. Moreover, the hearings conducted by the subcommittee may have a powerful impact on both public and congressional opinion. And subcommittee chairmen may tend to "gang up" on the chairman of the full committee, for the power of each of them is increased when they follow a policy of mutual assistance, supporting one another's positions in their respective spheres of influence.

Precisely because specialized subcommittees may pose a threat to his authority, the old-fashioned committee chairman sometimes insists that if subcommittees are to be created at all they should not be given subject-matter jurisdiction. When the chairman's wishes prevail and the subcommittees receive numbers instead of names, there is no opportunity for expertise to develop. In addition, the chairman of the full committee can exercise discretion and submit a bill to one subcommittee rather than another on the basis of how responsive its members ordinarily are to his wishes.[10]

But even when specialized subcommittees exist, the menace that they represent to the chairman of the full committee is subject to serious limitations. In most cases, the committee chairman decides how large a subcommittee shall be and what proportion of its seats shall be reserved for members of the minority party. It is he who determines, without necessarily following seniority, which members of the full committee shall serve on it and whether a particular bill should be withheld from it and considered right from the start by the committee as a whole. What is more, it is generally accepted that he himself may attend meetings of all the subcommittees he establishes.[11] And he must approve the hiring of subcommittee staff assistants, although some chairmen never invoke their veto.

Perhaps most important of all, the chairman may hold back money that subcommittees need to carry on their operations. This power stems from the practice in both houses of Congress of not making direct appropriations to subcommittees. Funds go instead to the full committee, and it is the full committee—actually the chairman in most cases—which allocates them to the various subcommittees. Only once in re-

[10] George Goodwin, "Subcommittees: The Miniature Legislatures of Congress," *American Political Science Review*, LVI (September 1962), p. 598.

[11] *Ibid.*, p. 601. The chairman of one House committee almost found a way to participate in two subcommittee meetings at the same time —and without even leaving his office. Congressman Adam Clayton Powell, Jr., chairman of the Committee on Education and Labor, toyed with the idea of having subcommittee hearing rooms wired for sound so that he could monitor meetings while sitting in his office, and participate in them, when the spirit moved him, through the mere flick of a switch. Mechanical problems proved insurmountable, however, and the idea had to be given up.

cent years has a different practice been followed. In 1963, all but 25 per cent of the funds for the Education and Labor Committee were earmarked for the direct use of its six sub-committees through House action. This was intended as a sharp rebuke to Committee Chairman Adam Clayton Powell, Jr. (D., N. Y.), who had come under attack for spending public funds on personal entertainment. In the absence of such an unusual motivation, neither house would think of depriving a chairman of control over his committee's purse strings. Usually it is taken for granted that the very existence of a subcommittee depends on the sufferance of the full committee chairman.

Myth and Reality

The power of the chairman is manifest in the legislative process wherever one looks. When hearings are held, he controls the time made available to both witnesses and members of Congress. When his committee recommends enactment of a bill, the report it submits has ordinarily been drafted by a staff subject to his will.[12] When a committee bill is being debated on the floor of the House, he may be its "manager," controlling half the time that is made available for speakers and doling it out as he pleases.[13] And when an effort is made to reconcile a committee bill passed by his house with a different version approved on the other side of the Capitol, he usually heads the "conferees" from his chamber.[14]

[12] Matthews, op. cit., p. 160.

[13] The other half is ordinarily controlled by the ranking minority member of the committee.

[14] To the extent that seniority need not be followed in selecting members of his committee to serve as conferees, the chairman has effective discretion in determining who they will be. The presiding officers make the formal choice of conferees in both the House and Senate, but they will tend to follow the recommendations of the chairmen. (A detailed description of the conference committee procedure appears in Ch. 11.)

Although the Legislative Reorganization Act of 1946 instituted some healthful reforms in Congress, one of the changes it made had the side effect of increasing the already great power of committee chairmen. As part of its effort to streamline Congress, the Act reduced the number of standing committees by more than half.[15] This necessarily involved a significant expansion of jurisdiction for the committees that remained, and in turn an enlargement of the domain ruled by each chairman. One of the most striking examples of this phenomenon was the Senate Judiciary Committee, which was handed jurisdiction over an almost incredible variety of subjects.[16] Today more than one-third of the total number of bills and resolutions introduced in the Senate are referred to this one committee.[17]

Committee chairmen have such great power that Presidents of the United States commonly make assiduous efforts to cultivate their good will, even when this entails the swallowing of considerable pride. In the 1960 election, Senator Harry F. Byrd (D., Va.), chairman of the powerful Finance Committee, had failed to endorse the presidential candidacy of Mr. Kennedy, and that act of party disloyalty contributed mightily to putting his state in the column of the Republican candi-

[15] The streamlining effects of this reform were short-lived, since subcommittees promptly sprang up to fragment congressional functions as seriously as had been the case in the past.

[16] The new jurisdiction of the committee encompassed claims, patents, judges, constitutional amendments, Federal courts, penitentiaries, antitrust measures, bankruptcy, mutiny, boundaries, civil liberties, immigration, and interstate compacts. The House Judiciary Committee was handed similarly wide jurisdiction.

[17] The committee's chairman, Senator James O. Eastland (D., Miss.), is thus the possessor of formidable power, particularly because the private immigration and claims bills that are referred to his committee are of great importance to individual senators who wish to oblige voters in their states.

date, Richard M. Nixon. Only six months later, however, Mr. Kennedy found it politic to let bygones be bygones and make a flamboyant gesture of friendship to the powerful senator. While Chairman Byrd was giving a big luncheon for friends at his country estate, a helicopter appeared out of the blue, and, when it landed, out stepped President Kennedy. The President's supporters did not believe that the salute would impel the ultra-conservative chairman to support the Kennedy program, but they hoped his opposition would be tempered by memories of the Kennedy visit.[18]

The power of a committee chairman is truly formidable. Still, it is not quite so great as some congressmen occasionally portray it. Rebellions against dictatorial chairmen have taken place before and could take place again, for in a real sense a chairman is dependent on the toleration of his committee, his party, and his house. When the will exists, the means can usually be found to get around him, and there are always means to get rid of him.[19] But the myth that the chairman is omnipotent continues to be cultivated by both members and party leaders, because it provides them with an effective device to evade responsibility: they can always blame the committee chairman for the fact that certain legislation never seems to get to the floor—while doing nothing themselves to force the chairman's hand. The power of a chairman is indeed great; but so is the power of those who can feign inability to accomplish precisely what they have no desire to accomplish.

With the very real power that a committee chairman does

[18] Edward P. Morgan, "O'Brien Presses on with the 'Four P's,'" *The New York Times Magazine*, March 25, 1962, p. 29. Mr. Kennedy also instituted the practice of inviting each committee chairman to a tête-à-tête in the White House at the opening of every new congressional session.

[19] The majority party could at any time deprive him of his chairmanship.

possess, one might think that he should be accountable for his actions to the public as a whole, or to his party, or at least to the legislative chamber that gives him his office. But far from that, a chairman is responsible only to the constituency that elected him to Congress. As long as his constituents continue to re-elect him, there is no other authority to whom he must account for his actions.

On superficial examination, there does appear to be at least a trace of accountability and responsibility in the system for selecting committee chairmen. For invariably committees are headed by members of the party commanding a majority in the chamber involved. This arrangement seems to be in accord with democratic parliamentary theory: the voters have indicated their sympathy with the program of a certain party by electing a majority of its candidates to Congress; members of that party should be placed in positions of power, so that they can promote the enactment of the program endorsed by the voters.

In practical terms, however, the system that exists in Congress is not even an approximation of this ideal. Committee chairmen may wear the *label* of the majority party, but they are not obligated to promote the *program* of that party. Some chairmen, indeed, have a far poorer record of party loyalty than members of Congress generally. This paradoxical situation comes about because the system that determines which members of the majority party serve as committee chairmen makes it likely that these men will be representatives of constituencies far removed from the mainstream of American political life.

Seniority System

The system that is responsible for this peculiar state of affairs rests on the principle of seniority. This principle requires that a committee chairmanship go to the majority party member with the longest record of continuous service on the committee. Intelligence, ability, party regularity— none of these have anything to do with the selection of a chairman. The only factor that counts is the ability to get elected over and over again, provided only that one stays on the same committee.[20] This rule makes it inconceivable that a member who is elected to Congress from a closely divided state or congressional district will ever become a committee chairman. Since his constituency is so marginal, the chances that his tenure in Congress will be long and uninterrupted are slim indeed. More probably, the seat he occupies will shift back and forth at frequent intervals between the two parties, and the state or district will never have a congressman with enough continuous seniority to be given a committee chairmanship.[21] In effect the constituency is penalized for a characteristic that is anything but blameworthy: the presence of two healthy and vigorous parties engaged in keen competition for votes. Conversely, of course, the kind of constituency whose representative will almost surely acquire a chairmanship is one that is irretrievably under the domination of a single party.

The seniority system affects profoundly the complexion of both houses of Congress. In the Senate, it tends to award chairmanships to members from one-party southern states when the Democrats are in the majority, and to members from rock-ribbed conservative states of the Middle West when the Republicans have won control. In the House, chairmanships

[20] A congressman who transfers to a new committee will be its junior member, regardless of the seniority he has built up in the chamber as a whole.

[21] In the Eighty-eighth Congress, chairmen of the most important Senate committees had an average of 23 years of continuous service. In the House, the average was 28.5 years. *The New York Times,* January 24, 1963, p. 4, col. 1 (Western edition).

go to Republicans from rural districts in which opposition voters are exceedingly scarce, or to Democrats from either one-party districts in the South or from those cities where political machines can keep incumbents in office indefinitely.

Many chairmen, therefore, are almost inevitably out of step with the national party to which they belong. Both national parties must address themselves to the problems of the closely divided urban states with their racial minorities and large working-class populations, for it is the electoral votes of these states that decide presidential elections. A disproportionately large number of congressional chairmanships, however, go to representatives and senators who are rural-oriented and accept no part of the liberal political ideologies of the cities.

Although the seniority system is used in both chambers, its impact is greater in the House than it is in the Senate, for the proportion of one-party congressional districts is higher than the proportion of one-party states. Since seniority is but a comparative concept, a senator who is only beginning his second term may find to his delight that he is already a somewhat senior member of a committee. In the House the situation is totally different. Because of the large number of safe seats,[22] even a member who has served continuously for more than a decade may still be very much of a junior in comparison with his colleagues. Chairmanships in the House are also somewhat more valuable than in the Senate, because the larger body has chosen to give its committees truly awesome power. A Senate committee that bottles up a bill can be thwarted if the bill is attached as an amendment to legislation already on the floor. No such avenue is open in the

[22] A study has revealed that from 1932 to 1956 more than half of the seats in the House never changed parties. Samuel Lubell, *Revolt of the Moderates* (New York: Harper, 1956), p. 212. Today, more than one-third of the seats can be considered safe for one party or the other.

House, where non-germane amendments are out of order. Woodrow Wilson's words are perfect as a description of what it means to send legislation to committee in the House. When a bill goes from the clerk's desk to a committee room, he wrote, "it crosses a parliamentary bridge of sighs to dim dungeons of silence whence it will never return. The means and time of its death are unknown, but its friends never see it again."[23]

When the Democrats are in the majority, the seniority system bestows an extraordinary number of chairmanships in both houses on southerners. In the Eighty-eighth Congress, for example, ten of the sixteen Senate committees were chaired by southerners, and twelve of the twenty committee chairmen in the House were also from the eleven states of the South. This bonus that the seniority system customarily awards to the Old Confederacy is the fact most often cited in criticism of the system. But other criticisms are made as well. For one thing, the seniority rule is sometimes derided as a "senility rule," which often gives power to the weak and enfeebled members of Congress instead of to those who are young and healthy. In addition, it is said, the rule has several times advanced to chairmanships men who were later proved totally unfit for public office.[24] And it is also charged by some that

[23] Wilson, *op. cit.*, p. 63.

[24] One example often cited is that of J. Parnell Thomas (R., N. J.), chairman of the House Committee on Un-American Activities in the 1940's. Chairman Thomas, who expected a high degree of patriotism on the part of others, went to jail for padding his congressional payroll and accepting "kickbacks." A somewhat similar case is that of Congressman Andrew Jackson May (D., Ky.), chairman of the House Military Affairs Committee during World War II. Chairman May was convicted of war frauds against the Government. Although another member of the committee—Congressman Ewing Thomason (D., Tex.)—possessed the same amount of seniority as May did, he had been passed over for the chairmanship because the first letter of his surname came after Mr. May's in the alphabet. Louis Smith, *American Democracy and Military Power: A Study of Civil Control of the Military Power in the*

the emphasis on seniority deters good men from seeking congressional careers because they do not relish what a legislator once called "the humble and unrewarding roles of freshmen. . . ."[25]

The principal argument that has been advanced in favor of the rule is that seniority is usually synonymous with experience, both in the subject matter of the committee and in the subtleties of the legislative process.[26] It is said, too, that resort to the seniority system, which provides a mechanical procedure for selecting chairmen, avoids the dissension and bitterness that would doubtless accompany any attempt to apply a less objective rule.[27]

Alternatives

Those who defend the seniority rule sometime challenge critics to suggest an alternative method of choosing chairmen. Several procedures have been recommended. One was proposed by Senator Kefauver, who would have had the majority party members of each committee elect their chairman by secret ballot.[28] Another senator, William Proxmire of Wisconsin, has urged that a frontal attack be made on the ten-

---

United States (Chicago: The University of Chicago Press, 1951), p. 251. For a discussion of the May case, see H. H. Wilson, *Congress: Corruption and Compromise* (New York: Rinehart, 1951).

[25] Richard L. Neuberger, "A Senator's Case against Seniority," *The New York Times Magazine,* April 7, 1957, p. 15. Senator Neuberger stated that this factor was to blame for the decisions of two former presidential candidates—Thomas E. Dewey and Adlai E. Stevenson—not to run for the Senate. *Id.*

[26] George Goodwin, "The Seniority System in Congress," *American Political Science Review,* LIII (June 1959), pp. 418-19. Yet experience does not count for a man who leaves Congress for a few years (to accept a position in the Executive Branch, for example) and later returns. Such an individual is considered to have lost the seniority he had accumulated.

[27] Udall, *op. cit.,* p. 64.

[28] Estes Kefauver and Jack Levin, *A 20th-Century Congress* (New York: Duell, 1947), p. 136.

dency of southerners to monopolize chairmanships. Proxmire favors adoption of a rule under which no more than half the major committees could have chairmen from a single section of the country. He also wants chairmen chosen by the majority party caucus instead of through seniority.[29] Others who have studied the problem have suggested that the House should return to an earlier system, under which the Speaker, as leader of the majority party, would pick the members who would become the heads of committees.

All these plans involve scrapping the seniority rule completely as the method of selecting committee chairmen. At least two other proposals have been made to retain the existing system but reform it significantly.

One of these proposals has been advanced by a political scientist, who wants to modify the seniority system to favor congressmen from two-party constituencies just as the present rule favors those from safe constituencies. The suggestion is that committee chairmanships should still be assigned on the basis of seniority, but with double credit given for election victories in which the opposition candidate received at least 20 per cent of the votes.[30]

A second idea for modifying the seniority system comes from a member of the House. Congressman Thomas B. Curtis (R., Mo.) advocates a constitutional amendment to limit the continuous tenure of a congressman to twelve years. After that time, the member would be compelled to take a two-year "sabbatical leave" before becoming eligible to serve again in Congress. This proposal, specifically designed to "overcome the detrimental aspects of the seniority system,"[31] received

[29] *Congressional Record,* February 2, 1959, p. 1395 (daily edition).

[30] Stephen K. Bailey, "The Congress and Majority Rule," *New Republic,* January 5, 1959, p. 8.

[31] *Congressional Record,* January 21, 1963, pp. 686-87 (daily edition). Congressman Curtis said, with apparent seriousness, that he believed his proposal would have a valuable by-product: the two-year "sabbatical"

the endorsement of only one prominent public figure. Former President Eisenhower, who had himself been precluded by the Twenty-second Amendment from seeking a third term in the White House, was struck by the thought that "what is good for the President might very well be good for Congress." President Kennedy, when asked for a comment on what Eisenhower had said, indicated that he was already having enough trouble with congressmen without challenging their right to remain in office as long as their constituents could tolerate them. He said diplomatically of the Eisenhower statement: "It's the sort of proposal I may advance in a post-presidential period, but not right now."[32]

As one might expect, criticism within Congress of the seniority system comes almost exclusively from junior members. House Majority Leader Carl Albert (D., Okla.) has put it this way: "Every new congressman is against the seniority system, but the longer he stays the more he likes it."[33] There is, however, another reason why there has been no widespread rebellion against the system. The conservatives, who benefit so much from it, often find themselves able to disarm critics by pointing to the existence of factors that make the power of a committee chairman something less than absolute. For example, a procedure exists under which the House or Senate may discharge a committee of further jurisdiction over a bill it refuses to report.[34] Another factor cited by conservatives is the existence of subcommittees, which tend to become

---

would permit the congressman "to get reacquainted with his constituents and their feelings." Mr. Curtis elaborated with a marvelously mixed metaphor: The congressman would benefit because the sabbatical "would put his feet back on the ground and would put him back into the mainstream of his community." *Ibid.*, p. 687.

[32] Press conference, January 24, 1963.

[33] Interview, September 24, 1962.

[34] The discharge procedure is described in detail in the following chapter.

fairly independent of committee chairmen. In Congress and out, those who are generally satisfied with the seniority rule emphasize the extent to which such adaptations allow abuses to be counteracted. Adaptations, they say, are infinitely preferable to radical reform, which might wreck the delicately balanced solar system of which the seniority rule is an important component.[35]

Committee Assignments

Seniority, although it is the sole determinant of who becomes chairman of a congressional committee, is only one of the factors behind the decision to put a congressman on a particular committee in the first place. The assignment power is an exceedingly important one, and those who exercise it have a potent weapon in their hands.

In each new Congress, a preliminary decision must be reached before new committee assignments can be made. That decision concerns the question of how the seats on each committee are to be divided between Republican and Democratic members. The basic system that prevails in both houses is that the seats on each committee are allocated to the two parties in rough proportion to the relative strength of each one in the chamber as a whole. There are exceptions. On the Rules Committee of the House, for example, the majority party always receives twice as many seats as the minority party, even though its margin in the chamber may be very slender. Fixed ratios exist, too, on House Appropriations and on Ways and Means. But in the case of the other committees, the usual practice is for the Republican and Democratic leaders to work out between themselves the precise ratio for each committee

[35] Ernest S. Griffith, in *Congress: Its Contemporary Role* (New York: New York University Press, 1961), pp. 29-31.

in their chamber. The agreements they conclude are then formally ratified on the floor.

Although this system of proportional representation on congressional committees is taken for granted, it rests on custom rather than any explicit rule. It would, as a matter of fact, be perfectly possible for the majority party to organize committees with only token representation from the opposition party, or even no representation at all. Both Jefferson and Wilson believed that such one-party committees would be highly desirable,[36] for the party with the popular mandate would then be in a better position to carry out its program. There would be no reason to fear that the minority on a committee would gain the support of a few dissidents from the other side and thus succeed in preventing the majority party from bringing its legislative proposals to the floor. Similarly, the electorate would know whom to praise or blame for the record that committees had made: responsibility would always be squarely on the shoulders of the majority party.[37]

A point of view similar to that of Jefferson and Wilson was expressed in 1950 by the Committee on Political Parties of the American Political Science Association. According to the political scientists, there is nothing so wonderful about a system that sometimes awards almost as many committee positions to the minority as to the majority. Such an arrangement, in fact, "gives individual members of the majority party the balance of power and invites chaos." To avoid undermining party responsibility, "the majority party in the house should have a comfortable margin of control within each committee,"

[36] Bertram M. Gross, *The Legislative Struggle: A Study in Social Combat* (New York: McGraw-Hill, 1953), p. 275, note 22.

[37] Wilson, *op. cit.*, p. 81.

regardless of the general proportion of party membership in the chamber as a whole.[38]

Congress, however, remains unconvinced. On committee after committee, the margin of the "majority" is razor-thin, and the party supposedly in control is in no position to enact its program. On even the most important legislative committees, decisions must often be made through bargaining and compromise rather than by a straight vote on the program of the party supposedly in power. It is natural, therefore, that committees regard themselves, in the words of one scholar, "as corporate bodies with collective opinions and wills rather than as instruments of the respective parties or of Congress as a whole."[39]

Once the ratios on the various committees have been established, it is left for each of the parties to fill its assigned seats by any method it cares to employ. There are at present four separate methods in use.

1. House Democrats

The Democratic Committee on Committees in the House consists of the party's representatives on the Ways and Means Committee.[40] The senior Democrat on Ways and Means is the chairman.[41] This Committee places Democrats on all the standing committees except Ways and Means itself (that function is

[38] "Toward a More Responsible Two-Party System: A Report of the Committee on Political Parties of the American Political Science Association," *American Political Science Review*, XLIV (1950), supplement, p. 63.

[39] Max Beloff, *The American Federal Government* (New York: Oxford University Press, 1959), p. 130.

[40] Ways and Means, because it has jurisdiction over tax legislation, is one of the most important committees in the House.

[41] Nicholas A. Masters, "Committee Assignments in the House of Representatives," *American Political Science Review*, LV (June 1961), p. 348.

performed directly by the party caucus, consisting of all Democrats in the House). Its decisions must be ratified by the caucus and the House as a whole, but these requirements are merely formalities.

The Committee performs two functions: it fills vacancies caused by deaths, retirements, or defeats; and it assigns additional members when a gain in over-all party strength in the House leads to an increase in the proportion of Democrats on the various committees.

Democrats who have just been elected to the House are encouraged to notify the Committee on Committees where they would like to serve, stating their first, second, and third preferences. Each application is screened initially by the member of the Committee on Committees who has been assigned primary responsibility for the geographical zone where the new member's district is located. In the course of considering a particular application, the zonal representative will confer with the senior Democratic congressman from the applicant's state (the "dean" of the state's Democratic delegation). When each of the zonal representatives is prepared to recommend assignments for members under his jurisdiction, the Committee on Committees is called into session. The Democratic floor leader is present, as well as the Speaker of the House, if he is a Democrat. As each vacancy is brought up for discussion, the various zonal representatives, speaking in the order of seniority, make their nominations and attempt to buttress them with supporting arguments. The Committee then holds an election, and the nominee who receives the highest number of votes gets the post.[42]

Any number of criteria may be employed by the House Democratic Committee on Committees in making its deci-

[42] *Ibid.*, p. 346.

sions. If a veteran representative has applied for transfer to a new committee, his seniority may tilt the scales against a freshman who has been nominated to the same committee. Often the determining factor is a desire to maintain some geographical balance on the committee. When a sensitive committee like Rules is involved, preference will usually be given to a representative from a safe district, since immunity from reprisal at the polls is considered desirable.[43]

The variety of criteria that may be employed means that broad discretionary power is vested in the members of the Committee on Committees. Only one rule must be followed, and even that one is often violated: a member who serves on one of the three most important committees of the House— Appropriations, Rules, and Ways and Means—is not supposed to be given a second committee assignment, and a member who serves on any one of ten other important committees is not supposed to be eligible for more than a single additional assignment.

In exercising their power, members of the Committee on Committees sometimes agree to follow the advice of the party leadership—the Speaker of the House (if he is a Democrat) or the Democratic Floor Leader. In case a vacancy on the Rules Committee must be filled, that advice will ordinarily be taken. To a lesser extent, this is true also of Appropriations and Ways and Means. If other committees are involved, however, the leadership's attempts to exercise influence may very well be rebuffed.

The Democratic Committee on Committees has been sharply criticized on the ground that its assignments seem to discriminate against liberal representatives. Undoubtedly such discrimination is to be expected, because the members

[43] *Ibid.*, pp. 352-54.

of Ways and Means are almost invariably representatives with considerable seniority on whom the passage of time has left its usual mark: a conditioned appreciation of the tried and true. Something of a conservative bias is thus built into the Committee. This situation will doubtless continue as long as the Democratic caucus, in the words of a Washington reporter, thinks of membership on the Committee on Committees "as a reward for seniority rather than as an assignment for articulate, hard-fighting proponents of [the caucus'] point of view."[44]

In addition to the criticism that it is not ideologically representative of the party as a whole, the Democratic Committee on Committees in the House has also come under attack for not being sectionally representative. The Committee, in fact, is often a caricature of the Democratic Party in the House, because no systematic effort is made to give representation to each state or region on the basis of its importance to the party. A state that has elected several Democratic representatives may be left out in the cold as far as membership on Ways and Means is concerned. On the other hand, a state that has only a single Democrat in the House may find this solitary soul plucked from obscurity and favored with assignment to the Committee on Committees. Year after year, only a small number of the states that have elected Democrats to the House are represented in the making of committee assignments. What is more, any sectional or ideological bias that creeps into the Committee has a way of becoming permanent, because as a matter of course the Democratic members of Ways and Means are reappointed to the Committee every

[44] Charles B. Seib, "Steering Wheel of the House," *The New York Times Magazine,* March 18, 1962, p. 146. "On the average, members [of Ways and Means] have served at least three consecutive terms, [or] five terms if computations are based simply on prior, rather than continuous, service before selection." Masters, *op. cit.,* p. 348.

time they are re-elected to the House. This continuity of membership means that it is sheer coincidence when the Democrats who wield the assignment power are even a reasonable facsimile of the party's membership in the House.[45]

There is no question about the power of the Democratic Caucus in the House to alter this situation whenever it cares to. At least a small step in that direction was taken in 1963, when it became necessary to fill a Ways and Means vacancy created by the retirement from Congress of a conservative Virginian. Disregarding the advice of House Speaker John W. McCormack (D., Mass.) that a conservative congressman from Georgia be given the seat, the caucus awarded it to a Kennedy Democrat.[46]

2. House Republicans

If the Democratic Committee on Committees in the House is open to criticism for not being at all representative of the party membership, no such blanket accusation can be made against the Republicans. Unlike the Democrats, who merely authorize their members on Ways and Means to double in brass as a Committee on Committees, the Republicans take pains to constitute at least on paper a group that will be a microcosm of their party in the House. Toward this end, a separate caucus is held by each state's contingent of Republican representatives before the opening of a new Congress. The caucus elects one of its members to represent the state on a Republican Committee on Committees, which will be

[45] *Id.*

[46] Although the caucus decision had an effect on the ideological composition of the committee, there was no break with the principle of sectional continuity: the new member, like the representative he replaced, was a Virginian. Similarly, in filling a second vacancy at the same time, the caucus selected one Tennessean to succeed another.

headed by the party's leader in the House.[47] When the Committee on Committees, meets, each of its members will be allowed to cast one vote for every Republican that his state has elected to the House. Nominations made by the Committee will be approved automatically by the House Conference of All Republicans, the equivalent of the Democratic Caucus.[48]

This arrangement appears to make it virtually certain that the Republican Committee on Committees will always be reasonably in step with the party membership in the House as a whole. No state that has elected a Republican congressman will go unrepresented. And the system of weighted voting guarantees that no member of the committee shall exercise more power than is warranted by the size of the Republican delegation from his state.

Yet, although it cannot be questioned that the Republican Committee on Committees rests on a more rational basis than the Democratic, the contrast should not be pressed too far. In actual practice the Republican machinery functions somewhat differently than what appears on paper. When, for example, a state delegation holds a caucus to select its representative, the result is often a foregone conclusion: the dean of the delegation will be chosen, in deference to his seniority. Furthermore, the Committee is generally content to ratify decisions made elsewhere. The custom has grown up of permitting the Minority Leader (or the Speaker, when the Republicans are in power in the House) to appoint a subcommittee to propose committee assignments. That subcommittee, or "executive committee," is dominated by representatives from the

[47] H. Bradford Westerfield, *Foreign Policy and Party Politics: Pearl Harbor to Korea* (New Haven, Conn.: Yale University Press, 1955), p. 99, note 10.

[48] The Republicans in the House do not like the term "caucus," which may conjure up a picture of a closed-door meeting at which party bosses lay down the law to cowed representatives.

seven biggest states, which also control the conference because of the number of Republicans they elect to the House.[49] But even conceding the gap that exists between theory and practice, it still remains true, as a Democratic congressman once admitted, that the Republican method comes closer than the Democratic "to ensuring that committee assignments will be made in accordance with the prevailing philosophy and sentiment of the party."[50]

3. Senate Democrats

The power of assigning Democrats to committees in the Senate is firmly in the hands of the floor leader.[51] He performs this function through a Committee on Committees, or Steering Committee, which is almost entirely his own creation: he is its chairman and he selects twelve of its fourteen other members,[52] subject only to *pro forma* review by the Conference (caucus).

Not quite so much competition exists in the Senate for committee assignments as in the House. The reason is simple: though the Senate has almost as many committees as the House,[53] it does not have even one-fourth as many members. Accordingly, there are almost enough desirable assignments to go around. Even a freshman senator will frequently be selected to serve on an important committee and begin to accumulate seniority there from his initial day in office.

This is particularly true for Democratic senators. Since 1953, the Democratic Steering Committee has followed the policy of giving every freshman Democrat an assignment on

[49] Masters, *op. cit.*, pp. 348-49.

[50] Kefauver and Levin, *op. cit.*, p. 109.

[51] His title is Majority Leader or Minority Leader, depending on whether his party controls the Senate.

[52] The two whom he does not select serve *ex officio:* the Deputy Leader (or Whip) and the Secretary of the Conference.

[53] Sixteen, compared with twenty in the House.

one major committee before granting even the most senior senator a second or third such assignment. This policy was instituted by President Johnson at the time when he was Majority Leader. Although liberals hailed his reform as a blow to the seniority system, southern conservatives did not appear at all alarmed. The reason for their sanguine attitude soon became apparent.

Under the new system, the Majority Leader had a completely free hand in giving deserving freshmen just the assignments they coveted. He could even place them on committees like Appropriations, Finance, and Foreign Relations, although these assignments had ordinarily been reserved in the past for senators with considerable seniority. What could a freshman do to convince Johnson that he belonged in the category of the "deserving"? Since little business is transacted by the Senate before committee assignments are made, the opportunities were somewhat limited. But it was made clear that there was at least one thing the newly elected senator could do: join the Majority Leader in opposing efforts by pro-civil rights members to change the cloture rule and make it easier to terminate filibusters.[54] Since the vote on liberalizing cloture was taken before committee assignments had been made, Johnson found himself in a commanding position. *The New York Times* was clearly guilty of understatement when it said that the order of events gave him "a powerful bargaining point to use for persuading the new men to follow his lead."[55] It was just as powerful a bargaining point for Johnson when he dealt with non-freshman senators who had requested transfers to new committee assignments. No one was surprised, therefore, when cloture reform was stymied in 1959.

Johnson's successor as Majority Leader, Senator Mike

[54] The filibuster question is discussed in Ch. 10.
[55] January 11, 1959 (weather edition).

Mansfield (D., Mont.), pursued a similar strategy when another major effort to soften the cloture rule was made in 1963.[56] The attempt failed again, and the accusation was made that the secret weapon of Mansfield's southern-dominated Steering Committee had been the same as the one used in 1959—the carrot of desirable committee assignments dangled in front of hungry senators.

This accusation was brought into the open by Senator Joseph S. Clark (D., Pa.) in a full-dress attack on the manner in which Democrats are assigned to standing committees. The burden of Clark's address, which he delivered on the Senate floor, was that the power to place senators on committees, like many other powers in the Senate, was in the hands of a conservative oligarchy that pursued goals unworthy of twentieth-century America. One of the goals of the "Senate Establishment," he said, was the preservation of the filibuster. That was the reason why the Steering Committee had meted out far better treatment to the friends of the filibuster than to its enemies. To prove his contention, Clark quoted from statistics he had compiled on non-freshman Democrats who had requested new committee assignments. Seven of the eight who had opposed making it easier to invoke cloture were rewarded with the transfers they wanted,[57] and all but one of these were placed on the committee they had listed as first choice. Those who had fought for reforming the cloture rule did not fare quite so well. Nine of the fourteen senators on the side of

[56] Johnson was no longer Majority Leader, for he had been elected to the Vice Presidency in 1960. The Vice President, however, is also president of the Senate, and this fact meant that Johnson was able to continue his war against majority cloture through parliamentary rulings that made the task of the reformers all but impossible. See Ch. 10.

[57] The only exception was Strom Thurmond (D., S. C.), Dixiecrat candidate for President in 1948, who had given the leadership a multitude of reasons for excluding him permanently from the Establishment.

reform were rebuffed when they applied for new committee assignments, and of the five who did receive transfers, only one—Mansfield himself—was given his first choice.[58]

That kind of discrimination in the making of committee assignments was only to be expected, said Clark, in view of the composition of the Democratic Steering Committee. Of its fifteen members, seven were southerners. Two western members of the committee were ideologically close to the southerners, so the conservatives had a majority in spite of the fact that only a little more than one-third of the Democrats in the Senate could be ranked as conservatives.

The indictment by Clark was particularly noteworthy because the senator himself was a member of the Steering Committee.[59] A second committee member, Paul Douglas, rose to associate himself with Clark's remarks. He was the only senator who did. The Senate hastily moved on to other business in a manner that indicated some embarrassment at the washing of so much dirty linen in public.

4. Senate Republicans

The Republican Committee on Committees in the Senate is appointed by the chairman of the party conference (or caucus). Conference approval of assignments made by the Committee on Committees is forthcoming as a matter of course.

Like the three other Committees on Committees in Congress, the Republican group in the Senate claims that it acts

[58] Clark was generous in listing Mansfield as a supporter of an easier cloture rule. Although the Majority Leader did vote that way, he made no fight for the reform.

[59] The "Establishment" address, which was spread over three days, appears on the following pages of the daily edition of the *Congressional Record:* pp. 2413-26 (February 19, 1963), pp. 2524-31 (February 20, 1963), and pp. 2703-13 (February 21, 1963). It was later published in book form as *The Senate Establishment* (New York: Hill & Wang, 1963).

on the basis of a number of objective criteria such as seniority, professional qualifications, and previous political experience.[60] Yet the very number of criteria employed means that considerable discretion rests in the hands of those who wield the assignment power. Since there is no rule that every freshman must be placed on a major committee, it was possible to give Senator Kenneth B. Keating of New York a coveted seat on the Judiciary Committee when he was only a freshman, while at the same time depriving his colleague, Jacob K. Javits, of a first-rank committee assignment until he had almost served out his initial six-year term. It was explained that Keating richly merited the excellent treatment because he had been on the Judiciary Committee in the House and also because he deserved a reward from his party for the totally unexpected election victory he had won.[61] The real difference, however, seems to have been that Keating was considered an organization man while Javits was something of a maverick.

Credence was lent to this view by an event that took place just two years after Javits had finally been assigned to a major committee (Appropriations). Although the Democrats gained a scant three seats in the Senate in the 1960 election, the GOP Floor Leader, Everett M. Dirksen (R., Ill.) agreed to drop one minority member from the Appropriations Committee, supposedly to make the party ratios on the committee reflect the strength of the Democrats and Republicans in the Senate as a whole. Javits, who was the most junior Republican on the committee, was, of course, the one who had to go. Like the Democratic senators who had been punished by their party

[60] Robert A. Dahl, *Congress and Foreign Policy* (New Haven, Conn.: Yale Institute of International Studies, 1949), pp. 9-10, note 2.

[61] *The New York Times,* August 19, 1962, p. 44, col. 4 (weather edition).

leaders, he had been in the forefront of the fight for majority cloture.

Each party in each house has its own method of making committee assignments, but both will generally try to give members appointments that will help them in their constituencies. Congressmen are not reticent about disclosing their preferences. A man from a farm state will probably seek membership on the Agriculture Committee rather than the Labor Committee, whose work is of no interest to his constituents. A seat on the Labor Committee, however, is exactly the place sought by a representative from an urban center. Similarly, the congressman from a mining or timber state will find the Interior Committee to his liking, while a member from a maritime district will be happiest on the Merchant Marine and Fisheries Committee. Assignment to a committee like House Appropriations or Senate Armed Services is considered a boon to any member, regardless of the makeup of his constituency. And there are certain committees on which practically no one wants to serve, notably those that deal with the District of Columbia.[62]

There is only one House-Senate committee with sufficient power to make it exceedingly attractive to almost any congressman: the Joint Committee on Atomic Energy. Alone among the joint committees, this one is empowered to report out legislation. So important has the committee become in making atomic energy policy for the nation that at times it has seemed to overshadow the Atomic Energy Commission, which is the executive agency supposedly charged with responsibility

[62] Matthews, *op. cit.*, p. 151. The only congressmen who generally want to serve on the committees that deal with the District of Columbia are those from nearby Maryland districts, and southern Democrats (whose motive is to block "home rule" for the residents of the District, a majority of whom are Negroes). Masters, *op. cit.*, p. 355.

over this field.[63] Only two other joint committees operate at the committee level instead of merely at the staff level: the Joint Committee on Defense Production and the Joint Economic Committee.[64]

[63] See Harold P. Green and Alan Rosenthal, *Governing the Atom: The Integration of Powers* (New York: Atherton, 1963), *passim*.

[64] The other joint committees: Internal Revenue Taxation, Reduction of Non-essential Federal Expenditures, Printing, Library, and Disposition of Executive Papers. Each of the joint committees is composed of an equal number of representatives and senators, with the chairmanship usually alternating each year between representatives from the two houses.

7

Committees and Congressional Staffing

DECISIONS OF UNPARALLELED IMPORTANCE in Congress are
framed by the standing legislative committees. Time has not
diminished the accuracy of Woodrow Wilson's observation
that "Congress in session is Congress on public exhibition,
while Congress in its committee rooms is Congress at work."[1]
Today, as in Wilson's time, there is no resemblance to the situation that prevailed during the early history of Congress. In
that era, Congress employed only select (or *ad hoc*) committees, and their function was of secondary importance. Before
such a committee could even be appointed, the chamber as a
whole would have to agree on the basic principles of the legislation to be considered. The task of the committee would be
merely to fill in the details of the proposed legislation.[2] This
order has now been reversed. It is in committee that legislation is really fashioned, while the House or Senate as a
body must usually be content to do little but tinker.

[1] Woodrow Wilson, *Congressional Government* (New York: Meridian,
1959), p. 69 (written in 1883).
[2] George B. Galloway, *History of the House of Representatives* (New
York: Thomas Y. Crowell, 1961), p. 76.

After a bill has been referred to committee and perhaps re-referred to a subcommittee, the first question that arises is whether hearings will be held to take testimony on its provisions. The failure to schedule hearings ordinarily indicates that a substantive decision has been made to pigeonhole the legislation and thus effectively kill it. If the committee or subcommittee does decide to hold hearings on a bill, it almost invariably wants to learn the views of the appropriate executive agencies, sometimes both in writing and in the form of oral testimony. An agency that is asked for comment on legislation never takes a position without first clearing its views with the Bureau of the Budget. The purpose is to obtain a certification that the opinions expressed are in accord with the program of the President.

Hearings

When the hearings themselves are held, the leading witnesses will very often be representatives of the Executive Branch. If a major Administration bill is under consideration, several members of the Cabinet may take the time to testify, in order to underscore the interest of the President in enactment of the measure. Certainly the head of the department that would administer the legislation will appear. An official of his rank, however, will ordinarily confine himself to broad and general principles, leaving specifics to be dealt with by his subordinates.

Except for Government witnesses, whose testimony is usually considered indispensable on bills affecting their jurisdiction, it is for the committee or subcommittee chairman to determine who will receive invitations to testify. He can, of course, use this power to good advantage to predetermine the kind of picture that the hearing will present. In most cases, however, he will allow testimony to be offered by the representatives of any organizations with a substantial interest in the bill under consideration. The result is that the typical hearing is dominated by testimony from spokesmen for pressure groups. Appearing before congressional committees and arranging for others to appear is, in fact, one of the principal tasks of a lobbyist. Spokesmen for the Chamber of Commerce, for example, testified on 25 separate occasions in 1962, and expressed opinions in writing an additional 81 times.

The manner in which an organization like the Chamber of Commerce presents its views to a congressional committee could not be duplicated by a less affluent group. Instead of using staff members of its national organization as witnesses, the Chamber prefers to speak through businessmen who belong to its component local organizations and who make the trip to Washington for the express purpose of offering testimony. The Chamber arranges to have such witnesses arrive in town at least one day before they are scheduled to testify. It has them observe the committee in action, so they can learn to identify its members and flatter them the next day by addressing each one by name. Staff employees of the Chamber's "legislative department" go so far as to conduct a mock hearing at which the arguments that the witnesses plan to present can be tested with searching and even hostile questions. They stress to the witnesses how desirable it is to tell committee members about the effects that proposed legislation will have on their own businesses and communities, instead of speaking in generalities about nationwide consequences.

A hearing usually takes place in the regular meeting room of the committee or subcommittee, which often adjoins the suite of offices housing the staff. If there is great public interest in the hearing and a large audience is expected, the meeting may be held where more spectators can be accommodated, perhaps in a caucus room. Wherever the location, members of the committee or subcommittee are grouped around the chairman in the order of their seniority, but with all Republicans seated on one side and all Democrats on the other. Seniority determines not only the seating but also the order in which members question witnesses. The chairman, who begins the interrogation, is followed by the ranking minority member, then by the ranking majority member, and so on— back and forth between the two parties.

Often testimony by a witness consists exclusively of answers to questions, without the presentation of any prepared statement. Some witnesses, however, come armed with lengthy written statements, and the chairman usually permits these to be read aloud, in spite of all the time that is thus consumed. The Legislative Reorganization Act made a valiant effort to save committee members from having to suffer through the oral rendition of statements that could be read much more quickly in their own offices. It did this by requiring that witnesses file written statements with the committee in advance of their appearance. The rule, though, is honored more often in the breach than in the observance, and witnesses continue to read their statements aloud.

Hearings are seldom models of decorum. Committee members wander in and out of the room, converse in loud voices with one another and with members of the press, and sometimes pay no attention whatever to the proceedings during the brief time they are present. Attendance is often skimpy and sometimes dwindles to the point where only a single member is left. Absenteeism is unavoidable in many cases, because several committees to which the congressman belongs may all be meeting at the same time. Frequently, however, the member has simply decided that he has more important things to do than put in an appearance at a hearing.

A deliberate decision to stay away does not necessarily reflect either laziness or lack of responsibility. For a great deal of what will take place at a hearing is easily predictable. The lobbyist of the AFL-CIO has been a witness on many previous occasions, and there will be few surprises in his testimony; the spokesman of the National Association of Manufacturers, too, will present a familiar case, and so will the legislative representative of the American Civil Liberties Union. Even congressmen will play familiar roles, with each one asking the questions that one expects of him—in some instances, questions prepared for him by the very lobbyist he is interrogating. Witnesses, too, may experience a sense of futility and even unreality if they are giving their testimony before "judges" who have announced in advance that their minds are made up. After all, even the presentation of utterly unanswerable arguments could not convince a Texas senator to vote against the interests of the oil industry.[3]

Still, this picture should not be overdrawn. Many hearings do succeed in eliciting information of value to the committee. In addition, hearings often furnish one of the earliest opportunities of ascertaining where bargains can probably be struck. They also help provide a method for adjusting group conflicts, since any legislative action will win more ready acceptance if there is a general impression that "it has been arrived at 'in the right way,' [with] 'everyone' [having] had a chance to be heard."[4]

From the point of view of the participants, hearings often serve purposes that have nothing to do with the legislation at hand. For a committee member, they may result in the strengthening of his position back home or the kind of pub-

[3] See Ralph K. Huitt, "The Congressional Committee: A Case Study," *American Political Science Review,* XLVIII (June 1954), pp. 344 ff.

[4] David B. Truman, *The Governmental Process* (New York: Knopf, 1960), p. 375.

licity that will make him talked about as a potential presidential candidate. For a pressure group, they may signify the beginning of a long and elaborate effort to condition public opinion favorably to a long-term legislative goal.

The information developed at a hearing is made available to members of Congress in the form of printed volumes which reproduce the testimony that was taken. Although these volumes appear on their face to contain verbatim transcripts, their contents often bear a somewhat distant relationship to what actually took place at a hearing. The reason is that committee members as well as witnesses are almost always given an opportunity to "correct" their remarks. In the absence of a rule that they must confine their editing to mistakes made in transcription and to matters of grammar, they often do a thorough job of rewriting. To diminish the value of the printed record still further, there is usually no subject-matter index to help one find at a glance the testimony that dealt with a particular point. Thus, from a practical point of view, the information obtained through a hearing is directly available only to members of the committee or subcommittee involved. Other congressmen, of course, would probably not have time to review it anyway, since they have their own committee work to keep up with.

"Marking-up" Process

If it is a subcommittee that has conducted a hearing, the decision its members must reach afterward is whether to advise the full committee to take favorable action on the legislation. With the subcommittee's recommendation before it, the full committee may hold supplementary hearings or go directly into executive session, just as it does after conducting hearings of its own on bills not referred by the chairman to a subcommittee. The basic question before the committee is whether to report the bill to the chamber with a recommendation that it be enacted into law.

It is during the executive session that the "marking-up" process takes place. This is the stage at which the committee discusses and votes on proposed amendments to the bill under consideration. The chairman reads the bill, line by line. At any point, members may offer amendments, and one after another the amendments are voted on. If the committee decides to alter the measure drastically, it may conclude that a completely different bill should be substituted for the original legislation referred to it. Such a draft, commonly termed a "clean bill," is then introduced by the chairman or another member as entirely new legislation, even to the point of being given its own number.[5]

If the committee is closely divided in the voting that takes place during the "marking-up" process, the hand of the chair-

---

[5] In each house, bills are given identifying numbers in the order in which they are introduced. "H.R. 18" will be the eighteenth bill introduced in the House during a particular Congress, and "S. 12" will be the twelfth bill offered in the Senate. Legislative measures that take the form of resolutions rather than bills are numbered separately, with a designation that indicates the type of resolution involved:

1. "H. J. Res." is a "joint resolution" originating in the House; "S. J. Res." is one initiated by the Senate. Joint resolutions have the same force as bills and, like them, are submitted to the President for his signature. They are usually simple, one-purpose enactments, such as extensions of statutes due to expire.

2. "H. Con. Res." and "S. Con. Res." signify "concurrent resolutions." These usually involve matters that directly affect only Congress, not the public (e.g., a resolution to schedule a joint session, or to adjourn at a particular time). One exception consists of proposed constitutional amendments. Concurrent resolutions are not submitted to the President.

3. "H. Res." and "S. Res." identify "simple resolutions," in which a single chamber takes an action within its own scope (e.g., the House creates a new committee, or the Senate expresses its opinion on a foreign policy issue).

man is often strengthened by the system of proxy voting accepted in a number of committees. Under such an arrangement, a congressman who knows he will be absent from a committee meeting may authorize one of his colleagues to vote on his behalf. Because members depend so heavily on their chairman for favors, it is a common practice for proxies to go to him.[6]

No publicity is given to the votes that are cast during a "mark-up." Yet the proceedings can by no stretch of the imagination be considered secret. There is nothing to prevent participants from disclosing details of an executive session to White House officials and even lobbyists in order to help assure that pressure will be applied in the right places. Favored newsmen, too, are often briefed on what has occurred.[7] Even when a committee goes to extreme lengths and excludes its staff members from an executive session, the newspapers in a matter of hours are usually peddling leaked versions of what took place. It is not the staff members but the congressmen themselves who would have to be excluded to assure secrecy. For to the congressmen, leaks are a part of the legislative game and one of the ways he exercises influence.[8] Leaks, of course, may be highly colored and even totally inaccurate, for there is no official record against which they can be checked.

It is by no means unlikely that the committee, after considering legislation in executive session, will come to the conclusion that no bill at all should be approved. If it makes that kind of decision, or if the chairman uses his power to prevent any action, the legislation for all practical purposes is dead.

[6] Bertram M. Gross, *The Legislative Struggle: A Study in Social Combat* (New York: McGraw-Hill, 1953), p. 316. See *Congressional Quarterly Weekly Report* (August 23, 1963), p. 1491.

[7] Gross, *op. cit.,* p. 310.

[8] Donald R. Matthews, *U. S. Senators and Their World* (Chapel Hill: University of North Carolina Press, 1960), p. 166.

The committee need not make an adverse recommendation and seldom does, for inaction will almost always suffice to kill the bill by preventing it from getting to the floor. Just as a bill on which the committee has declined to hold hearings is consigned to oblivion, so a bill that is not "reported out" is unlikely ever to see the light of day.

Discharge

Both the House and Senate, however, do provide techniques through which a determined majority can pry a bill out of committee, if its supporters can overcome the traditional reluctance of Congress to invoke extraordinary procedures. One such means enables the membership to "discharge" a committee of responsibility for a bill, thus bringing the legislation to the floor.[9]

In the House, this procedure is initiated through the filing of a "discharge petition" by any member. The petition remains on the Speaker's desk, available for signing by those congressmen who want to free the bill from committee. If at least a majority of the total membership feel strongly enough to inscribe their names, and if this majority retains its strength for a confirmatory vote on the floor, the bill is dislodged from committee and comes before the House for debate and decision. The discharge procedure in the Senate is similar, though no petition is required. Instead, a discharge motion may be made from the floor. In the event that it attracts support from a majority, the committee is forced to release the legislation.

Although no extraordinary majority has to be mustered in either house for a discharge attempt to succeed, few bills are wrested from committee through this procedure. Highly prac-

[9] The discharge procedure may also be used against the Rules Committee. See Ch. 8.

tical considerations make it difficult to obtain majority backing. There is, for one thing, universal recognition of how
dangerous it is to incure the displeasure of committee chairmen, who can often decide the fate of legislation affecting
a congressman's political future (such as private bills requested by important constituents). Every congressman
knows, too, that by supporting a discharge attempt he establishes a precedent he may regret, for someday one of *his*
committees may be threatened by a discharge petition against
a bill that *he* wants to keep from the floor. In addition, a general feeling exists in both houses that the discharge method is a
"departure from normal procedures." The fact that it is specifically sanctioned by the rules is not emphasized; the sophisticated congressman is expected to know that some things,
though permissible, simply are not done.

Use of the discharge device is even more of a rarity in the
Senate than in the House. Procedural obstacles of a formidable nature stand in the way of a senator who wants to offer
a discharge motion. Under the rules, such a motion may be
made only during the "Morning Hour," except in the highly
unlikely circumstance that unanimous consent can be obtained. A single obstructionist can prevent the making of the
motion by insisting that the period be devoted to a series of
formalities that are ordinarily waived by unanimous consent,
such as reading the Journal of the previous day's proceedings
(this is the single most time-consuming activity) and reading
communications from the executive departments.

Even if time is left for the senator to make his discharge
motion, another frustrating rule comes into play. Existing
procedure requires that a discharge motion "lie over" for one
day before being voted on. The word "day" in the Senate,
however, means something quite different than the time it
takes for the earth to complete a single turn on its axis.

Instead of lasting only 24 hours, a legislative day may go on for hundreds of hours, because it does not end until there is a formal adjournment.[10] As a consequence, the rule that a discharge motion must be held in abeyance for one day may in practice mean a delay of several weeks, if after the motion has been made the Senate chooses to recess from day to day instead of adjourning. Furthermore, no new discharge motion may be introduced during such an extended "day," because a "Morning Hour" is held only when the Senate has reconvened after an adjournment, as distinguished from a recess.[11]

In the light of such procedural complexities, a discharge motion has virtually no chance of success unless it has backing from the leadership. Even when such support is forthcoming, success is far from assured. In 1962, Majority Leader Mansfield personally moved to discharge the Committee on Government Operations of a resolution allowing a vote to be taken on President Kennedy's plan to establish a Department of Urban Affairs. But the action accomplished little more than to give the committee chairman, Senator McClellan of Arkansas, a chance to favor the Senate with the kind of oratory it loves: "The brightness of the legislative skies is clouded, the brilliance of statesmanship is dimmed, and the light of fairness and justice in this chamber is darkened today. . . ."[12] The Mansfield motion also provided an opportunity for those who really objected to the urban affairs plan on substantive grounds to hide behind the procedural argument that they

[10] The adjournment referred to is an adjournment to a specific date. It is not to be confused with an "adjournment *sine die*" (without a date fixed for reconvening), which concludes an annual or special session of Congress.

[11] Howard E. Shuman, "Senate Rules and the Civil Rights Bill: A Case Study," *American Political Science Review*, LI (December 1957), p. 956.

[12] *Congressional Record*, February 20, 1962, p. 2323 (daily edition).

did not want to undermine the Senate's committee system.[13]

In the House, the parliamentary problems are a little less forbidding. Still, a number of rules must be complied with. No committee, for instance, may be discharged of responsibility for legislation until after thirty days have passed without any action.[14] In addition, discharge may not be voted until the question has been on the calendar for a minimum of seven days. And even if the effort succeeds, the bill may not be brought up for debate except on two particular days of the month.[15]

In the House as in the Senate, discharge attempts succeed only infrequently. Of those few bills that do come to the floor by means of discharge petitions, virtually none can overcome all the other legislative obstacles and attain final congressional enactment. Actually, on only two occasions in the history of Congress have bills become law after successful discharge petitions in the House.[16]

The effectiveness of the discharge procedure in the House, however, cannot be measured in these terms alone. Once in a while it happens that a bill is reported out when a discharge petition is only a few signatures short of the necessary majority. A practical reason may impel the committee to bow to the inevitable. For the committee may not amend a bill that is forced from it through a discharge petition. If, on the other hand, the bill is released "voluntarily," there is an opportunity to introduce drastic changes before it is sent to the floor.

[13] The Mansfield motion was defeated, 58-42. From 1789 until 1959, only five discharge motions were approved by the Senate. On no more than twelve occasions were motions even made. George B. Galloway, *The Legislative Process in Congress*, (New York: Thomas Y. Crowell, 1959), p. 548.

[14] In the case of the Rules Committee, only seven days must elapse. *Ibid.*, p. 294.

[15] The second and fourth Monday.

[16] The Fair Labor Standards Act of 1938 and a 1960 statute increasing the salaries of Government employees.

Until 1910, the House had no discharge procedure at all. The discharge rule was adopted in that year as part of a major bipartisan effort to democratize the House. One reason the rule has not lived up to the expectations of its authors is that no provision was made to treat a discharge petition as a public document. Today a petition is given something of a semi-secret status. Although it is available for perusal by any congressman, it is concealed from the eyes of the press. Congressmen are strongly in favor of the secrecy, because publicizing the names of signers might mean that heavy pressure could be exerted against those who had refrained from affixing their names.[17]

Apart from the discharge procedure, the Senate and House have other devices for circumventing an obstructionist committee. Senate practice allows the substance of a bill that is immured in committee to be brought to the floor in the form of an amendment to legislation that has already been called up for debate. Since the Senate, unlike the House, has no rule of germaneness, the "rider" may concern a completely different subject than the measure to which it is offered as an amendment. The only restriction is that legislation may not be attached to an appropriation bill unless approval by two-thirds of the members is obtained.[18] Without such a provision, it would be possible to immunize a bill effectively against a presidential veto. This could be done by attaching it as an

---

[17] In 1960, a group of House liberals employed a ruse and learned the names of those representatives who had—and those who had not—signed a discharge petition to bring a civil rights bill to the floor. They turned the list over to *The New York Times*. After the *Times* published it, a flock of belated converts promptly found their way to the Speaker's desk to add their names to the petition. The incident is related in Daniel M. Berman, *A Bill Becomes a Law: The Civil Rights Act of 1960* (New York: Macmillan, 1962), pp. 74-75.

[18] In 1959, that majority was put together, and a bill to extend the life of the Civil Rights Commission was approved as a "rider" on a foreign aid appropriation bill.

amendment to an appropriation measure supplying funds desperately needed by a segment of the Government.[19] There are other ways for the Senate to deal with the problem of committee pigeonholing. A bill that has already passed the House can be kept from an unfriendly committee by putting it directly on the calendar.[20] Or the Senate can refer the bill to committee, but with instructions that it must be reported out by a given date.[21]

Suspending the Rules

The House, too, has an alternative to the discharge procedure: suspension of the rules. This device is uniquely a prerogative of the leadership. It cannot, in fact, be invoked without the direct cooperation of the Speaker. A member who wishes to move that the rules be suspended in order to pass a bill bogged down in committee will not be recognized for this purpose by the Speaker unless the strategy has been agreed on in advance. Suspension of the rules is thus in reality the Speaker's weapon against recalcitrant committees.

The weapon, however, is a cumbersome one. To begin with, the rules permit suspension motions to be made only on two days in the month—the first and third Monday. In addition, a bill that reaches the floor through the suspension route is not subject to amendment: the House must deal with it on a take-it-or-leave-it basis, and after only forty minutes of debate. To make matters still worse, the bill will go down

[19] No President has ever tried to exercise the power to veto a single section of a bill. There has been general agreement that legislation must be accepted or rejected in its entirety. (See Ch. 12 for discussion of proposals that the President be given an "item veto.")

[20] It was by this method that a civil rights bill was brought to the Senate floor in 1957. Shuman, *op. cit.*, p. 968.

[21] The Judiciary Committee was given such a deadline when a House-passed civil rights bill was referred to it in 1960.

to defeat unless it commands the support of two-thirds of the members who vote. But the suspension procedure assumes great importance when a congressional session is drawing to an end. For although suspension may ordinarily be moved only twice a month, this limitation can be waived during the days immediately preceding final adjournment.[22] The suspension device becomes a handy instrument for the Speaker during the annual end-of-session frenzy, when the drive for adjournment coincides with the realization that vital legislation has not yet been acted on.

None of these methods for getting around a committee is used successfully except at rare intervals. Tremendous pressure is generally required, either from the public or from the President or from both, to overcome Congress's traditional reluctance to bypass a standing committee. Under normal circumstances, a bill that has been buried by a committee stays buried. Thus a committee's decision on whether to report out a bill and, if so, on what provisions it should contain is one of the most important factors in the legislative process.

Committee Report

If a committee takes favorable action on a bill, it submits two documents to the House: the text of the bill it has approved and a report describing its terms. The bill is printed

[22] Under House rules, suspension is in order during the last six days before the end of a session. Prior to ratification of the Twentieth Amendment in 1933, this provision had applicability during the "short session" of Congress, which had a fixed date of adjournment (March 4). Today, in contrast, one never knows in advance when the two Houses will declare their session at an end by passing a resolution to adjourn *sine die* (without fixing a time to reconvene). But the Speaker is still able to use the suspension procedure in the closing weeks because the House customarily gives him a blanket authorization to do so, either by unanimous consent or through the adoption of an appropriate resolution reported by the Rules Committee.

in such a way as to indicate the changes made by the committee in the draft originally referred to it. Wording that the committee has added appears in italics, and any matter it has deleted is printed in "stricken through" type. The second document, the committee report, ordinarily contains a detailed explanation of the bill and argues the case for favorable action. In addition, it enumerates all existing laws that the proposed legislation would alter or repeal. The report is usually designed to rally support for the measure. Often, however, quite a different purpose may be discerned: to influence subsequent judicial interpretation by putting on record a statement that may later be used to establish congressional intent.[23]

Members of the committee who disagree with the report and oppose the legislation it deals with may explain their minority position in statements that accompany the report to the floor. Although it sometimes happens that the split between those who sign the committee report and those who subscribe to minority views follows party lines, the report can seldom be considered a party document. For on numerous issues, no party positions exist at this stage—or at any subsequent stage, for that matter. Woodrow Wilson deplored this evidence of party irresponsibility. Bills reported from committee, he said slightingly, "represent merely the recommendations of a small body of members belonging to both parties. . . . If they are carried, it is no party triumph; if they are lost it is no party discomfiture."[24] For better or worse,

[23] There is some question about whether it is logical to infer anything significant about the intent of Congress as a whole from statements made in a committee report. The report may only reflect the intent of those members of the committee who signed it. It may not necessarily reveal the intent of other members of Congress who voted for the legislation— or of the President who signed it into law. (See discussion in Ch. 14.)

[24] Wilson, *op. cit.*, pp. 78-79.

however, it is in the form of a committee bill and a committee report that a legislative proposal is presented on the floor.

The "Watchdog" Function

The screening of proposed legislation is not the only activity of congressional committees. Today more than ever before in their history, committees devote both time and energy to supervising operations of the Executive Branch. For Congress in the twentieth century, the function of passing new laws has become distinctly subordinate to the function of overseeing the manner in which existing laws are being executed. A major share of the responsibility for acting in the capacity of watchdog belongs to the legislative committees.[25]

The place of legislative committees in the supervision of administration was explicitly recognized by the Legislative Reorganization Act of 1946. Under that law, the committees of both houses were requested to keep careful track of how congressional policies are translated into functioning programs in the Executive Branch. Although some committees have taken this assignment less seriously than others, a prudent agency head is always prepared for committee inquiries into how he is interpreting and administering relevant legislation, for he may be in for serious trouble if he executes laws in disregard of the wishes of the committees. An expert in the field of Executive-Legislative relationships has explained this phenomenon in simple terms:

[25] Congressional supervision of the Executive Branch is not exercised in a unified or even in a coherent fashion. Typically, an agency must expect its activities to be scrutinized by the legislative committees and subcommittees that authorize its programs, by the appropriations subcommittees on which it depends for funds, and by the Government Operations Committees, which are licensed to roam about in the entire Executive Branch.

Since bureau leaders know that they will have to return again and again to their committees for renewals of their resources and for modifications of their authority, they usually try to follow, within reason, the intent of committee members who shape a given law.[26]

An agency will be especially concerned to maintain good relations with the chairmen of the committees and subcommittees empowered to oversee its activities. One thing that will be done as a matter of course is to give preferential treatment to the constituencies represented by the chairmen. Take, for example, the Department of Defense, which is supervised by the two Armed Services Committees. The chairmen of the committees—Senator Richard B. Russell and Representative Carl Vinson—both happen to be from Georgia. By a strange coincidence, the Defense Department seems to find their state a most congenial site for military installations. "When the Pentagon decides that a new air base or supply depot is needed," a newsman has written, "it naturally looks all over Georgia first to see if the right spot might happen to be there."[27] Chairman Vinson makes no effort to deny his power over the Pentagon. Reportedly he was once asked whether he would accept an appointment as Secretary of Defense. His reply was in the negative. "Shucks," he said, "I'd rather run the Pentagon from up here."[28]

Vinson and Russell are not the only committee chairmen who usually find executive agencies easy to get along with. A

[26] J. Leiper Freeman, *The Political Process: Executive Bureau-Legislative Committee Relations* (New York: Random House, 1955), pp. 49-50.

[27] Rowland Evans, Jr., "The Sixth Sense of Carl Vinson," *Reporter*, April 12, 1962, p. 27. It is a standing joke in Washington that if one more military installation were built in Georgia the state would probably sink beneath the Atlantic.

[28] Quoted by Russell Baker, *An American in Washington* (New York: Knopf, 1961), pp. 168-69.

conscious desire to curry favor with chairmen is not always the whole explanation for this compatibility. It may be that the agency head was originally recommended for his job by one or both of the chairmen. Sometimes the chairmen and he are obligated to the same interest groups or tend to think alike because of a common background. Thus relations between the Legislative and Executive Branches, far from pitting Congress against the President, are more often extremely cozy on the committee-department level and especially on the subcommittee-bureau level.

Since the typical subcommittee has no desire to alter this situation, it resists all efforts to integrate the bureau it supervises with the parent department. The result is a nightmare for experts in administrative management. But while congressmen are in favor of organizational efficiency as an abstract proposition, they are far more concerned with something else: maintaining access to the portion of the bureaucratic apparatus that deals with matters important to them. A theoretically sound organizational chart is simply not at the apex of a congressman's hierarchy of values.

Because Congress as an institution recognizes that a clientele relationship can be expected to develop between a legislative committee and the governmental unit supposedly being supervised, it has established two committees that are not tied to any special segment of the Federal bureaucracy. Instead, their responsibility encompasses the whole of the Executive Branch. The House and Senate Committees on Government Operations[29] have been given unparalleled supervisory power. They are authorized to oversee "the operation of govern-

---

[29] The committees have functioned under that name only since 1952. The Legislative Reorganization Act of 1946, which gave them their present responsibilities, used the name "Committees on Expenditures in the Executive Departments."

ment . . . at all levels with a view to determining its economy and efficiency." In accordance with their mandate, the committees have canvassed the Federal government's relationships with municipalities, states, and international organizations. Their primary concern, however, has not been in the field of intergovernmental relationships but rather with the activities of the Federal departments and agencies.

Both the legislative committees and the Government Operations Committees[30] are deeply involved in the supervision of administration. In some instances, Congress even provides that prospective Executive actions be subject to their approval."[31] Presidents have been deeply resentful of such congressional "interference" in administration. In several instances, they have vetoed legislation making committee approval a prerequisite for certain Executive actions. At other times, however, they have been obliged to concur in such arrangements or resign themselves to the defeat of legislation they favored.

The usual provision for a committee veto requires the department to submit a detailed report in advance of certain actions it plans to take. The committee is given a specific period of time in which it may disapprove the step. In practice, a committee sometimes chooses to delegate this veto power. The delegation may be to the committee chairman or to a subcommittee. On occasion it has even gone to professional staff members.[32] The two Committees on Government

[30] The role of the Appropriations Committees is discussed in Ch. 12.

[31] The first such provision dates from 1944, when the Secretary of the Navy was required to "come into agreement" with the House and Senate Naval Affairs Committees before spending money to acquire land for naval purposes. Joseph P. Harris, "Congressional Committee Veto of Executive Decisions," paper presented at the 1959 annual meeting of the American Political Science Association.

[32] Walter E. Rhode, *Committee Clearance of Administrative Decisions* (East Lansing: Michigan State University Bureau of Social and Political Research, 1959), p. 51.

Operations have often in effect subcontracted their veto to individual congressmen—whether committee members or not —whose constituencies would be directly affected by certain types of Executive actions. An agency plan to dispose of surplus property, for example, is usually referred to the representatives and senators from the area where the property is located. If the proposed action does not meet with their approval, one of the Government Operations Committees can usually be counted on to exercise its veto.[33]

Congress seems particularly concerned to give its committees a veto power over administrative action threatening the effectiveness of pork barrel legislation. Thus it has required committee clearance for military construction contracts, military real estate transactions, and the acquisition of public buildings.[34] In addition, it has used committee clearance when it is dissatisfied with the way in which established governmental programs are administered or when it is concerned about how new and untried programs will work out.[35]

Not content with preventing the President from taking certain actions, Congress has been toying with the possibility of attempting to compel him to take certain other actions. Legislators never feel more chagrined than when a Chief Executive declines to spend money that they have appropriated for a particular purpose. Presidents Truman, Eisenhower, and Kennedy each refused to spend funds voted by Congress for certain specific military projects that they did not consider

[33] *Ibid.*, p. 59.

[34] Galloway, *History of the House of Representatives, op. cit.*, p. 188.

[35] Rhode, *op. cit.*, pp. 48-49. Under the Reorganization Act of 1949, the President has the power to reorganize the agencies in the Executive Branch. A reorganization plan announced by the President, however, does not go immediately into effect. Instead, Congress has 60 days in which to express itself, if it so chooses, in opposition to the plan. If either house adopts a resolution against the plan, the President is prevented from putting it into effect.

desirable. In 1962, for example, the House Armed Services Committee reported out legislation in which the Pentagon was "directed" to use $491 million for development of the RS-70 bomber. Defense Secretary McNamara had requested only about one-third of that amount, and the Kennedy Administration made it clear that it would feel under no compulsion to spend any more than that on the project. A serious constitutional collision between the President and Congress was averted, however, when a "summit conference" attended by Mr. Kennedy and House Armed Services Committee Chairman Vinson resulted in an agreement, which, though called a compromise, really represented almost total victory for the Executive Branch. Congress abandoned its attempt to direct the spending of the money, and the President agreed to institute a new review of whether more money should be devoted to the project than had been originally budgeted.

Investigations

In the performance of their legislative and supervisory functions, congressional committees are immensely aided by their investigatory power. Investigations are sometimes instituted at the behest of a President who may wish to create a favorable atmosphere for a program he is promoting. The bulk of them, however, originate in Congress itself. They are, in fact, one of the principal devices enabling Congress to supervise the Executive Branch and compete with it for public attention. The upsurge of congressional investigations in recent decades has accurately been termed "one of the unanticipated consequences of the Presidency's enlargement."[36]

The congressional power to investigate, though nowhere mentioned in the Constitution, was already taken for granted

[36] Andrew Hacker, "Voice of Ninety Million Americans," *The New York Times Magazine* (March 4, 1962), p. 80.

when Congress was only in the third year of its existence. The first investigation was conducted in 1792, after a band of American soldiers, under the command of Major General Arthur St. Clair, experienced a disastrous defeat at the hands of the Indians. Six hundred American lives were lost. The House of Representatives proceeded to empower a select committee to investigate the debacle. It gave the committee authority to compel witnesses to appear, testify, and turn over relevant papers.[37]

In this very first inquiry, Congress came up against a problem that was to recur frequently: how to compel the President to produce documents needed in an investigation. When Washington was asked for certain papers relating to the St. Clair campaign, he enunciated the principle that the President "ought to communicate only such papers as the public good would permit, and ought to refuse those the disclosure of which would hurt the public." Jefferson, Monroe, and Jackson chose to follow this precedent, and "executive privilege" became a firmly established constitutional principle. It is generally conceded to mean that the President cannot be ordered to appear before a congressional committee. In addition, both the substance of conversations in which he has participated and the content of White House files are beyond the reach of Congress.[38]

But the metes and bounds of "executive privilege" are by no means clearly delineated. It is in dispute, for example, whether the privilege extends beyond the office of the President himself and encompasses the departments and agencies. For although the departments and agencies are, indeed, "mere

[37] Telford Taylor, *Grand Inquest* (New York: Simon and Schuster, 1954). pp. 19, 22.

[38] Joseph P. Harris, *The Advice and Consent of the Senate* (Berkeley: University of California Press, 1953), p. 103.

creatures of the Congress, dependent on the Legislative Branch . . . for their very existence,"[39] they are organizationally a part of the Executive Branch and it is difficult to see what Congress could do to prevent a President from throwing the cloak of executive privilege around their actions. A House subcommittee[40] has kept alive the issue of what is sometimes called the "right to know," but there is in Congress a high degree of realism regarding the inability of the Legislative Branch to force from the Executive any information that it wants to keep secret.

Not all congressional investigations, of course, are directed toward supervision of executive activities, although that was most frequently their subject during the first century of the nation's history. Toward the end of the nineteenth century and in the first three decades of the twentieth, Congress turned increasingly to quite another matter: economic and social problems that might call for legislative solutions.[41] The "muckraking" atmosphere that characterized the period of Theodore Roosevelt's administration prompted investigations into such important sectors of American society as the stock market, the railroads, and the giant financial combines. Investigations of the same type were important to the administration of Franklin Roosevelt, too. Senators, for example, conducted a sensational investigation in 1935 into the high-handed methods employed by power companies to defeat a bill providing for the regulation of public utility holding companies. This investigation was carried on under the chairmanship of Senator Hugo Black of Alabama.[42] The facts it

[39] *Ibid.*, p. 104.

[40] The Subcommittee on Foreign Operations and Government Information of the Committee on Government Operations.

[41] Taylor, *op. cit.*, p. 51.

[42] Black later became a Justice of the United States Supreme Court and one of the most scathing critics of congressional investigations that are lacking in legislative purpose.

turned up helped convince Black that proper investigations were an invaluable adjunct of the legislative process. On many occasions, he said, they had resulted in the enactment of salutary legislation, the saving of public funds, and the focusing of "the rays of pitiless publicity" on special interest groups, "who can defy every other power."[43] These words indicated that Congress had come to accept a broad view of its investigative authority during the century and a half following the inquest into General St. Clair's defeat.

That first congressional investigation was carried out by a House committee, but important investigations today are often conducted by committees of the Senate. In part this is so because senators have enough time for such things: the six-year terms give them a degree of freedom from electoral cares that members of the House can only dream about. An even more important reason is that the relative lack of centralized control in the Senate makes each member, in a sense, a power unto himself. The leadership needs his vote or, at the very minimum, his cooperation, because the smooth functioning of the Senate depends on ready acquiescence in the unanimous consent requests that enable the body to do most of its work. Thus even a single senator who is interested in a particular subject may not find it too difficult to persuade the leadership that it should endorse an investigation, perhaps by a select (or special) committee headed by him. Even if the investigation is distasteful to other senators, they will be reluctant to register any objection, for someday they might want approval for investigations of their own. A Senate committee is especially likely to take the lead when the subject matter of an investigation is supervision of the Executive Branch.[44]

[43] Hugo L. Black, "Inside a Senate Investigation," *Harper's Magazine*, February, 1936, p. 275.

[44] A leading place in Senate investigations of the Executive Branch has been taken by the Permanent Subcommittee on Investigations, a unit

A dominant role for the Senate was assured by a provision of the Legislative Reorganization Act of 1946, under which Congress still operates. Every standing committee of the Senate was given a regular annual appropriation of $10,000, earmarked for investigations. House committees were put at a distinct disadvantage: before one of them could institute an investigation, it had to obtain approval (as well as funds) through a special resolution.[45]

Contempt of Congress

Money was not the only gift that the Legislative Reorganization Act bestowed on the committees of the Senate. Without exception, each of them was given the power to subpoena both witnesses and documents needed to investigate "any matter within its jurisdiction." This was something of a revolutionary development, for previously no congressional committee had ever been granted the subpoena power on a permanent basis. Whenever either house had felt that a matter warranted investigation by a committee, it had been obliged to pass a special resolution describing with particularity the subject to be studied. Under the 1946 law, however, every Senate committee was given blanket authorization to issue subpoenas. The break with the past was especially sharp because the use of the subpoenas would no longer have to be confined to a specific subject certified by the Senate as ripe for investigation; subpoenas could now be used throughout

---

of the Senate Committee on Government Operations. It was as chairman of this subcommittee that Senator McCarthy of Wisconsin earned his reputation.

[45] See Gladys M. Kammerer, *The Staffing of the Committees of Congress* (Lexington, Ky.: The Bureau of Government Research, University of Kentucky, 1949). Speaker Rayburn and Minority Leader Martin insisted on this arrangement in order to retain control over House investigations.

the length and breadth of the spacious area over which each committee was given jurisdiction.[46] In the House, the situation is completely different. There, only three committees have authority to issue subpoenas: Appropriations, Government Operations, and Un-American Activities.

The importance of the subpoena power, of course, is that it enables a committee to compel the presence of an unwilling witness and to insist, under threat of punishment, that he answer its questions and produce records it wants. A recalcitrant witness runs the risk that he will he held in contempt.

Congress today handles contempt quite differently than it once did. In the nineteenth century, it did not usually involve the Executive and Judicial Branches in the process. Although a witness committed a criminal offense if he defied a demand for information by either house, violations were seldom referred to the Department of Justice for prosecution. Instead, the contumacious witness would be brought before the bar of the House or Senate for summary punishment. The punishment was imprisonment, but the witness would be freed when the congressional session ended.

In the present century, Congress has wholly abandoned the practice of punishing contempt on its own. It now prefers to rely on the Justice Department to prosecute balky witnesses and on the Federal courts to punish them. Congressmen play a part only during two preliminary stages of the process:

[46] The authority of the various committees was described in broad and general terms, since the pertinent section of the Act was designed to spell out jurisdiction over bills and was not drawn up with investigations and subpoenas in mind. The Committee on Labor and Public Welfare, for example, was entrusted with "public welfare generally," the Committee on Armed Services with "common defense generally," and the Committee on Interstate and Foreign Commerce with "interstate and foreign commerce generally." See Taylor, *op. cit.*, p. 232.

1. If the witness offends a subcommittee, the members of this body may recommend that the full committee issue a contempt citation. It is most unusual for such a recommendation to be turned down.[47]

2. The chairman of the full committee then asks the House or Senate, as the case may be, to issue the citation for which the committee has voted. With little discussion and with even less doubt as to the outcome, the chamber will agree and refer the citation to the United States attorney for the District of Columbia.

An examination of the *Congressional Record* makes it clear that neither the House nor the Senate really makes an independent judgment as to whether there is justification for the contempt citations it approves. The clubby atmosphere that suffuses so many areas of the legislative process is never more in evidence than here. Only rarely does even a single member vote against a contempt request, for there is reluctance to rebuke the chairman and members of a standing committee. The fear seems to be that this would not only be a discourtesy but, more important, would invite the members of the committee to retaliate against whoever had been foolhardy enough to oppose them. Even senators who attacked the late Joseph R. McCarthy (R., Wis.) as a character assassin would vote dutifully to confirm the contempt citations requested by the Government Operations Committee on behalf of his subcommittee. Many ostensible opponents of the House Committee on Un-American Activities do the same thing today.

[47] That kind of episode, however, did take place in 1962, when the Senate Anti-Trust and Monopoly Subcommittee recommended contempt proceedings against four steel companies that had defied subpoenas calling for the production of cost data. The subcommittee and its chairman, Senator Kefauver of Tennessee, were repudiated by the parent Judiciary Committee, which rejected the contempt recommendation and thus prevented it from reaching the Senate floor.

The casual way in which both the House and Senate place their stamp of approval on committee requests for contempt citations is open to serious criticism in view of the fact that the offense being dealt with is contempt of *Congress,* not contempt of *committee.* In such circumstances, logic would seem to demand a carefully considered independent determination by the house of Congress that brought the committee into existence.[48] In practice, however, it has been left to the courts, and especially the Supreme Court, to look beyond the simple fact that a witness has refused to answer a question or produce certain records, and determine whether contempt of Congress has indeed been committed.

The first occasion on which the Supreme Court made a ruling on contempt on Congress took place in 1880. A select House committee had been investigating certain financial dealings between the notorious Jay Cooke and a real estate pool in which he was involved. The committee had justified its interest in a private financial relationship on the theory that the Government was one of Cooke's creditors and had been injured as a result of the transactions in question. The manager of the real estate pool took a different view of the issue. Claiming that the House could not look into an essentially private matter, he declined to answer questions or produce documents, and when he was jailed for contempt he sued for damages because of false imprisonment. The Supreme Court upheld his position.[49] Its decision seemed to mean that the courts would carefully review the use made of

[48] Representative John V. Lindsay (R., N. Y.) has introduced legislation to establish special screening committees in both houses. The committees would "study requests for contempt citations sought by committees and . . . report with recommendations on such requests . . . if further action is deemed advisable." *Congressional Record,* July 2, 1963, p. 11459 (daily edition).

[49] Kilbourn v. Thompson, 103 U. S. 168 (1880).

the contempt power, in order to keep congressional committees within the boundaries established by the Constitution.[50]

"Un-American"?

The committee that has most often been accused of straying beyond these boundaries is the House Committee on
Un-American Activities. Instead of confining itself to tasks
that serve legislative purposes, this committee has gone so
far as to stage carefully prepared melodramas that could not,
by their very nature, inform congressmen of anything they
did not already know. The most widely publicized example
was a series of hearings on "Communist propaganda" passing
through the United States mails. The committee held hearings in a number of major cities throughout the country, but
virtually the same script was used regardless of locale. The
script called for the deputy collector of customs, who accompanied the committee on its travels, to open a mail sack and
horrify his audience by pulling out item after item of "Communist propaganda" sent into the United States from abroad.

The Un-American Activities Committee, which has been
functioning since 1938, operates under an extremely broad
authorizing resolution. It is empowered, among other things,
to investigate the "objects of un-American propaganda activities in the United States," as well as "propaganda that . . .
attacks the principle of the form of government as guaranteed
by our Constitution. . . ." This authorizing resolution was
derided by the Supreme Court in 1957, when for the first
time it reversed the contempt conviction of a witness who had
declined to answer questions of the committee. In a scathing
opinion by Chief Justice Earl Warren, the Court referred
deprecatingly to the authorizing resolution: "Who can define
the meaning of 'un-American'?" it asked. "What is that single,

[50] But see McGrain v. Daugherty, 273 U. S. 135 (1927), in which the
Court accepted a broad interpretation of Congress' investigative power.

solitary 'principle of the form of government as guaranteed by our Constitution'?" Since the committee had made no effort to compensate for the deficiencies of its authorizing resolution by informing witnesses of how its questions were serving a valid legislative purpose, the Court held that contempt had not been committed when one man declined to provide answers.[51]

The sharp language employed by Chief Justice Warren made it seem that the Court would subject to the most critical scrutiny all future contempt-of-Congress convictions that related to the Un-American Activities Committee. The impression was heightened by the fact that only one member of the Court[52] dissented from the majority decision. The checkered career of the committee was far from over, however. A change in the personnel of the Court and a switch in the votes of two Justices who had been on the majority side in 1957 combined to give the committee a new lease on life only two years later. With the Chief Justice now forced into dissent, a 5-to-4 majority affirmed the conviction of a professor who had been uncooperative with the committee.[53] By the same vote, the committee proceeded to win other important Supreme Court victories.[54] The Court now seemed inclined to reverse a contempt conviction only when a narrow and fairly technical ground for decision was available.[55] But the replacement of Justice Felix Frankfurter by Justice Arthur J. Goldberg may presage a return to the more critical attitude toward the Committee that the Court displayed in 1957.[56]

[51] Watkins v. United States, 354 U. S. 178 (1957).
[52] Justice Tom Clark, who had been Attorney General in the Truman administration.
[53] Barenblatt v. United States, 360 U. S. 110 (1959).
[54] Braden v. United States, 365 U. S. 431 (1961) and Wilkinson v. United States, 365 U. S. 399 (1961).
[55] Russell v. United States, 369 U. S. 749 (1962).
[56] See Yellin v. United States, 374 U. S. 109 (1963).

In the House itself, few members have been willing to risk political oblivion by opposing the Committee. When Representative James Roosevelt (D., Calif.) tried to persuade the House to cut the Committee's appropriation in 1961, only five of his colleagues supported him. In 1963, the number rose to twenty, but that was still an insignificant minority in the 435-member House of Representatives.[57]

The Fifth Amendment

The Committee on Un-American Activities holds the undisputed record for the number of contempt citations it has generated.[58] Any of the witnesses who have gone to jail for defying the Committee could have avoided prosecution by the simple expedient of invoking the Fifth Amendment to the Constitution. The idea behind this Amendment, which forbids forcing a man to testify against himself, was to make it hard for officials to pursue inquiries into religious heresy or political heterodoxy. Anyone who seeks the protection of the Amendment, however, risks being humiliated and degraded by the congressional committee before which he is appearing. Some committee members and their staffs, prevented by the letter of the Fifth Amendment from compelling a witness to help send himself to jail, persistently violate the spirit of the Amendment by holding up such a person to ridicule. Incidents of this sort have been a commonplace during hearings of the Senate Select Committee on Improper Activities in

[57] The death of Committee Chairman Francis E. Walter (D., Pa.) later that year may make a difference. Colleagues were always afraid to offend Walter, who had power over private bills (as chairman of the Immigration Subcommittee) and Democratic patronage (as chairman of the Democratic Patronage Committee). He was also chairman of the Democratic caucus and often chairman of the Committee of the Whole.

[58] Carl Beck, *Contempt of Congress* (New Orleans: The Hauser Press, 1959), p. 17.

the Labor or Management Field, headed by Senator McClellan of Arkansas. Particularly when Attorney General Robert F. Kennedy was chief counsel of the Committee, the technique reached a high stage of development. The following interrogation by Kennedy and McClellan was typical:

KENNEDY	And you defraud the union . . . ?
WITNESS	I respectfully decline to answer because I honestly believe my answer might tend to incriminate me.
KENNEDY	I would agree with you.
MCCLELLAN	I believe it would.
KENNEDY	You haven't got the guts to [answer], have you . . . ?
WITNESS	I respectfully decline. . . .
MCCLELLAN	Morally you are kind of yellow inside, are you not? That is the truth about it?
WITNESS	I respectfully. . . .[59]

A related technique employed by McClellan and Kennedy was to fire dozens of obviously futile questions at a witness who had already made it clear that he would refuse to answer any of them. This procedure made it possible for the newspapers to report that the witness had invoked the protection of the Fifth Amendment not once but many times, as though the ignominy was compounded with every mention of the Constitution. Senator McClellan made no secret of the fact that his motive in asking questions was not always to obtain information. During one hearing, he announced that he would continue asking questions of a recalcitrant witness. The senator explained:

It is anticipated that we will get the same kind of response that we have been getting. But just so the public will know that there is more, and yet more, I am going to indulge this

[59]Alexander M. Bickel, "Robert F. Kennedy: The Case against Him for Attorney General," *New Republic,* January 9, 1961, p. 16.

session a little longer so that Counsel may ask some of these very pertinent questions and let the witness continue to take the Fifth Amendment.[60]

Since this kind of treatment is customarily reserved by McClellan and others like him for those who have been publicly branded in advance of the hearing as criminals or Communists or worse, there has been no widespread indignation about it either in Congress or elsewhere.[61]

Yet a witness who uses the Fifth Amendment does at least immunize himself against criminal prosecution. No such immunity is conferred on anyone who claims the protection of another provision of the Bill of Rights: the portion of the First Amendment which places freedom of expression beyond the reach of Congress. In no instance has the Supreme Court upheld a refusal to testify before the Un-American Activities Committee on First Amendment grounds. As a consequence, anyone who makes such a claim puts himself in the most serious jeopardy.

One member of the Senate has proposed that a witness be allowed to challenge the propriety of a committee's questions without having to run the risk of going to jail if the courts later rule against him. Senator Keating of New York has suggested that a Federal judge should pass on the witness' constitutional claim *before* the committee orders that a question be answered. In this way there would be a disinterested judicial determination as to whether the question was permissible, instead of an arrangement under which the committee itself is allowed to be the arbiter of its own conduct. An additional

---

[60] *Id.*

[61] Although McClellan has made abundant use of this technique, the master of the method was the late Senator McCarthy. It was he who popularized the term "Fifth Amendment Communist" to describe a witness who exercised his constitutional right to remain silent.

virtue that Keating sees in his plan is that it would afford the witness "an opportunity, if the Court orders him to furnish the requested information, to decide whether he really wants to defy the order."[62]

Immunity from Libel

Senator McCarthy, who heaped so much scorn on witnesses invoking the constitutional protection of the Fifth Amendment, did not himself hesitate to use another constitutional protection that is available to congressmen: the right to make defamatory statements without worrying about being sued for libel. The Constitution provides that "for any Speech or Debate in either house, [representatives and senators] shall not be questioned in any other Place."[63] This privilege against suits for defamation was designed to prevent the Executive Branch from harassing its critics in Congress by means of legal action.[64]

It serves a quite different purpose for a demagogue. For McCarthy it converted the Senate chamber into a sanctuary from which he was able to make unsubstantiated charges of subversion, espionage, and even treason, while remaining secure in the knowledge that he could not be brought to book for his slanders. Not only what he said on the floor but also the words he uttered in committee and the charges he made in official congressional reports were

[62] *Washington Post*, September 5, 1962, p. A14, col. 1.

[63] Article I, Section 6.

[64] William S. White, *Citadel: The Story of the U. S. Senate* (New York: Harper, 1956), p. 265. The privilege was not intended to exculpate completely a congressman who had indulged in defamation, for the House and Senate were each given the power to punish members "for disorderly Behaviour, and, with the Concurrence of two-thirds, [to] expel a Member." Article I, Section 5. But in actual practice, the power of each house to punish its members has all but atrophied through disuse.

beyond the reach of the law. The Wisconsin senator established himself as a national figure by making the most promiscuous use of his own constitutional privilege.[65]

The news media helped him.[66] Under ordinary circumstances, a publication that reports a defamatory statement is just as guilty of libel as the person who made the statement in the first place. This does not apply, however, to reports of congressional deliberations. A newspaper being sued for reporting a defamatory charge by McCarthy had to prove in its defense only that the senator had actually made the statement in an official proceeding, not that the statement was true. No serious consideration has ever been given to the possibility of revoking by statute the right of the press to disseminate congressional slanders.[67]

Oddly enough, any witness who appears before a committee is as invulnerable to libel suits as a congressman is. The courts have bestowed this privilege on him by drawing an analogy with the immunity that he would enjoy in a Federal court. While the comparison has superficial plausibility, it can easily be challenged on the ground that significant differences exist between the two situations. For one thing, a witness in a trial is inhibited by the knowledge that he will be subjected to

[65] In 1954 the Senate voted to censure him for his actions toward other senators.

[66] McCarthy, of course, made his hearings available for broadcast on radio and television. The Senate permits each committee to decide for itself whether to admit cameras and microphones. The House at the present time prohibits both. The late Speaker Rayburn was a vigorous defender of the ban. His successor as Speaker, John McCormack, has given no encouragement to those who favor relaxation of the rule.

[67] The judiciary usually takes an extremely broad view of the congressional privilege, but a New York court awarded libel damages against Congressman Powell of New York in 1962 on the basis of statements he had made during a television interview, even though the statements constituted discussion of a speech he had delivered in the House.

cross-examination. In addition, he may not go beyond the limits established by the rules of evidence. Such restraints are ordinarily absent when a congressional committee takes testimony from a friendly witness.[68]

Reforming Investigations

If Congress ever acts to end the unconscionable practices in which some of its investigating committees indulge, it may very well be influenced by the realization that such methods bring into disrepute the legitimate use of congressional investigations. One student of the House Committee on Un-American Activities observed as early as 1952 that the Committee had already "discredited the investigating power of Congress and thereby weakened what has always been one of the most important and useful congressional functions."[69]

Congress has not been completely insensitive to this argument. In 1955, the House took notice of widespread criticism by adopting a code of fair play for its investigating committees. The code contained provisions such as these: a single committee member could not take testimony and receive

---

[68] There are other important differences between the positions of judicial and legislative witnesses. In court, "there is a greater likelihood that all controverting evidence will be presented. . . . And, unlike many committee investigations, legal proceedings are resolved by a final verdict which ordinarily will be given much more publicity and credence than charges made in the course of the trial." Edwin H. Goldberger, "Protection from Defamation in Congressional Hearings," *University of Chicago Law Review*, XVI (Spring 1949), p. 544.

[69] He went further and declared that the reputation of Congress as a whole had been tarnished, for the committee, "by providing an opportunity for certain of the most incompetent and thoughtless members of Congress to run hog-wild and to obtain almost unlimited publicity for their irresponsible acts, has unquestionably encouraged many people to hold the national legislature in contempt." Robert K. Carr, *The House Committee on Un-American Activities, 1945-1950* (Ithaca, N. Y.: Cornell University Press, 1952), p. 458.

evidence on behalf of the full committee; the chairman, in his opening statement, would have to announce the subject of the investigation; a copy of the committee rules would be made available to witnesses; after the hearing was over, a witness would be able to obtain at cost a transcript of his testimony. Some provisions of the code, however, were most noteworthy for what they omitted. A witness could bring an attorney to advise him—but not to speak for him; a witness could submit a brief sworn statement—but only if the committee approved; a person who had been defamed in testimony before a committee would have the right to appear and answer the charges—but the committee could reject his request that additional witnesses be subpoenaed.

The House code fell far short of the remedies proposed by Dr. George B. Galloway, who was in a real sense the author of the Legislative Reorganization Act of 1946.[70] Dr. Galloway's list included the following reforms: a witness making a claim of constitutional privilege before a subcommittee should have the right to argue his point before the full committee; a person who has been the target of criticism by a witness should be allowed to submit written questions that the witness would have to answer; except in the case of a public official, no individual should be subpoenaed without the concurrence of a majority of the committee members; and a person injured by false testimony before a committee should have the right to sue the witness for libel.[71]

In the final analysis, what is needed is the formulation of a set of standards based on traditional rules of evidence, which

[70] Dr. Galloway was staff director of the Joint Committee on the Organization of Congress. He is now a senior specialist in the Legislative Reference Service of the Library of Congress.

[71] Galloway, *The Legislative Process in Congress, op. cit.,* p. 638. Other proposals for reform are contained in Julia E. Johnson, ed., *The Investigating Powers of Congress* (New York: Wilson, 1951), *passim.*

are designed as a compromise between ferreting out the truth and protecting the dignity of all concerned. But the discovery of truth is not always the aim of congressional investigators. A civil liberties lawyer has written of investigations that had "no purpose or effect other than to expose individuals to public contumely, and the loss of their jobs and perhaps of their livelihoods. . . ."[72] Even William S. White, a writer who can seldom bring himself to admit that the Senate is guilty of any wrongdoing, has taken cognizance of investigations that are "punitive and in the spirit of prosecution."[73] And a reporter with wide experience says this of committee investigations:

> They are planned deliberately to move from a preconceived idea to a predetermined conclusion. The skill and resourcefulness of the chairman and a sizable staff are pitted against any effort to alter [their] destined course. Whatever investigation is done takes place well in advance of the public hearing. The hearing is the final act in the drama.[74]

If this analysis is correct, Congress will probably continue to display a monumental lack of interest in suggestions for basic reform of its committees' procedures.

Committee Staffs

Whether it is conducting an investigation or considering a bill that has been referred to it, a congressional committee today relies heavily on its professional staff. Members of the staff perform such varied tasks as preparing background in-

[72] Taylor, *op. cit.*, p. xiv.

[73] White, *op. cit.*, p. 254. In White's view, the Senate has "every right to indict issues, policies, systems, executive departments," but it has no right at all to indict men—particularly when they are outside the Government. *Ibid.*, p. 257.

[74] Douglass Cater, *The Fourth Branch of Government* (Boston: Houghton Mifflin, 1959), p. 58.

formation in the form of "committee prints," setting up hearings, suggesting questions to be asked of witnesses, participating in interrogations, and writing committee reports.[75] Oddly enough, professional staffs, which are so important today, were almost unknown in Congress before 1946. In those days, committees had no more than clerical and secretarial assistance. Even an investigating committee was compelled to assemble a staff of experts on a temporary basis every time it embarked upon an investigation, or perhaps borrow experts from the Executive Branch.[76] This situation might have continued indefinitely had not the Joint Committee on the Organization of Congress recommended the introduction of professional staffing as part of an effort to redress the imbalance that had come to exist between Congress and a highly professionalized Executive bureaucracy. The recommendation was accepted and included in the Legislative Reorganization Act. During the period since 1946, appropriations for staff assistance have increased steadily. Today not only the committees but also most of the active subcommittees are staffed.

It is not too difficult for committees to recruit competent staff members, since congressional salary schedules are generous. The chief clerk of a committee may be paid more than $18,000 a year. Investigators, consultants, attorneys, research assistants—all receive salaries that are highly respectable. Even the secretaries are paid well: salaries of $7,000 are far from unusual.

The Joint Committee on the Organization of Congress had recommended that employment of committee staff members

[75] See Kenneth Kofmehl, *Professional Staffs of Congress* (Lafayette, Ind.: Purdue University Press, 1962), *passim*.

[76] Ernest S. Griffith, in *Congress: Its Contemporary Role* (New York: New York University Press, 1961), p. 83.

be placed on a completely nonpolitical basis. Under its proposal, a director of personnel, who was to be in charge of the system, would see to it that merit alone determined the selection of employees. This proposal for a nonpartisan personnel director ran into a storm of opposition, however, and was not written into the 1946 law. Still, an effort was made to minimize the impact of patronage considerations on professional committee staffing. This effort took the form of a provision that only the staffs of the two Appropriations Committees were to be considered the patronage of the respective chairmen. In the case of all other committees, staff selection was to be the responsibility of the committee as a whole, not merely of the chairman. Moreover, appointments were supposed to be made on a completely nonpartisan basis. The criterion was to be fitness, and the tenure was to be permanent.

If nonpartisan committee staffing was the goal of the 1946 law, things have not worked out as Congress intended. To some extent, the failure was pre-ordained. For the law set no standards for the "fitness" that it established as the test for employment. Moreover, the "permanence" of staff employment was rendered meaningless by a provision that any staff member could be dismissed, even without cause, by a majority vote of the committee. The result was that committee staffing in practice soon bore little resemblance to the supposedly nonpartisan and nonpolitical system introduced in 1946.

Minority Staffing

What has happened, as might have been expected, is that committee staffs usually bulge with employees who are chosen by the chairman and often serve the majority party members only. Since in recent decades the Republicans have been consigned to minority status so often, it is they who have suffered most from this development, and not surprisingly it is they who have demanded reform. The demand has come principally from those Republicans who want their party to play a positive role by offering constructive alternatives to Democratic programs instead of confining itself to mere opposition. The members of this group, consisting mostly of relatively junior congressmen, have insisted that the shortage of staff assistants for minority members is a crippling blow to efforts at refurbishing the "image" of their party. The lack of minority staffing, they have noted, is particularly damaging when a Democratic President is in the White House, for that means that access to the vast research facilities of the Executive Branch is cut off.

The Republicans concede that on a few committees they have received fair treatment with regard to staff. There is general agreement, for example, that staff members of the House and Senate committees dealing with foreign policy have been selected on a nonpartisan basis and have served minority members effectively. But on the more typical committees, the claim is that Republicans have been able to count on an average of only a single staff member, as against the average of ten professionals who are responsible to the majority.

Whatever staff the Republicans are allowed to select on committees has generally gone to ranking minority members. As a consequence, senior Republicans have not joined the "Young Turks" in their campaign against prevailing staff practices. Nor at first was the Republican leadership in the House and Senate particularly concerned over the inadequacy of minority staffing.[77] When dissatisfaction continued to grow

[77] Meg Greenfield, "Charles A. Halleck and the Restless Republicans," *Reporter*, March 29, 1962, p. 30.

among the party's rank and file, however, the leadership joined, at least publicly, the movement for reform, and the party then began a drive to give Republicans 40 per cent of the staff jobs on congressional committees. Although the campaign ran immediately into a solid wall of Democratic opposition, the younger Republicans have shown no intention of giving up the fight.

Significantly, the Republicans have not chosen to attack the principle of partisan staffing, demanding instead a fair share of the jobs. Their resort to this approach seems to erase the possibility that the dream of nonpartisan staffing will ever be realized. It is also doubtful that the Republican goal of "adequate" staffing for the minority party will be achieved. Democratic Presidents have experienced so much difficulty with Congress even under present circumstances that their supporters in the House and Senate have no intention of increasing still further the strength of the conservative opposition.

Nor should advocates of strong and responsible party government be expected to lend any support to the Republican campaign for increased minority staffing. If party government means anything at all, it involves giving the majority party the opportunity to enact its legislative program. The voters can then decide at the next general election whether the program has been a good one and should be continued, or whether the opposition party should be elected and allowed to enact *its* program. From this point of view, it is serious enough that members of the minority are given a sizable number of seats on the standing committees; to give them massive staff assistance as well would make it even more difficult than it is at present to get Administration measures out of committee and onto the floor.

Legislative Reference Service

When research assistance is desired, the facilities of the Legislative Reference Service are available on a nonpartisan basis to committees, committee staffs, and individual congressmen. The Service, which is administratively a unit of the Library of Congress, was created on the theory that easy access to research facilities for all members of Congress could not but improve the legislative product.

The Legislative Reference Service came into existence in 1914, when Congress appropriated the modest sum of $25,000 for research purposes. The research was to be of a limited and somewhat mechanical type, for the work of the Service was to consist only of the preparation of indices, digests, and compilations of laws. In the decades that followed, however, the problems with which Congress had to deal increased steadily in complexity. There came to be greater awareness that a serious "information gap" existed, and that because of it Congress did not command sufficient expertise to deal with the Executive Branch on an equal footing.

The members of the Joint Committee on the Organization of Congress shared this point of view, and one of their major aims in drafting what was to become the Legislative Reorganization Act of 1946 was to redress the imbalance that existed between the Executive and Legislative branches. The creation of professional committee staffs was designed to serve that purpose, and so was the strengthening of the Legislative Reference Service.

The Joint Committee considered providing each congressman with one additional staff member who could be assigned to do research on pending legislation. Obviously, however, no single staff employee could be expert in every field. There was, moreover, a general expectation that more than just a few congressmen would interpret an authorization to expand their staffs as an open invitation to hire campaign aides. Persuaded by these considerations, the Committee decided to support the creation of a pool of experts who would be available to all committees and members of Congress. An expansion and invigoration of the somewhat anemic Legislative Reference Service became the means through which this goal was pursued. For the first time, LRS was placed on a permanent statutory basis and authorized to recruit a sizable professional staff. Today the Service has 220 staff members and an appropriation of almost $2,000,000. Yet there is still a serious question as to whether it is supported with sufficient generosity to handle the growing responsibilities that are thrust upon it.

Among virtually all classes of congressmen, there appears to be a tendency to turn increasingly to LRS for assistance. At present, about 100,000 congressional inquiries pour in each year. Many of these, however, are not really congressional requests at all, but rather constituent requests that are passed along by members. Their subjects are often far removed from proper legislative concern. Some even come from schoolchildren—and college students—who need help with their academic work. All, of course, must be answered, to help the congressman perform his function as Washington errand boy for his constituency.

About two-thirds of the inquiries put to LRS can be handled with printed materials taken from office files. Many others are spot questions that can be answered on the telephone (and some of which could have been answered by the congressman's own staff by referring to nothing more recondite than a commercially published almanac). But the remainder of the requests cannot be handled that easily. Some require the preparation of extensive research papers that are often as comprehensive as scholarly monographs. Each month there are in addition about 150 requests for speech "drafts," which more often than not are used verbatim by the congressman.

In general, LRS will try to give each member precisely what he asks for. Depending on what is requested, for example, the Service will prepare a report giving both sides of a question, or an exposition that is nothing more than a brief for one side. Its expert on civil rights must be able to produce a speech one day advocating strong anti-discrimination legislation, and another the next day denouncing the Supreme Court and all its works. There are, however, certain things that LRS declares it will not do. It says that for motives of self-preservation, it must decline to prepare campaign speeches or any material that is derogatory to a political figure. Issues, not personalities, have to remain its exclusive concern.

The Legislative Reference Service is organized into divisions that cover various subject-matter areas. There is only one exception: the Senior Specialists Division. Under the law, LRS is authorized to employ a limited number of research analysts of the highest professional competence, paying them not less than individuals in "the highest grade in the Executive Branch to which analysts and consultants without supervisory responsibility are currently assigned."[78] The Senior Specialists Division, more than any other part of LRS, was intended to furnish congressmen with professional research assistance equal to that which the Executive Branch was empowered to command. Today there are nineteen senior specialists, each generally maintaining a special relationship with the committees of Congress that are concerned with his field, and ready to assist in the preparation of hearings, the drafting of committee reports, and the writing of major speeches.

[78] Galloway, *The Legislative Process in Congress, op. cit.,* p. 408. Senior specialists are today paid between $18,000 and $20,000.

Bill Drafting

Another staff service is performed for both committees and individual members by the two Offices of Legislative Counsel. The job of these offices is the drafting of bills, amendments, and conference reports (which reconcile differing House and Senate versions of bills). Like LRS, the Offices of Legislative Counsel function on a nonpartisan, professional basis. The lawyers on their staffs cultivate an attitude of studious uncon- cern for policy matters. When an individual congressman or one of the standing committees requests assistance, their only wish is to ascertain the precise intent of the proposed legisla- tion and to translate that intent into a tight, well-drawn bill. The skilled draftsman, of course, must have a fine sense of the English language—of the shadings of words, and of the subtle nuances of meaning that a particular grammatical construc- tion may convey. He must also, however, possess expert knowl- edge of the subject matter with which the legislation is to deal. It is indispensable for him to know about previous legislation in the same area, about existing statutes that will have to be modified to achieve the results that are desired, and about court decisions that bear on the problem.

All of this is so obvious that it is surprising Congress chose to forego the services of professional legislative draftsmen until 1919. If the delay was occasioned by fear that a drafting serv- ice might be unable to remain nonpartisan, such apprehen- sion has been entirely dispelled. Today there is no one in Congress whose tenure is more firmly established than the 22 lawyers in the two Offices of Legislative Counsel. In the House, for instance, although control has shifted back and forth between Democrats and Republicans many times since 1919, the present Legislative Counsel is only the third man to have held that position.[79]

[79] *Congressional Record,* January 22, 1962, p. 497 (daily edition).

Although no one would quarrel with the excellence of the work performed by the Offices of Legislative Counsel or the importance of their function, one consequence of somewhat dubious value flows from their existence. The fact that it is now so easy for any individual member of Congress to fashion a bill has contributed in some measure to the sharp increase in the volume of legislation being introduced in every congressional session. The most readily observable result—that committee calendars are flooded—is not the only one. An additional consequence is the further strengthening of what have been called "the centrifugal forces in Congress."[80] Because the Offices of Legislative Counsel furnish such effective assistance, the individual congressman does not have to depend on any party organ for the drafting of bills that will help him politically. This may please congressmen, but it is not a source of unalloyed joy to one who favors strengthening party leadership in Congress in order to make the architects of legislative policy more readily identifiable than at present.[81]

General Accounting Office

In addition to the Offices of Legislative Counsel and the Legislative Reference Service, there is a staff agency of a very different kind serving Congress. As part of an effort to ascertain whether the money it appropriates is spent for the purposes it has in mind, Congress in 1921 established the General Accounting Office. It was placed in the Legislative Branch and told to review expenditures in the Executive Branch to be certain that they had been made in compliance with the law.[82]

[80] Stephen K. Bailey and Howard D. Samuel, *Congress at Work* (New York: Holt, 1952), pp. 7-8.

[81] To some extent, the existence of the Legislative Reference Service, too, results in weakening party organization in Congress. For LRS gives the individual legislator access to research facilities instead of limiting such access to the party.

[82] Robert Ash Wallace, *Congressional Control of Federal Spending* (Detroit: Wayne State University Press, 1960), p. 10. GAO was created

Congress had previously attempted to perform this function through other devices, all of which had proved unsatisfactory. The last attempt preceding the establishment of GAO was to assign supervisory powers to the Department of the Treasury. Members came to doubt, however, that this department, which is of course in the Executive Branch, could act with sufficient independence in checking on the expenditures made by other units of the same branch. Since taking the control function away from the Treasury Department constituted something of a slap at the Executive, it was not surprising that President Wilson vetoed the first bill to establish GAO as Congress' own agency. In order to win the President over, Congress then provided that the head of GAO—the Comptroller General—would be a presidential appointee.[83]

Some of the later Presidents have obviously regretted that Wilson allowed himself to be persuaded so easily. President Herbert Hoover, for example, had a number of conflicts with the Comptroller General of his day. Similarly, President Franklin Roosevelt once permitted the office to remain vacant for three years, after the term of one Comptroller General had expired. The fact that the head of GAO is not eligible to succeed himself tends to make him independent, since there is no reason why he should try to curry favor with any President.

The principal function of GAO is to audit the accounts of the executive departments and agencies. Most of the 4,500-member staff is involved in the carrying out of this responsibility.[84] Originally, an effort was made to audit every

---

by the same Budget and Accounting Act that brought into existence the Bureau of the Budget.

[83] The Comptroller General is nominated for a 15-year term by the President, subject to confirmation by the Senate. Reappointment is not allowed. He can be removed from office only by Congress, either through a joint resolution or impeachment proceedings.

[84] Another responsibility of GAO is to settle financial claims by and against the Government when an agency is unable to do so. It has other

department and agency on an annual basis. When it became evident that this was impossible to do, GAO imposed standard accounting procedures on all government agencies, and carried out the auditing only on a selective basis.

As part of its auditing function, the Office evaluates the management of agencies in terms of the economy and efficiency of their operation. It is always on the alert for instances of waste, extravagance, and maladministration.[85] Thus it does far more than merely audit vouchers in order to determine whether documentation is sufficient and whether expenditures were authorized and made in accordance with law. Its comprehensive review encompasses studies of the over-all management of an agency and the detailed administration of a program or function. This is what differentiates its activities from those of public accounting firms, which never question the policy decisions of management.

The General Accounting Office does not confine its attention to government agencies. Since colossal sums of Federal money are spent under contracts with private enterprise, GAO has an understandable interest in such contracts. When one of them has been let on a competitive basis, it is assumed that its provisions do not disadvantage the government.[86] But when there is only a single company which can do the work that the government requires and it is thus necessary to negotiate a contract, GAO has a reason to check on whether the terms were unfavorable to the government. Although it

---

functions as well: it lays down accounting principles and standards for all governmental units; it issues rulings as to the legality and propriety of payments made by governmental disbursing offices; and it works with congressional committees when financial matters are to be looked into.

[85] Wallace, *op. cit.*, p. 158.

[86] If what is apparently competition is actually collusion, prosecution under the antitrust laws can, of course, result.

may appear to be strange procedure for a Federal agency to audit the accounts of a private business, the law requires that a provision to allow auditing by GAO be included in every negotiated contract. As a consequence, a business concern that does not want to show its books to GAO has only one course of action open to it: not to enter into negotiated contracts with the government.

So much waste, inefficiency, and worse does GAO discover that in a recent year[87] it caused to be turned back to the Treasury the grand sum of $48 million. In addition, action taken by departments and agencies that were investigated by GAO resulted in "either definite, measurable savings or possible savings of $114,656,000."[88] Yet the work of the agency is seldom publicized widely except when sensational revelations are involved. There was an abundance of publicity in 1962 when GAO discovered that both a brothel and a nudist colony were flourishing in National Forests which were controlled by the Department of Agriculture. The brothel (in the Tonto National Forest in Arizona) and the nudist colony (in the Boise National Forest in Idaho) were being conducted under the guise of mining claims.[89] The newspapers were also interested when GAO found out that cotton brokers employed to act as government agents had made illegal profits by selling government cotton to themselves.[90] And a full-fledged Senate

[87] Fiscal year 1962.

[88] *Congressional Record,* May 2, 1963, pp. 7197-98 (daily edition).

[89] *Washington Post,* June 2, 1962, p. A4, col. 1. It was not the immorality that distressed GAO, but rather the fact that a mining claimant "has no right to use any part of the surface of his unpatented location for other than mining purposes. . . ." "Review of Administration of Mining Claims Located on National Forest Lands Reserved from the Public Domain," Report by the Comptroller General of the United States, May, 1962.

[90] *The New York Times,* July 3, 1962, p. 1, col. 1. (late city edition).

investigation ensued when GAO ascertained that a company owned by former Secretary of the Treasury George H. Humphrey had made a profit of 457 per cent under contracts to sell nickel to the Government for stockpiling.[91]

[91] *Ibid.*, August 15, 1962, p. 1, col. 4. (late city edition).

8

Sending Bills to the Floor

THE POWER OF STANDING COMMITTEES to obstruct legislation they dislike is greater than their power to advance legislation they support. A bill that has been favorably reported by a committee may not even get to the floor for discussion and decision by the entire membership. For procedures have been established in each house to examine committee-approved bills and determine which of them should be scheduled for chamber action. The need for such procedures is evident: since the legislative committees in every Congress report out many more bills than there is time to debate, someone must decide which ones deserve to be cleared for floor action and the order in which these should be taken up. In the case of the House of Representatives, however, grave doubts have been expressed regarding the particular way in which the scheduling function is performed.

When a bill is reported out by a House committee, it is listed on one of three regular "calendars," depending on the nature of the material that it concerns. "Public bills," which deal with general problems, are placed on the Union Calendar if they directly or indirectly involve the raising or spending of money;[1] all other public bills will appear on the House Calendar; and private bills go on the Private Calendar. On each of the three calendars, bills are arranged according to the order in which they were reported out of committee. But, except in the case of the Private Calendar, this order does not determine when they will reach the floor.[2] Nor does a listing even assure that a bill will ever be debated or voted on, unless it falls into one of the special categories which are recognized by the House.

One such category consists of bills reported out by certain committees. The committees on Appropriations and Ways and Means, for example, may bring bills to the floor at any time. A similar privilege has been given to three other committees: Public Works, when it has approved rivers and harbors bills (the favorite type of "pork barrel" legislation); Veterans' Affairs, on general pension bills; and Interior and Insular Affairs, for certain bills within its jurisdiction.[3] A second preferred group is made up of relatively minor bills to which there is no opposition. Any such apparently noncontroversial bill can be transferred to the special Consent Calendar on the motion of a single member of the House.[4] Twice a

[1] The full name of the Union Calendar is the "Calendar of the Whole House on the State of the Union."

[2] Once a month the bills on the Private Calendar are called. If as many as two members object to a particular bill, it is killed by being sent back to committee.

[3] Only the Appropriations Committee makes regular use of the privilege and takes bills directly to the House floor. The other committees almost always prefer to go through the Rules Committee. That way, a bill will be considered under parliamentary rules which are favorable to the legislative committee. (The Rules Committee procedure is described *infra*.)

[4] The Consent Calendar was introduced in 1910 as part of a revolt against the Speaker, who had assumed near dictatorial power. The idea behind the reform was that members would "no longer need to go to the Speaker, or any other majority leader, seeking a promise of recognition

month, the bills on that calendar are brought to the floor, one by one. Those to which no objection is registered are without further ceremony considered to have passed. A bill that provokes opposition from even a single member is laid aside for two weeks, when the Consent Calendar will next be called. At that time, it will take three negative votes to block its passage. If those three votes are cast, the bill is then dropped from the Consent Calendar for the rest of the congressional session and reverts to the regular calendar from which it was taken.[5]

Rules Committee

A bill that does not fall into one of the privileged categories —and most bills do not—will probably never reach the floor unless the Committee on Rules recommends that the House take it up. Such a recommendation comes to the House in the form of a resolution that is reported out by the Rules Committee and offered for the approval of the House. The resolution (which is more commonly referred to as a "rule") specifies, among other things, how much time will be allowed for debate and whether floor amendments will be in order. If the Rules Committee is so inclined, it can compel legislative committees to make substantial changes in bills they are framing, as the price for obtaining a rule. A committee with this kind of power is a force to be reckoned with in the House.

. . . in order to get unobjectionable bills through the House." Arthur N. Holcombe, *Our More Perfect Union: From Eighteenth-Century Principles to Twentieth-Century Practice* (Cambridge: Harvard University Press, 1950), p. 175.

[5] A procedure has been developed to prevent major or controversial legislation from slipping through on the Consent Calendar. The majority and minority leaders each designate three members of their respective parties as "objectors." These men must be in attendance each day that the calendar is called, to block passage of major bills and of other bills to which any members have indicated opposition.

For almost a century, the Rules Committee has enjoyed the right to report privileged resolutions making it possible for bills to be scheduled for debate without waiting their regular turn. During most of this period, the committee operated as an instrument of the majority party in performing the scheduling function. Since it seemed reasonable that the party which had captured control of the House should be master of the legislative program, the majority party was always given the right to name two-thirds of the members of the Rules Committee, regardless of how slender its majority might be in the chamber as a whole.

An entirely new factor was introduced, however, during the mid-1930's. In revolt against the New Deal, southern Democrats on the Rules Committee began to vote with their Republican colleagues. The alliance thus forged made the Committee a graveyard for liberal legislation in the years that followed. When the Republicans had a majority in the House, the conservative domination of the Committee was assured, and liberal measures on both economic issues and civil rights could not even reach the stage of floor consideration. The situation was not significantly different when a resurgence of liberalism in the country gave a majority in the House to the Democrats. For the conservative Republicans still had exactly the number of southern Democratic allies they needed to prevent the Committee from clearing liberal legislation. One of these was the Committee chairman, Howard W. Smith (D., Va.). Chairman Smith did not hesitate to use his committee position for the purpose of advancing conservative causes. As he once put it, his constituents had not sent him to Washington to be "a traffic cop." He would not be content with the relatively insignificant job of keeping the legislative highways open on an impartial basis.

When Mr. Kennedy was preparing to take office as President in 1961, he announced his support for a drive to reshape the Rules Committee so that it could not emasculate the legislative program he planned to present. By a slim five-vote margin, the House agreed to institute a limited reform. It added two Democrats and one Republican to the committee, thus increasing the membership from twelve to fifteen and supposedly giving the liberals a one-vote majority. The majority was an unreliable one, however. During the Eighty-seventh Congress, the "reformed" committee was responsible for some of the most important defeats suffered by the Administration, including the blocking of bills on aid to education, the establishment of a Department of Urban Affairs, youth employment, and mass transit.[6]

The Two Faces of Congress

The Rules Committee is seldom the target of Republican criticism, for when the Republicans are the majority party in the House, it customarily serves as the faithful agent of their leadership. It is the Democrats who find it impossible to use the Committee to promote their party's program, and it is therefore only they who profess indignation at the present state of affairs. It is they who say they resent the fact that after a legislative committee has approved a bill its chairman must appear before the Rules Committee to argue the case for the legislation all over again. It is they who say they are disturbed that legislative committees will often rewrite bills with the aim of making them acceptable to the Rules Committee, instead of considering amendments on their merits.[7] It is they,

[6] The 1961 enlargement of the Rules Committee was a temporary measure, due to expire after two years. In 1963, however, the House voted to make the expansion permanent. The vote was 235 to 196. The committee's place in the House is examined in James A. Robinson, *The House Rules Committee* (Indianapolis: The Bobbs-Merrill Company, 1963).

[7] Clem Miller, *Member of the House,* John W. Baker, ed. (New York: Scribner's, 1962), p. 45.

also, who say there is no reason why seniority should determine the selection of the Rules Committee's chairman. For if the rationale behind the seniority system is that it usually means the chairmen of substantive committees are experts in their fields, that factor possesses little relevance where the chairmanship of the Rules Committee is concerned.[8]

But Democratic members of the House are far more critical of the Rules Committee on the public platform than they are privately. In candid conversation, many express their pleasure at the existence of a committee with the power to keep from the floor legislation on which they have no desire to stand up and be counted.

For example, a congressman's largest contributor may be strongly opposed to a pending bill, while the overwhelming majority of his constituents are just as strongly in favor of it. In such a situation, the congressman will be impaled on the horns of a dilemma if the bill comes to a vote. Accordingly, he may very well be tempted to approach the chairman of the Rules Committee with a request that the bill be kept from the floor. He will, of course, inform the contributor about his request, and appreciation will doubtless be expressed in more than merely verbal terms. The Rules Committee may decide to honor the request, particularly if other members have importuned it similarly or if the committee majority itself does not like the bill.[9] If, indeed, the bill is denied clearance, the congressman may be expected to denounce the Rules Committee for its intolerable obstructionism. That way he will appear in the eyes of his constituents as a courageous defender of their interests, while at the same time not alienating the contributor.

[8] Interview with Congresswoman Edith Green (D., Ore.), March 1, 1962.

[9] Since Rules Committee members usually come from safe districts, *they* need not be troubled about retaliation at the polls.

Members of the House are quick to insist that the Rules Committee serves another, presumably more noble, purpose. Some bills, they explain, are clearly against the public interest but have so much support from selfish or uninformed groups that a negative vote on the floor might prove fatal to an individual member. In such circumstances, say the congressmen, recourse to the Rules Committee enables a member to accomplish what his conscience demands without at the same time subjecting himself to punishment at the polls.

Thus, contrary to appearances, the chairman of the Rules Committee is by no means an unpopular figure in the House. Chairman Smith, whom liberal representatives habitually portray to their constituents as an arch villain, was exaggerating only a little when he told an interviewer that sometimes congressmen actually urge him to leave town and thus prevent his committee from even meeting to consider bills that members find embarrassing. Smith declared:

> Some folks might be surprised to know the number of people from both sides of the aisle, who have, under deep stress about bills, come to me and said: "Judge, we wish you'd take another vacation. We'll get up a pot and pay for it." This year, everybody I think that came to see me wanted to help paint my barn or something like that.... [10]

If the rank-and-file voter knew how frequently his congressman used the Rules Committee to camouflage the role he was actually playing, decisive retribution might conceivably ensue. But with such knowledge difficult to come by, the voter tends to take at face value the frequently demagogic

[10] Smith would frequently oblige those who urged him to make himself scarce. He did just that in 1957, vanishing into the Virginia countryside during one of the most important phases of the civil rights struggle. When he gave as the reason for his absence the fact that he had to inspect a barn which had caught fire on his farm, Speaker Rayburn commented: "I knew Howard Smith would do most anything to block a civil rights bill, but I never suspected he would resort to arson."

assertions that the Rules Committee is constantly thwarting the will of the House. It is for this reason that there is considerable popular support for curtailing the powers of the Rules Committee. Such a demand for reform impelled the House to approve a "21-day rule" in 1949. The rule provided that the chairman of a legislative committee could bring a bill directly to the floor after it had been blocked by the Rules Committee for three weeks. Although the conservative coalition succeeded in repealing the rule after only two years, there continues to be support for it, most notably from Speaker McCormack.[11]

Advocates of such a reform may be ignoring an exceedingly important point. The most significant issue regarding the Rules Committee is not whether it possesses too much power but rather whether a body with this much power should not be directly responsible to the elected leadership of the House. The case for giving *someone* the power is unassailable, for priorities must be assigned in a legislature where thousands of bills and resolutions are introduced in every session. The basic question, therefore, is why this power should rest in the hands of members who are not responsible to the majority party.

Circumventing the Rules Committee

The leadership is not totally powerless to bring a bill to the floor against the opposition of the Rules Committee. In addition to informal pressures, several procedural devices are available, although none is simple and the use of any is infrequent.

One of these devices is the Calendar Wednesday rule. This rule dates from 1910, when House members organized a revolt against the autocratic power of the Rules Committee and Speaker Joseph Cannon (R., Ill.).[12] Calendar Wednesday

[11] Interview, October 3, 1963.
[12] See discussion in Ch. 9.

makes it possible for the chairman of a legislative committee to bring a reported bill directly to the floor without going through the Rules Committee. Every Wednesday is supposed to be set aside for chairmen to "call up" measures that have been approved by their committees. Most chairmen, however, have never had the opportunity to make use of the procedure. In practical terms, it seems open only to those whose committees have names that start with letters near the top of the alphabet, for committees are invited *in alphabetical order* to present bills for floor consideration. Thus, for example, before a committee like Judiciary can be reached to place a civil rights bill before the House, each of the eleven committees with alphabetical priority must be given a chance to bring up bills of its own. If the chairmen of any of those eleven committees are hostile to civil rights, they can force the chairman of Judiciary to wait for weeks by simply insisting that bills from their committees be considered first. Many Wednesdays may go by in this way. Moreover, a bill cannot be passed under the Calendar Wednesday procedure unless it is voted on during the same legislative day when it is brought up. A decision to adjourn thus has fatal consequences.

Even if these obstacles can be surmounted, a committee that attempts to use Calendar Wednesday lets itself in for a trying experience. So many dilatory motions are in order—including motions to adjourn—that it is necessary for a cohesive majority in favor of the bill to remain on hand all day if sudden death is not to befall the measure they support. In 1960, the House did pass a bill under the rule—the first time in ten years that this feat was accomplished.[13] But before the bill could be brought to a vote, the reading of its full 36-page text

[13] The bill, providing Federal assistance for economically depressed areas, had been reported out by the Banking and Currency Committee, which of course enjoys an extremely favorable alphabetical listing.

was ordered (as well as the reading of the Journal), and three points of order were made regarding the absence of a quorum. It was not until 9:30 p.m. that the voting could begin. All in all, it was necessary for the House to remain in continuous session for ten hours, although the actual substantive debate consumed only a fifth of that time. A proponent of the bill commented wryly: "The lesson was well impressed on us that Calendar Wednesday is not a royal road to congressional objectives."[14] Little wonder, then, that the procedure is scarcely ever used. Rarely is there an objection when the Majority Leader asks unanimous consent in advance that Calendar Wednesday be dispensed with for the week.[15]

Another way to bring a bill to the floor without the consent of the Rules Committee is by means of the same discharge procedure that can be used to free bills from legislative committees.[16] The identical requirement, however, must be met: a majority of the total membership of the House has to sign a discharge petition, and there must be majority approval on the floor as well. Such success is difficult to achieve. When a petition manages to come within striking distance of success, however, the Rules Committee often decides to cease its obstruction and give the bill a rule. For a bill pried from the Committee by a discharge vote is open to floor amendment, and that may result in the framing of a measure even more offensive to the Committee than the original bill. If, on the other hand, the Committee consents to release the bill, it can foreclose amendments by reporting out a closed (or "gag") rule. No order reported to the House by the Rules Committee can go into effect unless it receives majority approval on the

[14] Miller, *op. cit.*, p. 43.

[15] In the last two weeks of a congressional session, Calendar Wednesday cannot take place at all.

[16] The discharge procedure is discussed in Ch. 7.

floor, but everyone understands that a negative decision will mean the death of the bill. The choice is between considering the bill under the terms laid down by the Rules Committee, and not considering it at all.

Apart from Calendar Wednesday and a discharge petition, the only other device for circumventing the Rules Committee is "suspension of the rules"—the same procedure that can be used to free a bill from a legislative committee.[17]

Scheduling in the Senate

In the Senate, the scheduling of legislation is handled in a completely different manner.[18] The basic decisions are made by the Policy Committee of the majority party. A bill reported out by a legislative committee is placed on a calendar, but the Senate turns to the "call of the calendar" only under one set of conditions: when it wants to obtain swift approval of innocuous legislation. Controversial bills do not come before it unless they are taken from the calendar and brought to the floor. Although any senator may "call up" a bill, it is ordinarily left to the Majority Leader to perform this function. He may ask for unanimous consent that the bill be considered, or he may accomplish the same purpose by means of a motion; either way, he acts only when the Policy Committee of his party has determined that the legislation should be brought to the floor. The Policy Committee, however, obstructs bills far less frequently than the Rules Committee does in the House.

Before the Majority Policy Committee makes its decisions

[17] See description in Ch. 7.
[18] The nominal counterpart of the House Rules Committee, the Senate Committee on Rules and Administration, exercises no jurisdiction over the scheduling of bills.

about which bills should be cleared for floor action, the Minority Leader is always consulted. More than mere courtesy accounts for the fact that such consultation takes place. For if the Majority Policy Committee's decisions are not to be thwarted, the Minority Leader will have to cooperate. In the event that he feels slighted, he is in a position to block the Majority Leader and prevent him from using successfully the most common device for bringing a Senate bill to the floor—unanimous consent. As long as the feathers of the Minority Leader remain unruffled, the Majority Leader can count on the fact that his request for unanimous consent to call up a bill will be granted by his colleagues. Although there will be many senators who oppose the bill and will do their best to defeat it, none will challenge the right of the Majority Leader to formulate a legislative program for the Senate (except in the case of civil rights, when every device for obstruction can be expected).

In a very real sense, the Democratic Policy Committee functions as an arm—and even as a shadow—of the leadership. The Leader is chairman of the committee, and he appoints twelve of its fifteen members.[19] If he decides to exercise firm control, the power of the Committee becomes seriously attenuated. When the Republicans have a majority in the Senate, much the same situation obtains. Again the Policy Committee makes the decisions, but again a strong Majority Leader tends to dominate that committee. In one respect, however, the Republican Policy Committee differs from its Democratic counterpart: its chairman is elected by the Conference (or caucus), while among the Democrats the position goes automatically to the Floor Leader. The chairman of the Republican Policy Committee has the power to appoint six of the

---

[19] The other three members serve *ex officio:* the Leader himself, the Whip, and the Secretary of the Conference.

remaining thirteen members who will serve with him on the Committee. The others hold their positions *ex officio.*[20]

Since both the Democratic and Republican Policy Committees are party organs and treat the scheduling function as a party responsibility, a wide gap separates the Senate from the House regarding the way in which decisions are made as to which reported bills will reach the floor. The majority party in the Senate can never claim that it lacks the power to enable the entire membership to vote on a bill. In the House, however, the majority party can always blame the Rules Committee. But as long as this blame is not accompanied by a serious attempt to re-establish the Rules Committee as an instrument of the majority party, it cannot be taken seriously.

[20] The *ex officio* members are the Floor Leader, Whip, chairman of the Conference, secretary of the Conference, chairman of the Senatorial Campaign Committee, chairman of the Patronage Committee, and chairman of the Committee on Committees. Interview with David Kammerman, counsel, Senate Republican Policy Committee, May 1, 1963. Each of the Republican Party Committees is aided by a small staff.

9

Party Organization in Congress

THE WEAKNESS OF POLITICAL PARTIES in Congress is typified by what has happened to the Senate Policy Committees. Their name indicates that these committees were intended to formulate the positions of the senatorial parties on legislative issues, but the tendency in practice has been to move away from that function—partially, in the case of the Republicans, and totally, in the case of the Democrats.

The creation of party policy committees in each house was one of the recommendations of the Joint Committee on the Organization of Congress. The hope was that formulation of over-all legislative policy by responsible party organs would be a step in the direction of party responsibility in Congress. The proposal, however, did not find its way into the Legislative Reorganization Act. Although the Senate approved it without hesitation, the House, with just as little hesitation, killed it. Neither Speaker Rayburn nor the Rules Committee was desirous of introducing a new power center into their domain.

In 1947 the Senate obtained legislative permission to establish party policy committees for itself, without attempting to impose them on the House. It accomplished this by attaching a "rider" to a bill providing money for the Legislative Branch: $15,000 would now be available for the functioning of policy committees for the two parties in the Senate.

The amount appropriated for the policy committees has risen steadily until in 1963 it exceeded a quarter of a million dollars.[1] At the same time, the functions of the committees have become completely different from what was originally expected. The appropriation, in fact, is being spent for purposes that have nothing in common with what the Joint Committee had in mind in 1946.

The difference between original intent and actual function is especially pronounced among the Democrats, who are afraid that any attempt to enunciate policy will split irrevocably a party whose members see eye-to-eye on only a pathetically small number of issues. As a consequence, the only sense in which the Democratic Policy Committee establishes party policy today is through its recommendations that certain legislation be scheduled for floor action. The Republican Policy Committee comes a little closer to the original conception. This is so because that party is less seriously divided than the Democrats are, and also because it is easier for the party that is out of power to strike ideological poses than it is for the party that must run the Senate.[2] Thus it was possible for the Republicans in 1963 to adopt a policy statement on civil rights, while the Democrats, as usual, stood mute. The staff of the Republican Committee, too, turns out fairly extensive policy studies for the party.

Occasionally protests are heard against the fact that the policy committees have wandered so far from what was sup-

---

[1] *Congressional Record,* August 2, 1962, p. 14403 (daily edition).
[2] The Republican Policy Committee in the House is discussed later in this chapter.

posed to be their principal purpose. Senator Proxmire of Wisconsin has been particularly critical of this development, and one of his fellow Democrats, Senator Douglas of Illinois, has lamented that the Policy Committee of his party does not have a sufficient number of members from the large, urban states. "When the kissing takes place," he has said, these states "are never under the mistletoe."[3] It will require a major revolution for the policy committees to be given functions consonant with their names. Until such a revolution comes about, the real policy committees, in the Senate as well as the House, will continue to be the coalition-dominated standing committees.

Majority Leader

What power the Senate Democratic Policy Committee has today is really the power represented by the Majority Leader. Oddly enough, the typical Leader is reluctant to admit that he possesses any power at all. Senator Mansfield, who became Majority Leader in 1961, speaks on this theme at the drop of a gavel. "The Senate is not an army, with the leader giving orders and the rest of the troops carrying them out," he has said.[4] "The powers of the Majority Leader under the rules are no greater than the powers of any individual senator. The leadership . . . functions on the basis of the self-restraint of equal members and mutual accommodation with equal members."[5] Mansfield emphasizes that the Majority Leader must use persuasion and reason, for there are no other weapons in his arsenal.[6]

[3] *Congressional Record,* March 9, 1959, p. 3198 (daily edition).

[4] *Ibid.,* August 1, 1962, p. A-5926 (daily edition).

[5] *Ibid.,* August 10, 1962, p. 15088 (daily edition)

[6] There is evidence that Mansfield has long accepted, or professed to accept, a wholly passive philosophy of leadership. Senator Barry Goldwater (R., Ariz.) has told his colleagues that he once heard Mansfield discuss his concept of leadership in a training session for armored troops. Mansfield had used a visual aid:

On the surface, Mansfield's argument seems plausible. It is not he, but rather the standing committees, that make the decisions as to whether to report out legislation. He has no direct power to punish recalcitrants. He certainly is not assured of the support of a united party in whatever he does.

But even though he lacks these powers and is totally devoid of constitutional credentials, the Majority Leader is far from the helpless figure he so often tries hard to impersonate. A Democratic Majority Leader is particularly powerful, since his position, unlike that of the Republican Leader, confers on him the chairmanship of no fewer than three party organs: the Policy Committee, which schedules legislation; the Steering Committee, which places party members on all the standing committees; and the Conference, which is the organization of all party members in the Senate. Whether he is a Republican or a Democrat, however, a Majority Leader cannot safely be trifled with. A senator who covets a choice committee assignment had better stay on good terms with him. One would be well advised to do the same if he wants to attract a respectable vote for a bill or an amendment that is important to his constituents. Assignment to a special committee; an appropriation for one's subcommittee; appointment to represent the Senate at an international meeting;[7] assurance that an absence will not be called to the attention

---

He would hold a . . . plate in his hand . . . and he had on it a wet noodle. He tried to push it, and it would go nowhere. Then he would put his two fingers around the noodle and pull it across the plate. He said, "Gentlemen, you have to pull a noodle; you can't push it." That is the kind of leadership we have had under Senator Mansfield.

Ibid., October 3, 1962, p. 20911. Goldwater apparently thought he was paying Mansfield a compliment.

[7] Ralph K. Huitt, "Democratic Party Leadership in the Senate," *American Political Science Review*, LV (June 1961), p. 338.

of one's constituents through a roll call vote or a quorum call; the allocation of desirable office space—for all of these, the good will of the Majority Leader is a prerequisite. Moreover, an unwritten rule requires that the Leader be recognized on the floor in preference to any other member who is seeking recognition at the same time. And when his party controls the White House, it is the Leader who is the principal liaison between the Senate and the President.

Each individual Majority Leader must determine for himself how much use he is going to make of these powers. Lyndon Johnson used them to the hilt.[8] Under him the office was such a center of power that there was general surprise in 1960 when he chose to give it up to run for the Vice-Presidency. Johnson's successor as Majority Leader, Senator Mansfield, has used the prerogatives of the office much more sparingly, but under him, too, the leadership is at least to some degree a focal point of power.

Yet the authority available to a Majority Leader is different from what he would be able to exercise under a system of party responsibility. Then he would be recognized as the Senate leader of a party with a program that he was charged with advancing. His power would be great, for it would derive from a disciplined and united majority party. It would not be necessary for him to resort to the petty punishments and trivial rewards that now must be the stock in trade of "leadership."

When his party is in the White House, the Majority Leader to some extent assumes the burden of acting as the surrogate of the President in the Senate. Along with other

[8] "His Senate was a six-ring circus, with Lyndon Johnson performing in every ring—pulling a last-minute tie-breaking vote out of the Democratic cloakroom at midnight . . . , forcing some chastened and humiliated nonentity to change his vote and tip the scales while the galleries chuckled." *The New York Times,* July 17, 1961, p. 11, col. 4 (city edition).

leaders of his congressional party, he participates in a weekly breakfast meeting to discuss with the President the legislative program of his Administration and the strategy that should be employed to assist in its enactment. In discharging this responsibility, the Majority Leader helps to maintain communications between his party colleagues in the Senate and those in the White House.[9]

Just as the Majority Leader is something of a mediator between the Senate and the President, he must also serve—especially among the Democrats—in the capacity of broker between divergent wings of his party in the Senate. Even more than that, it would be undesirable for him to be *persona non grata* with the opposition party, for often he has to depend on votes from "the other side of the aisle." That is why the caucus hesitates to select an extremist or a doctrinaire for the leadership position. The ideal leader is one who has learned to subordinate all ideological values to the welfare of his party.

Speaker of the House

Unlike the Majority Leader, the Speaker of the House holds a position that was created by the Constitution. There is nothing in that document, however, to indicate that the

[9] His role is somewhat ambiguous, with his colleagues assuming that he speaks for the President, while at the White House he is regarded as an emissary of the Senate. In 1944, one Majority Leader demonstrated dramatically that he was not the tool of the White House. Resentful at the sharp language used by President Franklin D. Roosevelt in vetoing a tax bill, Alben W. Barkley (D., Ky.) registered a resounding protest by announcing his resignation as Majority Leader. The resignation was such a blow that Mr. Roosevelt felt obliged to humble himself by urging the Democratic Caucus to give Barkley a vote of confidence and re-elect him as Majority Leader. The Caucus proceeded to do just that. Never again could it be taken for granted that Barkley was "the President's man." For a colorful description of this episode, see Barkley, *That Reminds Me* (Garden City, N. Y.: Doubleday, 1954), pp. 169-82.

framers expected the Speaker to be an active participant in the political process. The title "Speaker" made it inevitable that comparisons would be drawn with the impartial presiding officer of the British House of Commons. Yet the office developed in a surprisingly different fashion in the United States. Here the Speaker, in addition to serving as an officer of the House, became the undisputed leader of his party in that chamber. It is the combination of his powers as a constitutional officer and his powers as a party leader that continues to define the Speakership today.

The election of a Speaker, on the opening day of a new Congress, marks one of the rare occasions when party lines in the House hold firm. Every Democrat votes for the nominee of his caucus, and every Republican votes for the man whom his party has agreed to support. The result, of course, is a foregone conclusion: the nominee of the majority party is elected to the Speakership, and the defeated candidate becomes the Minority Floor Leader. Just as there is no suspense at all regarding the election of the Speaker, there is seldom any doubt as to who will be the nominees of the two party caucuses. For only in an extraordinary situation will a party choose to abandon its leader in favor of someone new.[10]

The powers that today belong to the Speaker of the House, although they are impressive, cannot compare with those which came with the office for 30 years before a successful

[10] Extraordinary circumstances do occur, however. In 1959, for instance, the Republicans, with White House support, turned their backs on Congressman Joseph W. Martin of Massachusetts, who had been their leader for more than twenty years and had actually served as Speaker for four of these years. The party's alleged aim in elevating Congressman Halleck of Indiana to the leadership was to make Republicanism in the House more vigorously partisan and put an end to the psychology of many Republicans that their party had been relegated to the status of a permanent minority.

revolt took place in 1910. The Speaker, for example, used to have the right to assign representatives to the standing committees; that function is now performed by the Committees on Committees. It was he who selected the chairman of each standing committee; now the selection is made automatically and mechanically, through the seniority system. He was once chairman of the Rules Committee, and was thus in a position to decide what legislation the House should consider; for the past half century he has not even been permitted to serve on the Rules Committee (or on any other committee, for that matter). In addition, the Speakership formerly carried with it the unrestricted power of recognition, which was often employed to punish and to discipline; today this power is restricted by reforms such as Calendar Wednesday, which compels the Speaker to extend recognition to committee chairmen.

So vast were the powers of his office in the first decade of this century that the Speaker was commonly referred to as a czar. There was no doubt that his authority was surpassed only by that of the President of the United States. Even the anecdotes that were told about him related to his power. It was said, for example, that a constituent who requested a copy of the rules of the House once received a picture of the Speaker.[11]

But in the era when the Progressives were inspiring the country with the irresistible rhetoric of majoritarianism and direct democracy, this kind of dictatorial power was an anachronism. After "Czar" Thomas B. Reed (R., Maine) had arrogated despotic power to himself, and when his autocratic practices were later continued and even expanded under Speaker Joseph Cannon (R., Ill.), a rank-and-file revolt took

[11] Thomas N. Schroth, "A New Speaker Faces a Changing House," *The New York Times Magazine*, January 7, 1962, p. 83.

place. An alliance of liberal Democrats and insurgent Republicans succeeded in reducing the Speakership to a mere skeleton of what it had been.

Resurgence of the Speakership

Although the reforms of 1910 were far-reaching, the Speaker was left with certain of his prerogatives intact. What is more, in the decades that have since intervened, the office has tended to regain, bit by bit, a great deal of the authority it once enjoyed. Today the Speaker appoints all the members of special committees, as well as the chairmen of the Committee of the Whole;[12] he selects a Speaker Pro Tempore to take his place when he is absent; he refers bills to the standing committees; he can refuse to recognize a member who intends to move that the rules be suspended in order to pass a particular bill; he rules on points of order; after a bill has been cleared by the Rules Committee it is up to him to decide exactly when it will be brought to the floor; and his opinion usually carries decisive weight when majority-party representatives are being selected for the Rules Committee. It has been said, in fact, that the House has become the private preserve of the Speaker, and that he runs everything in it, "from the nature of its legislative program to the conduct of its dining room. . . ."[13]

In large measure the resurgence of the Speakership is a tribute to the tact with which Cannon's successors have acted. They would never think of boasting, as Speaker Reed was

---

[12] He also appoints House members of conference committees, although in practice this power is more formal than real. See Ch. 11.

[13] William S. White, "Sam Rayburn—the Untalkative Speaker," *The New York Times Magazine*, February 27, 1949, p. 48. The death of President Kennedy reminded the country that the Speaker is also high in the order of presidential succession: immediately after the Vice President.

said to have done once, that no man was his peer and that only God was his superior.[14] The contemporary Speaker realizes that he must at least give the impression of influencing events through persuasion and reasonableness rather than through arbitrary dictation. He has learned to use the carrot as once he used the stick. Speaker Rayburn would tell freshman representatives: "If you want to get along, go along." Rayburn, without doubt the most successful of the "New Speakers," believed that "the old day of pounding on the desk and giving people hell is gone. We've all grown up now."

Rayburn followed the precedent established by a former Speaker[15] who had wanted to make sure that members of the House were always "educated" as to his views. Each day "Mr. Sam" would preside over a little assemblage popularly known as the "Board of Education." During the cocktail hour, those representatives who were in his good graces would gather informally in a room on the floor immediately below the one on which the House chamber is located. With Scotch and bourbon available in plentiful quantities, the "Board of Education" meetings generally tended to be spirited affairs. Since Rayburn found them an exceedingly useful adjunct of his leadership over the party as well as the House, it was not purely out of tribute to his memory that his successor, Speaker McCormack (himself a teetotaller), decided to continue holding them.

So powerful is the Speakership today that no incumbent would dream of forsaking it to run for the Senate (which a good representative will never refer to as "the Upper House"). There still seems to be widespread agreement with Speaker Reed that "the Senate is a nice quiet sort of place where good

[14] *Time,* January 19, 1962, p. 17.
[15] Nicholas Longworth (R., Ohio), occupant of the office from 1925 to 1931.

Representatives go when they die."[16] Speaker Rayburn even made something of a fetish of not crossing over to the Senate side of the Capitol any more than he absolutely had to. A Washington newspaper reported that "the only time he was seen there in recent years was eating dinner during one late session when the House restaurant was closed."[17]

The Impotent Caucus

For each party in each chamber, the source of the leadership's power is supposed to be the caucus, or conference, to which all party representatives belong. In practical terms, however, the power of the caucus today is largely an amiable myth. The contrast with one period of the past is striking, for during the first Wilson administration Democratic caucuses functioned with great effectiveness in both houses of Congress. They were an important factor in helping the Democrats achieve sufficient unity to enact the legislative program referred to by Wilson as the New Freedom.

Democratic caucuses were so important in Wilson's time because they exercised the power to compel members to support party positions. The "binding caucus" would operate in this manner: by a two-thirds vote, the Democrats in either house could take an official party position and obligate all party members to support it on the floor. There were exceptions. The caucus, for one thing, could only bind members on issues it formally characterized as involving a party policy or principle. For another thing, a member would not be bound by a caucus decision if he believed that it involved a construction of the United States Constitution or was one

[16] Hubert Bruce Fuller, *The Speakers of the House* (Boston: Little, Brown, 1909), p. 215.

[17] *Washington Post,* April 24, 1962, p. A1, col. 2.

on which he had made specific pledges during the election campaign.[18]

But even with these exceptions, the caucus was a potent party instrument. During the Wilsonian era, Democratic caucuses not only helped determine the outcome of floor action; they also exercised their influence at an earlier stage, to affect the shape of the legislation that would come to the floor. To an extent they converted the standing committees into instruments of their will, even going so far as to forbid them to make reports not sanctioned by the party. And in the House, the Democratic caucus felt free to issue instructions to the Rules Committee on which bills to clear for floor consideration.[19] The result was that in the brief span of a single Congress Wilson saw the enactment of such historic legislation as the Clayton Antitrust Act, the Federal Reserve Act, the Federal Trade Commission Act, and the Underwood tariff.

Although the Republican caucuses, too, were important party organs during the Wilson administration, they could not compare with those of the Democrats in terms of effectiveness. Today the shoe is on the other foot. The power of the caucus in both parties has been severely attenuated, but on the Democratic side the caucus has become so completely insignificant that its formal abolition would hardly be noticed. Virtually the only function that the Democratic caucus performs today is organizational: it selects the party leadership and ratifies assignments to the standing committees. The party that once used the "binding caucus" now hardly ever uses any caucus at all.

[18] A congressman was similarly free to disregard a caucus decision if it contradicted instructions he had received from the body that gave him the nomination.

[19] George B. Galloway, *History of the House of Representatives* (New York: Thomas Y. Crowell, 1961), p. 140.

The principal reason for the demise of the Democratic caucus is a fear that only negative results could ensue from policy discussions in a party so sharply split by sectional and ideological differences. At the time when President Johnson was Majority Leader and therefore chairman of the Senate Democratic Conference, he said that any attempt to resolve party differences on legislative policy would lead to nothing but the exaggeration of those differences and the opening of new rifts. "Party members," he explained, "frequently stand together for different reasons, but talking about those reasons may only open old wounds and drive them apart."[20]

Not through coincidence, therefore, the Senate Democratic Conference sank into almost total decrepitude during the reign of Johnson as party leader. It would meet only once a year, and that single meeting served for little more than to provide an audience before which Johnson would deliver what was sometimes referred to as his "little State of the Union address." Senator Proxmire of Wisconsin was appalled that events had come to such a pass. He took the Senate floor to make a full-dress attack on Johnson. The speech assailing Johnson contained a description of the proceedings at a typical Conference.

> After the Leader's speech, the only real caucus business that has transpired since I took office . . . took place. The President Pro Tempore was renominated. The President Pro Tempore then declared that the Majority Leader, his assistant, and the Secretary of the Conference had done a fine job last year, and without objection were elected again. The business of the caucus was over. The only business of the entire caucus had taken less than two and one-half minutes.[21]

Proxmire did not go so far as to advocate a return to "bind-

[20] Huitt, *op. cit.*, p. 341.
[21] *Congressional Record*, February 23, 1959, pp. 2544-45 (daily edition).

ing caucuses." He did not even suggest that Conferences should vote on questions of legislative policy. His only point was that more frequent meetings should be held. From these meetings, he hoped, the point of view of a majority of Democratic senators would emerge as an expression of the party's general orientation.

Stung by the Proxmire attack, Johnson replied that he was always willing to call the Conference into session, even at the request of a single senator. This, however, was rhetoric rather than reform, and the long-range effects of the Proxmire campaign were non-existent. Senator Mansfield, Johnson's successor, looks no more kindly on the caucus than the man whom he replaced. "I believe that caucuses are a waste of time," he has said bluntly. In a speech that he delivered even before becoming Majority Leader, he explained: "We would lose more votes than we would probably gain, because stories will get out of the Conference which will over-emphasize something of perhaps a somewhat spectacular nature, or contain only partial truths."[22]

Perhaps because there are fewer ideological fissures in their party than among the Democrats, the Republicans in both the House and Senate are less afraid to hold meetings. Particularly during periods when they are in the majority, frequent conferences are the rule. And even when they have only minority status, there is confidence in the possibility of presenting a reasonably united front. Adoption in 1962 of a declaration of "principles and policies" by the two Republican caucuses was a case in point."[23] Yet the party evinces no

---

[22] *Ibid.*, January 11, 1959, p. 197.

[23] The document, which was drawn up by a committee of senators and representatives in consultation with national party leaders outside Congress, furnished a useful campaign document for Republicans running that year.

desire to make the "binding caucus" a part of its congressional machinery.[24]

The low state to which the caucus has sunk reflects an important fact: both houses of Congress are today dominated by men who regard their political party as a vehicle for winning elections, not for securing the adoption of a program. The resuscitation of the caucus will almost surely come about only as part of a major effort to emphasize the programmatic function of political parties. But the only one of the four caucuses that is showing even the slightest sign of being more than casually interested in program is the House Republican Conference. In 1963, that group elected a new chairman (Gerald R. Ford, Jr., of Michigan), who favors encouraging the Conference to help mold a Republican viewpoint and publicize it to the Nation.

Campaign Committees

In both the House and Senate, each party has a fairly elaborate organization between its caucus, which constitutes the base of its pyramidal hierarchy, and its floor leadership, which sits at the apex. One unit in this structure is of special concern to each member: the campaign committee that exists in his chamber. Campaign committees in Congress originated as the result of almost unbearable strain between President Andrew Johnson and the so-called radicals who dominated the Republican Party in Congress during his term of office.

---

[24] The Republicans have never employed the device of a "binding caucus." On occasion, however, a Republican Conference has taken strong action to discipline recalcitrant members. In 1925, for example, the Conference in the House voted to punish representatives from Wisconsin who had bolted the party to support Senator Robert M. La-Follette of their state in his 1924 campaign for the Presidency. The punishment was twofold: demotion in rank on the standing committees of the House, and exclusion from the Republican Conference. Galloway, *op. cit.*, p. 103.

For fear that President Johnson would use the power of the national party to help crush their re-election hopes, the radicals organized their own campaign committee to assist them in the 1866 election. Before long, the Democrats in Congress chose to emulate the Republicans. Campaign committees were at first concerned only with House elections; members of the Senate did not yet face the problem of appealing to a popular electorate, since their selection was still in the hands of the state legislatures.[25] When the Seventeenth Amendment introduced the popular election of senators in 1913, it was only a matter of time before senatorial campaign committees were created.[26] Today, as in 1866, the congressional campaign committees act with considerable independence of the national parties. Their function is to work for the election to Congress of as many party members as possible, completely without regard to whether candidates have anything in common except the label "Democrat" or Republican."[27]

The two Republican Campaign Committees work more closely with the national party than the Democratic groups do. Behind this difference is the more centralized financial structure that the Republicans maintain.[28] A high degree of organization enables the GOP to conduct a unified fund-raising campaign, never soliciting prospective contributors more than once. Although the responsibility for raising the money is in the hands of the Republican National Committee, funds are turned over to the party's Senatorial and

[25] Article I, Section 3.

[26] V. O. Key, *Politics, Parties, and Pressure Groups* (4th ed.; New York: Crowell, 1958), pp. 355-56.

[27] Frank Church, "Campaign Money—How Much? From Whom?" *New York Times Magazine*, August 26, 1962, pp. 11-12.

[28] David B. Truman, *The Congressional Party: A Case Study* (New York: Wiley, 1959), p. 102.

Congressional Committees for allocation to particular candidates. The Democrats, in their financial activities, have been "less systematic and more variable in their practices," as one student has put it,[29] although in 1962 the White House under Kennedy insisted on exercising some control over the disbursement of National Committee funds to the congressional committees.

Money is quite obviously the principal commodity that the campaign committees have to offer, but it is not the only one. The permanent staffs that the committees employ, for example, may analyze the record of one's opponent, assist with publicity, and write campaign speeches. And in order to help candidates who were running in 1962, the committees participated in organizing schools for congressional candidates. Hundreds of hopefuls descended on Washington from all over the country, many accompanied by their campaign managers. They attended pep rallies, indoctrination meetings, and workshops, all designed to help them run successful campaigns. Each Democrat who showed up was granted a ten-second audience with Mr. Kennedy, so that a photographer could record for posterity—and for campaign posters—the beaming face of the candidate as he was awarded a smile and a handshake from the President (who, at the same time, was adeptly propelling him toward the exit). Republican candidates had to settle for speeches by the leading contenders for their party's presidential nomination.

In the Senate, there is frequent rotation of the campaign committees' membership, for neither party wants to place additional burdens on an incumbent who is seeking re-election and may have to devote all his efforts to keeping his own seat. The decision as to which senators shall serve on the campaign committee is made for the Democrats by their floor leader; among the Republicans, selections are in the hands

[29] Key, *op. cit.*, p. 357.

of a chairman, who is elected by the party Conference. The campaign committees in the House consist generally of one representative from each of the state delegations. Usually every committee member is the dean of his delegation.[30]

To some extent, the campaign committees perform a mechanical function as they pick the races into which to pour party money. For they are motivated first and foremost by a desire to place the funds where they will do the most good: in contests that could go either way. Yet considerable room remains for subjective judgment, and when campaign committees exercise their discretion they almost always favor incumbents. Usually they also seem willing to bow to the judgment of the chairman when it is necessary to make a difficult decision on who will receive major contributions and who will receive only token sums. The chairmanship of a campaign committee is thus a position that is by no means lacking in power.[31]

Party Whips

While the Campaign Committees concern themselves only with elections, there are other party organs that are in-

[30] Interview with Kenneth Harding, director of Democratic Congressional Campaign Committee, October 26, 1962.

[31] In the Second Session of the Eighty-seventh Congress, the chairman of the Democratic National Congressional Committee (as the Democrats have named their campaign committee in the House), Michael J. Kirwan of Ohio, decided in his role as a member of the appropriations committee to recommend that Congress provide $10 million to establish an aquarium in the Nation's Capital. The aquarium would, he said, serve as a tourist attraction. Although it was generally assumed that government and not fish would continue to draw tourists to Washington, congressmen hastened to approve Mr. Kirwan's "gold-plated fishbowl," as Senator Morse of Oregon called it. Some uncharitable observers concluded that congressmen had been less impressed by the merits of the proposal than by the fact that Kirwan was chairman of the Democratic Campaign Committee—as well as chairman of the Appropriations Subcommittee on Interior and Related Agencies.

volved in the day-to-day aspects of the legislative process. One such organ is the whip system maintained in each house by both Democrats and Republicans. The peculiar title "whip" is an English importation. Across the Atlantic, it means a functionary who is charged with the responsibility of seeing to it that party members are present and vote as they should on legislative issues, even if this means whipping them into line by threatening to invoke the considerable sanctions that the party possesses.[32] Here, by contrast, the title is a grotesque misnomer for an official who exercises powers that are not substantial in behalf of a party program that is not clear.

The duties of a Whip do, however, bear at least a faint resemblance to those of his British counterpart. The principal similarity is the fact that the Whip is expected to produce his party's members on the floor when an important vote is scheduled. To help accomplish this aim, he circulates each week a "Whip Notice," containing information about the legislative program for the week to come. In addition, he conducts polls among the members of his party to ascertain how they plan to vote on pending issues. The information produced through such polls is helpful in determining whether —and where—pressure should be applied in order to achieve the results desired by the leadership. If a head-count shows that defeat is certain on a particular bill, the party may try to put off the vote until the auguries are favorable.

The lot of a Whip is by no means a happy one. Since congressmen seldom feel any urgency about being present for a vote on which their individual positions will not be recorded, it is only when roll calls are scheduled that the Whip

[32] The name "whip" is a short form of "whipper-in." It was borrowed from the hunting field, "where the whipper-in is supposed to keep hounds from straying out of the pack when they ought to be after the fox." *The New York Times*, June 18, 1963, p. 15, col. 4 (city edition).

can safely count on good attendance. A Democratic Whip in the House[33] once complained that he could depend on his colleagues to be present for a vote only when he could predict precisely when the vote would be taken; otherwise, as many as 150 Democrats could be expected to vanish rather than remain on the floor for as long as a quarter of an hour.[34] To help solve this problem, the Majority Whip is frequently authorized to dispatch pointed telegrams with the following message: "The Speaker urgently requests that you be present [on a particular date] for all teller votes on [a named] bill. . . ."[35]

The large membership of the House creates an exceedingly difficult task for the Whips in that chamber. Accordingly, each party has instituted a system of assistant whips. Among the Democrats, every assistant whip is given responsibility for the party's members from a particular geographical zone. Customarily, the assistant is selected by the senior Democrats from his zone, though in some instances the "deans" allow the choice to be made by all the representatives in the zone. The Republican system for selecting assistant whips in the House is neither as decentralized nor as geo-

[33] Carl Albert of Oklahoma, who later became Floor Leader.

[34] *Congressional Quarterly Weekly Report,* June 16, 1961, p. 995. One Democratic congressman, the late Clem Miller, of California, felt nothing but sympathy for his party's Whip. He wrote:

> If he puts out a call too soon . . . many members will assemble, take a quick look, and then begin to fade. . . . Yet he cannot defer too long, because a vote might come unexpectedly. When ten speakers might be scheduled . . . the Republicans could yank six all of a sudden and the vote would be upon us twenty minutes before it was expected and at a time when our members are dispersed.

Clem Miller, *Member of the House,* John W. Baker, ed. (New York: Scribner, 1962), p. 53.

[35] *Congressional Record,* June 13, 1962, p. 9637 (daily edition).

graphically oriented as the Democratic. The Republicans leave it completely to the Whip to pick his own assistants. Although three of the twelve assistants whom he selects are placed in charge of geographical regions, even these are hand-picked by him, instead of being chosen by the delegations of the regions they will oversee.[36]

Regardless of party, the functions of the assistant whips in the House are essentially the same. Their principal responsibility is to get party members to the floor when their presence is needed. In addition, they often conduct informal polls and can thus help keep the leadership informed of sentiment on a particular issue among the rank and file of the party.[37]

Democratic Study Group

When Whips are alerting the members of their party to be on the floor for a particular vote, they are expected to communicate with one and all, not only with those members who can be expected to follow the party line on the issue. Among the Republicans, who enjoy a significant degree of party regularity, this presents no serious problem. The Democratic Whips, on the other hand, are constantly faced with the embarrassment of having to urge the attendance of men who are certain to join the fight against their party's program. So grave has the problem of Democratic disunity become that those party members in the House who in general support the program of the national party have felt compelled to create a formal whip organization of their own—the Democratic Study Group.

For this organization to call itself a "study group" is not entirely inaccurate, because the whip function is not the only

[36] *Congressional Quarterly Weekly Report,* June 16, 1961, p. 992-93. The Whip also chooses one deputy.

[37] Truman, *op. cit.,* p. 227.

one it performs. Its staff, which is considerably augmented each summer by student volunteers, turns out studies that supplement the material produced by the Legislative Reference Service and the individual office staffs. Research papers that it produces are designed to assist Study Group members not only in their legislative work but in their election campaigns as well. Congressmen snap up Study Group "fact sheets," for these provide material for speeches and campaign "literature" on the issues that can be expected to dominate a campaign. They also may attend seminars on subjects of interest.

But the most distinctive activity of the Democratic Study Group is the informal whip system that is maintained. The organization claims that when an important amendment is unexpectedly brought to a vote it can fetch the bulk of its 100 members to the floor "within minutes."[38] Since it is unusual for more than 150 representatives to be present when the House is considering amendments on the floor, the bloc of votes that the Study Group can deliver is sometimes decisive.

The Democratic Leadership in the House reacts with some ambivalence to the activities of the Study Group. On the one hand, there is recognition that those Democrats who support the program of the national party must maintain an extraordinarily good record of floor attendance if they are to stand a chance of outvoting the dedicated coalition of southern Democrats and conservative Republicans. On the other hand, however, there is concern that the very existence of the Study Group hardens the division between the two wings of the Democratic Party in the House—the moderately liberal, White House-oriented members of the Study Group, and

[38] Interview with William G. Phillips, staff director of Democratic Study Group, March 7, 1963.

the conservative Democrats who represent the southern states. Moreover, the no-nonsense pragmatists who constitute the official House Democratic Leadership shy away instinctively from an organization whose commitment to programmatic principles gives it an almost long-haired appearance.

Parties and Legislative Issues in the House

Liberals in the House have expressed their dissatisfaction with existing party organization not only through creation of the Democratic Study Group but also by agitating for the formation of a party Steering Committee. Such a committee had been established in 1933, but when Sam Rayburn became Speaker in 1940 he made no effort to conceal his hostility to it. The result was that the committee began to lose strength at a steadily increasing rate, until it passed from the scene entirely in 1956. Rayburn's death five years later was the signal for the liberals to launch a campaign for the establishment of a new Steering Committee. They hoped that such a group would amplify their voice in party councils. Speaker McCormack allowed himself to be persuaded by the liberals, and a Steering Committee was created with a membership that was fairly representative of the Democratic Party in the House.[39] In retrospect, however, the Democrats who promoted the establishment of the Committee are not certain that they really accomplished anything. For apart from sev-

[39] Eighteen of the twenty-four members are chosen as representatives of geographical zones and are elected to the Steering Committee by Democratic congressmen who represent states in those zones. Unlike the old Steering Committee, it does not include among its *ex officio* members the chairmen of the Appropriations, Rules, and Ways and Means Committees; the only Democrats who are automatically members of the Steering Committee by virtue of other offices they hold are the Speaker, Majority Leader, Whip, Chairman of the Caucus, Secretary of the Caucus, and Chairman of the Congressional Campaign Committee.

eral organizational meetings that were held shortly after its formation, the Committee has simply not met. Its chairman explains that "there just haven't been any issues that the members wanted to discuss."[40]

The Republicans in the House have a group that is to some extent a counterpart of the Democratic Steering Committee. At one time it, too, was called a Steering Committee. In 1949, however—three years after the Joint Committee on the Organization of Congress had recommended the creation of policy committees in each chamber—its name was changed to the Republican Policy Committee. Of its 33 members, 10 serve by virtue of other positions they hold. These *ex officio* members are the Floor Leader, Whip, Chairman of the Conference, Secretary of the Conference, Chairman of the Congressional Campaign Committee, and the five Republicans on the Rules Committee. Eighteen additional members are elected from nine geographical zones into which the party is divided. These 28 members of the Steering Committee are the only ones with the right to vote. In addition, there is one non-voting member for each of the five "classes" of Republicans most recently elected to the House. In the Eighty-eighth Congress, for example, the Republicans of the "Class of 1962" —those who were first elected to Congress in that year—chose a representative to serve on the Steering Committee, and each of the four preceding "classes" (or "clubs") did the same.[41]

The Republican Policy Committee in the House is much more influential than the parallel Democratic committee, partly because it has had more time to develop and partly because the Republicans are not so seriously divided as the Democrats are. It meets on a regular weekly basis, and is not

[40] Interview with Representative Ray J. Madden (D., Ind.), August 13, 1963.

[41] *Congressional Quarterly Weekly Report,* March 16, 1962, pp. 451-52.

averse to a practice that horrifies the Democrats more than any other: taking votes on legislative issues. Although the results of such votes are not binding on party members, they are generally considered to be official statements of the party's position, and Republicans are reluctant to disregard them. Recommendations of the Policy Committee are communicated officially to Republican House members either at meetings of the Conference or by means of the whip organization. Particularly during the years that Congressman Charles A. Halleck of Indiana has been the Republican leader, the Policy Committee has been a significant unit of Republican party organization in the House.[42]

The "Out" Party

From at least one point of view, the rather elaborate apparatus maintained by both Democrats and Republicans in Congress is less important to the party that occupies the White House than it is to the "out" party. For the party that is in control of the Executive Branch has an acknowledged leader to formulate its policies: the President of the United States. The messages that the President sends to Congress, the speeches he delivers, the statements he makes at press conferences—all these are taken to constitute the program of the party. The President may very well experience great difficulty in convincing Congress to accept this program, or even in persuading members from his own party to stop obstructing it; but seldom is any doubt raised that it is *party policy* for which he is campaigning.

There is thus little controversy about who is the spokesman of the party in the White House. But it is not easy to decide who can legitimately speak for the other party. The defeated

[42] Meg Greenfield, "Charles A. Halleck and the Restless Republicans," *Reporter,* November 8, 1962, p. 29.

presidential candidate is considered the "titular leader" of his party, but the fact that a limiting adjective is attached to the word "leader" signifies that he leads in name only;[43] a former President may be listened to with respect, but as an elder statesman rather than a policy-maker; and the man who will be his party's standard-bearer in the next presidential election might be recognized as leader, but there is never any general agreement as to who he is. Almost by default, therefore, the "out" party tends to depend on its leadership in Congress for the formulation of its policies. Accordingly, it was the Democratic Leader in the Senate, Lyndon Johnson, and the Democratic Speaker of the House, Sam Rayburn, who stood at the helm of their party during the eight years of Mr. Eisenhower's presidency. And it was the minority leaders of the House and Senate, Congressman Halleck and Senator Dirksen, who began to speak for the Republican Party after Mr. Kennedy became President in 1961.

But there are a number of Republicans who do not like the image of their party that Halleck and Dirksen project. The two leaders are criticized on the grounds that they are too conservative and too negative—and too unphotogenic as well. The picture that Dirksen and Halleck present on the television screen is considered a fit subject for comment because the two leaders make a point of inviting extensive broadcast coverage of their news conferences. An unkind newspaperman once referred to the weekly "performance" as the "Ev and Charlie Show," and the name has stuck. Liberal Republicans as well as younger party members of every ideological hue are distressed that many have come to look

[43] Even if some considered Richard M. Nixon as the leader of the Republican Party after his defeat in the presidential election of 1960, only a few took this position after he was beaten two years later in the race for the governorship of his home State of California.

on their congressional leaders as a pair of vaudeville comedians with a regular, if unsponsored, television program.[44] Nor is any satisfaction taken from the fact that people are tending to regard the nay-saying of Dirksen and Halleck as the best the Republican Party has to offer. Some Republicans are concerned that their party will continue to lose elections as long as voters identify it with the philosophy of its leaders in Congress.

No satisfactory solution to the Republican problem, however, has yet been devised. One party leader who has interested himself in the subject is former President Eisenhower. In 1962, Mr. Eisenhower brought together about 150 party leaders at his Gettysburg farm to announce the establishment of an All-Republican Conference. The idea was that the party should speak between its quadrennial conventions through an organization which would include Republican office-holders of both the past and present as well as the party's current candidates for office.

Republican National Chairman William E. Miller was an enthusiastic supporter of the Conference: the job of a National Chairman, after all, is to help the party win presidential elections, and the Eisenhower organization was almost bound to be dominated by the "presidential wing" of the party. Not surprisingly, though, the love of Dirksen and Halleck for the Conference was noticeably undemonstrative. The leaders' lack of enthusiasm guaranteed that the first meeting of the Conference would also be its last. In 1963, a successor group, the Critical Issues Council, was created under the

[44] The belief that there was such a thing as a weekly television program entitled the "Ev and Charlie Show" was widespread. Television stations received countless letters from irate Republicans demanding to know why the "program" was not being carried locally. The letter-writers often hinted darkly that it was being suppressed by Democrats.

chairmanship of Dr. Milton Eisenhower, brother of the former President. It promised to "articulate a Republican citizens' position on the great problems that face our Government and our people."[45] Only "presidential Republicans" were announced as members.

Democratic Advisory Council

While it is still too early to assess the effectiveness of the Critical Issues Council, the prospects of the group are not favorable if the fate of a similar Democratic effort is any indication. The Democratic attempt, designed to cope with much the same problem, was made after the 1956 election, when the party suffered its second consecutive defeat at the hands of Mr. Eisenhower. National Chairman Paul Butler inspired the creation of a Democratic Advisory Council, which would function between national conventions to express what might fairly be considered Democratic positions on important policy matters. The Council was to include among its members prominent White House-oriented Democrats such as former President Truman, Eleanor Roosevelt, and Adlai Stevenson, who had twice been the party's presidential candidate. Seats on the Council would be reserved as well for the seven principal leaders of the congressional party, particularly Speaker Rayburn and Senate Majority Leader Johnson.[46]

Rayburn and Johnson, however, declined to serve, and the other congressional leaders chose to do the same. None of them wanted to lend their support to an organization that would doubtless press them to respond more to the program-

---

[45] *The New York Times,* July 5, 1963, p. 1, col. 1 (late city edition).

[46] The other congressional representatives on the Advisory Council were to be the House Floor Leader, the two Whips, and the chairman of the two Campaign Committees. Truman, *op. cit.*, p. 301.

matic preferences of voters in the North and less to those of the southern wing, which was so powerful in the congressional party. Perhaps the leaders also feared that their legislative effectiveness would be seriously diminished if they showed any willingness to use their positions in the House and Senate to secure approval for programs formulated outside the halls of Congress.[47] Without the participation of the congressional leaders, the Advisory Council was reduced to little more than a star-studded discussion group operating on the fringes of the party. As soon as the Democrats reclaimed the White House in 1961, the Council formally dissolved, for there was now a Democratic President to speak for the national party.

The difficulty of creating an organization that will unite the Democrats or the Republicans in a meaningful way is basically one of bridging the gap between the congressional and presidential wings of each party.[48] The two are very different. The congressional wing is responsive to the pressures of hundreds of constituencies, while the President is supposed to be the representative of a single nationwide constituency. The problem of producing majorities in the House or Senate, where the constituencies are not weighted, is very different from the problem of gaining a majority in the Elec-

[47] As one student of legislative politics has written:

> Even after conferences with the President, the leaders of his legislative party—though they may head a majority— normally avoid specific public commitment about what the congressional party will do. Rather, they report what the President wants and indicate an intent to help get it for him if they can. What they do not do as spokesmen for the White House, they clearly cannot appear to do as members of a group created by the National Committee.

Ibid., pp. 301-02.

[48] See James M. Burns, *Deadlock of Democracy: Four-Party Politics in America* (Englewood Cliffs, N. J.: Prentice-Hall, 1963), *passim.*

toral College, where the large urban states predominate. Thus people such as the national party chairmen, who think in terms of winning the next presidential election, are likely to espouse more liberal policies than the congressional leadership.

But a national chairman is in no position to impose his more liberal, or at least more national, viewpoint on his party's representatives in Congress. Neither he nor the National Committee he heads has the power to give orders to county chairmen or state chairmen, not to mention members and leaders of Congress. In reality, therefore, each of the national parties is little more than a loose confederation. A member of Congress worries only about staying on good terms with his constituents, not with the national chairman of his party. As long as this situation continues and each party remains an uneasy alliance of state and local organizations, a national chairman will experience nothing but frustration if he attempts to use his office to promote what he deems to be the ideology of his party.

Coalition Politics

Because party lines are so lax in Congress, it is extremely rare for all Democrats or all Republicans to vote the same way on any significant issue. Far more commonly, alliances that cut across party lines are forged on particular issues. The most enduring of these alliances is the coalition of Republicans and conservative southern Democrats.[49] This collaboration has given a degree of operational unity to the southerners and Republicans, both of whom generally seek identical goals: an end to positive Federal legislation on social and economic issues. The southerners, who want to defeat civil rights legis-

[49] "We should realize that some Democrats have voted with the Republicans for a good 25 years," President Kennedy once noted sadly.

lation, and the Republicans, whose principal desire is the scrapping of social welfare proposals, cooperate closely to insure the death of both types of measures. The coalition has been most successful in preventing the passage of strong civil rights laws, but it has functioned almost as smoothly on issues such as education, immigration, taxes, regulation of business, and regulation of labor. The identity of views between the partners in the coalition is so close that liberals in the House sometimes refer to the Democratic Chairman of the Rules Committee, Howard Smith of Virginia, as the Assistant Republican Leader. Senate Minority Leader Dirksen denies that any coalition exists. The southerners, he says, simply "see through the same spectacles as Republicans do."[50]

There is often much better rapport between the Republicans and the southern Democrats than between the national and congressional wings within each party. To help the Republicans overcome the lack of coordination between the national party and the congressional party, President Eisenhower thought it would be a good idea to select the national chairman from the ranks of the Republicans in Congress. Accordingly, a senator—Thruston B. Morton of Kentucky—was chosen for the national chairmanship in 1959. Any improvement in coordination that may have resulted was not visible to the naked eye; Senator Morton, after all, held no position of authority in the Republican *congressional* hierarchy, and his influence with other members of Congress was therefore minimal.[51] The Republicans tried again when they

[50] Interview, March 1, 1962.

[51] Moreover, the job of national chairman was a serious political liability to Senator Morton in Kentucky, for that state is more likely to elect a Republican who acts somewhat like a Democrat than one whose job calls for him to be the most rabidly partisan Republican in the party. To make matters worse, Morton's duties as National Chairman were so time-consuming that he was unable to return to Kentucky

named Congressman William Miller of New York to succeed Morton as national chairman in 1961. The results were no more impressive.[52] Party unity, it seems, is not to be purchased either easily or cheaply.

---

to mend political fences as often as a prudent concern for his re-election prospects seemed to require. The Kentuckian seemed genuinely surprised when he was re-elected to the Senate in 1962, only two years after giving up the national chairmanship.

[52] Mr. Miller did not, however, lose any favor with his congressional constituency. He represents an Up-State district that appreciates the partisan hyperbole in which a Republican National Chairman is expected to indulge.

10

Debate on the Floor

THE TOURIST WHO VISITS WASHINGTON and feels that he should "see Congress" hardly ever thinks of visiting a committee meeting. His natural inclination is to attend a plenary session of the House or Senate. It is on the floor, after all, that final decisions seem to be made. This intuition is not entirely defective, for sometimes the floor is indeed the place of decision, and almost always what is done there is far more than a mere formality in the legislative process.

At no time are the differences between the House and Senate more evident than during proceedings on the floor. The House, in accommodating its 435 members—more than four times as many as the Senate has—provides neither desks nor individual seats: only the elected party leadership and the committee members presenting a bill have even a table on which to take notes. Representatives are clustered together on benches that emphasize the collectivity, not the individuals who compose it. Each senator at least has his own seat and desk to give him an air of individuality.

The difference in the size of the two houses helps explain many dissimilarities in their respective modes of operation.

Without doubt, the most significant of these dissimilarities is that senators enjoy the privilege of unlimited debate, while in the House debate is conducted under rigid restrictions. Not only does this affect oratorical styles in each house; it also creates the conditions under which the Senate's most peculiar institution—the filibuster—can flourish.

Limitation on House debate is so drastic that loquacious members constantly chafe under its restrictions. Except when they are on a committee that is reporting a bill, representatives seldom have an opportunity to take the floor while legislation is being considered. The House agreed a long time ago that full and free debate is less important than expeditious decision. It certainly will not tolerate obstruction by a minority.

Normally, such House discussion as is allowed takes place in three distinct stages.[1] First comes an hour-long debate on whether to adopt the Rules Committee resolution containing the conditions under which the bill will be considered. Approval of this resolution, or rule, is followed later by "general debate" on the measure. And perhaps the most critical discussion takes place in the final stage, when amendments are debated and voted on.

Accordingly, it is the members of the all-powerful Rules Committee who set the scene for the debate on most bills before the House. The issue at this point is supposedly not substantive but rather procedural: whether to agree to the terms recommended by the Rules Committee for considera-

---

[1] These stages are not to be confused with the three "readings" which a bill must undergo in each house. The term "readings" is today something of a misnomer. The first consists merely of an announcement of the title when the bill is referred to committee or sometimes just the printing of the title in the *Congressional Record*. The second, at the time the bill is open to floor amendment, is usually the only real reading. The third, by title only, precedes the final vote.

tion of the bill. But the members of the Rules Committee, who dominate this phase of the debate, are no more interested than the rest of their colleagues in procedure for its own sake. The substance of the legislation is what really concerns them. So the discussion, even at this preliminary stage, tends to deal with the merits of the bill and of the amendments that will be offered to it. And the members of the Rules Committee, though they may possess no special competence in the subject with which the bill deals, are in the enviable position of key-note speakers.

The remarks that Rules Committee members deliver at this juncture are heard by more representatives than one generally finds on the floor of the House at other times. The reason is that this phase of the debate takes place before the House itself—not before the Committee of the Whole, into which the House will soon resolve itself. The importance of this distinction is that a more exacting quorum requirement is in effect when the House meets *as the House* than when it functions as the *Committee of the Whole*. For the House itself to be in session, at least 218 representatives—a majority of the total membership—must be present. In the Committee of the Whole, on the other hand, the attendance of only 100 members is sufficient.

Since only the debate on the adoption of the rule occurs in the House as distinguished from the Committee of the Whole, it is strange but true that the only floor discussion heard by some members is directed by the Rules Committee, not by the committee that specializes in the subject-matter of the legislation. Once the rule has been adopted, a mass exodus from the House chamber may take place. Many members will not return until all debate on the measure as a whole has been terminated and the voting is about to begin on amendments. Some will not put in an appearance even at that time.

Committee of the Whole

After the discussion of the rule is over, the House votes on whether to accept the conditions for debate that the Rules Committee has laid down. Affirmative action is assured, since the resolution of the Rules Committee is not subject to amendment and its outright rejection would almost surely mean that the bill would never come before the House. When the resolution has been adopted, the chairman of the committee from which the bill was reported moves that the House resolve itself into the Committee of the Whole House on the State of the Union. That motion is adopted, and the general debate begins.

From this point on, the members of the legislative committee that reported out the bill replace the members of the Rules Committee as directors of the debate. The time that is available for discussion on the floor is almost always equally divided between proponents and opponents of the bill. A senior committee member on each side of the fence parcels out time to his colleagues on the committee. If extra time remains, perhaps a representative or two from outside the committee will be allowed to speak. But there is seldom any extra time. Even for the members of the committee, general debate does not furnish the opportunity for exhaustive analysis of the legislation before the House. No representative may take the floor more than once, and his single speech is limited to a few brief minutes.

The third and generally most informative stage in House debate occurs at the time amendments are considered. Priority is given to amendments that were approved in committee. These are frequently debated and voted on as a package.[2] When this *"en bloc"* method is used, it is extremely unlikely that any of the committee amendments will be defeated, be-

[2] Methods of voting are discussed in Ch. 11.

cause it is necessary for members to vote against all in order to vote against even one. A theoretical possibility always exists, however, that the amendments will be turned down. To guard against such an eventuality, the committee may choose to produce an entirely new bill of its own instead of reporting out with amendments the bill originally referred to it. Such a reworked committee draft is referred to as a "clean bill."

From the standpoint of the committee, the advantage of writing its views into a "clean bill" instead of advancing them in the form of amendments is simple: in Congress, it is always easier to block action than to promote it. The "clean bill" tactic saddles opponents of the committee measure with the burden of trying to make changes on the floor instead of putting this burden on the committee.

After disposing of any committee amendments that might have been reported out, the House next turns its attention to amendments offered from the floor, if the Rules Committee has not foreclosed such a procedure in the order it reported out.[3] The proponents of far-reaching amendments always face an uphill fight, for there is a widely held conviction that bills should be written in committee and not on the floor. In part, this conviction stems from the idea that the expert work of specialized committees should not casually be undone. Many congressmen, however, are heavily influenced by a very different factor: they know that if they vote today to undo the handiwork of a committee, they can expect that tomorrow favorite projects of their own committee will be dismembered on the floor.

[3] If the Rules Committee has reported out a "closed rule," there is still a chance to alter the bill on the floor, by offering a motion to recommit it with instructions that a particular change be made by the committee. In addition, the minority on the committee that reported out the bill may offer a single substitute for the committee bill.

Neither of these considerations, however, prevents amendments from being offered on the floor in great profusion. Many are submitted by representatives who know there is no chance of passage and would in all honesty have it no other way. Their aim is merely to convince constituents that the congressman is "in there, battling all the way."

The representative who introduces an amendment has only five minutes to argue for its adoption. The same amount of time is also given to one opponent of the amendment. Yet this apparently rigid time limit and the rule that only two speakers may address themselves to a given amendment are not so confining as they appear. Extensive debate can still take place under the five-minute rule, and it often does. For the absence of any ceiling on the number of amendments that may be offered makes it possible for a congressman to maneuver his way into the debate by offering a *"pro forma* amendment."* Even though the section of the bill on which he wants to comment has already been debated by two speakers, he offers an amendment to "strike out the last word" of the provision under consideration and thus wins the right to speak for five minutes. The *pro forma* amendment he has offered, of course, is not even put to a vote.

Thus it is in this third and last stage of House debate that the most meaningful floor discussion takes place. As a matter of fact, such debate often possesses a lively, give-and-take quality that would probably be absent if the reading of long speeches were the rule.

Special Order

Yet it remains true that only a small percentage of representatives manage to speak on any particular bill, and those who are thus favored often feel they have had insufficient time to explain their position fully. Safety valves, however, make it unlikely that such resentment will ever assume serious proportions. The principal such outlet is the "special order."

After all legislative business on a given day has been transacted, time may be made available to an individual representative to hold the floor under a "special order" for a far longer period than the rules allow at other times. Unanimous consent must be secured in advance, but this is seldom more than a formal requirement. Of course, the value of a "special order" is adulterated by the time of day at which it permits a member to speak. The cocktail hour is not a time when one can reasonably expect a large audience.[4]

Occasionally a fairly sizable group of like-minded representatives reserve many hours of "special order" time in order to bring their ideas to public notice. This was the case, for example, when Republicans were granted fifteen hours in April 1962 for "Operation Spring Thaw," in which they happily recounted the "failures of the Kennedy Administration" far into the vernal night. Considerable press coverage is sometimes given to such a marathon effort.

What amounts to a miniature "special order" is available to members of the House at an earlier hour of the day, when better attendance is likely. Shortly after the House convenes at noon, unanimous consent will be given to any member who asks permission to speak for no more than a single minute. The member customarily uses the sixty seconds that have been granted him by his generous colleagues to read through the

[4] Although in the Senate members do not have to confine their oratory to such an unlikely hour, Wayne Morse of Oregon chooses voluntarily to schedule his major forensic efforts for the late afternoon, because of his reluctance to slow down the legislative machinery with speeches not relevant to bills under consideration. He has been speaking late in the afternoon for so long now that he refers to himself as "the five o'clock shadow."

first few sentences of a lengthy speech. He then obtains unanimous consent for the entire address to be printed in the *Congressional Record* as though it had been delivered on the floor in full. It is not surprising if members of the public who wander into the House gallery at this hour start to doubt their sanity as they listen uncomprehendingly to a succession of fragmentary observations that bear even less of a relationship to each other than the components of an unusually bizarre dream.[5]

For the representative who wishes to play an important part in floor action, "special orders" and the like serve to mitigate only slightly the frustration he suffers because of the strict limitations that the House imposes on debate. Sometimes even the author of a bill is not allowed to speak in support of his own measure. But debate limitation in the House has been the object of criticism for another reason as well. Members of the Senate look with lofty disdain on House practice because they are convinced that it often allows demonstrably bad and irresponsible legislation to slip through, simply because debate is too fragmentary to expose its bad features. Senators like to cite cases where it was not until such legislation reached *their* chamber that there was time for sufficient discussion to expose its evils and prevent its passage. In 1946, for example, President Truman's request that he be empowered to draft railroad strikers into the Army was approved by the House after only 40 minutes of debate; it was left for the Senate to introduce a note of caution, to insist on deliberation—and to kill the bill. An admirer of the Senate has described what often happens after the House is stampeded by talk of crisis

[5] At any time of the day, a representative may be given the floor on a "point of personal privilege" if the Speaker agrees with him that he has been subjected to a personal attack, perhaps in the press, that is sufficiently serious to justify a public response.

into passing a bill with virtually no debate: "Time passes, the frenzy evaporates, the fantastic hysteria of the House is revealed in all its bald outline. The bill dies—in the Senate."[6] It has been said that the House acts with full consciousness of its irresponsibility, confident that the Senate will save it from its own folly. One critic has written: "The House ought to legislate as if the Senate were not there. Far too often . . . it legislates as if nothing *but* the Senate were there."[7]

The rules under which debate is conducted in the House have one great advantage over those of the Senate: It is not possible for speeches to be used as a device for obstruction. The anti-filibustering rules of the House assure that a majority can bring to a vote any measure on the floor. A "previous question" motion enables the House to vote when a majority is ready. The motion is made by the manager of the bill—the committee member who has been charged with the responsibility of guiding the legislation on the floor—and it is put to an immediate vote. If approval is forthcoming from more than half of those present, it is no longer in order to speak on the bill or to offer amendments, and a vote is taken at once.[8]

[6] Allen Drury, "Is the House a Rubber Stamp?" *The New York Times Magazine,* August 11, 1957, p. 32. Former Congressman (and later Interior Secretary) Stewart L. Udall admits that in each of three consecutive years the House took legislative action with unseemly haste: in 1955, it was inveigled into "rubberstamping the Formosa resolution with only the slightest pretense of real debate"; in 1956, it approved an incredibly expensive bill that would have awarded automatic pensions to all veterans at least 65 years of age; and in 1957 a bill to revise the effect of a Supreme Court decision on the inviolability of Federal Bureau of Investigation files was "whipped through committee" and promptly endorsed by the House. "A Congressman Defends the House," *The New York Times Magazine,* January 12, 1958, p. 69.

[7] Drury, *op. cit.,* p. 35.

[8] Voting is discussed in Ch. 11.

Unlimited Debate

The Senate has no "previous question" rule. It operates, instead, under a rule of unlimited debate. Senators take pride in this rule. They say it is the principal reason why the Senate deserves to be considered the greatest deliberative body in the world. Debate should not be cut off, they argue, as long as a single member has something that he wants to say. Senators should be courteous enough to hear out patiently any colleague who wishes to speak. Whatever sacrifice in time may be involved is more than outweighed by the benefits that result from preserving full and free debate in at least one chamber of the National Legislature.

In the terms in which it is presented, this argument may well be unanswerable. It is, however, almost totally irrelevant to the only serious criticism made of the unlimited debate rule: that it enables a Senate minority to kill a bill by refusing to stop talking. The case against unlimited debate thus does not rest on any skepticism about the benefits to be derived from exhaustive discussion. It is predicated instead on the belief that a Senate minority should not be permitted to prevent the majority from enacting legislation it favors. The issue, in short, is the filibuster.

The term "filibuster" is often used somewhat loosely. When, for example, a single senator talks around the clock on a particular issue, his impressive oratorical effort will often be labeled a filibuster. Yet such a speech is not designed to obstruct legislation but rather to dramatize an issue. Only in the closing days of a congressional session might an individual senator's threat to hold the floor for 24 hours frighten his colleagues into dropping the bill to which he objects. At other times, when there is no danger that adjournment plans will be wrecked, the one-man "filibuster" is regarded more with amusement than with dismay. The Senate seems a bit proud that a number of its members are equipped with leather lungs and iron constitutions.

Probably the most famous senator thus endowed was Huey P. Long (D., La.), who was an expert at delivering interminable speeches on irrelevant subjects. Once, for instance, he used a wastebasket as a theatrical prop in instructing his colleagues on how best to prepare "potlikker," which he defined as "the residue that remains from the commingling, heating, and evaporation—anyway, it's in the bottom of the pot." In more recent years, the Long tradition has been carried on by two other senators: Strom Thurmond of South Carolina, whose 24-hour speech against civil rights legislation in 1957 was apparently the lengthiest oration ever delivered in the Senate; and Wayne Morse of Oregon, who once spoke for twenty-three hours against a tidelands oil "give-away" bill. Thurmond may have held the floor longer than Morse, but the latter never once left the chamber for the brief excursions taken by his fellow senator, whose flesh was evidently weaker than his spirit.

Although it is not easy to stay on the same subject from one dawn to the next, senators like Thurmond and Morse try hard to stick to the point, from the first word of the exordium to the last word of the peroration. The era seems to have vanished when a senator had no qualms about wasting the Senate's time by reading the Manhattan Telephone Directory, or the *World Almanac,* or even the *Congressional Record* of the previous day. The late-model senator who is waging a one-man war of words takes pains not to roam too far from the subject under discussion. His intention, after all, is to educate and influence public opinion.

Filibusters

The molding of public opinion, however, is not the aim of a real filibuster—one conducted by a sizable number of members to prevent the Senate from functioning until a bill they oppose is withdrawn from the floor or amended to make it satisfactory to them. Such a filibuster only takes place, of course, when the senators know that the legislation to which they object would be approved if it came to a vote. Their aim, therefore, is to hold the floor indefinitely in order to prevent a vote from being taken. Lengthy speeches are designed to convey one simple thought: until the objectionable bill is laid aside or modified drastically, the Senate will not be allowed to transact any of its business.

Some say that a filibuster of this type constitutes a senatorial form of blackmail. In its most acute form, it may even pose a threat that vital national functions will have to grind to a halt for lack of funds unless the will of the minority is done.

But the filibuster does not lack for defenders. One of the most effective of them is the columnist, Walter Lippmann. In his customarily cogent manner, Lippmann has defined the issue involved in the quarrel over the filibuster. This is his frame of reference:

> The real issue is not whether measures shall be fully debated. The question is how they can be passed. . . . The . . . question is what are you to do with a minority which is not open to being converted by the debate. Under what conditions should you override it?[9]

Lippmann believes that a determined minority should not be overridden by a simple majority, as opponents of the filibuster

[9] Column reprinted in *Congressional Record,* January 9, 1959, p. A-18 (daily edition).

desire. He considers it sensible to require an extraordinary majority when a significant minority is convinced that a proposed law is hostile to its vital interests. For such a law, he believes, can be readily enforced only if "a very large majority" accepts it.

Lippmann's defense of the filibuster is reminiscent of the doctrine of the "concurrent majority," expounded in the last century by John C. Calhoun. Rule by a simple majority, said Calhoun, made no sense at all in a heterogeneous nation such as the United States. The counting of heads would merely legalize exploitation by the numerically largest interest groups. If a society consisted of four shoemakers and three tanners, for example, crass exploitation by the more numerous shoemakers would be a certainty unless the principles of majoritarian democracy were modified. In any complex society, therefore, it is logical to give each interest group a defensive veto over actions affecting its fundamental concerns.

A serious weakness may be perceived, however, in the attempt by Lippmann and others to defend the filibuster in Calhounian terms. Obviously the filibuster does not protect *all* interest groups, but only those that are supported in the Senate by a significant fraction of the membership. Since a filibuster can be broken by a two-thirds vote, any group that cannot count on the support of more than $33\frac{1}{3}$ per cent of the Senate's members cannot make effective use of the weapon. That was proved in 1962, when a two-thirds vote smashed a filibuster against legislation opening the door to private development of a communications satellite system. Not every determined minority can defend itself or the Nation against laws that it considers undesirable. Only a minority with sufficient votes in the Senate can do that.

The filibuster should not be spoken of in purely abstract or philosophical terms, for in practice it is not a protection that is available on a continuing basis to every minority whose interests are threatened by a tyrannical majority. Rather, there is really only one issue on which the filibuster today seems to offer protection to a minority. That issue is civil rights. And the minority that enjoys the protection is not, of course, the subjugated Negro, but rather the very southern white who is the immediate cause of the Negro's distress. Lippmann, himself an antisegregationist, has admitted this. The rule permitting unlimited debate, he has written, "is in effect a veto, held by the southern states, on Federal legislation dealing with the relations of Negroes and whites."[10]

The veto represented by the filibuster and the threat of the filibuster has allowed southern senators to prevent the enactment of any civil rights legislation to which they have had strong objections, from the end of the Reconstruction until the present day. No bills at all were enacted until 1957, and the two that have been enacted between that year and the present—the Civil Rights Acts of 1957 and 1960—were stripped in the Senate of those provisions to which southern members were really opposed. As long as it requires a two-thirds vote to terminate a filibuster, civil rights legislation will continue to be enacted only with the sufferance of southern senators.

That the filibuster is highly prized by southern whites is only to be expected. It is, however, fervently defended elsewhere as well. Senators from small states look to it as a means by which they can protect their interests in case the large states should ever try to team up against them. Others believe that only the latent power of the filibuster prevents the Senate

[10] *Washington Post,* January 4, 1957. The Senate as a whole has been described even by one of its most enthusiastic admirers as "a southern institution" and as "the South's unending revenge upon the North for Gettysburg." William S. White, *Citadel* (New York: Harper, 1957), p. 68.

from becoming a rubber stamp for the Executive Branch. And in addition there are those who do not mind blocking a Senate majority because, they say, it does not necessarily represent a majority of the Nation.[11]

Cloture

Never was the Senate's tolerance of the filibuster more evident than in 1945, when the Joint Committee on the Organization of Congress was created. At the insistence of the southerners, the Committee was specifically prohibited from making "any recommendations with respect to the rules, parliamentary procedures, practices and/or the precedents of either house. . . ." This was a roundabout way of telling the Joint Committee that it was not to suggest making it easier to invoke cloture, which is the only way it is even theoretically possible to choke off a filibuster.[12]

Cloture is a device sanctioned by Senate Rule XXII for terminating filibusters. Until 1917, the rules provided absolutely no method for accomplishing this end. No matter how many senators wanted to close debate and take a vote, the participants in a filibuster needed nothing more than physical stamina to tie the Senate in knots until it agreed to do their bidding.

But in 1917, a dozen senators waged a filibuster which was so unpopular that it stimulated irresistible pressure for reform. The filibuster was carried on by anti-war senators against a bill allowing President Wilson to arm American merchant ships against German submarines. When the bill was blocked, Wilson directed a stream of invective against the

[11] The arguments for the filibuster are canvassed in Franklin L. Burdette, *Filibustering in the Senate* (Princeton, N. J.: Princeton University Press, 1940), pp. 233-40.

[12] Estes Kefauver and Jack Levin, *A 20th-Century Congress* (New York: Duell, 1947), p. 45.

senators who were responsible. "A little group of willful men, representing no opinion but their own," he raged, "have rendered the great Government of the United States helpless and contemptible." The Senate was "the only legislative body in the world which cannot act when its majority is ready for action." The presidential denunciation excited public opinion to such an extent that the Senate decided to trim its sails before the wind. It proceeded to adopt the first cloture rule in its history.

The rule that was approved in 1917 is almost identical to the one in force today. On several occasions the Senate has altered it, but the changes have not been in any one direction. Indeed, they have tended to cancel each other out. The rule, now as then, provides that cloture proceedings may be initiated by a petition bearing the names of sixteen senators. Two days after the petition is filed, the Senate votes on whether to impose a limitation on debate. If approval is voiced by two-thirds of those present and voting, cloture goes into effect. Under its terms, each senator is bound to confine his further comments on both the bill and any proposed amendments to a single hour.

Although the adoption of the 1917 cloture rule seemed to represent a reform of revolutionary proportions, it soon became evident that appearances were deceiving. In the first ten years of its life, the rule was successfully invoked only four times. After 1927, it remained a dead letter for 35 years, until it was revived in 1962 to throttle the liberal filibuster against the communications satellite bill sponsored by the Kennedy Administration. Never had the cloture rule made it possible to break an anti-civil rights filibuster.

In the course of the years, battle after battle has been fought over attempts to liberalize the rule and make it a little easier to terminate debate. The campaign has involved the Senate in some of the most intricate parliamentary maneuvering of its history. Perhaps the most important struggle took place in 1949. Pro-civil rights senators attempted in that year to close a loophole in the 1917 rule. The Senate in Wilson's time had provided that cloture could be imposed on a *measure,* but not on a *motion to take up a measure.* Only if opponents allowed a bill to be called up for debate before beginning their filibuster could cloture be attempted. But there was no reason for the opponents to be so cooperative. They could start talking at an earlier stage, when a motion was made to bring the bill to the floor. Nothing could then be done, for cloture made it possible only to close debate on a bill, not on a motion to consider a bill.

The liberals sought to erase this distinction in 1949. They succeeded in their effort, but only at a price. For when the Senate agreed to allow cloture on a procedural motion to bring up a measure, it did so as part of a package agreement. There were two other items in the package: henceforth, cloture could be imposed only by a two-thirds vote of the entire Senate membership, not merely those senators present and voting; and cloture could not be imposed at all when the business before the Senate was a proposal to change a rule, such as the cloture rule itself. The effect of this last provision was to freeze the two-thirds requirement into the Senate rules. Any attempt to substitute a majority rule for the two-thirds rule would provoke a filibuster, and that filibuster would not be subject to cloture, regardless of how many senators were ready to vote.

Struggling desperately for some way to extricate themselves from the straitjacket into which they had been laced, the liberals hit on a rather ingenious solution. A provision of the Constitution was their point of departure. The Constitution says plainly that "each House may determine the Rules of its

Proceedings. . . ."[13] The liberals interpreted this as meaning that every two years, when a new Congress comes into being, a majority in each house has the right to adopt new rules by a simple majority vote. It can terminate debate the same way, they maintained. No two-thirds requirement in the Senate could carry over automatically, because that would be denying to a majority in the new Senate its constitutional right "to determine the rules of its own proceedings. . . ." That right would be hollow, they said, if one Senate could bind its successors.

Opponents of this view took the position that there is no such thing as a "new Senate." The Senate, they claimed, is a continuing body. Since two-thirds of its membership is renewed automatically from Congress to Congress, there is never a point in time when an old Senate goes out of existence and a new Senate is born. On this theory, the argument was advanced that even at the opening of a new Congress a simple majority in the Senate does not have the power to bring a matter to a vote.

Nixon vs. *Johnson*

In 1957, Vice President Nixon, in his capacity as President of the Senate, rendered an informal advisory opinion that accepted the theory promulgated by the liberals. The gist of the Nixon opinion was that in each new Congress a current majority of the Senate has the right to adopt its own rules. Since this right is derived from the Constitution itself, Nixon said, it cannot be restricted or limited by rules adopted in a previous Congress.

The liberals, however, were unable to take advantage of this opinion. At the opening of the Eighty-sixth Congress in 1959, they made a major effort to persuade the Senate that it could act on the basis of the Nixon analysis and overhaul the cloture rule. The two-thirds requirement, they said, should be

[13] Article I, Section 5.

trimmed to a simple majority, or at least to three-fifths. Victory was denied them, however, largely through the efforts of the Democratic Majority Leader, Lyndon Johnson, who was later to become President of the United States. Mr. Johnson persuaded the Senate to adopt another "compromise," which was no more beneficial to the liberals than the compromise of 1949 had been. The Johnson proposal called for a return to the pre-1949 formula: it should again be possible to impose cloture on a filibuster against a proposal to change the rules; and two-thirds of those present and voting should be allowed to invoke cloture, instead of requiring the approval of two-thirds of the entire membership. This plan, said Johnson, represented a middle-of-the-road approach that avoided the extreme positions of the northern liberals, who demanded majority cloture, and the southern intransigents, who opposed any change whatever in the rule.

The liberals denounced Johnson's "compromise" on the ground that it would make little difference in the existing situation. On a question as controversial as imposing cloture, they said, few if any senators would absent themselves. Thus "two-thirds of those voting" and "two-thirds of the entire membership" might well turn out to be the same thing. In any event, the liberals noted, the arrangement Johnson wanted to revive had proved almost totally useless during the period when it had been in effect, from 1917 to 1949. But Johnson had the votes, and he won. Some liberals felt that he had struck them a foul blow. Recognizing that there was enough pressure to make *some* revision in the cloture rule inevitable, he had contrived to satisfy the demand for action with the mere appearance of change.[14]

[14] The liberals were further angered by another ingredient of the "compromise": a provision which established the principle that all Senate rules "continue from one Congress to the next Congress unless they are changed as provided in these rules."

In 1961, the liberals tried once more to amend the cloture rule, but with President-elect Kennedy remaining cau-
tiously in the background they failed again.[15] Perhaps the
most futile effort of all to liberalize the rule was made in
1963. Although for the first time a majority of senators went
on record as favoring an easing of the rule, defeat for the proponents of civil rights was virtually guaranteed by the presence in the chair of Vice President Johnson, who as Majority
Leader had labored so long and hard to prevent effective cloture reform. Although the 1960 Democratic platform, on
which he had been elected Vice President, had endorsed majority cloture,[16] Johnson chose to play a familiar role. Instead
of reiterating the Nixon opinion, he held that questions of
constitutional interpretation were for the Senate to dispose of.
By leaving it to the Senate to make the decision, he made it
certain that the decision would not be made. For the constitutional question he put to the Senate was debatable, and
the debate could be ended only by the very two-thirds vote
that the liberals had never been able to muster. The inevitable filibuster developed, and the effort at reform was
dropped.

The events of 1963 were a bitter pill for the liberals to
swallow. For the first time, a clear majority in the Senate had
been ready to vote for reform of the cloture rule. Johnson,
however, had contrived to create a parliamentary situation
in which this majority was helpless. The ironic fact was this:

[15] The story of the 1961 struggle is told in detail by Alan Rosenthal
in a case study prepared for the Eagleton Institute of Politics, *Toward
Majority Rule in the United States Senate* (New York: McGraw-Hill,
1962).

[16] "In order that the will of the American people may be expressed
upon all legislative proposals, we urge that action be taken at the beginning of the Eighty-seventh Congress to improve congressional procedures so that majority rule prevails and decisions can be made after
reasonable debate without being blocked by a minority in either house."

while Nixon was in the chair, a majority could have revised the cloture rule but that majority did not exist; when, on the other hand, a majority was finally pieced together, Johnson was in the chair, and approval by a majority was insufficient.

President Kennedy had remained completely aloof from the struggle over cloture in 1963, as he had done two years earlier. Thus, when the threat of widespread violence over the racial issue later erupted and persuaded him to announce his support for a new civil rights bill, that bill was immediately faced with a filibuster that could be broken only by a two-thirds vote in the Senate. That became Mr. Johnson's problem, too, when he succeeded to the presidency in November 1963. Somewhat belatedly, he had concluded with Mr. Kennedy that only a strong civil rights law could prevent the pent-up resentment of the Negro from tearing the country asunder. But through a supreme irony, the most serious obstacle that the Administration civil rights bill faced was the two-thirds cloture rule that Johnson had worked so diligently to preserve.

Double Standard

To some extent, the pressure on the Senate to liberalize the cloture rule was eased in 1962, when for the first time in 35 years an attempt to terminate a filibuster met with success. The bill that was involved provided for the development of a system of communications satellites by a corporation whose stock would be held on a 50-50 basis by the public and the communications companies. Liberals, who wanted the system controlled by a government agency, attacked the idea of a mixed private-public corporation on the ground that it would give away a tremendously valuable system developed with public funds to a monopoly dominated by the American Telephone & Telegraph Company. Aware of the fact that the votes were available to override their objections, they decided to make use of the filibuster weapon. Although all but one of them[17] objected in principle to obstructionism and wanted to make it easier to impose cloture, they saw no reason to refrain from using the filibuster as long as the conservatives kept it on the books.

The liberal filibuster never had a chance, however, because the leaders of both parties—Senators Mansfield and Dirksen —decided to make the first determined effort in many years to impose cloture. One of the liberals commented on the contrast between the single-mindedness with which the leadership pursued cloture on the satellite bill and the near-absentmindedness with which it would approach a "fight" to impose cloture when civil rights was the issue. Senator Douglas of Illinois made the point this way: "Some members of the Senate think that the right to filibuster is exclusively the property of those who are opposed to civil rights, and that when others engage in extended discussion, they should be immediately cut off."[18] Russell Long of Louisiana was even blunter. What the leadership was unwilling to do for the NAACP, he said, it was happy to do for the AT&T. Liberal bitterness against the leadership was unprecedented. Senator Morse went so far as to disown publicly his own party leader, Senator Mansfield. "I do not believe the Majority Leader," he said at one point. "So far as I am concerned, [he] will never represent me as my Majority Leader in protecting my rights again."[19] At one point there was a near physical clash between two Democratic senators on opposite sides of the issue.[20]

[17] Senator Russell B. Long (D., La.), a son of Huey Long.

[18] *Congressional Record,* August 1, 1962, p. 14215 (daily edition).

[19] Morse subsequently apologized for his outburst. *Congressional Record,* August 1, 1962, pp. 14182-83 (daily edition).

[20] *The New York Times* described Senator John O. Pastore (D., R. I.) laying down the gauntlet to Senator Morse with the words, "Any time,

The massive campaign launched by the bipartisan leadership against the filibuster was successful, and cloture was approved by more than the necessary two-thirds vote. Senator Long expressed fear that a precedent had been set for frequent invocations of cloture in the future. "Imposing cloture upon the Senate," he said, "is somewhat like getting olives out of a bottle. After one gets the first olive out of the bottle, the others come out easily."[21] The same consideration was uppermost in the mind of another southern senator, Richard Russell of Georgia, who favored the satellite bill but refused to vote for cloture. "I'll vote to gag the Senate when the shrimp start whistling 'Dixie,' " he explained.

---

anywhere, any place!" According to the newspaper, "Each man pointed a finger at the other's bristling moustache, but they stopped short of bodily contact." August 16, 1962, p. 14, col. 6 (late city edition).

[21] *Congressional Record,* August 15, 1962, p. 15531 (daily edition). Long provided reporters with an abundance of material sometimes even worthy of his father Huey. He could not resist the urge to recite poetry about the communications satellite:

> This star is here to make a buck,
> It's here for monopoly;
> Tell all poor people they're out of luck,
> A man's got to pay to see.

The Russians, he predicted, would advertise their communications satellites differently:

> Come on, everybody, make your telephone calls for free;
> Look! it's our television program, this ain't pay TV.

Ibid., August 15, 1962, p. 15531. A newspaper reported that Long had composed an additional verse for the Russian version:

> You're listening to the peoples' star,
> It's put here for you and me;
> Don't tune in on that satellite,
> It's owned by AT&T.

Washington Post, August 16, 1962, p. A2, col. 1.

Yet there is considerable doubt about whether the invocation of cloture to rescue the satellite bill made it more likely that cloture would be approved in the future on behalf of a strong civil rights bill. The two types of legislation simply do not have the same status in the Senate.

The filibuster will continue to be an all-important part of Senate procedure as long as it is impossible to bring it to an end by simple majority vote. A three-fifths rule would probably not have too significant an effect on the present situation. According to a 1961 study, on only four occasions since 1917 would a three-fifths vote have made any difference. On the other hand, there were eleven times when a majority cloture rule would have turned defeat into victory.[22]

Trial by Ordeal

When the votes to impose cloture are not to be had, it is virtually impossible to shut off a filibuster. The only other method available is to keep the Senate in session day and night in an attempt to wear out the filibusterers physically. At the time such a drive is in progress, senators may try to make things difficult for the filibusterers by strict enforcement of rules that on other occasions are freely disregarded. For example, a speaker may be required to stand while he is addressing the Senate, instead of being permitted to walk about or even to sit down. In addition, the filibusterer may be deprived of the opportunity to conscript a Senate clerk to read the text of documents he wants to incorporate into his speech.

If the filibuster is being conducted by a large enough group, however, there is only a slight chance that 'round-the-clock sessions will have their desired effect. The filibusterers can make such efficient use of their manpower that no individual

[22] Individual views of Senator Kenneth B. Keating of New York in Rules and Administration Committee Report No. 870 (1961), p. 5.

senator of their number is even subjected to any strain. In 1960, for instance, 18 southern filibusterers followed a battle plan that entitled each of them to a three-day respite after he had spoken for only four hours. Even while one senator held the floor, another would allow him to rest periodically by interpolating lengthy questions.

As a matter of fact, it is the anti-filibusterers who are really subjected to a major physical ordeal when the device of continuous sessions is employed. It is they who must remain within reach 24 hours a day lest the filibusterers, by making the point that a quorum is not present, compel the Senate to adjourn.[23] It is the anti-filibusterers who must sleep on cots in the Senate cloakroom, subsist on sandwiches in the Senate cafeteria, and in general incarcerate themselves on Capitol Hill for days and weeks on end. The filibusterers, of course, will stay away from the Senate floor in droves, in order to help by their absence to push attendance below 51, which is the number required to transact business.

Occasionally it is so difficult to rustle up a quorum that the physical arrest of absentees by the Sergeant-at-Arms will be ordered. In 1942, Majority Leader Alben Barkley persuaded the Senate to adopt this course. The order resulted in dragging one of Barkley's colleagues[24] out of bed at 3:40 a.m. The senator did not speak to Barkley for two years.[25] No arrests were ordered during the 1962 filibuster over the communications satellite bill, but extreme measures were taken to pre-

[23] An adjournment is valuable to the filibusterers, for when the Senate again convenes several time-consuming formalities must take place. Unless there is unanimous consent—and an objector is always available to block that—the Journal of the previous day must be read, for instance, and more time is frittered away by the "Morning Hour," in which senators introduce bills and insert items in the *Congressional Record*.

[24] Senator Kenneth D. McKellar (D., Tenn.).

[25] *Washington Post*, July 29, 1962, p. A1, col. 1.

serve a quorum. During one Saturday session, the leadership had planes commandeered to bring in errant members, and even dispatched a PT boat to return three senators from an atomic-powered merchant ship on which they were cruising.[26]

Senate Debate

When senators are not abusing the rule of unlimited debate to prevent legislation from coming to a vote, they are generally willing to enter into agreements in advance on a cut-off point when discussion will end and voting begin. Such agreements, adopted by unanimous consent, are commonplace. Their use means that the Senate often functions under the same sort of tight limitation on debate as the House. What is more, the time available for debate under a unanimous consent request is normally divided between proponents and opponents of the measure, just as it is in the House.

Even without a unanimous consent agreement, Senate debate is strictly regulated when the issue is whether to disapprove a presidential plan for reorganization of the executive departments. Under several Reorganization Acts, the President is authorized to transfer, consolidate, or even abolish governmental agencies as long as neither house of Congress disapproves the action within sixty days. In this procedural context, a positive expression of congressional disapproval is required to kill a plan submitted by the President. A filibuster would prevent the Senate from blocking the President, and that is a position in which senators never like to find themselves. Provision has therefore been made to limit debate on a disapproval resolution to ten hours, with the time equally divided between those who favor the resolution and those who oppose it.

When the Senate is not operating under limitation of de-

[26] *Id.*

bate, its discussion of bills is significantly different in tone from that which takes place in the House. It is different in that it is more leisurely, and it is different also in that it is replete with non-germane digressions.

Forty per cent of Senate debate is not germane to pending business, according to an estimate by the Legislative Reference Service.[27] When a senator has the floor, he may usually speak on any subject that appeals to him. Moreover, when he gets tired of one topic he may shift gears and start on another. A Washington reporter has described what happened one day in 1962 during what was billed as a great debate on the United Nations. The "deluded crowds" that expected a forensic feast, he wrote, actually heard "one senator pay tribute to the Jewish women of America, denounce the service of hard liquor on the Capitol premises, discuss capital punishment in the District of Columbia, deplore highway construction in park lands, and discuss a California water project. Not a word about United Nations."[28]

The value of Senate debate is diminished still further by what has been described as the tendency on the part of the men "who know the most and wield the most influence [to] speak the least."[29] One succinct explanation for this phenomenon has come from the dean of the Senate, Carl Hayden (D., Ariz.), who has represented his state in Congress since its

[27] "Proposed Amendments to the Standing Rules of the Senate," Hearings before the Subcommittee on the Standing Rules of the Senate of the Committee on Rules and Administration, 87th Congress, 1st Session, June 16, 1961, p. 18.

[28] *The New York Times,* April 7, 1962, p. 9, col. 1 (city edition). In 1963, thirty senators sponsored a resolution to provide for a rule of germaneness in their chamber. Hearings on the resolution were held by the Committee on Rules and Administration. The committee reported out a recommendation that three hours each day be reserved for germane debate. In January 1964, the resolution was adopted by the Senate.

[29] *Wall Street Journal,* February 7, 1963.

admission to the Union in 1912. "When you've got the votes you needn't talk," he has said.

The decline of Senate debate was sharply accentuated as a result of the influence exercised by Lyndon Johnson during his years as Majority Leader. A Washington columnist once summarized Johnson's philosophy of the proper role of debate in the Senate in these words: "You have to work things out in the cloakroom and then when you've got them worked out you can debate a little before you vote."[30] A political scientist who once worked for the former Majority Leader has said that, according to Johnson, "good legislation is not the product of oratory and debate but of negotiation and discussion, designed not to make issues but to find common ground that equal, independent, and dissimilar men could occupy."[31] Whatever may be the merits of the Johnson position, its widespread acceptance has obviously done little for the art of Senate debate and the reputation that the Senate once enjoyed as the greatest deliberative body in the world.

Sparse attendance on the floor is certainly one of the factors that prevent debate in the Senate from approximating the parliamentary ideal. Frequently, the only senators present are those who agree with the speaker's point of view, and thus the questions they ask seldom provide a test of his mettle. The speaker, in fact, can shield himself from hostile questions by simply declining to yield to colleagues on the other side of the issue.[32] Too often, what purports to be a debate is nothing

[30] Marquis Childs, quoted in *Congressional Record*, March 9, 1959, p. 3188 (daily edition).

[31] Ralph K. Huitt, "Democratic Party Leadership in the Senate," *American Political Science Review*, LV (June 1961), p. 341.

[32] The word "yield," which is used in the House as well as the Senate, lends itself to some fairly obvious punning. Congressman Joseph Cannon, the former Speaker of the House, was in his eighties at the time he was involved in the following incident: A lady member of the House,

more than "an exchange of mutually agreeable remarks."[33] Sometimes it is only when the hour for taking a vote approaches and the Senate chamber begins to fill that any real controversy arises.[34]

Brothers Under the Skin

On the rare occasions when true debate does take place, it is unusual for tempers to be lost or passions aroused. In both houses of Congress, members are tolerant of the positions others feel compelled to take in the interests of electoral survival. Under such circumstances, only simulated acrimony is possible. The northern liberal and the southern segregationist who shout at each other in public may in reality be good friends. Each benefits from the verbal brawls in which they engage when reporters are present. The Negroes will applaud the integrationist and vote for him; the southern voter will react in the same manner to the white supremacist. The two congressmen are really involved in a symbiotic relationship. What, indeed, would each do without the other?

But if a political scientist criticizes congressional debates for being nothing but sham battles that seldom change any

---

asked by Cannon if she would be good enough to yield, replied with apparent ardor, "The lady will be delighted to yield to the gentleman from Illinois." Cannon then demanded of one of his colleagues, in a stage whisper that could be heard in every corner of the chamber: "My God! Now that she has yielded, what can I do about it?" Alben W. Barkley, *That Reminds Me* (Garden City, N. Y.: Doubleday, 1954), pp. 97-98.

[33] Donald R. Matthews, *U. S. Senators and Their World* (Chapel Hill: University of North Carolina Press, 1960), p. 245.

[34] *Id.* A Capitol Hill reporter overstated the case only slightly when he defined debate in the Senate as "a procession of senators talking to themselves." When senators really want to talk to one another rather than to themselves, he said, "they get together in a private room or pick up a telephone. [They] do occasionally assemble on the floor, of course, but rarely during a debate." Russell Baker, *The New York Times,* April 7, 1962, p. 9, col. 1.

votes,[35] the rules of both the Senate and House appear to be predicated on the assumption that fratricidal conflict and not debilitating friendliness is the danger that must be guarded against. Accordingly, a speaker is never to address himself directly to another member; instead, his remarks must always be addressed to the presiding officer. Preferably also, a member of Congress never refers to a colleague—or to himself, either, for that matter—by a pronoun. It is never "I," but rather "the senior senator [or the gentleman] from New Jersey"; it is never "you" or "he," but rather "the distinguished junior senator [or the gentleman] from California." A member must be careful lest he become confused and refer immodestly to himself as distinguished.

For words that are unbecoming to a member of Congress, one may be compelled to take his seat. Irony is thus the only course that is open to one who has an utterly irresistible impulse to insult a colleague but is unwilling to pay the price of being called to order. Alben Barkley once advised a freshman senator that if he thought a colleague was stupid, he should refer to him as "the able, learned, and distinguished senator"; if, however, he was certain of his estimate, he should refer to him as "the *very* able, learned, and distinguished senator."[36] There was a time when no such circumlocutions were resorted to. Before the Civil War, for example, this was the way in which Senator Charles Sumner (R., Mass.) once spoke on the Senate floor about a southern colleague:

The Senator from South Carolina . . . has chosen a mistress to whom he has made his vows, and who, though ugly to others, is always lovely to him; though polluted in the sight of the world, is chaste in his sight—I mean the harlot, Slavery. For her, his tongue is always profuse in words. Let her be impeached

[35] Votes are most likely to be changed in debate when the issue is only of peripheral interest to the member and his constituents.

[36] Barkley, *op. cit.,* p. 255.

in character, or any proposition made to shut her out from the extension of her wantonness, and no extravagance of manner or heartiness of assertion is then too great for this senator. . . .[37]

The speech so inflamed a representative who was related to the senator under attack that he assaulted Sumner on the floor of the Senate with blows from which the abolitionist never fully recovered.[38] In the blander era in which we live, congressmen need fear neither physical nor verbal attack. The only serious risk that they run in attending a floor debate is that of being bored. The result is an extremely high rate of absenteeism. Attendance is not impressive even during record votes and quorum calls, when official note is taken of those who are absent. Demands that are made on a congressman's time are endless, and almost to a man members decide that floor attendance is the most expendable item on the list.

Congressional absenteeism is not discouraged even slightly by a statutory provision directing officials of the House and Senate to "deduct from the monthly payment of each member . . . the amount of his salary for each day that he has been absent . . . unless such member . . . assigns as the reason for such absence the sickness of himself or of some member of his family." The statute, which was passed in 1872, remains on the books, but no prospect exists that it will ever be enforced. When Huey Long suggested in 1935 that every senator be compelled to remain in the chamber to listen as he was filibustering against the National Industrial Recovery Act, Vice President John Nance Garner replied: "In the opinion of the chair, that would be cruel and unusual punishment, as forbidden in the Bill of Rights."[39]

[37] Burdette, *op. cit.*, p. 29.
[38] *Ibid.*, p. 30.
[39] *Washington Star*, September 17, 1961, p. 2, col. 2. Senators who were present while Long carried on his 1935 filibuster were treated to quite a

Congressional Record

For interested citizens, for historians, and for congressmen themselves, the only available source for extensive reporting of debates on the floor is the *Congressional Record*.[40] The *Record* is an undertaking in which the Government Printing Office takes justifiable pride, for it is truly one of the miracles of modern publishing. The law requires that daily copies be delivered to every member of Congress by 8 o'clock in the morning. The Printing Office meets the deadline religiously; during non-stop Senate sessions, it even manages to include all proceedings up to midnight. Each issue reports the debates of both the Senate and House.[41] Also included are a handy digest of the contents,[42] announcements of committee

---

show. Among other things, the senator told this story:

> They started to baptize my uncle out in the old milling bottom, and as they led him out, there floated out of his pocket the ace of spades. As he turned around and walked a little further, the king of spades came out, then the queen of spades, and just as the preacher was ready to baptize him, the jack and ten-spot of spades came out. His wife was standing over on the bank. She became frantic and threw up her arms and she said, "Don't baptize him, parson. My husband is lost. He is lost." But the young man was sitting on the bank, and he said, "Hold on, Ma. Don't get excited. If he can't win with the hand he's got there, he can't win at all!"

Edward Boykin, ed., *The Wit and Wisdom of Congress* (New York: Funk & Wagnalls, 1961), p. 190.

[40] The task of recording debate was originally entrusted to a private printing firm. Not until 1855 did the reporters of what was then called the *Congressional Globe* begin to be paid at public expense, and only since 1873 has the enterprise been entirely a governmental undertaking.

[41] Prior to 1961, the proceedings of the Senate always appeared at the beginning of the *Record*, but in that year the House finally won equal billing. Now its proceedings are printed first on alternate days.

[42] Howard N. Mantel, "The Congressional Record: Fact or Fiction of the Legislative Process," *Western Political Quarterly*, XII (December

meetings that are scheduled, brief reports of those already held, and—an almost indescribable Appendix.

It is suggestive that the *Record* contains an Appendix even more voluminous on some days than the report of the floor proceedings. This fact indicates that members do not think the exclusive, or even the primary, function of the *Record* is to report what transpires during plenary sessions of the Senate and the House. They see the *Record* rather as a tool that serves an entirely different purpose: enabling members to circulate to their constituents, with the help of a generous public subsidy, all sorts of material that they hope will improve their election prospects.[43]

The Appendix is ideally suited to this end. What does Congress care if this portion of the *Record* has been called the "national wastebasket"? The slur certainly did not affect the warm feelings harbored by the late Congressman Leon H. Gavin (R., Pa.) for a publication allowing him to defend the weather-forecasting abilities of a groundhog apparently indigenous to his state against the "petty, prevaricating pretenders [who] have pecked peevishly at his position as the pre-eminent prognosticator. . . ."[44] Similarly, it would require more than mere name-calling to persuade congressmen that they should abandon a device conferring on them the opportunity to preserve for posterity local recipes, prize-winning high school essays, editorials from home-town newspapers, and poetry that might otherwise remain unread.[45]

1959), p. 982 (reprinted in *Congressional Record,* January 19, 1960, p. 652).

[43] See discussion in Ch. 1.

[44] *Washington Post,* February 13, 1962, p. A14, col. 5.

[45] Occasionally a member recognizes that this kind of material possesses too much merit to be consigned to the Appendix and will have it published in the body of the *Record* instead. For example, Congressman J. Floyd Breeding (D., Kans.) reported that in honor of Kansas Pancake

A great deal of money is spent on printing the *Congressional Record,* and the voluminous Appendix accounts for no small part of the total. The cost of the average issue of the *Record* is about $16,000. The Public Printer, who is head of the Government Printing Office, has estimated that every page added to the *Record* entails an expenditure of $90.[46] Because of these costs, which continue to rise steadily, Congress has prohibited members from inserting in the Appendix any items that will occupy more than two pages unless they obtain an estimate of the expense from the Public Printer and inform their colleagues of the sum involved when making the necessary request for unanimous consent to print the material.[47]

The inhibitory effect of this provision, however, is almost entirely nonexistent. For one thing, hardly any congressman even dreams of objecting to a request by one of his colleagues to insert an item in the *Record,* regardless of how astronomical the cost; if he acted otherwise, he would be exposing himself to retaliation in kind. Furthermore, when a member wishes to avoid the embarrassment of publicly announcing

---

Day "delicious pancakes made from Kansas high-protein wheat flour [would be served] at either the House restaurant or the House Office Building cafeteria. . . . " Reminding his colleagues that two years earlier "Kansas pancakes were served and they did not last long," he urged them to "come early. . . . " *Congressional Record,* March 5, 1962, p. 3095 (daily edition). In a similar vein, Senator J. Glenn Beall (R., Md.) testily informed his colleagues: "I resent the crabcakes being served in the Senate dining room being called 'Maryland crabcakes.' . . . No Marylander would recognize what is served. . . . Patrons of our dining room should be protected from deception." *Ibid.,* January 18, 1963, p. 593. Three days later, Senator Beall spread on the *Record* a detailed recipe for "some real Maryland" crabcakes, submitted to him by no less an authority than the wife of the Governor. *Ibid.,* January 21, 1963, p. 632.

[46] *Washington Post,* February 13, 1962, p. A1, col. 3.

[47] Mantel, *op. cit.,* p. 986.

the amount of money his insertion will cost, he finds it easy to circumvent the requirement for an estimate by dividing the document being placed in the *Record* into individual sections of shorter length, which he offers in piecemeal fashion in the course of several days or parcels out to friendly colleagues for simultaneous insertion in the *Record* on a single day.

In only one respect has Congress acted to economize on the Appendix: by excluding the large volume of extraneous material it contains from the permanent bound volumes of the *Record*.[48] No one pays any attention to the Public Printer, who has pointed out that complete elimination of the Appendix would mean not only the saving of money but also the availability of additional time for his staff to organize the rest of the *Record* and present it in more readable form.[49] Certainly those congressmen who constitute the 5 per cent of the membership that takes up 80 per cent of the space[50] cannot be expected to campaign very enthusiastically for reform.

Rewriting History

The expense involved in publishing the Appendix is not the only criticism that is made of the *Congressional Record*. A more basic complaint is that, as one senator put it, "the

[48] Interview with Carper W. Buckley, Superintendent of Documents, Government Printing Office, September 19, 1962. The Appendix does appear in the bi-weekly compilations of the *Record,* which merely bind together two weeks' issues of the daily edition. Accompanying this bi-weekly volume is an index for the two-week period.

[49] *Washington Post,* August 3, 1962, p. A2, col. 2.

[50] This is the estimate of Congressman Paul C. Jones (D., Mo.). The same congressman has pointed out that the material inserted in the Appendix by some members costs more to publish than their yearly salary of $22,500. *Ibid.,* February 13, 1962, p. A1, col. 3.

Congressional Record is *not* a record,"[51] for the supposedly verbatim reports of debates frequently bear little resemblance to what actually took place on the floor.

This situation does not arise because those who put out the *Record* are sloppy in their work. On the contrary, there is universal recognition of the great skill demonstrated by each of the 14 reporters for the *Record*. A reporter makes every effort to produce a completely accurate verbatim transcript. For fear that he might not be able to record peripatetic orators with complete fidelity if he were anchored to a stenographic machine, he uses shorthand, so that he may move around easily in the chamber. After five or ten minutes, when he is relieved of floor duty, he reads his notes into a recording device for transcription by a typist. He then reviews the transcript to make sure that it is completely accurate.[52] His skill and efficiency are legendary.

It is precisely the speed with which the typewritten transcript of a speech is produced that opens the door to a practice frowned on by almost everyone—except the congressmen, who are the only ones with power to change it. The speed permits the transcript to be made available for editing by the member before the material has to be set up in type, and the editing is often so extensive that it results in a speech entirely different from the one delivered on the floor.

By statute, the *Record* does not have to contain more than a "substantially" verbatim report of proceedings.[53] The editing practice, however, means that it often falls considerably short of even that modest goal. Permitting members to revise their remarks would not be necessary if the only aim were

[51] Richard L. Neuberger, "The Congressional Record Is *Not* a Record," *The New York Times Magazine*, April 20, 1958, p. 14.

[52] *Ibid.*, p. 95.

[53] Mantel, *op. cit.*, p. 982.

to rescue congressmen from the errors in style, syntax, and grammar with which their speeches are commonly pock-marked, for this function is discharged by employees of the Government Printing Office.[54] The reason why members of Congress insist on their right to edit their speeches is not to perfect the style but rather to alter the content.

Although substantive editing is practiced by senators as well as representatives, it is in the House that the relationship between what is actually said and what appears in the *Record* is particularly tenuous. House custom allows a member to speak on the floor for just one minute and then on the basis of unanimous consent, "revise and extend" the text of his original remarks. Such permission authorizes him to convert the few paragraphs actually spoken on the floor into a major full-length address. When the *Record* appears on the following morning, there is absolutely no way of differentiating between what was spoken and what was later added.[55] Also it is almost always agreed unanimously after a bill is passed that members should have several days to "revise and extend" their remarks on the legislation.[56]

This House practice is sometimes justified on the ground that representatives should be conceded the right to express themselves in print since in a body of 435 members they can-not be permitted the luxury of delivering long speeches on the floor. The need to conserve time in the House is obvi-

[54] Neuberger, *op. cit.*, p. 95. "Once a congressman leaped to his feet in a farm debate [and] said that the time had come to take the bull by the tail and look the situation squarely in the face. As discreetly as pos-sible, the *Record* reporter straightened things out." *Time,* March 21, 1960, p. 63.

[55] Neuberger, *op. cit.*, p. 94. Only when the representative submits the phantom material at a late hour of the day will the speech appear in the Appendix instead of in the body of the *Record*. Mantel, *op. cit.*, p. 985.

[56] *Id.*

ously real. Yet it has been argued by at least two members that this objective could readily be achieved wthout bequeathing a mangled *Record* to the historian. Congressmen John Lindsay of New York and Thomas Curtis of Missouri want to require that words not actually spoken on the floor appear in the *Record* in type of a reduced size. In this way, the House would continue to be spared serious interference with its legislative business, while members would still not be deprived of the opportunity to bring their ideas to public attention.[57]

In the Senate, too, the *Record* does not necessarily reflect what happened on the floor. A senator may read only a portion of his speech and have the remainder printed in regular-size type. Only when he wants to interpolate extraneous matter (such as newspaper articles) will reduced-size type indicate that the material was not read on the floor.[58] And senators, like representatives, may edit their speeches before the *Record* is printed. The late Senator Richard Neuberger of Oregon was the foremost critic of this practice. He wrote of having seen many senators, after a major debate, "virtually rewriting the speeches and reports just delivered on the floor." Neuberger's description was caustic:

Some will totally expunge comments made in the heat of debate that may seem indiscreet or unwise in the cold, gray light of the next dawn and in the inflexible type of the *Congressional Record*. Others will be adding afterthoughts, which may furnish an extra fillip to a reply that was flat or

[57] *Congressional Record*, January 30, 1962, p. 1047 (daily edition).
[58] This practice has been subjected to scathing criticism by Senator Clark of Pennsylvania, who says it compels senators to assail the ears of their colleagues with material they would be happy to insert quietly in the *Record* if that would not bring into play the reduced-type requirement.

ineffective. . . . [A congressman] is evidently the only person on earth who can sigh, "I wish I'd said that," and then actually say it![59]

In an effort to eliminate the make-believe from the *Congressional Record,* Neuberger introduced a resolution that would prohibit members from making changes of a substantial nature in their speeches.[60] The proposal, however, was almost totally ignored. Congressmen are generally more expert with words than men of lesser clay, but they are terrified lest they say something absurd—and be deprived of the opportunity to unsay it. Thus, although colleagues paid eloquent tribute to Senator Neuberger on his death in 1960, they gave no thought to honoring his memory by turning the *Record* into a publication that will not belie its name.

Face Lifting

Congress does appear willing to consider sympathetically some lesser criticisms that have been made of the *Record.* In 1962, for example, the House adopted a resolution authorizing a study of how to improve the appearance and the usefulness of the *Record* by modifying its format, typography, organization, and indexing. Although only comparatively minor and technical subjects would be covered by such a study, the project might nonetheless not be totally lacking in importance. Despite all its imperfections, the *Record* still purveys some information about what Congress is doing, and any innovations that would make it less forbidding to the voter can only be applauded.

Some of the suggestions for improvement are intended to make the *Record* more attractive and readable. At the present

[59] Neuberger, *op. cit.,* p. 14.
[60] *Id.*

time, its design is a triumph of unimaginativeness. There is virtually no variation in the kind or size of type. Anyone who is skimming a debate hastily may well be confused as to whose speech he is reading at a particular moment, since not even a bold-face caption heralds the arrival of a new participant in the discussion. The reader may possibly even blunder into a debate on a completely different subject because, as Senator Neuberger put it, "it requires virtual 20/20 vision to pick out at a glance the headings which separate one topic . . . from another."[61] In addition, a great deal of extraneous material clogs the *Record,* so that it is necessary to wade through a mass of tables, letters, and other inserts in order to get at the actual proceedings. The inserts and Appendix also help to make the daily *Record* so bulky that only compulsive neurotics and professional students of Congress (the categories overlap) will not be discouraged from the start.[62]

All things considered, it is not surprising that the *Record* today has only about 3100 cash subscribers. Part of the reason is that most of the people who want to read it can avoid paying the monthly subscription price of $1.50 by having their congressman place their names on a complimentary list.[63] Undoubtedly, the more significant factor, however, is the singular unattractiveness of the publication. Some years ago, the late Senator Kefauver, who was then a member of the House, had the idea that democracy would be served if the *Record,* with an improved design, were put on sale at

[61] *Ibid.,* p. 95.

[62] The amount of time that those who are addicted to the *Record* must sacrifice to their vice is steadily increasing. While the Eighty-sixth Congress filled only 35,958 pages, the Eighty-seventh set a new record with 42,496 pages. The average page of the *Record* contains about three times as many words as a page of this book.

[63] A senator can give away as many as 100 free subscriptions, while a representative is limited to 68. *Id.*

newsstands throughout the country.[64] A wider distribution would no doubt serve the purpose of helping to create an informed electorate, but the improvements in the *Record* will have to be substantial before Americans start lining up to buy copies.

[64] Kefauver and Levin, *op. cit.*, p. 204.

11

Enactment of Legislation

IN ANY PARLIAMENTARY BODY, mastery of the rules confers substantive power on members who have succeeded in acquiring it. In Congress this is particularly true of the House, where the rules and precedents are as important as they are formidable.

The almost incredible complexity of House procedure is related to the size of the body, for in the absence of carefully delineated procedures a 435-member assembly might soon dissolve into anarchy. In preference to such a state of affairs, the members of the House seem willing to subordinate themselves to a corpus of procedural rules and to the men charged with the responsibility of interpreting and enforcing them.

As the population of the Nation has grown, the size of the House has until recently grown along with it. The practice used to be to enlarge the membership every time a new state was admitted to the Union. In this manner, a body that originally had only 65 members became almost seven times that large.

There are signs, however, that a ceiling has now been imposed. In 1962, Speaker McCormack tried in vain to persuade the House to expand its membership by adding three new seats. His campaign was prompted by the fact that a reapportionment of House seats, based on the census of 1960, was about to go into effect. Under the reapportionment, the number of representatives from the Speaker's own state was to be cut, since Massachusetts' share of the national population had dropped during the decade of the 50's. With the state's Democratic legislature and Republican governor seriously deadlocked over how to redistrict in order to conform with the new apportionment, the danger existed that all candidates for the House from Massachusetts—including Speaker McCormack—would be compelled to run on a state-wide basis.[1]

Since McCormack did not relish this prospect, he urged the House to approve an expansion that would have the effect of permitting the Massachusetts delegation to remain at full strength. He argued that an increase in the size of the House was warranted because two new states—Alaska and Hawaii—had recently been admitted to the Union. But the McCormack proposal foundered, for representatives were confused as to how its adoption would affect states in which redistricting had already taken place in obedience to the reapportionment that the Speaker wanted to upset.

Even without adding any new members, however, the House is already so large and its procedures so complex that whoever presides over its deliberations must be thoroughly conversant with its rules and precedents. Senate procedures are a model of simplicity by comparison: the job of presiding over a Senate debate can be performed by any member, and

[1] When a state gains or loses seats in the House as a result of a reapportionment, its legislature is expected to pass a redistricting law before the next election. If it fails to do so, any additional representatives to which the state is entitled must run "at large" (on a state-wide basis), while if it has lost representation all the seats it still retains must be filled in a state-wide election.

since it is nothing but a time-consuming chore it is usually given to freshmen. That rarely happens in the House.

The question of who shall occupy the chair during proceedings of the House and Senate arises even though the Constitution makes provision for presiding officers—the Speaker in the case of the House, and the Vice President of the United States in the case of the Senate. For in the House the Speaker does not preside when the Committee of the Whole is meeting (which is the case about 90 per cent of the time) and is not always present when the House convenes. And the daily meetings of the Senate are often too lengthy for one to expect the Vice President alone, even with his burden shared by a President Pro Tempore, to be in the chair at all times.

Presiding Officers

To preside over the Committee of the Whole as it takes up a major bill, the Speaker often selects a senior representative whose political orientation is similar to his own. The member's philosophy is an important consideration because it will inevitably affect the rulings he will make on parliamentary questions possessing substantive significance. For example, the fact that the House operates under a rule of germaneness means that the chairman may have to determine whether certain amendments that are offered on the floor are pertinent to the main purpose of the bill or whether they deal with another subject and must therefore be ruled out of order. Although the chairman will confer with the parliamentarian before making such rulings, it is taken for granted that on matters of high political importance he will be influenced by more than precedents or technical legal interpretations. Nonetheless, the House will seldom vote to reverse the chairman on what purports to be a parliamentary ruling. Since the chairman's word is therefore in a real sense the last word, the Speaker will exercise meticulous care in deciding who he shall be.

On the Senate side, the situation is very different. The rules there are simpler and they restrict the individual member far less. The presiding officer has little to do other than call on senators who ask for recognition. Even this power is more formal than real, since recognition must go to the first senator who addresses the chair. It is not surprising, therefore, that the assignment of presiding over the Senate invariably goes to a freshman. Never is a senator more strongly smitten by pangs of conscience than when he boasts to his constituents that despite his juniority he was singled out to preside over the deliberations of the United States Senate.

Just as temporary occupancy of the Senate chair confers neither prestige nor authority, the officials whom the Constitution[2] designates to preside over the Senate on a regular basis do not by that token wield any appreciable political power. In the same sentence in which the Constitution names the Vice President of the United States as the President of the Senate, it informs him that he "shall have no Vote, unless [the senators] be equally divided." The Vice President, of course, is not even a member of the Senate, and with rare exceptions his ability to influence its actions bears only a formal resemblance to what the Speaker of the House can do. No one has written more scathingly—or more accurately—about the Vice President and the limitations of his role in the Senate than Woodrow Wilson:

> He is simply a judicial officer set to moderate the proceedings of an assembly whose rules he has had no voice in framing and can have no voice in changing. . . . His chief dignity, next to presiding over the Senate, lies in the circumstance that he is awaiting the death or disability of the President. And the chief embarrassment in discussing his office is, that in explaining

[2] Article I, Section 3.

how little there is to be said about it, one has evidently said all there is to say.[3]

The Vice President may not leave the chair to participate in floor debate, and his rulings on points of order and on referring bills to committee are more frequently overturned than those of the Speaker of the House. No wonder that he chooses to spend so little time in the Senate chamber.

The Constitution empowers the Senate to choose a President Pro Tempore, who shall serve when the Vice President is absent or has succeeded to the Presidency. The Senate often chooses the senior member of the majority party to fill this position. A senator with so much seniority is probably already a powerful and influential member of the chamber; adding the title of President Pro Tem to whatever others he may have accumulated does not enhance his importance. For example, Senator Carl Hayden, the President Pro Tem for many years, derives far more of his power from his chairmanship of the Appropriations Committee than from his status as presiding officer.[4]

Enough has already been said about the Speaker of the House[5] to indicate how much more significant he is in the congressional process than either the Vice President of the United States or the President Pro Tem of the Senate. If the Speaker is no longer in a position to exercise the autocratic controls that belonged to him before 1910, his office is still so laden with authority that he seldom covets any other one, except perhaps that of the presidency of the United States. As

[3] Woodrow Wilson, *Congressional Government* (New York: Meridian, 1959), p. 162 (written in 1883).

[4] Congress has provided by law that the President Pro Tem shall be high on the list of those in the line of the presidential succession. He ranks third, preceded only by the Vice President of the United States and the Speaker of the House. There is no regular Speaker Pro Tempore in the House.

[5] Pp. 221 ff.

presiding officer of the House, he can exercise with considerable effectiveness both the power of recognition and the power of appointment: as leader of the majority party in the House, he has favors of considerable worth to dispense; and as a member of the House, he may participate in debate and also cast his vote whenever he chooses to do so.[6]

Planning Ahead

The House, because of both the tight rules under which it operates and the power exercised by the Speaker, customarily uses its time well and keeps abreast of its work. Many days during each session, in fact, it does not even meet, to give the Senate a chance to catch up. On Mondays and Fridays, for instance, it is a rarity for the House to take any votes or transact any important business when it schedules any meeting at all.[7] The leaders will occasionally go so far as to announce an unofficial recess, during which only *pro forma* meetings will be held every three days, to comply with the constitutional provision banning a lengthy adjournment by one house without the consent of the other.[8]

[6] In practice, the Speaker generally votes only in case of a tie. Moreover, some Speakers have followed the general policy of not participating except when the question before the House concerns the essential character of the chamber. Speaker Rayburn, for example, abandoned the chair of the presiding officer on several occasions to speak from the well of the House on proposals to cope with the Rules Committee. Speaker McCormack has elected to take the floor more frequently than his predecessor.

[7] This provision for what amounts to a four-day week end helps accommodate those members who are not too far from their home districts and like to return to them regularly to attend to private business affairs and maintain contact with the voters. Cynics on Capitol Hill refer to these congressmen as members of the Tuesday-Thursday Club.

[8] Article I, Section 5. To accord with the letter of this requirement, the House is called to order every three days and immediately adjourned. A single sentence by the presiding officer is enough to begin the meeting and to end it as well.

But such informal vacations and long week ends come to be a little less frequent when the summer sun begins to beat down on the Nation's Capital. Each year, sometime in July, Congress seems suddenly to discover what everyone else has known all along: that the July 31st adjournment date which is prescribed by the Legislative Reorganization Act will have to be ignored, as it has been since 1956. The session may have to continue right through the summer and autumn and into the winter as well, for Congress has once again fallen hopelessly behind in its work. The 1963 session of the Eighty-eighth Congress did not end until eight days before the 1964 session began.

On any level of inquiry, deplorable consequences flow from this perennial inability to plan ahead. The need to schedule evening sessions to make up for lost time means that congressmen, including the large proportion who are of advanced years, are subjected to considerable physical strain and compelled to remain at their jobs during months when the climate of Washington is anything but salubrious. Some refuse to submit to such an ordeal, but the flight of these few from the city only aggravates the problem of absenteeism. The most damaging consequence of all is that a frantic drive to adjourn leads each house to abandon any pretense of being a deliberative body or even a responsible legislative body. Every extraordinary device is used to stifle debate and hasten action. Bills are ground out on a wholesale basis, with members compelled to vote on many measures they have not even had time to digest. Congressmen admit that they sometimes pass bills in the dead of night without knowing what is in them.

Is there any solution to this problem? The situation could obviously be eased by foregoing or at least curtailing some of the vacations taken by congressmen while the session is still relatively young.[9] At least a little more time could be saved if Congress did not have to serve as the city council of the District of Columbia. Because it refuses to grant home rule to the residents of the Capital City, it must assign a difficult and time-consuming chore to the District Committees of the two houses. While other congressmen concern themselves with atomic energy legislation, foreign affairs, labor problems, and taxation, the members of these two committees are preoccupied with the propriety of stand-up drinking in local bars and an appropriate salary scale for members of the Sanitation Department. Elaborate committee work must be done on these matters, and valuable floor time is consumed when the District Calendar is called in the House and when the Senate deals with District affairs.

The Joint Committee on the Organization of Congress suggested in 1946 that Congress extricate itself from responsibility for District of Columbia business. The recommendation was the obvious one: residents of the Capital should be given the power to conduct their own affairs. Home rule would mean that the District Committees could be abolished, with their functions assumed by elective officials who would be responsible to the people they served.

Congress, however, turned a deaf ear to the home rule proposal. A determined campaign for its adoption would have provoked passionate opposition from southern members. In 1946 the Negro population of Washington was approaching—and since then it has come to exceed—50 per cent of the total. Southern congressmen were fearful that a Negro majority

[9] "If a Republican, the congressman takes Lincoln Week off in February; if a Democrat, he needs a week to praise Jefferson and Jackson. These are followed by an Easter recess, days off to attend the Kentucky Derby and the baseball season opener, a long Memorial Day holiday, and a long July Fourth holiday." Russell Baker, *The New York Times,* August 6, 1962, p. 24, col. 3 (city edition).

would elect Negro public officials. The lift that this would give to Negro aspirations, and the idea of foreign dignitaries being greeted at the National Airport by a Negro mayor, were too outrageous to contemplate. For southern members, of course, these considerations far outweighed the desirability of cutting Congress loose from some of the extracurricular activities preventing it from devoting full time to its legislative work.[10]

To do away with the pre-adjournment rush, it has also been proposed that Congress make better use of the time available in each session, perhaps devoting the first few months exclusively to committee hearings and only then proceeding to plenary sessions. And adoption of a Senate rule requiring all debate to be germane would help, too. It might save time, and it would certainly improve the quality of floor discussion.

Voting on the Floor

No clearly defined point can be discovered in either the House or Senate at which the debate ends and voting begins. Probably the most important voting takes place while debate is still in progress, when decisions are made on amendments that have been offered to a committee bill. The outcome of these votes determines the shape of the bill on which a final verdict will have to be rendered.

Although action on amendments is such an important aspect of the legislative process, it is carried on in the House of Representatives under procedures that assure members of virtual anonymity as they cast their votes. The voting takes place when the House is sitting as a Committee of the Whole. If the members were meeting *as the House,* one-fifth of those present could insist on a roll call vote, in accordance with

[10] The campaign for home rule is especially important to Washington Negroes because the House District Committee is dominated by southerners.

a constitutional provision;[11] when they meet *as a committee,* however, a record vote is not in order. A considerable amount of time is saved because roll call votes may not be demanded. To call the roll takes more than thirty minutes, for after the names of all 435 representatives have been read off, the names of those who did not respond must be read once again. Conserving time, however, is not the only reason why many congressmen appreciate the absence of roll-call votes. A far more basic consideration is involved.

Without roll call votes, a member can conceal from his constituents the actual part he is playing. A bill may have strong backing in his district, but he can safely support an amendment to cripple it, for no official tabulation of that vote will be made. Then, when the Committee of the Whole has finished its work and the House itself takes a publicized roll call vote on the entire bill, he can vote in favor of final passage and thus indicate to his constituents, on the basis of that publicized vote, that he has acted in accordance with their wishes.

Although it is true that some time is saved in the Committee of the Whole by avoiding roll call votes, this point is strictly secondary. If time were really on its mind, the House would have long since installed a system of electrical voting, as a number of state legislatures have done. Through the use of such a device, its members could complete a recorded vote in no more than a few seconds. Electrical voting would take up even less time than the systems presently employed in the Committee of the Whole. Not infrequently three separate votes must be taken today on a single amendment before a decision is considered final. First, the chairman of the Committee of the Whole puts the question to a voice vote, in which the outcome often seems to depend more on lung power than on numbers. A single member may then force a

[11] Article I, Section 5.

division, or standing vote, in which a fairly accurate tabulation may be made. But even that does not always end the matter. On the demand of a mere 20 members—one-fifth of the 100-man quorum in the Committee of the Whole—the chairman must order a teller vote. This is a lengthy and undignified procedure, in which first all those supporting a bill and then all those opposing it march between two members, usually one from each party, who are designated as "tellers." The teller method provides an accurate count without revealing the position taken by each individual member.

It is not unusual for the result of a teller vote to be reversed in subsequent proceedings. This can happen if the parliamentary situation permits a roll call vote on the same question when the House itself meets to pass on the recommendation of the Committee of the Whole. One reason why such switches occur is that typically many members participate in a roll call who did not bother to attend for the teller vote, which perhaps drew only a bare quorum. The extra votes may have made the difference. But there is another and more important reason. The anonymous vote cast in the Committee of the Whole may have reflected the personal thinking of House members, while the vote on a publicized roll call reflects more their perceptions of what constituents want them to do.

The voter is in no position to take steps against such practices of concealment. On one occasion, however, a newspaper chain managed to overcome the secrecy of an important teller vote. In 1935, the Scripps-Howard staff in Washington included a young reporter with an unusual memory for names and faces. During the teller vote on a crucial provision of the Public Utilities Holding Company bill, this reporter sat in the House press gallery and calmly identified each of the 286 representatives who participated. Within forty minutes, newspapers were on the street with a tally of votes that later proved to contain only a single error. Some congressmen shook their fists at the press gallery, but they need not have been too concerned: it was obviously not feasible for such a *tour de force* to become an everyday occurrence.[12]

In the Senate, details of floor proceedings cannot readily be concealed. Because the rules do not authorize any procedure comparable to the Committee of the Whole device, senators work under the conditions prescribed by the Constitution for plenary proceedings whether they are voting on amendments to bills or on the bills themselves. Accordingly, a roll call vote must be taken if one-fifth of the members request it. No one can complain that a great deal of time is being wasted, since only 100 names have to be called instead of the 435 that must be canvassed in the House. Even when no roll call is demanded and a division (or standing vote) takes place, it is not too difficult for reporters in the press gallery to combine their resources and ascertain how each member has voted. The faces of senators are better known than those of representatives, and, even more to the point, there are far fewer of them.

In both the House and Senate, an elaborate system of signals notifies members that a vote is under way. Whether a congressman happens to be in his office, at a committee meeting, in a Capitol restaurant, or even in the Senate swimming pool, he will be informed of what is happening on the floor by an electronic system that makes use of both buzzers and lights. Prior to 1963, there was only a bell system, with the number of rings indicating what was about to take place: a teller vote, a division, a roll call vote, a quorum call, an adjournment, or a recess. Now buzzers have replaced the bells, supplemented in some parts of the Capitol by rows of star-shaped

[12] Estes Kefauver and Jack Levin, *A 20th-Century Congress* (New York: Duell, 1947), p. 63.

lights. To learn what is occurring on the floor, a congressman need only glance at the panel and observe which light is on.

Although voting *in absentia* is not allowed, provision is made to accommodate one who wants his position recorded on a bill though he is unable to be present. Such a congressman may take advantage of a device known as "pairs." Under this procedure, he enters into an advance agreement with a colleague who differs with him on the bill. The agreement is that both members will refrain from voting even if the anticipated absence does not materialize. Thus pairing actually amounts to something almost indistinguishable from absentee voting, for through its use a member can neutralize the vote of someone on the other side just as effectively as if he were present. One who is approached does not have to agree to a pairing request, but courtesy requires a favorable response, and only in extreme circumstances does the party leadership pass the word that no pairing agreements are to be made.[13]

After a vote has been taken, a motion calling for reconsideration is always in order. Such a motion is customarily made right after the result has been announced. Oddly enough, it almost always comes from a member who has voted with the majority and is by no means desirous of upsetting the decision. His motive is quite the opposite. Under the rules, no chamber action is final until there has been an opportunity to reverse it. A prompt motion to reconsider meets the technical requirement while at the same time not subjecting the bill to any real jeopardy. The motion inevitably fails, because almost all the members who took part in the original

---

[13] The kind of pair described above is generally known as a "live pair" to differentiate it from other types of pairing agreements that do not reveal how the parties to them would have voted, and merely constitute announcements of absence.

decision are still on the floor and not enough time has elapsed
for any of them to have changed their minds. From the point
of view of those who support the decision that has been taken,
an immediate vote is far preferable to a period of delay, for
then opponents of the action might be able to rally their
forces and undo the action at a time when many of those
who voted for it are absent from the floor.[14]

While one house is debating and voting on a bill, its members generally act as if the other house did not exist. Seldom
is there any reference to words that were spoken or actions
that were taken on the other side of the Capitol. On the rare
occasions when it is impossible to avoid conceding that Congress is bicameral, a circumlocution will be called into play
to avoid mentioning the proper name of the sister chamber.
The references invariably will be to "the other body." And
even such references will be few and far between.

But after the debate is over and approval of a bill has been
voted by one house, "the other body" can no longer be so
cavalierly ignored. An "engrossed copy" of the bill is printed
on blue paper, and a clerk is commissioned to deliver it to
the second chamber. When the clerk arrives and his presence
is announced, floor proceedings are interrupted to hear him
report that his house has completed action on the bill he
carries with him.

Legislation approved by one chamber has the official status
of an "act," rather than a "bill." No great deference is accorded to it, however, merely by virtue of its new designation.
Like any bill, it is ordinarily referred to committee and begins
to negotiate the same kind of legislative obstacle course that
it had to run in the house where it originated. It must complete its journey before the two-year Congress expires, or else

[14] Bertram M. Gross, *The Legislative Struggle: A Study in Social Combat* (New York: McGraw-Hill, 1953), p. 362.

it will have to begin all over again its struggle to be born.

Because the act is subject to amendment both in committee and on the floor, it will almost surely be revised before receiving the approval of the second house. No legislation, however, may go to the President for final action unless it has been passed in identical form by the two houses. Of necessity, therefore, the House and Senate must harmonize their two bills if what has already been done is not to become an exercise in futility.

Conference Committees

The changes that are made in a bill already passed by one house are ordinarily submitted to the originating house in the form of "engrossed amendments," with a request that they be approved. Only when the changes are minor, however, can approval be expected. What is more likely is that a "conference" of representatives from each chamber will be requested by the house that wrote the original bill. When rejection of the "engrossed amendments" can be taken for granted, the second house may not trouble to go through the motions of seeking concurrence in the actions it has taken. It may instead notify the originating chamber of its amendments and of its intention to insist on them, and itself request a conference.

In the Senate, it is theoretically possible for diehard opponents of the bill to filibuster against the appointment of "managers" to a conference committee,[15] but this happens only rarely. The blocking of a conference is much more common in the House. One of two things has to happen there to allow participation in a conference: unanimous consent must be obtained, or a resolution must be reported by the Rules

[15] Gilbert Y. Steiner, *The Congressional Conference Committee: Seventieth to Eightieth Congresses* (Urbana: The University of Illinois Press, 1951), p. 8.

Committee. By interposing an objection to a unanimous consent request, a single member can therefore reintroduce the Rules Committee at a most critical stage in the legislative process.

The power of the Rules Committee at this point is truly awesome. Both houses have passed legislation on a given subject and the two bills may not even be far apart, but a simple majority on the Rules Committee can assure that nothing will come of all this. Sometimes legislation of the most vital significance is involved. Federal aid to education is an example. In the Eighty-seventh Congress, one unimportant member of the House objected to a conference on an education bill, and it then proved impossible to muster a majority on the Rules Committee in favor of issuing a rule until there was advance agreement to cut out one of the key sections of the measure. Yet the House staunchly opposes adoption of an amendment to its rules permitting conferences to be authorized by a simple majority vote of the membership.

If all obstacles can be overcome and each house expresses willingness to compromise differences on a bill, a House-Senate conference committee is formed and given the task of hammering out legislation that will be acceptable in both chambers. Since the compromise devised by a conference committee will be submitted to each house on virtually a take-it-or-leave-it basis, the conferees are obviously entrusted with enormous power. In all probability, their handiwork will become the law of the land. To be appointed to a conference committee, therefore, is more than an honor; it is a grant of legislative power in one of its least adulterated forms.

Technically, the presiding officer in each house has free rein in selecting the members who will serve on a particular conference committee. His range of choice, however, is actually extremely limited. Custom constrains him to accept the recommendations of the chairman of the legislative committee that originally reported the bill. In the Senate, where the Vice President is always acutely aware that he is very much of an outsider, the members designated by the committee chairman to serve on a conference will always be approved. In the case of the House, the Speaker is not compelled to be an entirely silent partner in the selection of conferees, but only in extreme instances will he be inclined to challenge the recommendations of the chairman. Thus the committee chairman, who occupied such a commanding position at an earlier stage in the legislation's life, again plays a central role. In effect he selects the congressmen who will represent his chamber in the writing of the final bill.

Almost always the chairman will name himself to the conference committee. Almost always, too, he will appoint the ranking majority and minority members of the committee. It is at this point, though, that his effective discretion begins. If he is satisfied that the three members he has selected for the conference committee on the basis of seniority will effectively promote the point of view he favors, he may decide to appoint no others. If not, he may add two, four, or even six members to the three already picked on the basis of seniority. He is not compelled to choose any particular number, since the size of the contingent that is sent to a conference can have no effect on voting strength; the delegation from each house will be entitled to only a single vote, and that vote will be cast in favor of the position approved by a majority within the delegation. More than half of the conferees must be from his own party, but within that limitation the chairman can pick almost anyone he likes. Often he will settle on the senior members of the subcommittee to which the legislation was first farmed out.

The Third House

This system for appointing conferees makes it highly unlikely that a junior member of Congress will ever represent
his house at the time when legislation is being put into final
form. Senator Proxmire of Wisconsin discovered that only
26 of the 64 Democrats in the Senate were serving on conference committees on a particular day which he studied. Many
of the select few were participating in several conferences
at the same time, although 38 Democratic senators had no
assignments at all.

The procedure used for selecting conferees has been subjected to criticism for a second reason. Senator Clark of Pennsylvania has condemned as totally illogical the arrangement
under which a member may be chosen to participate in a
conference and defend a bill passed by his chamber, although he himself may have voted against it on the floor.
What makes him a conferee is his senior status on the standing committee, not a passionate resolve to fight to the death
for the bill his colleagues have passed. Clark thinks it makes
no sense for either chamber to be represented by someone
whose sympathies are really on the other side. As he sees it,
"an attorney must believe in his client's case. If he does not,
he should not take the case." He told the Senate about one
conference he had attended. He had seen how "a proposal
which the Senate had adopted by a Yea and Nay [roll call]
vote was discarded within minutes after the discussion began,
because a majority of the conferees had opposed the action
which the Senate had taken in the first place."[16]

According to the rules, what Clark has seen is not supposed
to happen. The Senate Manual contains a provision that on
each conference committee the majority of the "managers"

[16] *Congressional Record*, September 24, 1962, p. 19306 (daily edition).

from the Senate shall represent the prevailing opinion of their chamber on the bill under consideration. In practice, however, the conferees from one house sometimes retreat from their chamber's position so quickly that it seems their commitment could not have been very firm. Senator Eugene McCarthy (D., Minn.) once said that he had heard of a conference that consumed less than half an hour—and that included the time it took members to get from their offices to the conference room. In McCarthy's view, 27 minutes, portal to portal, was insufficient to convince observers that a real battle had taken place:

> I do not believe that is the way to operate. At least, when we go to conference, we ought to walk slowly on the way . . . and very slowly on the way back, so at least one hour would elapse from the time we sent the conferees to negotiate for a settlement and the time they came back to the Senate to tell us that they could not do anything against the firm stand of the House of Representatives.[17]

The indictment of conference disloyalty should not be overdrawn. Instances exist of members who have declined to serve on conference committees because they could not in good conscience support provisions of a bill enacted by their chamber. Moreover, the membership in either body may once in a while have the temerity to reject a slate of conferees named by the presiding officer.[18] It is usual, however, that protests

[17] *Ibid.,* March 29, 1962, p. A-2490.

[18] "Proposed Amendments to the Standing Rules of the Senate," Committee Print, Report of the Subcommittee on the Standing Rules of the Senate of the Committee on Rules and Administration, 87th Congress, 2nd Session, 1962, p. 5. In 1952, Vice President Barkley's choice of Senate conferees on a tidelands oil bill was challenged by Senator Russell Long of Louisiana on the ground that the members did not in the main represent the prevailing views of the Senate. Long won his point the next day when, at the request of the committee chairman, an additional con-

against the appointment of particular members are withdrawn on assurance by the nominees that, regardless of their private views, they will support faithfully the position taken by their colleagues.

As far as Senator Clark is concerned, such "demeaning public assurances" are worthless, since a bill that must depend on unwilling advocates is in the same plight as "the child ... put to a nurse that cares not for it."[19] Clark would require flatly that a majority of the senators on each conference committee "represent the prevailing view of the Senate in matters in disagreement with the House."[20] A fox, he believes, should not be commissioned to guard the henhouse.

Neither the Senate nor the House, however, has demonstrated any sympathy for the Clark position. It is still true, as it was in 1953, that "many conference committees include members who voted against the bill in their own house and are equally opposed to the version adopted by the other house and are fully committed to having no legislation whatsoever."[21]

If the House or Senate feels strongly enough about a bill it has passed, it may issue instructions to its managers that they are not to retreat. Such a step is not taken very often, because there is general agreement that, unless conferees are free to compromise, their work is unlikely to be productive. Occasionally there are instructions on a selective basis: The conferees may be told, for example, that they are not to accept

feree favorable to the position of the Senate was appointed. "Proposed Amendments to the Standing Rules of the Senate," Hearings before the Subcommittee on the Standing Rules of the Senate of the Committee on Rules and Administration, 87th Congress, 1st Session, June 16, 1961, p. 11.

[19] *Ibid.,* p. 10.

[20] *Congressional Record,* August 31, 1960, p. 17211 (daily edition).

[21] Gross, *op. cit.,* p. 322.

some particular amendment approved in the other chamber. This practice, too, runs into the objection that there must be freedom to give and take, or the outlook for a conference will not be promising.

The right to compromise and trade points is not supposed to mean that conferees can come up with legislation completely different from the two bills they have been asked to harmonize. Their proper function is to seek out middle ground on which both houses can stand, not to explore entirely new territory. Accordingly, conference committees operate under procedures that are intended to restrict the leeway available to them. The basic rule is that they are not to delete material that has been accepted by both houses, and they are not to incorporate into their compromise any material that goes beyond the action of either house. In the event that this rule is violated, the report produced by the conference may be blocked on the floor by a point of order.

The rule does not apply, however, in an important class of cases: those in which the second house has chosen to amend a bill by striking out everything after the "enacting clause"[22] and inserting instead what amounts to a completely new bill. In this situation, when the second house has adopted "an amendment in the nature of a substitute," conferees find themselves almost entirely free agents, for they are at liberty to include in their report any matter which is "a germane modification of subjects in disagreement."[23] Because the members of any conference committee are understandably delighted with such permission to roam far and wide, it is not surprising that those congressmen who may expect ap-

[22] Each bill begins with a standard "enacting clause": "Be it enacted by the Senate and House of Representatives of the United States of America in Congress assembled. . . . "
[23] Section 135 of the Legislative Reorganization Act.

pointment as conferees on a particular measure sometimes maneuver to have their chamber embody its ideas in "an amendment in the nature of a substitute."

Conference committees enjoy such great latitude that they are sometimes characterized as a third house of Congress. Rank and file senators and representatives occasionally experience feelings of complete futility at the realization that conferees can and do completely disregard what has taken place on the floor and write their own bill. Senator J. William Fulbright (D., Ark.) once said sarcastically that Congress could save both expense and trouble by not going through "the archaic ritual of pretended legislation." Instead, it could just have everything settled by conference committees.[24]

Regardless of how broadly conferees interpret their mandate, they can be fairly certain that, if they reach an agreement, the bill they produce will receive quick approval when it is reported back to the floor. Prompt action is assured, because in both houses a conference report is a matter of high privilege: it is always in order to bring it up. Favorable action is almost as sure, because a conference report is not subject to amendment, and must thus be accepted or rejected in its entirety. The large number of significant conference reports that are not brought up until the closing days of the congressional session seldom can receive more than the most cursory review, for members are anxious to adjourn and leave for home. If a congressman does make the point that his chamber appears to have yielded too much, he will generally find it difficult to convert his colleagues to this view. They are usually willing to accept at face value the assurance of the conferees that "it was this bill or nothing."[25] In only an in-

[24] George B. Galloway, *The Legislative Process in Congress* (New York: Thomas Y. Crowell, 1959), p. 321.

[25] Gross, *op. cit.*, p. 324.

finitesimal number of cases are conference reports rejected.[26]
Faced with a choice between the conference report and no bill
at all, congressmen generally accede to the argument that part
of a loaf is better than none.

One of the most serious criticisms of conference committees
pertains to the secrecy of their meetings. At no other point in
the congressional process can so little be learned about why
actions are taken and by whom they are promoted. The committees do not even keep minutes or other formal records.[27]
This situation is made to order for a lobbyist, either from an
executive agency or a private organization. He has only a
small number of congressmen on whom to work, he knows
that what they decide cannot be effectively challenged, and he
has an atmosphere of secrecy in which to campaign. Because
of the absence of publicity, conferees need not fear being
held accountable for what they do. One of the earliest studies
of the conference system declared:

> In the privacy of the conference, mutual concessions may be
> made [involving] provisions which would never pass if con-
> sidered openly in the House or the Senate. The conference
> committee has much power of independent action, but it is
> not held responsible. . . .[28]

The Veto Power

After a bill has been approved in the same form by both
houses, it is printed on parchment and is signed on behalf of
the House by the Speaker, and for the Senate by the Vice
President. A clerk of the chamber in which it was first passed
delivers the document to the White House, where within ten

[26] On September 20, 1962, the House did reject a conference report,
on a compromise college aid bill.

[27] Steiner, *op. cit.*, p. 10.

[28] Ada C. McCown, *The Congressional Conference Committee* (New
York: Columbia University Press, 1927), p. 16.

days the next and perhaps final step will be taken in the bill's passage through the legislative labyrinth.[29]

The President does not have to wait until the official copy is actually delivered before setting in motion the machinery that will help determine the action he will take. The Public Printer, who is head of the Government Printing Office, submits facsimile copies of every "enrolled bill" to the Executive Branch immediately after the original has been printed and referred to the Speaker and the Vice President for their signatures. The copies go to the Bureau of the Budget, which serves as the President's right arm at this ultimate point of the legislative process just as it did when the President first submitted his recommendations to Congress. The Bureau collects the views of interested agencies and also makes its own independent recommendation to the President.

The role of the Bureau of the Budget at the "enrolled bill" stage has expanded greatly in recent years. Presidents Harding, Coolidge, and Hoover sought the advice of the Bureau only on appropriations bills. Franklin Roosevelt instructed the Bureau to assume wider responsibilities, first by screening certain private relief bills and later by examining all "enrolled bills" regardless of their nature.[30]

From the time that Roosevelt took this action in 1938, the

[29] The Constitution requires that Congress submit to the President every positive bicameral action taken, except an agreement to adjourn. Yet the very first Congress initiated the practice of ignoring the President where proposed constitutional amendments were concerned. This precedent is still followed, and amendments are sent directly to the states. Early in the nation's history the courts rejected a challenge to the constitutionality of this procedure. Hollingsworth v. Virginia, 3 Dallas 378 (1798). Congress also disdains to send concurrent resolutions to the President. Gross, *op. cit.*, p. 393.

[30] Richard E. Neustadt, "Presidency and Legislation: The Growth of Central Clearance," *American Political Science Review,* XLVIII (September 1954), pp. 648-49.

Budget Bureau has been in charge of distributing the facsimile copies of "enrolled bills" to interested agencies and of seeing to it that the agencies reported their recommendations while enough time remained for the President to consider them. The Bureau has proved to be a hard taskmaster. It insists that replies be made within 48 hours, and it discourages adopting an "on the one hand, on the other hand" approach. Agencies are told that specific recommendations are expected, for the President must make a decision; an analysis proving that there is equal merit on both sides of the argument is of utterly no value.[31] On the basis of the often divergent views submitted by the agencies, the Bureau of the Budget advises the President as to whether he should approve or disapprove the measure before him. The President, of course, is under no obligation to accept the advice. During his second term, Franklin Roosevelt grew to feel that his advisers in the Budget Bureau were getting too soft. "Tell them to stiffen up," he ordered. On sixteen occasions, he vetoed bills on which the Bureau had submitted a favorable report.[32]

The early Presidents used the veto power only infrequently. Washington rejected but two bills during his eight years in office, and his two immediate successors, Adams and Jefferson, did not turn down a single measure during their twelve years in the presidency. Madison's six vetoes seemed bold indeed.

The theory under which the early Presidents operated was that the veto power should be used primarily, if not exclusively, to prevent Congress from enacting unconstitutional legislation. It was believed particularly that it should be employed by the President in self-defense—to keep Congress from usurping his constitutional power. Alexander Hamilton,

[31] The agency is encouraged to support its recommendation with factual information that the President may want to consider. *Id.*

[32] *Id.*

always a proponent of a strong presidency, said that without this weapon the Chief Executive "would be absolutely unable to defend himself against the depredations" of Congress.[33]

But at an early stage it was anticipated that the veto power could be legitimately employed even when the President perceived no constitutional infirmity in a bill. Hamilton said flatly before the Constitution was ratified that the veto power furnished security "against the enaction of improper laws." The community would benefit, he believed, if the President used his power against potentially harmful bills that Congress had passed either through haste, inadvertence, or design.[34] Starting with Andrew Jackson, Presidents began to embrace the Hamiltonian viewpoint. And though vetoes up to the time of the Civil War were occasionally based on the argument that the legislation was unconstitutional, since that time they have rested almost without exception on policy grounds.[35]

The number of vetoes has risen spectacularly since Washington's time. The acme was reached during the administration of Franklin Roosevelt, who turned down more than 600

[33] Alexander Hamilton, John Jay, James Madison, *The Federalist* (New York: Modern Library, 1941), No. 73, p. 476.

[34] *Ibid.,* p. 477.

[35] A distinguished scholar has offered this explanation for the change:

> For the first seventy years of national life, the most important questions with which Congress had to deal were constitutional. There were wide differences of opinion as to the proper settlement of great fundamental lines of policy. . . . After the war, the nature of the questions before Congress changed. The result of that struggle was to leave permanently in the hands of the general government powers up to that time disputed. Questions as to the administration of the government then became important, and the veto accordingly became a weapon of expediency.

Edward Campbell Mason, *The Veto Power: Its Origin, Development and Function in the Government of the United States, 1789-1889* (Boston: Ginn, 1890), pp. 129-30.

bills.[36] In the course of the years, vetoes came to be used against appropriations bills as well as legislative bills. No President had ever vetoed a tax bill until Roosevelt broke with this precedent in 1944.[37] FDR used the veto power without any feeling that he was trespassing on legislative territory over which Congress was supposed to rule. Instead, he considered the veto, as one analyst has put it, both "an independent and responsible act of participation in the legislative process, and a means of enforcing congressional and agency respect for presidential preferences or programs."[38] The Roosevelt vetoes almost equalled the total number cast by all his predecessors.[39]

When the President vetoes a bill, the Constitution requires him to return it to the house where it originated along with a statement of his objections.[40] The chamber that first passed the bill, adds the Constitution, "shall enter the objections at large on their Journal, and proceed to reconsider [the bill]."[41] If two-thirds of those present do not vote to override the veto, the bill is dead. It is not even sent to the other house, for approval there could make no difference.

Only in unusual circumstances is there much of a chance

[36] Arthur N. Holcombe, *Our More Perfect Union: From Eighteenth-Century Principles to Twentieth-Century Practice* (Cambridge: Harvard University Press, 1950), p. 276.

[37] Gross, *op. cit.*, p. 408.

[38] Neustadt, *op. cit.*, p. 656.

[39] Bailey and Samuel, *op. cit.*, p. 414. A high percentage of presidential vetoes is directed against private bills. In the wake of the Civil War, a large number of questionable private claims bills succumbed to vetoes. Throughout American history, about two-thirds of the vetoes have concerned private legislation. There is seldom enough political force behind the campaigns for private bills to muster the two-thirds vote that is necessary for a veto to be overridden.

[40] Article I, Section 7.

[41] In neither house is it possible to prevent an effort to override a presidential veto by recourse to a filibuster or other dilatory tactics. Action on a presidential veto is given the highest priority. Gross, *op. cit.*, p. 345.

that a vetoed bill will be repassed, "the objections of the President to the contrary notwithstanding," because of the necessity at this stage to obtain a two-thirds vote in favor of the legislation in place of the simple majority that sufficed when the earlier vote was taken. In addition, all the powers of the presidential office are customarily brought into play to spare the Chief Executive the embarrassment of having a bill enacted over his strong and publicly expressed disapproval. Only during a period of the most acute tension between President and Congress are a large number of vetoes overridden. More than one-fourth of the instances in which Congress overcame presidential vetoes took place during the Reconstruction Era feud between Congress and President Johnson. Since the very first Administration, vetoes have failed to stand up in only about one case out of every ten.[42]

Even such an impressive statistic, however, does not do full justice to the effectiveness of the President's veto power. Often the mere threat of a veto, or even the knowledge on the part of Congress that the President is turning over the possibility in his mind, leads to the framing of legislation in accordance with the President's wishes. The Democratic Congresses that were elected during the Eisenhower years, for example, always kept a weather-eye peeled toward the White House when they were seriously interested in the enactment of a bill and not merely in the creation of a campaign issue.

The framers of the Constitution were alert to the possibility that Congress might try to keep the President from exercising his veto by passing legislation he did not like and then promptly adjourning its session. That way the President would have insufficient time to disapprove the bill and send his veto message to Congress.[43] To prevent such high-handed

[42] Edward S. Corwin, *The President: Office and Powers* (New York: New York University Press, 1941), p. 286.

[43] Mason, *op. cit.*, p. 113.

action from succeeding, the Constitutional Convention voted to give the President what is popularly known as a "pocket veto." It provided that any bills passed by Congress during the last ten days of a session would not become law unless the President made an affirmative decision to sign them. No positive action would be required on his part; he would merely have to do nothing, and the bill would die.

Allowing the President to deal with a bill in this manner was no insignificant grant of power. For the pocket veto is essentially an absolute veto, since no congressional majority, however mighty, can overcome it. Ironically, an extraordinarily large number of major bills are subject to the pocket veto: because Congress always lets its work pile up, it must invariably approve dozens of bills in the closing days of a session.

The invulnerability of a pocket veto sometimes makes the President's supporters in Congress try to postpone action on a measure that he opposes if Congress is sure to approve it by an overwhelming majority. When this strategy of delay is successful, the bill dies as the result of a pocket veto instead of being enacted through the overriding of a conventional veto. But Congress can prevent this from happening by prolonging its session for the necessary ten days. For if the President neither signs nor vetoes the bill within that period and Congress remains in session, the measure becomes law without his approval.[44]

Nonetheless, the veto and the threat of the veto are so effica-

---

[44] A President may allow a bill to become law without his signature if: (1) he lacks enthusiasm for it but considers it better than no legislation at all; (2) he disapproves only portions of it (he is presumed powerless to exercise an item veto); or (3) he opposes the bill, but is deterred from exercising a veto by the certain knowledge that there are enough votes in Congress to override. Under such circumstances, the President may issue a statement announcing that he is permitting the bill to become law without his signature and explaining at least some of his reasons.

cious that Congress can seldom succeed in enacting legislation to which the President really objects. Thus presidential frustrations do not ordinarily stem from the necessity of accepting obnoxious legislation, but rather from the inability to obtain passage of desired legislation.

When Congress does approve a measure about which the President is enthusiastic, he may show his pleasure by signing it into law as part of a ceremonial occasion. He may fill his office with Cabinet members and congressmen who were influential in winning approval for the bill. Often he will use a different pen for each letter of his name, so that every guest may carry away a souvenir of the occasion.[45] A President who chooses to dramatize the birth of a new law in this way may invite reporters and photographers to record the event. Considering the number of obstacles that a bill must surmount before it is enacted, it is easy to understand the irresistible urge to celebrate when, at long last, a bill becomes a law.

Publication of Statutes

The original copy of the law, containing the signatures of the Speaker of the House, the Vice President, and—if he has approved it—the President, is submitted by the General Services Administration to the National Archives for safekeeping. The first form in which copies are printed for general distribution is the "slip law"—the text of the statute published as a single sheet or an unbound pamphlet.

A "slip law" is, of course, invaluable for one who must have

[45] Although President Truman lacked a middle name, he still managed to use 26 pens in signing the British Loan Act of 1946. President Kennedy went through 22 pens for the resolution establishing the Arms Control and Disarmament Agency, but to do that he had to make use of his middle name and the precise place where he performed the signing (the Carlisle Hotel in New York City). President Johnson once used 169 pens to sign three bills, an average of 56.3 pens per bill.

immediate access to the contents of legislation, but it is unsatisfactory as a permanent record. The General Services Administration takes care of that by publishing the United States Statutes at Large. In this massive series of volumes are printed the texts of Federal laws in the order in which they were enacted. These volumes are official. Congress itself has provided that they may be used in any court as legal evidence of the laws they contain. A lawyer who wishes to call the attention of a court to a particular legislative enactment will identify the measure in terms of the volume and page on which it appears in the Statutes at Large.

The very exhaustiveness of the Statutes at Large, however, diminishes the usefulness of the work. The legal historian may greatly appreciate a chronological encyclopedia of Federal legislation, but the lawyer requires something quite different from what is offered in this series. The lawyer has to know what the law is at present or what it was at the time of the events in his case. Although he may find a pertinent law in the Statutes at Large, he cannot know whether this legislation was subsequently modified by amendments adopted in a later Congress or whether, indeed, it was repealed outright. For legal purposes, therefore, the bulky volumes of the Statutes at Large leave much to be desired. What the lawyer needs is an up-to-date collection of the laws still in force on a given subject. This function is served by the United States Code.

In the Code, general and permanent laws are arranged topically, so that the lawyer can readily ascertain the current status of the law in any field. The Code is thus indispensable as a research tool. Yet it must be used with care by the practicing lawyer, for it possess only semiofficial status. Although it is prepared by a subcommittee of the House Judiciary Committee,[46] annual supplements are compiled in consultation

[46] The Subcommittee on the Revision of the Laws.

with a private publishing company.[47] No court would presume conclusively that the codifiers' version of the law necessarily coincides with what the law actually is. A Code provision as such is, therefore, only *prima facie* evidence of the law and is subject to rebuttal. Congress, however, has been so impressed with the extent to which the Code has managed to capture the intent of its actions that it has decided to give official status to at least some of the "titles," or sections, of the work. This process began only in 1943,[48] but eighteen of the Code's fifty "titles" have already been enacted by Congress into positive law. These "titles" are now accepted by the courts as proof of the laws they contain.[49]

[47] The West Publishing Co. of St. Paul, Minnesota.

[48] The first edition of the Code itself was published in 1926.

[49] A privately published series, United States Code Annotated, reproduces the provisions of the Code, and explains how they have been judicially interpreted. This series is prepared by the West Publishing Company.

12

Appropriations Process

AFTER SURVIVING all the trials and tribulations of the congressional process, a Federal statute may still remain for all time a complete nullity, its purposes frustrated and its provisions mocked. This lamentable condition will exist unless Congress bestirs itself a second time and appropriates money to finance the program it has approved. The bill that has been enacted into law is only an *authorization*. It signifies approval of a program, but by itself provides no funds for putting that program into effect. What must come next is an *appropriation*. Countless bills never get the appropriation that would be required to give them meaning. As a general proposition, it is far easier to obtain approval for programs or constituency projects from legislative committees and from Congress as a whole than to convince the Appropriations Committees to recommend that the necessary funds should be provided.

The appropriations process is as complicated—and as important—as all the other parts of the legislative process combined. But it can be described much more briefly at this stage because an appropriation bill goes through many of the same steps as an authorization bill.

It has become a commonplace to say that Congress' power over the Federal purse is the most important source of its authority. During times when the Legislative Branch is overshadowed in many ways by the Executive, it can console itself with this thought: although governmental initiative belongs almost exclusively to the President, he can never act to translate an idea into an activity unless Congress provides the necessary funds. Without "supply" bills, not a wheel of Government can turn. This is so because of the existence of a short and simple constitutional provision: "No Money shall be drawn from the Treasury, but in Consequence of Appropriations made by Law."[1] In the course of its history, Congress has experimented with various devices designed to make the most effective use of this power. But always its aim has been effective supervision of the functions exercised by the Executive Branch.

To a considerable extent, Congress has delegated the power of the purse to its Appropriations Committees. Few committee assignments are more coveted than an appointment to one of them. In a very real way, those who supervise the appropriations process sit as a committee of review over all the other committees of Congress. Legislative committees in both houses may have recommended the enactment of a bill and the two chambers may have approved it, but before the program that has thus been authorized can go into effect it must undergo the scrutiny of the Committees on Appropriations.

Since the House exercises primary responsibility for "supply" bills, a seat on its Appropriations Committee is particularly attractive. Almost never is such a place relinquished voluntarily in favor of membership on another committee. Conversely, congressmen who do not sit on Appropriations

[1] Article I, Section 9.

are in a continuous state of readiness to transfer to the more desirable committee. The members who are selected are seldom freshmen. A recent study of the committee revealed that its members had served an average of more than thirteen years in the House.[2]

The Pork Barrel

Not only because of their seniority but also because of their power, Appropriations Committee members receive considerable deference from their congressional colleagues. One of the first facts of congressional life is that it does not pay to antagonize the committee to which one will someday have to appeal for funds to support a local project. Such projects are commonly referred to as "pork." The word is not inappropriate, for Federal programs that pour money into a constituency and give contracts to its businessmen and jobs to its people are indeed juicy political morsels for the congressman whose state or district will benefit.

So important a part of the legislative process is this kind of legislation that congressmen on the Appropriations Committees almost all want seats on subcommittees dealing with "pork" projects for which their constituencies might be eligible. Probably the most important of these subcommittees are the ones that supervise the Departments of Defense, Interior, and Agriculture, the "civil functions" of the Army, and the scientific and space programs. Each of these subcommittees handles spending programs that have an immediate economic impact on particular geographical areas. The programs that the Army is in charge of, for example, include rivers, harbors, and flood control projects, which always have an exhil-

[2] Richard F. Fenno, "The House Appropriations Committee as a Political System: The Problem of Integration," *American Political Science Review*, LVI (June 1962), p. 314.

arating economic effect on the areas in which they are built.[3] Water projects constructed by the Bureau of Reclamation of the Department of the Interior have a similar effect where they are established.[4]

Every such project represents the use of tax money, obtained from the country at large, to benefit a particular locality and, even more directly, private concerns situated there. Why does a congressman vote to spend money that was taken from his constituents on projects that will be of value only to constituents of other members? The answer, of course, is that he is likely to do so only in exchange for a similar "courtesy" that will redound to the benefit of his own district or state. That is why logrolling—or what congressmen like to call "mutual accommodation"—is the order of the day. It is practiced when the original authorization legislation is being formulated; it is practiced among members of the Appropriations Committee; and it is practiced when the appropriation bill comes to the floor.

Logrolling is not a new phenomenon. In the last century, Woodrow Wilson spoke of how a group of representatives, each one anxious for certain projects in his district,

> put their heads together and confirm a mutual understanding that each will vote in Committee of the Whole for the grant desired by the others, in consideration of the promise that they will cry "Aye" when his item comes on to be considered.[5]

More recently, Senator Douglas of Illinois described public works appropriation bills as the product of "a whole system of mutual accommodations in which the favors are widely dis-

[3] Robert Ash Wallace, *Congressional Control of Federal Spending* (Detroit: Wayne State University Press, 1960), pp. 32-33.

[4] *Ibid.*, pp. 94-95.

[5] Woodrow Wilson, *Congressional Government* (New York: Meridian, 1959), p. 121 (written in 1883).

tributed, with the implicit promise that no one will kick over the apple-cart; that if senators do not object to the bill as a whole, they will 'get theirs.' "[6]

There was a major stir in Congress in 1963 when the president of the Chamber of Commerce joined the critics of pork-barrel legislation by delivering a speech brimming with highly quotable quotes. "Bagmen" and "bribers," for example, were the words he used for congressmen who promise pork in return for votes.[7] Even before the speech was given, congressmen reacted irately, on the basis of an advance text. The Chamber president was called "a man of vast ignorance and unlimited ill will."[8] Senate Majority Leader Mansfield spoke of his "wild statements" and termed them an "affront to the citizens of this Nation."[9] In the same month that the Chamber president delivered his speech, *Life* devoted 14 pages to an exposé indelicately headlined, "Now— See the Innards of a Fat Pig."[10] The halls of Congress again echoed with violent denunciations. One member spoke of the article's "distortions, slanders, and misstatements of fact."[11] Another made a thinly veiled threat to work for revocation of "the heavy subsidies enjoyed by the users of the second-class mail such as *Life* magazine."[12] It is evident that when one speaks of pork, he exposes a sensitive nerve in Congress.

Defenders of the pork barrel and of logrolling are as few as its practitioners are many. The practice has been stigmatized

[6] Donald R. Matthews, *U. S. Senators and Their World* (Chapel Hill: University of North Carolina Press, 1960), p. 100, quoting *Congressional Record,* February 16, 1956, pp. 2300-01.

[7] Address by Edwin P. Neilan, National Press Club, Washington, August 7, 1963.

[8] *Congressional Record,* August 7, 1963, p. 13599 (daily edition).

[9] *Ibid.,* p. 13630 (daily edition).

[10] August 16, 1963, p. 21.

[11] *Congressional Record,* August 15, 1963, p. 13968 (daily edition).

[12] *Ibid.,* p. A-5230.

as "extravagant, wasteful, and occasionally dishonest."[13] It has even been said that the network of "improvements" resulting from the process are not really improvements at all. Certainly there is a real question as to whether national purposes are served "when navigation works on an empty river [are] made possible by harbor works in an empty port."[14] But regardless of how wasteful and irrational such projects may be, the fact that the President does not possess an item veto forces him to make his usual difficult choice between accepting or rejecting a large omnibus bill. On one occasion, when President Eisenhower made the decision to veto a pork-barrel bill, Congress managed to override the veto. It was the first time in the six and one-half years Eisenhower had been President that Congress felt strongly enough about a disapproved bill to pass it over his veto.

The President, however, cannot be compelled to establish a particularly noisome project merely because Congress has authorized it and appropriated funds. If he wants to, he may simply decline to spend the money. But this is not always an easy step for the President to take, since many pork-barrel projects were originally developed with the support of an agency in his own Executive Branch: the Army Corps of Engineers. In practice, the Corps has much closer relations with Congress than with the Department of the Army, of which it is administratively a unit. So solid is its alliance with Congress that any President who proposes a reform of its structure and functions runs up against a stone wall. Powerful support for the Corps comes not only from Congress but also from local contractors, private power companies, and state and municipal officials. These allies of the Engineers have been organized

[13] Stephen K. Bailey and Howard D. Samuel, *Congress at Work* (New York: Holt, 1952), p. 169.

[14] Denis W. Brogan, *An Introduction to American Politics* (London: Hamish Hamilton, 1954), p. 368.

since 1901 in the National Rivers and Harbors Congress, which includes in the ranks of its active members many congressmen and, of course, officers of the Corps of Engineers.[15] The success enjoyed by the organization represents a significant triumph of localism over national need. The Corps has a way of doing exactly the things individual congressmen want, while at the same time professing to be engaged in the pursuit of objectives that will benefit the entire country. Its projects are sometimes meritorious. But that is not the principal reason why Congress approves them.

House Appropriations Committee

The key role in the development of supply bills is played by the House Appropriations Committee. This committee is almost always far more conservative in its attitude toward the expenditure of public funds than the legislative committees of the House. It has, in fact, a tradition that its proper function in the legislative process is to stand at the door of the Federal treasury to guard public funds against raids by legislative committees as well as executive agencies and special interest groups. Even if a congressman has a reasonably tolerant attitude toward public expenditures when he is named to Appropriations, committee tradition is so strong that he tends in time to fall in line with his economy-minded colleagues. But both parties have generally picked congressmen for the Appropriations Committee who are conservative to begin with. Quite consistently, both the chairman and the ranking minority member are unfavorably disposed to Government spending, especially for social and welfare purposes.

[15] Not until 1963 did the organization elect a president who had not been a member of Congress. *Congressional Record,* July 11, 1963, p. 11768 (daily edition). See Arthur A. Maass, *Muddy Waters: The Army Engineers and the Nation's Rivers* (Cambridge: Harvard University Press, 1951), *passim*.

The size of the House Appropriations Committee is greater than that of any other committee of Congress: 30 members of the majority party and 20 members of the minority. The extraordinary size, however, does not constitute a serious impediment to effective functioning, since most of the real work is done by subcommittees.

Committee practice makes it possible for the chairman and ranking minority member of House Appropriations to create subcommittees in their own conservative image, for the chairman selects the majority party members of each subcommittee, and the ranking minority member performs the same function for his party.[16]

The basic document around which the entire appropriations process revolves is the annual presidential budget. Even before that document is submitted to Congress, advance page proofs are made available to the House Appropriations Committee so that its exceedingly complex work may begin at the earliest possible moment. The committee chairman, assisted by his staff, then parcels out the various sections of the budget to the proper subcommittees, and a meticulous, line-by-line examination at once begins.

Subcommittee Hearings

It is at the subcommittee level that hearings are conducted in the House on the appropriation for an agency. The hearings are generally dominated by the subcommittee chairman.

[16] The situation in the Senate is very different. Subcommittee vacancies there are filled strictly on the basis of seniority. A senator who wants to serve on a particular subcommittee will in time earn a place on it, as long as he manages to remain a member of the chamber for a sufficient number of years. The subcommittee he chooses will doubtless be one that is in a good position to authorize the spending of money in his state. A relative degree of profligacy thus tends to characterize the Senate Appropriations subcommittees, while greater penuriousness is the hallmark in the House.

The chairman is looked on by "his" portion of the bureaucracy with feelings compounded of respect and fear: respect for his specialized knowledge of the agencies that must appeal to him for funds, and fear of the cuts he may insist on. The negative feelings of the bureaucrat are often entirely reciprocated by the chairman. Commonly, chairmen look on agency heads as empire-builders who seek to obtain larger and larger appropriations only because they want to expand the realm over which they rule. In view of the mutual disdain that characterizes the relationship between some administrators and the congressmen who handle their appropriations, the annual subcommittee hearings on the budgetary requests of the Executive Branch are often anything but models of harmony and tranquility.

For the agency head, the hearings can be particularly trying. Although the appropriation that the White House requested for his work may be smaller than the amount he favored, the subject for discussion at the hearings is almost invariably not whether the budgetary figure should be increased but by how much it should be decreased. The figure that the President has accepted is treated by the subcommittee as the point of departure for further cuts.

The confrontations before the House Appropriations subcommittees take place in executive session, except in the case of the Subcommittee on the District of Columbia. Neither reporters nor members of the general public are admitted. When this secrecy is attacked, the Appropriations Committee replies that the problem is one of space: since several subcommittees frequently meet at the same time, a large number of commodious rooms would have to be available for public hearings, and the House simply does not have them.

Yet this is by no means the only reason for the secrecy. A feeling exists that executive officials are generally more candid when reporters are not present. There is also less of a temptation—for both witnesses and congressmen—to "play to the galleries." And perhaps most important of all, open hearings, covered on a day-to-day basis by the press, might generate irresistible pressures on committee members to abandon their role as guardians of the public purse. That congressmen prefer arrangements under which they are free from pressure is, of course, understandable. From the viewpoint of individual voters in a representative democracy, however, to insulate congressmen from pressure is to deprive citizens of the right to make their views known to their representatives in an effective manner. A careful student of the House has explained the consequences of secret appropriations hearings in the area of foreign policy:

> . . . Public support for adequate financing of particular foreign policies cannot make itself felt until after the committee has reported. When the committee reports a bill, action comes so swiftly in the House that only weak and ineffective pressure can be exerted to bring the bill into line with the professed foreign policies of the United States if the group . . . has tampered with them.[17]

Even members of the House leadership may sometimes find it difficult to ascertain what an Appropriations subcommittee is doing until it is too late.[18]

In spite of the fact that House Appropriations subcommittees continue to hold only closed meetings, they are now compelled to make transcripts of their hearings available to the members of the House in time for the data to be examined

[17] Holbert N. Carroll, *The House of Representatives and Foreign Affairs* (Pittsburgh: University of Pittsburgh Press, 1958), pp. 144-45.

[18] H. Bradford Westerfield, *Foreign Policy and Party Politics: Pearl Harbor to Korea* (New Haven, Conn.: Yale University Press, 1955), p. 98.

before floor debate takes place. Until 1946, the committee followed the practice of not releasing transcripts of hearings until the bill that had resulted came before the House for debate and decision. Since representatives who did not serve on the particular subcommittee had no access to the information elicited at the hearings, there was little they could debate and only one thing they could decide; to accept the figures recommended by the subcommittee and approved by the full committee. The Legislative Reorganization Act of 1946 put an end to this odd state of affairs. It provided that an appropriation bill could not be considered in either house until both the printed hearings and the committee report had been available for at least three days.[19]

The bill that the House Appropriations Committee brings to the floor is, in an overwhelming number of instances, precisely the one that was recommended by the relevant subcommittee. To a great extent, each subcommittee functions as a completely autonomous unit. None need fear that its recommendations will be overruled. Partly this is so because the full committee is not inclined to substitute its own judgment for that of men it acknowledges as experts. Another factor is that no member of the committee is inclined to invite retaliation against the subcommittee on which *he* serves. Logrolling on the committee is a highly developed art.

The only centralizing influence that makes individual Appropriations subcommittees something less than absolutely sovereign over their territories is the part played by the chairman of the full committee. By keeping open the lines of communication with the chairmen of his subcommittees, he attempts to exercise something of a coordinating function.

[19] Bertram Gross, *The Legislative Struggle: A Study in Social Combat* (New York: McGraw-Hill, 1953), p. 308.

Through his efforts, subcommittees are prevented from going their separate ways in complete disregard of how their individual actions affect the over-all appropriations picture.

Because only the committee chairman can influence the formulation of all governmental appropriations, his place is assured in the hierarchy of the House leadership. Even Presidents take pains to avoid antagonizing him. James B. Reston of *The New York Times* has related an incident that illustrates the respect with which President Kennedy treated Committee Chairman Cannon. In 1962, Cannon asked Vice President Johnson to make a trip to his congressional district in Missouri and deliver an address to a college audience. The Vice President begged off: he had already agreed to speak on the same day in his own state of Texas. Reston continues the story:

> Mr. Cannon was resentful and made his views widely known. As a result, President Kennedy himself called Johnson and said he did not think it wise to ruffle Chairman Cannon, and insisted that Johnson take a special Air Force jet plane to Missouri to meet Cannon's wishes.[20]

Subcommittee chairmen, too, are not to be trifled with. A chairman can even reach over to the other side of the Capitol to punish a senator who has offended him. In 1962, Senator Morse of Oregon made the mistake of opposing an appropriation to finance the establishment of an aquarium in the Nation's Capital. Unfortunately for Morse, the aquarium was a pet project of Congressman Kirwan of Ohio, chairman of the Appropriations subcommittee that deals with the Department of the Interior. In retaliation for Morse's action, Kirwan persuaded his subcommittee to eliminate from its bill all the

[20] *The New York Times,* August 19, 1962, p. E-8, col. 4 (weather edition).

public works appropriations that had been earmarked for the senator's State of Oregon.[21]

Floor Action

A bill reported out by the Appropriations Committee is certain of passage when it comes to the floor, since its outright defeat would be tantamount to a death warrant for all the agencies waiting breathlessly for their funds. Floor consideration takes place under procedures similar to those applying when a legislative committee produces a measure. First comes a period of general debate, with the time controlled by the chairman and ranking minority member of the subcommittee in charge of the appropriation. This is followed by the "second reading," when the bill is read paragraph by paragraph, with its provisions open to debate and amendment under the five-minute rule.

Not too often is an appropriation bill modified in any significant fashion on the floor. For amendments are acted on in the Committee of the Whole, where there are no record votes.[22] This affords an opportunity for individual congressmen to deceive their constituents about what really takes place during the voting on amendments to a bill. Members are free to engage in the familiar congressional practice of doing one thing and letting the folks back home think they are doing quite another: they can vote to retain the cuts made by the Appropriations Committee, and at the same time issue public statements denouncing the committee for pinching pennies in

[21] *Washington Post,* October 12, 1962, p. A16, col. 6. Kirwan was also chairman of the House Democratic Congressional Campaign Committee. See Ch. 9.

[22] Only when such amendments are adopted or on a motion to send the bill back to committee (perhaps with instructions) is there a constitutional right to demand a roll call vote, after the Committee of the Whole rises and the House itself is called to order to act on the bill.

disregard of pressing national needs. These tactics may bring them votes in their constituencies while at the same time permitting them to avoid offending the Appropriations Committee.

The "Upper House"

Only after an appropriation bill has been approved by the House does the Senate begin its committee hearings. These hearings are neither as lengthy nor as comprehensive as those held in the House. One obvious reason is that the soil has already been plowed, first by the House Appropriations Committee and then during floor debate. But there is another reason. Although senators are seldom overly modest about their talents and capabilities, they generally concede to the members of the House Appropriations Committee superior knowledge on the subject of supply bills.

That there should be an "expertise gap" between the two committees is natural. In the House, a member of Appropriations almost never sits on a second committee; he is thus able to devote himself almost exclusively to supply matters, and may make himself a genuine expert, particularly in the subjects with which his subcommittee deals. In the Senate, on the other hand, the smaller membership of the chamber means that it would be impossible to man all the standing committees without giving several assignments to each senator. The result is that the typical senator, serving as he does on a group of committees, is almost always a jack-of-all-trades. If he manages to become master of one, the field in which he makes the grade is seldom appropriations.[23]

Because House action often results in cutting the funds requested for an executive agency, most hearings in the Senate are dominated by a campaign to restore money that has been

---

[23] Ernest S. Griffith, *Congress: Its Contemporary Role* (New York: New York University Press, 1961), pp. 91-92.

eliminated. Members of the Senate Appropriations Committee, in fact, often refer to their hearings as "reclama" sessions, because in them the effort is made to reclaim money that the House has denied.[24]

In effect, the Senate committee sits as something of a board of review. Except where security material is involved, hearings held by its subcommittees are open, and so the Executive Branch—and other interested parties as well—can apply pressure for the restoration of funds eliminated by the House. There is an even more important reason why the Senate is so much more generous with public money than the House: the chairmen of some Senate Appropriations subcommittees also serve as chairmen of the parallel legislative committees and subcommittees which maintain close clientele relationships with the very executive agencies that are requesting more funds.

In trying to explain the prodigality of senators, members of the House attach importance to still another factor. Representatives, they note, must face their constituencies every two years, and do not want to be confronted by the charge that they have voted to squander tax money. A senator, on the other hand, may reasonably expect that long before his six-year term is up his constituents will have forgotten how free and easy he was with the taxpayers' money.

Senators, quite naturally, deride this explanation. It is not they who behave in an unethical way, they say, but rather the House. Since representatives act first on appropriation bills, they can make utterly unconscionable cuts in executive estimates, confident that the Senate can be counted on to put back the money which is needed. The House thus attempts to work both sides of the street: while relying on the Senate to cancel out cuts that would be damaging to the Nation, it man-

[24] Interview with Vorley M. Rexroad, professional staff member, Senate Appropriations Committee, October 11, 1962.

ages at the same time to establish a reputation as the only Federal unit striving constantly to introduce economy into government.

Whatever the explanation, it remains true that in case after case the Senate subcommittee and full committee and later the Senate itself vote to appropriate a considerable portion of the money cut out by the House. So predictable is this sequence of events that cynics insist the Senate is known as the Upper House primarily because of its tendency to "up" the appropriations approved in the other chamber.[25]

After the Senate has acted, a conference committee is called into being to compromise the bills passed by the two houses. The conferees will, perforce, recommend an appropriation that is somewhere between the amounts voted by the House and Senate, and its report will be accepted in both chambers. Thus the end result is usually that the amount requested in the executive budget is decreased, but sometimes not by much more than the padding with which it may have been provided in anticipation of cuts.[26]

[25] J. Leiper Freeman, *The Political Process: Executive Bureau-Legislative Committee Relations* (New York: Random House, 1955), p. 26. At the time Wilson wrote his book on Congress, it was already understood that this would be the pattern. The Senate, wrote Wilson, could be counted on to increase expenditures voted by the House "almost, if not quite, to the figure of the estimate." Wilson, *op. cit.*, p. 114.

[26] Senator Douglas of Illinois has summarized what usually happens:

> One of the common jokes around Washington is that an agency will request more than it actually needs, depending on the House to cut its request by 50 per cent, the Senate to restore the amount to 100 per cent, and the conference committee to compromise at 75 per cent, which is the figure actually wanted by the agency in the first place.

Paul Douglas, *Economy in the National Government* (Chicago: University of Chicago Press, 1952), pp. 58-59, quoted in Wallace, *op. cit.*, pp. 27-28.

A Senate Challenge to the House

Nothing makes senators angrier than to be attacked as free spenders. That was why Senate members of every political hue were enraged when the House in 1962 made precisely that accusation, and in an official resolution, at that. During the preceding ten-year period, the House charged, "Senate conferees have been able to retain $22 billion out of the $32 billion in increases which the Senate added to House appropriations. . . ." The House resolution stigmatized the Senate as "the body consistently advocating larger appropriations, increased spending, and corresponding deficits." Senator A. Willis Robertson (D., Va.) called the resolution "the most insulting document that one body has ever sent to another." Senators know, however, that they will continue to be portrayed as spendthrifts as long as appropriation bills originate in the House and it is left for them to restore vitally needed funds. This realization has sometimes prompted them to inquire whether the framers of the Constitution really intended to subordinate the Senate to the House in the appropriations process.

It is strange but true that the Constitution does not say in so many words what has generally been assumed: that the House has exclusive power to originate appropriation measures. What the Constitution does say is this: "All Bills *for raising Revenue* shall originate in the House of Representatives" [emphasis added].[27] On its face, this provision gives the House priority only on tax legislation, which is designed to raise money, and not on appropriation legislation, which determines how money is to be spent. Nor can it be argued that "bills for raising revenue" was a generic term, embracing appropriation measures as well as tax measures. A statement

[27] Article I, Section 7.

by a delegate to the Constitutional Convention makes it impossible to maintain this position seriously. George Mason of Virginia, in explaining his reasons for refusing to sign the Constitution, objected specifically to the fact that "the Senate [would] have the power of altering all money bills, *and of originating appropriations of money* . . . although they are not representative of the people or amenable to them."[28] The Constitution thus seems to furnish no authority for the contention that only the House may originate appropriation bills.

Right from the start, however, the House became in practice the exclusive originator, and the Senate acquiesced in the arrangement. This situation obtained because at first—and for 75 years—appropriations and revenues were handled in a single package. One committee in the House—Ways and Means—dealt with both the income and the outgo. By considering both at the same time, it was writing appropriations legislation as well as revenue legislation. Although the House decided in 1865 to establish a separate appropriations committee, it continued to be the exclusive source of supply bills. Sporadic protests were to be heard, but no major effort was made until recently to press the Senate's case.

In 1962, the Senate started to insist seriously that it, too, should have the power to originate appropriation bills. It did

[28] Jonathan Elliott, *Debates on the Federal Constitution* (2nd ed., Philadelphia, 1861), Vol. I, p. 494. Quoted by Eli Nobleman in his staff memorandum, No. 88-1-27, to the Senate Committee on Government Operations, April 3, 1963, "Authority of the Senate to Originate Appropriation Bills," published as Senate Document 17 (88th Congress), and also in "Create a Joint Committee on the Budget," Hearings before the Committee on Government Operations, 88th Congress, 1st Session, March 19-20, 1963, reprinted in *Congressional Record,* April 25, 1963, pp. 6684ff. (daily edition). For an opposing view of the issue, see John Sharp Williams, "The Supply Bills," Senate Document 872, 62nd Congress, 1912. Williams argued that the phrase "raising money" was equivalent to the phrase "raising money and appropriating the same."

so, however, only as a tactical response to the House, which had tried to aggrandize further its already dominant role in the appropriations process. The House move and the Senate countermove plunged Congress into one of the most ridiculous situations in its history.

It all started over the question of where to hold meetings of conference committees on appropriation bills. For a century, the meetings had taken place on the Senate side of the Capitol. House members, who had gotten no younger during that century, suddenly registered a complaint against the prevailing practice. They pointed out that during conferences it was frequently necessary for them to trudge back to the House several times to answer quorum calls and roll calls. What could be fairer, they wanted to know, than to hold half the conferences on the House side?

Members of the Senate Appropriations Committee offered to strike a bargain: they would accede to the House request if the House in turn would recognize their right to originate half the appropriation bills. The senators suggested that each year the two houses could alternate in initiating the major supply measures.

The Senate proposal was, of course, totally unacceptable to the House. Not only did the representatives reject it, but they also put forward a demand of their own: the custom of permitting a senator to preside over each conference, they said, should be abandoned in favor of a 50-50 arrangement.

That this was not to be a merely academic argument soon became evident. With various departments and agencies threatened with imminent paralysis unless funds were made available to them, representatives and senators were unable to agree on the ground rules for even a single appropriations conference. The Small Business Administration stopped making loans, the State Department held up issuance of travel funds, and the chief of the Secret Service asked 700 members of his staff to volunteer for work without pay.[29]

If the situation was deadly serious for the executive agencies, it had its comical aspects as far as the general public was concerned. The idea that grown men, and members of Congress at that, could get so exercised over where to hold meetings was absurd enough; but for each of the warring sides to be represented by a champion in his eighties made the whole thing utterly ludicrous.[30] Cartoonists had a field day, portraying the "battle of the octogenarians" in terms of physical combat between the two Appropriations chairmen.[31] Week after week, the newspapers played up the farcical elements of the clash. Indeed, there was not much hard news to report, since each of the two chairmen was content to stand on what he had already said.[32]

The deadlock continued for weeks, but two days before the expiration of the fiscal year both houses approved a stop-gap resolution providing funds to keep the executive agencies going for another month on the same basis as during the past. And within that month a compromise was reached to end the impasse, at least for the Eighty-seventh Congress. Conferences

[29] *Congressional Quarterly Weekly Report,* June 22, 1962, p. 1062.

[30] Clarence Cannon, chairman of the House Appropriations Committee, was 83 years old, and Carl Hayden, his counterpart in the Senate, had passed his 84th birthday.

[31] In actuality, Cannon never tangled physically with Hayden, but when he was in his sprightlier seventies he did have an encounter during an appropriations conference with another ancient, Senator Kenneth McKellar (D., Tenn.). According to a press account, the fight "wound up with the two elderly statesmen chasing each other around the table with gavels as weapons. Nobody was hurt." *The New York Times,* June 25, 1962, p. 17, col. 1 (city edition).

[32] Hayden, particularly, was not very much given to loquacity. Although he participated in a filibuster in 1927, which was his first year in the Senate, he amply atoned for this garrulousness by refraining from taking the floor again for the next twenty years. From 1927 on, he has averaged one formal floor speech every twelve years.

would be held almost midway between the House and Senate wings of the Capitol—in the old Supreme Court chamber, which is only a few yards on the Senate side of the boundary between the two houses. The question of whether a senator or a representative would preside over a particular conference would be left for the chairmen of the two subcommittees in charge of the bill to decide. A joint committee would be created to recommend a permanent solution before the new Congress convened.[33]

In the first conference held under the terms of the agreement, a truly Solomon-like solution to the problem of who was to preside was reached: a coin was tossed. The winner was Representative Albert Thomas (D., Tex.), so history was made as a member of the House was authorized for the first time to chair an appropriations conference. Chairman Cannon of the House Committee did not think that the question of who presided was merely a matter of prestige. Viewing every conference as a tug-of-war between House economizers and Senate spenders, he wanted a representative to preside as often as possible because "the chairman frequently decides what the compromise will be. . . ."[34] The "temporary" arrangement was continued during the Eighty-eighth Congress, although no more coins were tossed and senators were almost invariably chosen to preside. Cannon told reporters: "I don't think another thing will be done."[35]

Joint Committee on the Budget

The House thus has no intention of permitting the Senate to originate appropriation bills. It is determined that this must not come about either directly or indirectly. The in-

[33] A summary of the appropriations dispute appears in the *American Bar Association Journal,* December, 1962, p. 1167.

[34] Quoted in *Congressional Quarterly Weekly Report,* June 22, 1962, p. 1062.

[35] *Washington Post,* January 9, 1963, p. A8, col. 5.

direct method that it fears most is the establishment of a joint committee on the budget. Creation of such a committee has been approved by the Senate on six separate occasions, only to die each time in the House. Senators, however, are growing progressively more enthusiastic about the idea. In 1963, a bill to establish a joint committee was co-sponsored by no fewer than 76 members of the Senate.

Proponents of the joint committee idea believe that under present circumstances Congress is unable to use effectively its power of the purse. For at no point in the appropriations process is a comprehensive look taken at the entire complex of Federal expenditures. The presidential budget, instead of being examined in its totality, is divided into what appear to be its component parts, and each of these is turned over to a subcommittee. But like Humpty Dumpty, the budget will never really be put together again. Each subcommittee holds its own hearings, develops its own bill, steers that bill through the chamber, and continues in charge as a conference committee puts the measure into final form. The parent committee, with a small staff and little more than formal control over its subcommittees, is in no position to exercise much of a coordinating influence. To make matters still worse, the two houses work at cross-purposes with each other. What they eventually agree on is a series of compromises that do not even purport to make sense as details of a master plan.

Advocates of a joint committee on the budget wish to inject the element of planning into the appropriations process. They believe that the committee they favor would do for Congress what the Bureau of the Budget does for the President: create a program that can rationally be defended in its entirety and not merely on a piecemeal basis. They are horrified to see Congress content to make patently irrational slashes in presidential requests instead of basing its budgetary decisions on a carefully formulated over-all plan. Congress is squandering a golden opportunity, they believe, for only the appropriations process offers a chance to review the entire program of the President and assess the specifics it contains in relation to the totality. They look on their campaign as part of a general effort to restore the effectiveness of Congress in the face of the continuing enlargement of the presidency.

Those who seek to establish a joint committee are led by Senator McClellan of Arkansas. The committee that the senator favors would be composed of 16 members of the Senate and House Appropriations Committees. A staff of non-partisan fiscal experts and technicians would study the programs and expenditures proposed by the Executive Branch, and on the basis of their research would provide congressmen with data on which they could rely. McClellan emphasizes that Congress would no longer have to depend on the testimony of Executive officials, "who formulate the programs and present them in a light most favorable to their requests [and] are apt to tell us only as little or as much as they desire to disclose."[36]

The pleas of Senator McClellan and his associates, however, fall on deaf ears in the House. Representatives are convinced that a joint committee would subvert their power in appropriations matters and lead to the breakdown of their exclusive authority to originate supply bills.[37] They are not impressed with Senator McClellan's proposal that 9 of the 16 members of the proposed joint committee should come from the House.

[36] "Create a Joint Committee on the Budget," Hearings, *op. cit.*, p. 2.
[37] This is a manifestation of the serious rivalry that exists between the two chambers—rivalry that is sometimes so intense as to make it difficult to speak meaningfully of Congress as a single institution.

Legislative Budget

The idea of a joint committee on the budget is the most recent of the proposals made to strengthen Congress' power over Federal appropriations. An earlier suggestion was adopted as part of the Legislative Reorganization Act of 1946. The aim was to provide for a degree of coordination among the four committees in both houses that deal with the money the Government raises and the money it spends. The two Appropriations Committees and the two tax-writing committees (House Ways and Means and Senate Finance) were to meet together at the opening of each congressional session. Their purpose would be to produce a resolution establishing guidelines for bills on taxation and appropriations. The resolution would include an estimate of revenues that could be expected in the next fiscal year, and it would also establish a ceiling on appropriations. If receipts were not expected to cover expenditures, the resolution was to recommend an increase in the public debt. Proponents of the procedure said it would allow legislative decisions on fiscal policy to be made with an understanding of all the factors involved, for Congress would have before it a *legislative* budget as an alternative to the *presidential* budget. Clearly the existence of such an alternative would have important political effects: the legislative budget would compete with the White House budget for the support of congressmen who belonged to the President's own party.

The high hopes with which the legislative budget was created were soon dashed. When the procedure was first put into effect in 1947, it was greeted with almost universal dissatisfaction. Complaints were made that the time allowed for adoption of a legislative budget (from the day Congress convened until February 15th) was insufficient. There was also criticism of the unwieldy size of a body combining the memberships of four large committees. Most important of all, however, there was deep anxiety in congressional hearts about the effect that an appropriations ceiling would have on the budgets for favored agencies. In the abstract, congressmen could find no objection to the legislative budget, but they could not reconcile themselves to what it would mean in practice. As a consequence, the first such budget was also the last.

Consolidated Appropriations

The demise of the legislative budget led to the consideration of other methods for reversing the trend toward congressional impotence in the establishment of broad fiscal policies. A new approach was tried three years later. Instead of making an effort to harmonize revenues and appropriations, it was confined to a narrower problem: the fact that under existing procedures each house is able to consider appropriations only in a fragmented form. Since the bills produced by the several appropriations subcommittees come to the floor separately, neither house has an opportunity to achieve perspective in the evaluation of a particular departmental budget. To cope with this problem, it was proposed that Congress be asked to approve not a series of ten or twelve separate appropriation bills but rather one omnibus measure for the entire Executive Branch. In 1950, the omnibus approach became a reality.[38]

Protests, however, were soon heard on all sides. It had been expected, of course, that the subcommittee chairmen would be in considerable pain. But rank-and-file congressmen were upset, too. They felt that the power of an individual member to influence appropriations legislation, not very

[38] See Dalmas H. Nelson, "The Omnibus Appropriations Act of 1950," *Journal of Politics*, XV (May 1953), p. 274.

great to start with, had now been reduced almost to the vanishing point. Under the old system, a member had at least had time to study the budget recommended for an executive department. Now, with a consolidated bill reported out, he would be in the impossible position of having to absorb the equivalent of a dozen bills at one time. Moreover, he would have to complete his study quickly. For the Appropriations Committee would not report out any of its measures until the very last one was ready, and there would thus be no bill on the floor until late in the session. Only a few days might be available to study hundreds of important items.[39]

Faced with such extensive opposition, the omnibus procedure quickly evaporated. It had lasted just as long as the legislative budget: a single year.

Today, far from dealing with one omnibus appropriation measure, Congress must handle a multitude of individual bills as well as an increasing number of "deficiency" and "supplemental" bills. Deficiency bills are emergency calls for help by agencies that have found they are running out of money needed to continue their operations until the end of the current fiscal year. Such a situation may arise because of either unforeseen circumstances or simple mismanagement. Although some congressmen feel that no mercy should be shown, the gentlemanly thing is to throw a life preserver to the drowning man. In practice, therefore, deficiency requests are almost always granted. So many are made each year[40] that the House Appropriations Committee has a special subcommittee to scrutinize them.

[39] Wallace, *op. cit.*, p. 135.

[40] They were already sufficiently common before the turn of the century to impel Woodrow Wilson to comment that it was "as if Congress had resignedly established the plan of making semi-annual appropriations" instead of annual appropriations. Wilson, *op. cit.*, p. 116.

Supplemental bills constitute another type of extraordinary appropriation. A supplemental bill may represent a presidential request that Congress reconsider the appropriation it has already approved for a particular segment of the Executive Branch, or it may be designed to finance a program authorized after submission of the presidential budget.

Chagrin is occasionally expressed in Congress at the appropriation of billions of dollars each year through the indirect methods of "deficiencies" and "supplementals." Yet some members regard these bills with mixed feelings. For under the prevailing system Congress can make political hay by reducing the size of regular appropriations bills, to the accompaniment of cheers from an economy-minded public; then, since some of the money that was cut was necessary for the continuation of important programs, it can act later in the year to restore the funds through supplemental and deficiency bills, to which the press seldom pays as much attention.[41]

"Back-door Spending"

An even more controversial appropriations procedure makes it exceedingly difficult for Congress to obtain a broad overview of the spending requests it is asked to endorse. This practice is usually labelled "back-door spending." Some of its critics charge that it is a patently unconstitutional device, and all of them condemn it as a calculated effort to destroy the influence of the Appropriations Committees.

"Back-door spending" is a method by which a program authorized by Congress may be financed without resort to the Appropriations Committees. This is done by providing for the financing of the program in the original authorization bill. Under ordinary circumstances, an authorization bill touches only incidentally on the subject of money: it does

[41] Douglass Cater, *The Fourth Branch of Government* (Boston: Houghton Mifflin, 1959), p. 56.

nothing more than establish a ceiling beyond which Congress may not go in appropriating funds to finance the undertaking. A "back-door spending" bill, however, deals directly with the question of financing, usually by sanctioning direct borrowing from the Treasury to defray the costs of a program.[42]

Treasury borrowing has been authorized on many occasions for programs that involve the making of Government loans. Such lending programs have been carried out, for example, by the Department of Agriculture, the Housing and Home Finance Agency, and the Veterans Administration. Under a "back-door spending" arrangement, the agency borrows money from the Treasury and in turn lends it out—to veterans who want to purchase homes, for example. When, in time, the lenders pay back the money they have borrowed, the agency will discharge its debt to the Treasury. The theory is that a program financed this way does not require a congressional appropriation because in the long run it is not expected to cost the Government anything. Not only will the Treasury recoup the funds it has lent out, but it will also receive from the agency the accumulated interest that the money has earned. Since there is supposedly no actual spending taking place, defenders of such Treasury borrowing consider the name "back-door spending" a misnomer. The term they prefer is "public debt transactions."

Although the first use of Treasury borrowing to finance a Federal program took place during World War I,[43] not

[42] Another method of financing a program "through the back door" is to provide that the agency administering it may contract for the goods and services it will need. When it comes time to pay the contractors, Congress will have no alternative but to make the necessary appropriation, since the costs will have already been incurred. The Federal urban renewal program is financed this way. Another "back-door" method is the establishment of a revolving fund from which loans may be made on the agency's own authority.

[43] The purpose was to finance the Federal land banks. James Reichley, "Battle at the Back Door," *Progressive,* January 1960, p. 29.

until the New Deal era was the method employed with any degree of frequency. For President Roosevelt and for President Truman after him, the approach was tempting because it offered a way to finance welfare programs approved by Congress without seeking funds from the highly unsympathetic House Appropriations Committee. Liberals were conscious that they were employing questionable means, but they despaired of finding any other way to prevent the members of the Appropriations Committee from frustrating the expressed will of Congress merely on the basis of their own political preferences. The Appropriations Committee, they said, should confine itself to strictly fiscal matters and not become involved in substantive legislative problems on which Congress had already spoken.

In what amounted to an expanding revolt against the power of the Appropriations Committees, Congress resorted to short-circuiting the appropriations process time and time again. "Back-door spending" came to be used to sustain a wide variety of Federal programs. The high point was reached in 1961, when bills involving the colossal sum of $19 billion were enacted with self-financing provisions. Some of the programs authorized loans that were exceedingly risky at best. The *Wall Street Journal* was stating an obvious truth when it said: "No one . . . really expects the Commodity Credit Corporation to recover the money it has sunk into surplus crops."

Congressmen hostile to "back-door spending" always return to one critical argument. When the Appropriations Committees are bypassed, they say, the legislative committees are free to make the most important decisions regarding new Federal expenditures.[44] But the legislative committees, they

[44] Between 1885 and 1920, the authority to report appropriations bills had belonged to the legislative committees. The situation in other years was as follows: (1) until 1865, appropriations—like revenues—were

add, are congenitally incapable of making decisions on the basis of broad national requirements and capabilities. Instead, they are special pleaders for particular interests. As far as the Agriculture Committees are concerned, for example, it is impossible to spend too much money on the farmers; the Veterans Committees feel the same way about veterans; and, most serious of all, the Armed Services Committees have an unbridled enthusiasm for military expenditures. The opponents of "back-door spending" warn that these committees will propel the nation into bankruptcy if they are allowed to make the basic decisions on how much money their "clients" may spend.

Not surprisingly, the chairmen of three important legislative committees—Agriculture, Armed Services, and Banking and Currency—appeared before the House Rules Committee in 1959 to oppose a resolution intended to forbid "back-door spending." The battle lines were thus drawn between the conservative Rules and Appropriations Committees on the one hand and the legislative committees on the other. Decisive opposition to the resolution came from Speaker Rayburn, however, and the attack on "back-door spending" collapsed.

Yet many congressmen were impressed by the argument that they were making themselves the tool of special interests by undermining the authority of the Appropriations Committees. As a consequence, the pendulum that had swung so far in the direction of "back-door spending" in 1961

---

handled by the House Ways and Means Committee; (2) from 1865 to 1885, the newly created House Appropriations Committee framed all general supply bills; (3) since 1920, the present system has been in operation. It was given statutory sanction in the Budget and Accounting Act, which also created the Bureau of the Budget (see Ch. 4) and the General Accounting Office (see Ch. 7).

careened just as far in the other direction in the very next year. At the close of the Second Session of the Eighty-seventh Congress, Chairman Cannon exulted: "Back-door appropriations provisions dropped to a mere fraction of the past several years." The fraction was a small one. In contrast to the more than $19 billion that "back-door" bills involved in 1961, less than one-half billion dollars was provided in this way in 1962.[45]

Although the Appropriations Committees have at least temporarily won their point on the subject of "back-door spending," other aspects of the situation in which they must function continue to be sources of grievous frustration. One of these relates to the common congressional practice of establishing programs that are permanent by their very nature, for this makes them effectively independent of the Appropriations Committees. Such programs include veterans' pensions, compensation payments, the farm price-support program, payments to the Civil Service Retirement Fund, maritime subsidies, and public assistance grants to states. Since the congressional commitment in these programs is essentially contractual, the annual role of the Appropriations Committee is reduced to that of a rubber stamp. It would be as unthinkable for Congress to withhold funds as it would be to refuse money for the payment of interest on the national debt.

Because of such arrangements, the Appropriations Committees find that a significant proportion of the Federal budget is beyond their effective control. They are also burdened by the realization that the President's budget is too vast and complex for them to call into question the basic policy considerations on which it rests. Perhaps that is why members of the Appropriations Committees fluctuate some-

[45] *Congressional Quarterly Weekly Report,* October 13, 1962, p. 22211.

what violently between two extreme modes of behavior. At the one extreme, they sometimes concentrate on the most trivial details of administration when questioning an official of modest rank regarding the budget for a relatively insignificant project. It is not unheard of for questioners to ask about why more long-distance calls were made last year than in the past. But at the other extreme is the "across-the-board" or "meat-ax" technique, through which a predetermined percentage reduction is applied to the budget of an entire agency.

Presidential Frustrations

Largely as a result of the feelings of inferiority under which Congress functions in the appropriations process, it has no intention of weakening its power still further by allowing the President to exercise an item veto on appropriations bills. It is thoroughly familiar with all the arguments. It knows that there is absolutely no logic in compelling the Chief Executive to choose between a bill containing some provisions that are anathema to him and no bill at all; but it is more interested in power than in logic, and it prizes the way in which the existing system permits it to flex its muscles. It knows, too, that the item veto would discourage pork-barrel appropriations and logrolling; but it is quite sure that this would be an undesirable result from the standpoint of the individual congressman. What is more, it believes that the item veto would be positively harmful in at least one way. As an expert on the appropriations process has explained:

> To allow the President to say that one city can have a post office, that another city cannot, [and] that still a third city can . . . is to confer on [him] an extremely broad type of legislative discretion.[46]

[46] Wallace, op. cit., p. 142.

Congressmen fear that the President would use such power to force a member to do his bidding by threatening to veto one of his pet projects. With such strong prejudices against the item veto, Congress is not impressed when it is told that the chief executives of all but nine of the states enjoy this power. It raises an anguished outcry, too, when it hears that the President already possesses somewhat comparable authority in that he may impound appropriated funds which he does not believe should be spent.[47]

The lack of an item veto is only one aspect of the appropriations process that annoys most Presidents, regardless of party.[48] For one thing, the two separate stages of authorization and appropriation often compel witnesses who speak for the Administration to give testimony at four different sets of hearings. The valuable time of officials as high in the Executive Branch as Cabinet members is thus frittered away. For another thing, the Appropriations Committees are almost always far more parsimonious with Federal funds than the President. Not only Mr. Johnson but also Mr. Eisenhower was obliged to do battle with Congressman Otto Passman (D., La.), chairman of the House Appropriations Subcommittee on Foreign Operations.[49]

[47] On this question, see Robert E. Goostree, "The Power of the President to Impound Appropriated Funds: With Special Reference to Grants-in-Aid to Segregated Activities," *American University Law Review,* XI (January 1962), p. 32.

[48] Democratic Presidents are particularly upset by the role of House Appropriations. For in the eyes of the committee there is no higher good than a budget balanced on an annual basis. Little sympathy exists, of course, for the suggestion in liberal economic theory that budgeting should take place over a business cycle instead of a calendar year.

[49] So dedicated an economizer is Congressman Passman that in 1962 he would not permit a painful physical injury to prevent him from leading the floor fight to cut the foreign aid appropriation. Although he had fractured a humerus in four places on the previous day, Passman made

Passman is not the only House Appropriations subcommittee chairman who feels that his chief responsibility is to keep the spenders at bay. Almost all his colleagues think along the same lines. A change in party makes only a relatively slight difference in this connection, for there is little partisanship on the committee. One indication of this is the long tenure of staff members, who retain their positions in spite of shifts in party control of the House. An even more significant indicator of a lack of partisanship is the almost complete absence of minority reports in either the subcommittees or the full committee. In a recent ten-year period, only 5 per cent of the appropriation bills reported to the House were accompanied by minority views.[50]

Presidents might be more impressed with the congressional passion for economy were it not for the generosity, verging on profligacy, that the Legislative Branch manifests when it is appropriating money for its own use. In recent years, Congress has helped itself freely to some $20 million from the public treasury to extend the East Front of the Capitol by 32 feet and thus provide itself with more office space, and has erected a second Senate Office Building (at a cost of $26 million) and a third House Office Building (costing $80 million). The newest House Office Building, named in honor of the late Speaker Rayburn,[51] has been called "one

---

a dramatic entrance on the House floor seated in a wheelchair and wearing a plastic cast on his arm and shoulder. *The New York Times,* October 7, 1962, p. 1, col. 4 (weather edition). He told awed colleagues that he questioned whether he was "in as much pain as about 187 million Americans who are going to have to foot the bill [for the foreign aid appropriation]." *Congressional Record,* October 6, 1962, p. 21498 (daily edition).

[50] Fenno, *op. cit.,* p. 317.

[51] The older House Office Buildings bear the names of Speakers Cannon and Longworth.

of the most lavish construction jobs since the Great Pyramid of Cheops."[52]

Although Presidents can thus compile a long list of grievances against the Appropriations Committees, there is at least one area in which they can have no complaints. The committees are entirely cooperative in furnishing funds for the Central Intelligence Agency, and in helping the White House conceal from the general public and from most congressmen as well the amounts they are appropriating and the purposes for which the funds are to be spent. This feat is performed by padding legitimate budget items, or by peppering the Budget with wholly fictitious items that are really CIA appropriations in other guises. Congress may have thought it was voting funds for wall-to-wall carpeting in the American Embassy in Tokyo, when it was actually financing the purchase of poison-tipped needles for U-2 pilots to carry in their espionage flights over the Soviet Union. Because the funds for CIA are enormous—estimates range to $1 billion—this sleight-of-hand means that each year Congress is dealing with budget items whose integrity is open to the most serious question. Even more important, it means that congressmen know pathetically little about what CIA is doing, either in its intelligence-collecting activities or in the "operations" that it carries out. In spite of the fact that some recent CIA operations have terminated in disaster,[53] Congress shows little desire to bring the activities

[52] Russell Baker, *The New York Times,* August 6, 1962, p. 24, col. 3 (city edition).

[53] The U-2 flight over the Soviet Union on May 1, 1960 wrecked a scheduled summit meeting and ushered in a period of heightened international tension. It also exposed the calculated use of mendacity by the United States Government, which at first denied that an espionage flight had taken place but was then compelled to reveal the truth. Another CIA operation, the invasion of Cuba at the Bay of Pigs in April

of the agency under scrutiny. Proposals to establish a joint committee as something of a watch-dog have never obtained wide support.[54] At present there is only a very informal arrangement under which a few members of the Appropriations and Armed Services Committees are told anything of what CIA is doing. The agency continues spending money on the personal voucher of its Director.[55]

Just as Congress is not inclined to reform the system for appropriating money for CIA, it does not seem ready to make any basic changes in the appropriations process generally. It continues to be divided over the proper jurisdiction of the legislative and appropriations committees. The coexistence of the two types of committees leads inevitably to both duplication and conflict. These tendencies are somewhat abated in the Senate, because there a member may sit on both a legislative committee and the appropriations subcommittee that is responsible for the same general area. Also, the Senate permits certain of its legislative committees to assign several of their members to sit *ex officio* with appropriations subcommittees when bills in their area are being considered. The Armed Services Committee and the Foreign Relations Committee, for example, are represented when appropriations are being voted for the Departments of Defense and State.[56] What is

---

1961, ended in what was probably the most ignominious military defeat for which the United States Government has ever been compelled to assume responsibility.

[54] For details on a recent proposal for a joint committee by Representative John V. Lindsay (R., N. Y.), see *Congressional Record,* August 15, 1963, p. 14265 (daily edition).

[55] The most thorough study of CIA is Harry Howe Ransom, *Central Intelligence and National Security* (Cambridge: Harvard University Press, 1958). Ransom brought his material up to date in a paper, "American Secret Intelligence: Problems of Policy, Organization and Control," delivered at the 1962 annual meeting of the American Political Science Association.

[56] Westerfield, *op. cit.,* p. 114.

more, one of the *ex officio* members will sometimes be named to serve on the conference committee that will develop a compromise from the bills passed by the House and Senate.[57]

If these are real steps toward solving at least one problem, they are nonetheless small and unimpressive in relation to the work that remains to be done to rationalize the handling of appropriations bills.

Supervision of Administration

The strategic position that the Appropriations Committees occupy in the legislative process enables them to play a highly important role in congressional supervision of the Administration. If the committees were content to make lump sum appropriations to large departments and then leave it up to the administrators to determine how to spend the funds, their supervisory power would be only minimal. Although they could threaten to cut a budget total, they would be unable to express themselves effectively on a particular program being carried out by a bureau tucked away in one of the corners of a vast department. To avoid being equipped only with an ax when a scalpel might be needed, the Appropriations Committees often follow the practice of writing reports that describe in minute detail how funds are to be apportioned to the subordinate units of a department.

Such detailed specification has been called "the most positive and flexible single method of legislative control of administration."[58] Its effectiveness stems from the fact that no administrator can afford to forget that anything he does may be examined by the Appropriations Committees. He knows that if his actions displease the committees, he may be pun-

[57] Carroll, *op. cit.*, p. 225. These devices, which bring the Senate's legislative and appropriations committees closer together, also help make the Senate as generous as it is with public funds.

[58] James M. Burns, *Congress on Trial: The Legislative Process and the Administrative State* (New York: Harper, 1949), p. 104.

ished by a budget cut when the next appropriations bill for his agency is drawn up. He pays careful heed, therefore, when he receives unsolicited advice as to how his office should be administered. He may even try to fill vacancies in his agency only with personnel satisfactory to the Appropriations sub-committees with which he must deal. Sometimes the appropriators go so far as to "recommend" individuals for jobs with the agency. They also often issue what amounts to instructions as to how the work of the agency should be carried out—and require periodic reports to assure that their directions are not being ignored.[59]

On occasion, Congress has provided in so many words that certain executive actions were not to be undertaken without advance approval from the Appropriations Committees.[60] Regardless of party, Presidents have been up in arms over such provisions. There have even been threats that legislative vetoes would be ignored. But in the final analysis the Executive Branch has bowed to Congress, sometimes covering up its retreat by means of a face-saving formula.

Such was the case, for example, in 1955 when Congress attached a rider to the big Defense Appropriations bill. The rider gave the Appropriations Committees the right to prevent the Secretary of Defense from closing down certain local installations and activities of the military establishment. President Eisenhower, though violently opposed to the provision, had no real alternative but to sign it into law, for a veto of the entire bill was out of the question and it is generally accepted that the Constitution does not sanction the veto of only part of a bill. According to the rider, the Defense Department would have to justify to the Appropriations Committees any plan to close a facility that had been in existence for at least

[59] *Ibid.*, pp. 105-06.

[60] It has given the same veto power to other committees as well. See pages 170 f.

three years. If within 90 days either one of the committees disapproved the shutdown, the plan would have to be dropped. Although Executive officials at first let it be known that they would ignore the rider as unconstitutional,[61] they did nothing of the sort. Defense Secretary Charles E. Wilson kept the committees fully apprised of all closing plans, and when a committee expressed its disapproval—as was the case in nine instances—there was no defiance. In all nine cases, the Department contented itself with insisting, after it had capitulated, that its decision to cancel the closing plan had been arrived at independently of the Committees' action.[62]

Although the Defense Appropriations rider was repealed in 1956, the general approach it embodied continues to win favor. In 1962, for example, Congress wrote into a foreign aid appropriations bill a provision prohibiting the President from transferring money within the aid program unless the Appropriations Committees were notified 60 days in advance and did not object. Once again presidential defiance was threatened, but once again the Administration was in no position to make good on its threat.

The use of such a congressional veto has been subjected to serious criticism. Perhaps the most interesting argument, and certainly the most ironic, is that the practice actually impairs the ability of Congress to supervise administration effectively. For when an executive official clears an administrative decision with Congress, he is no longer fully responsible for that decision and cannot be held accountable if it turns out to have been unwise.[63] If this criticism possesses merit, Congress

[61] Edith T. Carper, "The Defense Appropriations Rider," in Edwin A. Bock and Alan K. Campbell, eds., *Case Studies in American Government* (Englewood Cliffs, N. J.: Prentice-Hall, 1962), pp. 47-48.

[62] *Ibid.*, pp. 67-81.

[63] Joseph P. Harris, "Congressional Committee Veto of Executive Decisions," paper presented at the 1959 annual meeting of the American Political Science Association.

would be well advised to allow executives to make executive decisions and then take the consequences of their actions.

Another criticism of the committee veto and of congressional interference with administration generally is that only an administrator is close enough to programs to make intelligent decisions as new problems arise. Unless he is given sufficient flexibility, he will be unable to act in response to an ever-changing situation. But the Appropriations subcommittees are not deterred by arguments resting on principles of effective administrative management.

13

Appointments and Treaties

IN TWO FIELDS, the Constitution assigns a role to the Senate alone rather than to the House and Senate together. Both these instances entail participation in executive power rather than the exercise of independent legislative power. They are accordingly described by the Constitution in Article II, which is devoted to the President, instead of Article I, which concerns Congress. In the two cases, the Senate is treated like the small, select council that the framers expected it to be: its "Advice and Consent" are made a requirement for the appointment of Federal officers and for the conclusion of treaties.[1]

For the Senate to confirm a nomination by the President, only a simple majority vote is needed. Approval is required for a vast number of governmental offices, from a Supreme Court Justiceship or membership in the Cabinet down to a postmastership or a commission as a junior military officer.[2]

[1] Article II, Section 2.
[2] For the overwhelming majority of Federal job-holders, confirmation is little more than a formality. The Senate, for example, confirms thousands of military commissions with just a single vote. The President makes the nominations, the Senate confirms them, and then the President makes the appointments and issues the commissions. The

Although the Senate takes very seriously its responsibility for screening nominees to the most important Federal offices, it is a rarity for confirmation to be withheld from one who has been named to a Cabinet position. The theory is that the President should have broad discretion in naming the members of his official family. Cabinet officers, after all, are expected ideally to be extensions of the President; the Chief Executive's unqualified power of removal is an index of the absolute trust and confidence that should characterize the relationship. As a student of the subject has pointed out, unless the President has around him Cabinet members of his own choosing, the country is denied "a definite center of responsibility for what issues from the Executive."[3]

There are, however, instances in which the Senate kicks up its heels and declines to confirm a Cabinet nomination. The first such case occurred in 1834, when President Andrew Jackson was rebuffed in his desire to appoint Roger B. Taney Secretary of the Treasury. In the most recent instance, the Senate in 1959 rejected Lewis L. Strauss, President Eisenhower's choice as Secretary of Commerce.[4] These, however, were extraordinary events. As a rule, a President—especially on first taking office—may feel free to select Cabinet officials according to whatever criteria seem appropriate to him.

---

procedure, however, is not completely devoid of meaning even in these instances. For if a senator from the President's party should object to a particular nominee from his state, the confirmation procedure gives him the opportunity to inform the Senate of his objection and thus prevent the appointment.

[3] Sidney Hyman, " 'With the Advice and Consent—'," *The New York Times Magazine*, July 5, 1959, p. 28.

[4] The only President who was frustrated repeatedly on his Cabinet nominations was John Tyler, who succeeded to the office on the death of William Henry Harrison, in 1841. Tyler, the first President who had not won the position on his own, had almost no political support in Congress. *The New York Times*, June 19, 1959, p. 126 (late city edition).

Similarly, the Senate hesitates to stand in the way of the President regarding the appointment of ambassadors, on the theory that these men are simply the President's personal representatives in the nations to which they are assigned. Accordingly, senators did nothing more than make snide comments when President Eisenhower named ambassadors whose only observable qualification was extreme generosity in contributing money to the Republican Party. The group even included one[5] who could not tell the Foreign Relations Committee the name of the prime minister of the country to which he was to be accredited. The Senate did turn thumbs down on Eisenhower's nomination of Clare Booth Luce as Ambassador to Brazil, but only after Mrs. Luce had insulted a senator and implied that his mental condition left something to be desired.[6]

Committee Hearings

If the Senate tends to resolve all doubts in the President's favor when a Cabinet office or an ambassadorship is at stake, it manifests no such inclination when considering a nominee for a judgeship or a seat on a regulatory agency. There is justification for this difference in attitude. A Cabinet officer or an ambassador is subject to peremptory dismissal by the President if his nomination should prove to have been ill-advised, while a Federal judge serves for life and a member of a regulatory agency is appointed for a fixed term.[7] Searching exami-

[5] Maxwell Gluck, Ambassador to Ceylon.

[6] Mrs. Luce had attached undue significance to the fact that her principal critic in the Senate, Wayne Morse of Oregon, had been kicked in the head by a horse.

[7] Both, of course, may be removed through the impeachment procedure, but an attempt at impeachment is unlikely unless an actual crime has been committed. During the entire history of the nation, only four men—all judges—have been convicted by the Senate after the House voted to impeach them. The procedure is for the House to bring formal

nations in these cases are therefore the order of the day, especially on judicial nominations.

Like a bill, a presidential nomination gets its most thorough screening at the committee level. The President of the Senate refers each nomination to the proper committee: judgeship nominations, for example, are considered by the Judiciary Committee, and ambassadorial nominations by the Foreign Relations Committee. Unless the chairman of the committee resorts to dilatory action to delay a nomination or perhaps to block it permanently, hearings are soon scheduled, either before the full committee or before a subcommittee. The nominee makes an appearance to answer questions regarding his qualifications, the senators from his state may testify, and other witnesses may be heard as well. In the course of time, the committee as a whole will vote on whether to report the nomination to the Senate floor. There, the support of a majority of those voting is necessary for confirmation.

A committee hearing sometimes concerns the nomination of a judge who is already sitting on the bench under a temporary recess appointment. The Constitution gives the President power to make such appointments to Federal offices when vacancies arise during the time that the Senate is in recess. The interim appointee serves, with pay, until the end of the next session of the Senate. If the Senate does not act on his permanent nomination during the congressional session, the individual may be given a second recess appointment, but this time the service must be uncompensated.

No one doubts the power of the President to issue recess commissions to political officers of the Government, including Cabinet members. But the practice of granting interim ap-

---

charges (by a majority vote to impeach) and then for the Senate to sit in judgment as a trial court. For a conviction, a two-thirds vote in the Senate is necessary.

pointments to Federal judgeships has been the object of sharp attack.

The criticism stems from the fact that under the Constitution judges are given life tenure.[8] The obvious intent of the framers was to enhance the independence of the courts by insulating judges from extraneous pressures.[9] A judge, however, can hardly feel secure and free from pressure if he is serving under a recess appointment. Every decision he makes can be subjected to the most minute scrutiny by senators who have the power to block his permanent appointment. He has to be brave, indeed, to withstand the pressure.

In spite of the argument that a recess appointment is in the interest of neither the nominee nor the litigants who appear before him, the device has been used extensively in recent years, even to fill vacancies on the Supreme Court. Within the space of only five years, President Eisenhower placed three men on the Court with interim commissions: Chief Justice Warren, Justice William J. Brennan, Jr., and Justice Potter Stewart. Although all the nominations were subsequently confirmed by the Senate, grave doubts were expressed by members of the Judiciary Committee regarding the propriety of the interim appointments.

One of the most telling criticisms was that the Judiciary Committee could not conduct a satisfactory interrogation of a nominee who was already sitting on the bench. The judge would be clearly within his rights if he declined to answer questions on matters that were pending in his court or might be expected to arise there. On this basis, the Judiciary Committee reported out a resolution in 1960 urging that recess

[8] Article III, Section 1.
[9] Just as a member of the bench is not subject to removal (except through the difficult impeachment route), neither can his salary be diminished. Article III, Section 1.

appointments be made only "under unusual circumstances and for the purpose of preventing or ending a demonstrable breakdown in the administration of the [Supreme] Court's business."[10] The proposed resolution was never acted on, however, and there is still no senatorial recommendation to the President against the use of recess appointments for judges or even Supreme Court Justices. Presumably, Presidents will continue to make such appointments, influenced by the knowledge that every judicial vacancy aggravates congestion in the Federal courts.

In recent years, two developments have contributed to making senatorial review of many presidential nominations somewhat more meaningful than in the past. For one thing, the Senate acts with greater deliberation today than it did at one time. In the early days of the Republic, a nomination was commonly approved on the same day that it was received from the President. Today, by contrast, a long delay is the norm, and it requires unanimous consent to act on a nomination on the very day that a committee has reported it out.[11] The second change in the screening of nominations has made committee consideration the rule rather than the exception. Until 1868, a nomination would be referred to committee only when special circumstances were present.[12] In the run-of-the-mill case, prompt and even casual confirmation was common. But for almost a century now, a completely different policy

[10] Senate Report No. 1893, on S. Res. 334, Calendar No. 1963, 86th Congress, 2d Session, August 22, 1960. The subject of recess appointments is thoroughly canvassed by Louis S. Loeb in a committee print of the House Committee on the Judiciary, "Recess Appointments of Federal Judges," 86th Congress, 1st Session, January, 1959.

[11] George B. Galloway, *The Legislative Process in Congress* (New York: Thomas Y. Crowell, 1959), p. 574.

[12] If an individual was completely unknown, for example, or if there was derogatory information about him, his nomination might go to committee. Another exception was made in the case of jobs that would involve the disbursement of public funds.

has been followed. Only under extraordinary circumstances is a nomination today *not* referred to committee. It takes positive action to bypass the stage of committee consideration, and such action is seldom forthcoming except when a member of the Senate itself has received a presidential nomination.[13]

When a senator has been honored by a nomination, his colleagues act like the members of a club. One senator after another rises to extol the virtues of the nominee in the most fulsome terms, and unanimous confirmation can be expected to follow at once. Never are senators so sure that the President is a pillar of wisdom as when he decides that one of their number merits a judgeship or a high post in the Executive Branch.

If senatorial consideration of most presidential nominations is today more painstaking than it used to be, it is also more widely publicized. Until 1929, the galleries were cleared and the Senate went into executive session when a nomination was laid before it.[14] Today the term "executive session" is still used, but the doors are open to the public and the press.[15]

"Senatorial Courtesy"

Before a President makes any nomination requiring senatorial approval, he consults a senator who is both from the nominee's state and the President's party (unless, of course,

[13] In 1937, the nomination of Senator Hugo Black of Alabama as a Supreme Court Justice was referred to the Judiciary Committee. According to the foremost authority on the confirmation power of the Senate, this was the first time in fifty years that the Senate "had not extended the courtesy of immediate confirmation of the nomination of one of its members." Joseph P. Harris, *The Advice and Consent of the Senate* (Berkeley: University of California Press, 1953), p. 307.

[14] For the first four years of its life, the Senate did all its work in secret. *Ibid.*, p. 249. Now the galleries are cleared only when a senator demands a private session. Strom Thurmond of South Carolina did so in 1963, to talk about missiles and argue for increased defense procurement.

[15] *Ibid.*, p. 255.

both senators from the state belong to the opposition party).[16] He will certainly not fail to do this if the office will primarily involve dealing with the people of the state. Never will he nominate a man whom the senator opposes. In the event that he did, the senator would announce on the floor that the nominee was "personally obnoxious" to him, and his colleagues would immediately rise in their wrath to deny confirmation. This is the practice known as "senatorial courtesy." The President usually does more than merely ask the senator's opinion of a prospective nominee; rather, he actually allows the senator to decide who will receive the nomination.

"Senatorial courtesy" can be traced all the way back to the first term of the first President. Washington made the mistake of nominating one Benjamin Fishbourne to be Naval Officer at the Port of Savannah. When word circulated that Fishbourne was *persona non grata* to at least one of the Georgia senators, the appointment was blocked.[17] A precedent was established that no one had foreseen. Certainly Alexander Hamilton had not anticipated the development. In *The Federalist*, he rested his defense of the President's appointment power on grounds that have been completely undermined by the practice of "senatorial courtesy." The President, said Hamilton, will have "fewer personal attachments to gratify, than a body of men who may each be supposed to have an equal number." Because of this, the President would be "less liable to be misled by the sentiments of friendship and affection."[18] Today it is precisely on the basis of "personal attachments" of one sort or another that the senators of the

[16] In such a case, no consultation is required. In the event that both senators belong to the President's party, the senior member is consulted.

[17] William S. White, *Citadel: The Story of the U. S. Senate* (New York: Harper, 1956), pp. 46-47.

[18] Alexander Hamilton, John Jay, James Madison, *The Federalist* (New York: Modern Library, 1941), No. 76, pp. 492-93.

President's party are usually conceded the right to fill Federal offices in their states.

"Senatorial courtesy," as it actually works out, often means that the senator himself simply rubber-stamps a selection made at a relatively low level of his state's party organization. For a Federal official to be hand-picked by no more exalted a personage than a county chairman is a far cry from the constitutional provision that the President, "by and with the Advice and Consent of the Senate, shall appoint . . . Officers of the United States. . . ."[19]

If "senatorial courtesy" is somewhat unseemly, the President finds it a source of frustration for another reason as well: he is effectively prevented from making use of the appointment power to strengthen the hand of the national party, of which he is the leader. Even worse, the senator who actually selects the nominee inevitably uses his power to strengthen his state party organization—and it is support by that very organization that makes the senator sufficiently independent to defy the President and oppose his legislative program with impunity. Quite understandably, Woodrow Wilson characterized "senatorial courtesy" as "the ugliest deformity in our politics."[20]

Treaty Power

The fact that the Senate and not the House participates in the confirmation process is one of the most important considerations that help make it the more powerful of the two chambers. In another field, too, the Constitution gives it primacy. That field is foreign affairs.

[19] Article II, Section 2.
[20] Woodrow Wilson, *Congressional Government* (New York: Meridian, 1959), p. 160 (written in 1883). For a further discussion of patronage, see Ch. 1.

The most significant power that the Senate possesses in the area of foreign affairs relates to the treaty-making process. Largely because the consent of the Senate is needed before a treaty can go into effect, Presidents have concerned themselves far more with senatorial reactions to their foreign policy than with reactions in the House.

The framers clearly intended to give the Senate an active role in the making of treaties. Before the President could commit the Nation to such solemn international obligations, he was to receive not only the consent of the Senate but also its advice.[21] President Washington accordingly went directly to the Senate during his very first term in office for consultation regarding the terms of a treaty to be negotiated with the Indians. Instead of being received with the kind of respect he thought fitting for the President of the United States, he was treated with casualness and almost with disdain. Furious with the Senate, he resolved that never again would he set foot within its precincts. He never did.[22]

What impelled the Senate to behave so badly to Washington was an idea that its prerogatives would be enhanced if treaties were discussed without the inhibiting presence of the Chief Executive.[23] Events proved, however, that this was a woefully shortsighted view. Washington, stung by his humiliating experience, abandoned his intention of consulting with the Senate in the early—and crucial—stages of the treaty-making process. Instead, he instituted the practice of

[21] "[The President] shall have Power by and with the Advice and Consent of the Senate, to make Treaties, provided two-thirds of the Senators present concur; . . . . " Article II, Section 2.

[22] Edward S. Corwin, *The President: Office and Powers, 1787-1957* (New York: New York University Press, 1957), p. 210.

[23] James A. Robinson, *Congress and Foreign Policy-Making: A Study in Legislative Influence and Initiative* (Homewood, Ill.: Dorsey, 1962), pp. 117-18.

not soliciting help until a finished treaty was in his hands. Only at that point would the Senate be asked to "advise and consent" to the treaty. Senators would still be in possession of the admittedly formidable power to reject a treaty, but they would no longer be invited to help frame the agreement that they would eventually be asked to pass upon.[24]

Treaties accordingly are hammered out today in a manner that bears little resemblance to what the framers intended. In *The Federalist,* the hope had been expressed that the Senate would bring to bear qualities such as "talent, information, integrity, and deliberate investigation."[25] It was with such thoughts in mind that the delegates to the Constitutional Convention brought the Senate, instead of the House, into the treaty-making process. The more numerous House was considered too large for the kind of intimate consultation that was desirable for treaties. Moreover, there would be a better chance to preserve secrecy and act with expedition if only the members of the Senate were involved.

This line of thinking is today of only academic interest. The Senate at present has almost four times as many members as it did in 1789—more than half again as many as the first House, which was considered too large to be suitable. Not surprisingly, the House has chafed for decades about being excluded from treaty-making.

But there is an even more controversial aspect of the con-

---

[24] *Ibid.,* p. 118. Today, however, it is customary for members of the Senate Foreign Relations Committee to be consulted when a treaty is to be negotiated. And at times the Senate as a whole has helped to shape treaties by expressing itself in advance on the issues that would be posed. The Connally Resolution of 1943, for example, anticipated the treaty through which the United States would later join the United Nations, and the Vandenberg Resolution of 1948 foreshadowed the North Atlantic Treaty Organization.

[25] Hamilton, Jay, Madison, *op. cit.,* No. 64, p. 420.

stitutional provision on treaties: the requirement that two-thirds of the senators present must concur in their ratification. This provision was designed to enable two separate blocs of states to protect their particular economic interests against treaties harmful to them. The New England states would not find it difficult to block treaties threatening their fishery rights, and the southern states would similarly be able to protect navigation on the Mississippi River and the future of New Orleans as a port.[26] A general two-thirds requirement, however, meant far more than the ability of each of these two groups of states to exercise a kind of defensive veto. Any combination of senators totaling one third plus one of those voting could prevent ratification of a treaty that did not command their support, for one reason or another. Former Secretary of State John Hay once said bitterly: "There will always be 34 per cent of the Senate on the blackguard side of every question. . . ."[27] The authors of *The Federalist* had made a related point: "To give a minority a negative upon the majority (which is always the case where more than a majority is requisite to a decision), is, in its tendency, to subject the sense of the greater number to that of the lesser."[28]

The effect of the two-thirds requirement cannot adequately be measured in terms of the number of treaties which the Senate has actually refused to ratify (only 1 per cent of the total number submitted by the President). For on 250 occasions the Senate has by majority vote written important

[26] Robert A. Dahl, *Congress and Foreign Policy* (New Haven, Conn.: Yale Institute of International Studies, 1949), p. 24.

[27] Hay compared the prospects of a treaty in the Senate with those of a bull in the ring. "No one can say just how or when the final blow will fall, but one thing is certain: it will never leave the arena alive." W. R. Thayer, *Life and Letters of John Hay* (Boston: Houghton Mifflin, 1920), Vol. II, p. 393.

[28] Hamilton, Madison, Jay, *op. cit.*, No. 22, p. 135.

qualifications or reservations into treaties before ratifying them. A noted scholar tells us that most of the treaties rejected or amended by the Senate would have met a similar fate even if the two-thirds requirement had not existed.[29] The key word is "most." For an exclusively quantitative measurement conceals the fact that the treaties defeated by the two-thirds rule have been among the most important ones. It is clearly understatement to say that "the policy of the United States in these matters has been greatly affected by the attitude of the Senate."[30]

The most dramatic instance in which a treaty was done to death by the two-thirds requirement was the rejection of the Treaty of Versailles in 1919 because it provided for United States adherence to the Covenant of the League of Nations. Rejection of the treaty seemed due at least in part to President Wilson's failure to take influential senators with him to Versailles, where the negotiations had been held. Senatorial pique was particularly acute among the Republicans, who had long been irritated by what they considered Wilson's extreme partisanship.

At least two significant developments resulted from this monumental defeat of the President at the hands of the Senate. First, Wilson's successors sought to prevent a repetition of the Versailles debacle by resorting increasingly to the device of executive agreements, which are unlike treaties in that they do not require the concurrence of the Senate. And second, important steps were taken toward bipartisanship in foreign policy.

[29] Royden J. Dangerfield, *In Defense of the Senate: A Study in Treaty Making* (Norman: University of Oklahoma Press, 1933), *passim*. *Cf.* Kenneth W. Colegrove, *The American Senate and World Peace* (New York: Vanguard, 1944).

[30] Quincy Wright, "Introduction," in Dangerfield, *op. cit.*, p. xvi.

Executive Agreements

Executive agreements have become an increasingly popular presidential technique. Particularly during the administration of Franklin Roosevelt, when the United States abandoned its policy of isolationism and leaped onto the world stage, it became evident that only minimal use would be made of treaties in the formulation of international accords entered into by this country. The executive agreement had come into its own.

The term "executive agreement" does not appear in the Constitution. The authority of the President to negotiate such pacts is inferred from his constitutional powers as Commander-in-Chief of the American armed forces and from his position as what John Marshall called the "sole organ of the Nation in its external relations . . ."[31] The theory behind the executive agreement has been put well by an English student of American politics: "In any field in which the President as Commander-in-Chief or as director of foreign relations can act, he can permit himself to act by an agreement and can carry out this agreement."[32] On the basis of this theory, President Roosevelt traded American destroyers for British bases in World War II and President Truman committed American troops to the postwar occupation of Germany. And the Atlantic Charter, as well as the preliminary declaration of the United Nations, was created in the same way.

Agreements have been used in a wide variety of cases when treaties would have been in order. The precise difference between an executive agreement and a treaty is somewhat obscure. One possible distinction is that some question exists as to whether an executive agreement binds the successors of the

[31] Quoted in Corwin, op. cit., p. 177.
[32] Denis W. Brogan, An Introduction to American Politics (London: Hamish Hamilton, 1954), p. 308.

President who signed it; no such question can arise concerning the more solemn treaty obligation. Another observable difference is that in practice executive agreements have generally been used only for bilateral compacts; agreements that involve a joint enterprise of a group of nations have usually taken the form of treaties. It was by means of a treaty, for example, that American adherence to the United Nations Charter was accomplished; treaties were used also to authorize the participation of the United States in military alliances such as the North Atlantic Treaty Organization; and the partial nuclear test ban agreement of 1963 was submitted to the Senate in the form of a treaty.[33]

Although the constitutionality of executive agreements has been sustained,[34] the desirability of their almost unlimited use is open to serious question. For the American people can be kept completely in the dark regarding the contents of an executive agreement; a secret treaty, however, is almost inconceivable under the system requiring senatorial ratification.[35] At a time when foreign policy decisions may determine the

[33] Yet the United States joined "specialized organizations" of the United Nations (such as the Food and Agriculture Organization and the International Bank for Reconstruction and Development) not through treaty but by means of joint resolutions.

[34] United States v. Belmont, 301 U. S. 324 (1937), United States v. Pink, 315 U. S. 203 (1942). See also Wallace McClure, *International Executive Agreements: Democratic Procedure under the Constitution of the United States* (New York: Columbia University Press, 1941), pp. 368ff. and Elbert M. Byrd, *Treaties and Executive Agreements in the United States: Their Separate Roles and Limitations* (The Hague: N. V. Martinus Nijhoff's *Boekhandelen Vitgeversmaatschappij,* 1960), *passim.*

[35] Executive agreements, it has been said, expose the people to the "danger that the most important decisions affecting the foreign policy of the country will be made on the basis of facts not disclosed to the public and by methods so secret as to impair the practical capacity of the Senate and the House to ensure due deliberation." Arthur N. Holcombe, *Our More Perfect Union: From Eighteenth-Century Principles to Twentieth-Century Practice* (Cambridge: Harvard University Press, 1950), p. 282.

fate of the species, a curious paradox exists: the nation which once was unwilling to accept taxation without representation does not rebel today against the possibility that it may be consigned to extinction without representation.

Still, there will doubtless continue to be a temptation to resort to executive agreements if the two-thirds requirement for ratification of treaties is not modified. Senator Kefauver was one of those who perceived the ironical fact that the two-thirds rule, instead of operating to preserve the power of the Senate, is actually taking away that power. He warned that under strong Presidents who commanded wide public support, the rule "could lead to the virtual elimination of Congress from the vital field of foreign affairs, where the wisdom and experience of the peoples' representatives should be used as a check upon the powers and decisions of the Executive."[36] The most far-reaching reform of the two-thirds rule would be to authorize ratification of treaties by a simple majority in each of the two houses of Congress. With the support of Kefauver, at the time he was a representative, the House approved such a constitutional amendment, but the resolution was buried by the Senate Judiciary Committee.[37] It is understandable that the Senate does not relish the idea of accepting the House as an equal partner in the foreign policy field. But in time it may realize that to exercise a real power, even on a sharing basis, is better than to enjoy exclusive possession of a power that can hardly ever be used.

Bricker Amendment

Even if the Senate has not yet demonstrated any passion for reforming the system by which treaties are ratified, it has

[36] Estes Kefauver and Jack Levin, *A 20th-Century Congress* (New York: Duell, 1947), pp. 89-90.

[37] *Ibid.*, p. 91.

shown a lively interest in restricting the subject matter with which treaties may deal. Some senators are unhappy that the Constitution, which makes treaties "the law of the land," does not establish boundaries to define the subjects they may cover. Although an ordinary Act of Congress is invalid unless it is authorized by a constitutional grant of power to the Federal government, no such limitation is placed on what can be accomplished by treaty. Conservative senators think that there is no justification for permitting the Federal government to enlarge the area of its jurisdiction simply by acting through a treaty instead of a statute.

In line with this philosophy, a major campaign has been waged in favor of a constitutional amendment proposed by former Senator John W. Bricker (R., Ohio). The Bricker Amendment would in effect overturn a 1920 Supreme Court decision holding that a treaty can validly bestow on Congress powers that have not been granted by the Constitution. Justice Oliver Wendell Holmes, speaking for a seven-member majority, rejected the argument that "what an act of Congress could not do unaided, in derogation of the powers reserved to the states, a treaty cannot do." Holmes explained the Court's point of view in these words:

> It is obvious that there may be matters of the sharpest exigency for the national well being that an act of Congress could not deal with but that a treaty followed by such an act could, and it is not lightly to be assumed that, in matters requiring national action, "a power which must belong to and somewhere reside in every civilized government" is not to be found.[38]

Accordingly, the Court held that a Federal statute was valid although Congress' power to enact it rested on the provision of a treaty instead of a provision of the Constitution.

[38] Missouri v. Holland, 252 U. S. 416 (1920).

The Bricker Amendment would nullify the Supreme Court
decision with this provision: "A treaty shall become effective
as internal law in the United States only through legislation
which would be valid in the absence of a treaty." Although a
vociferous nationwide campaign was waged for the amendment, Senator Bricker could never convince even a simple
majority in the Senate[39] to give its consent. The Senate was
clearly unwilling to require that each state of the Union
would have to give its individual approval in order to validate
a treaty dealing with a subject not within the scope of the
enumerated powers of Congress.[40]

Without doubt, the general erosion of the Senate's treaty-
making power can be understood in part as a reaction against
the rejection of the Versailles Treaty in 1919. But that rejection had a second important consequence as well. It helped
bring about the phenomenon of a foreign policy supported in
its essentials by both Democrats and Republicans.

Bipartisanship in Foreign Policy

Franklin Roosevelt was one of the principal architects of
bipartisanship in foreign policy. Since it was generally accepted that the absence of Republicans at the peace conference in 1919 had almost guaranteed the defeat of the
Versailles treaty in the Senate, Roosevelt initiated the practice of soliciting the advice of Republicans and including their

[39] A two-thirds majority in both houses would have been needed to
submit the amendment to the states. Article V.

[40] The Bricker Amendment would also have placed serious restrictions
on the power of the President to enter into executive agreements. In
one of the many forms in which the Amendment was proposed to the
Senate, it contained this provision: "An international agreement other
than a treaty shall become effective as internal law in the United States
only by an Act of the Congress." In 1954, this provision won the approval of a majority in the Senate, but it fell one vote short of the
necessary two-thirds. The vote was 60-31. Noel T. Dowling, *Cases on
Constitutional Law* (5th ed.; Brooklyn: Foundation Press, 1954), p. 490.

foreign policy spokesmen in the most important postwar international conferences. The nearly unanimous ratification of the United Nations Charter by the Senate seemed to prove the wisdom of the practice.

In the years following World War II, bipartisanship in one form or another continued to be followed, by Presidents Truman, Eisenhower, Kennedy, and Johnson. A national foreign policy was formulated. Its fundamental tenets included containment of Communism, the building up of enormous military strength, and the creation of a system of alliances to encircle the Soviet Union. The fact that both political parties supported this policy meant that in a very real sense it was beyond public debate and insulated from revision at the polls. An atmosphere was created in which dissent against the basic elements of the policy was equated with woolly-headedness at best and with disloyalty at worst. In such conditions, criticism could come with impunity only from the bellicose right, which accepted the bedrock assumptions of the Cold War and limited itself to accusations that insufficient toughness was being exhibited.

In the days when bipartisanship in foreign policy was first conceived, there was already some fear that one of the consequences might be a stultifying uniformity of viewpoints. Such apprehension was expressed by Senator Arthur H. Vandenberg (R., Mich.), who had become the symbol of Republican acquiescence in President Roosevelt's foreign policy. Vandenberg warned that bipartisanship should not be taken to imply even the remotest surrender of free debate. Precisely because unity was desirable on foreign policy issues, he believed, discussion should be encouraged while policy was in the process of formulation.[41] This ideal, however, has not been achieved in practice. What has happened instead is that

[41] *The New York Times*, September 7, 1962, p. 28, col. 3 (city edition).

meaningful debate usually takes place only after policies have already been enunciated.

One of the principal results of bipartisanship and congressional-executive "cooperation" on international affairs has been to disarm Congress in general and the opposition party in particular. Each year, for example, the President appoints one senior congressman from each party as a member of the United States delegation to the annual session of the United Nations General Assembly. Service with the official delegation naturally helps convert the congressmen to Administration attitudes, and since the legislators are always influential members of the Foreign Relations and Foreign Affairs committees, the importance of the conversion cannot be exaggerated.

A serious question exists, however, as to whether Congress must reconcile itself permanently to an insignificant role in the shaping of American foreign policy. Power is there, waiting to be used. With the President obliged to depend on it for appropriations, Congress can exercise the same potent leverage in foreign policy as it does in other fields: executive agreements almost without exception require legislative implementation if they are not to remain pious expressions of intention; the hearings that are conducted by the Foreign Relations and Foreign Affairs committees can play a significant role in educating the American public on issues of foreign policy; the power to refuse confirmation to a presidential nominee is always present; and although the initiative in foreign policy is certainly in the hands of the Executive, Congress may use the device of the concurrent resolution to express its views.

Yet these weapons are seldom used in a creative sense. The concurrent resolution, for example, is hardly ever employed to check and criticize the conduct of foreign policy by the Executive Branch, but rather to "strengthen the hand" of the President as he pursues his own foreign policy objectives. It is almost as though Congress, recognizing that in the missile age its power to declare war is essentially meaningless,[42] has concluded that there is no self-respecting part left for it to play in foreign affairs.

Admittedly, it would be far from simple for Congress to act with imagination and originality in a field that has become highly specialized. Foreign policy has been increasingly preempted by executives at the expense of parliaments throughout the world. Doubtless there are objective factors that make it difficult to reverse this trend: only the Executive has access to the staggering volume of information that forms the basis for day-to-day decisions on foreign policy, and only the Executive is equipped to act with the speed that is often required in international politics. But neither of these factors casts any doubt on the competence of Congress to grapple successfully with the broad issues of foreign policy. The National Legislature could become the breeding ground for policy alternatives on the major issues. In this way, it would contribute far more to the Nation than it does by devoting itself to supervision of minute aspects of program administration.

[42] In 1950, President Truman committed the United States to one of the bloodiest wars in its history without even requesting congressional authorization, on the interesting semantic ground that the Korean conflict was not a war but rather a "police action."

14

Courts and Congress

THE BURDEN of interpreting congressional legislation falls on the Federal courts. In case after case, judges are called on to construe laws passed by Congress. The purpose sometimes is to ascertain whether a statute has been validly applied in the case being litigated. At other times, the courts are asked to make a constitutional determination: whether the enactment violates the Constitution and must therefore be invalidated. Only rarely is the wording of a Federal statute so clear and precise that reasonable men cannot differ as to its meaning. Ambiguity and imprecision can occasionally be traced to faulty draftsmanship, but the reason usually runs deeper.

Political realities in Congress are such that support for a measure tends to melt away with every effort to spell out exactly what is intended. In order to enhance the possibility that a bill will receive majority support, its sponsors are frequently led to sacrifice clarity for votes. In the words of one student of congressional behavior, "ambiguity and verbal compromise may be the very heart of a successful political formula, especially where the necessity for compromise is recognized but [where compromise] is difficult to achieve in explicit terms."[1] There may, that is, be majority support for some sort of bill to discourage secondary boycotts, but no agreement on what the bill should contain. The result in all probability will be a statute which is phrased in terms of calculated ambiguity. The allies in the uneasy coalition approving the bill agree tacitly to let the courts choose between the two or more interpretations that can validly be made of the legislative formula agreed on.

Even when Congress has thus almost commanded the courts to formulate policy, judges are unwilling to admit that they must perforce make a decision based in part on subjective factors. They accept the view that the courts can continue to play an important part in the American system of government only if they do not appear to be framing policy decisions.

This may help explain why judges, when engaged in the task of statutory interpretation, work so long and hard at what seems to be a completely objective aspect of their task: ascertaining the legislative intent. They pore through materials such as committee reports and statements made on the floor with such a consuming interest that they have been accused, only half in jest, of consulting the statute itself only when its legislative history is doubtful.[2]

Leaving to one side the nagging question of whether it is defensible to treat the heavily edited *Congressional Record* as if it were a verbatim account of floor proceedings,[3] a larger problem suggests itself. That problem goes to the heart of the

[1] David B. Truman, *The Governmental Process* (New York: Knopf, 1960), p. 393.

[2] Howard N. Mantel, "The Congressional Record: Fact or Fiction of the Legislative Process," *Western Political Quarterly*, XII (December 1959), p. 987 [reprinted in *Congressional Record*, January 19, 1960, p. 652].

[3] The unreliability of the *Record* is discussed in Ch. 10.

legislative process, for it is concerned fundamentally with the underlying assumption that such a thing as "legislative intent" exists at all. It is difficult enough to ascertain the intent of an action or statement by a single individual; when one goes a step farther and seeks to learn the intent of a group, he may be in quest of a philosophical absurdity. And the absurdity is compounded if Congress is the group with which one is dealing.

For Congress is so heterogeneous, its procedural machinery is so ill-adapted for rational decision-making, and the motives of its members are so unrelated to their verbal professions that it may be completely unreasonable to inquire after its intent. On what premise, for example, is it assumed that the chairman of a House committee speaks for his chamber as a whole, not to mention the Senate? What can one really infer about the will of the Senate from the fact that a certain provision was dropped from a bill in order to avert a filibuster? Can a compromise reached secretly in conference and presented to each chamber on an all-or-nothing basis really be said to reflect the will of a majority in each house? And in addition to such questions there is also the problem of whether presidential statements should be considered as part of the relevant record. The President, after all, may have had a completely different motive in signing the bill than any member of Congress did in voting for it.[4]

Alternatives Available

When Congress is offended by a Supreme Court decision based on an interpretation of the Constitution, it can do nothing by itself to prevent the Justices from having the last word.

---

[4] Supreme Court Justice Robert H. Jackson remarked: "It is not to be supposed that, in signing a bill, the President endorses the whole *Congressional Record*." He also attacked what he considered the common judicial policy of selecting "casual statements from floor debates, not always distinguished for candor or accuracy." Mantel, *op. cit.,* p. 653.

Only by initiating a constitutional amendment can it even attempt to overcome the decision. But when the Court rests its decision on statutory construction rather than constitutional interpretation, a quite different situation is presented. If the Court has found in legislation a meaning that members of Congress think unwarranted, an attempt may be made to reverse the effect of the judicial action by promoting passage of a new law. For instance, a Supreme Court decision that Congress had not meant to prevent the Department of Justice from obtaining access to copies of confidential Census reports was overturned by an act of Congress prohibiting such access.[5] In cases when Congress does not pass legislation to repudiate the judicial interpretation of a statute, the Supreme Court assumes that its interpretation has been accepted. Considering how much inertia and irrationality are built into the Federal legislative process, the Court, in refusing to desert an interpretation of the congressional will that Congress has failed to disown, may be inferring far too much from the failure of Congress to act.

If Congress gets angry enough at the Supreme Court, there are several courses of action available to it. One of these is the removal, by means of impeachment, of an offending Justice.[6] Not a single member of the Supreme Court, however, has been removed in this manner, and only one—Samuel Chase, in 1805—even had to undergo a trial in the Senate. Short of impeachment, Congress has no weapon it can use against individual members of the Court. The framers of the Constitution saw to that when they provided that all members of the Federal Judiciary should serve for life and be paid salaries that Congress could not diminish.[7]

[5] St. Regis Paper Company v. United States, 368 U. S. 208 (1961), overturned by 76 Stat. 922.

[6] The impeachment procedure is described on pp. 363-64, note 7.

[7] Article III, Section 1.

Even if the independence of the Supreme Court is constitutionally safeguarded, Congress is not entirely powerless to translate into action its displeasure with what the Court has done. For one thing, it can increase the size of the Court and thus enable the President to appoint members who will neutralize the incumbents.[8] President Franklin Roosevelt tried to persuade Congress to pack the Supreme Court in 1937, after the Justices who had been popularly labelled "The Nine Old Men" had invalidated some of the most significant New Deal measures. Congress declined to expand the size of the Court to conform with Roosevelt's wishes, but the President won his main point when the Justice whose vote had been crucial in giving the conservatives a majority[9] suddenly began to throw his support to the other side.

If Congress is averse to Court packing, it can try to curtail the appellate jurisdiction of the Supreme Court, thus preventing the Justices from handling cases in certain categories. Although this extreme action has not been taken since 1867,[10] it has been promoted vigorously in recent years as a way to prevent the Supreme Court from "interfering" with governmental activities directed against political dissenters.

Malapportionment

Contemporary criticism of the Supreme Court has centered around decisions involving "subversives" and racial segregation. In 1962, the Court earned itself still more criticism when

[8] This method, of course, is usable only if Congress does not find the political philosophy of the President as obnoxious as that of the Court. At times Congress has been in such violent disagreement with the President that it has wanted to prevent him from making any Supreme Court appointments at all. On such occasions it has sometimes provided that any vacancies arising on the bench were not to be filled until the number of Justices fell to a given level.

[9] Owen J. Roberts.

[10] See *Ex parte* McCardle, 7 Wall. 506 (1869).

it ventured into an area of direct concern to members of Congress. For the first time, the Justices opened the doors of the Federal courts to cases which involved malapportionment of legislative districts. The division of a state into districts varying significantly in terms of population has this baleful consequence for a democratic society: some citizens —those living in sparsely populated districts—have votes that mean more than others, although the political system of the Nation supposedly rests on the principle of one man, one vote.[11]

Malapportionment exists in the National Government as well as the various state legislatures. In Congress, the malapportionment of the Senate is constitutionally ordained: the equality of all states in the Senate was part of the "Great Compromise," under which the small states agreed to the creation of a strong National Government. But another type of malapportionment—completely unforeseen by the framers— is easily observable in the House of Representatives. The disparities in the size of congressional districts are so gross that the nearly one million constituents of the 5th Congressional District of Texas must be content with a single representative, although the mere 177 thousand residents of Michigan's 12th Congressional District are entitled to one representative, too.

On both the national and state levels, malapportionment is perpetrated by the legislatures of the individual states. For it is the task of a legislature to draw the lines that determine the size (as well as the shape) of congressional districts in its state, just as it is supposed to make appropriate alterations in its own composition to reflect shifts in population.

[11] Malapportionment is sometimes confused with gerrymandering, which means tampering with the shape of an electoral district to benefit one political party.

The rural portions of the state are commonly over-represented in the legislature. This is so because, although in state after state the population has been leaving the countryside and streaming into the cities, representatives of the non-urban areas have firmly refused to permit redistricting to take place. They have thus managed to retain in the Space Age numerical power that was given to them by virtue of the state's population distribution during the Horse-and-Buggy Age. And since they control the legislatures, they have also been able to favor the rural areas when dividing the state into congressional districts.

The malapportioned congressional districts that have been laid out by rural-dominated state legislatures have helped make the House of Representatives by far the more conservative branch of Congress. The framers anticipated that it would be the other way around, with the Senate representing the interests of economic conservatism against the radical tendencies which would probably exist in the popular legislative chamber. Contrary to what they expected, it has been the House rather than the Senate that has turned a deaf ear to the problems of the cities, for the rural legislator could not care less about subjects like urban decay, disorderly suburban growth, and critical conditions in education, housing, and transportation. The response made by the House to these problems might be significantly different if malapportionment were not present.[12]

The malapportionment that exists in the House does not confer any undue advantages on any states, but rather on particular areas within states. By act of Congress, the number of seats that a state is entitled to in the House is redetermined every ten years on the basis of census figures. If the percentage

[12] *Congressional Quarterly Weekly Report* has estimated that, in a numerically fair redistricting, rural areas would lose 16 seats in the House. September 20, 1963, p. 1642.

of the total national population living in a particular state has either increased or decreased significantly, the size of the state's delegation in the House will be altered accordingly, since—unless Congress decides otherwise—there are only 435 seats to go around. It is not states, then, that are the beneficiaries of the malapportionment which characterizes the House, but rather individual congressional districts.

Residents of the disadvantaged urban and suburban areas have long since abandoned hope that help will ever come voluntarily from the malapportioned state legislatures themselves. Since rights under the Federal Constitution are involved,[13] major efforts have been made to persuade the Federal Judiciary that the courts should step in to resolve the problem. Hopes that the courts would act were dashed, at least temporarily, in 1946. In a case in which gross disparities in the population of Illinois congressional districts were attacked as unconstitutional, the Supreme Court decided, by a 4-to-3 vote, that it would take no action.[14] Justice Felix Frankfurter, who spoke for himself and two other members of the majority, saw malapportionment as part of "an essentially political contest," in which judicial intervention would be highly improper. In his view, Congress was the only branch of the Federal government with power in this area. Political action, he hoped, would eventually solve the problem of malapportionment.

During the years that followed, however, the political action of which Frankfurter had spoken did not take place. Congress paid no attention to the problem,[15] while the mal-

[13] Section 1 of the Fourteenth Amendment provides that no state shall "deny to any person within its jurisdiction the equal protection of the laws."

[14] Colegrove v. Green, 328 U. S. 549 (1946).

[15] No serious consideration was given to a bill introduced repeatedly by Congressman Emanuel Celler (D., N. Y.) which would have imposed a requirement that congressional districts be both compact and con-

apportioned state legislatures themselves, of course, were content with the *status quo*. State courts generally did nothing,[16] and the Federal courts took their cue from Frankfurter's 1946 opinion.

It may have been this massive inaction that persuaded the Supreme Court to re-examine its position. Or perhaps it was merely that new members who had joined the Court after 1946 were not in accord with the judicial passivism of Justice Frankfurter. Whatever the cause or constellation of causes, the Court in 1962 acted to administer what may have been a fatal blow to at least the most extreme forms of legislative malapportionment. The Court's holding was not broad. The Justices did little more than decide that a Federal district court has jurisdiction to determine whether a state legislative apportionment is so unfair that it deprives some citizens of the equal protection of the laws.[17] Despite the narrow frame in which the majority opinion was cast,[18] it was widely recognized that the Court had initiated a process that would

---

tiguous. The bill would also have provided that the size of no congressional district could vary more than 20 per cent above or below the average for all districts in a state. At present there are variations far in excess of 20 per cent. The population of the 5th Congressional District of Texas, for example, is 118 per cent above the average district in the state. See Andrew W. Hacker, *Congressional Districting: The Issue of Equal Representation* (Washington, D. C.: The Brookings Institution, 1963), *passim*.

[16] One exception occurred in New Jersey, where the State Supreme Court gave the legislature a precise deadline (5 p.m. on February 1, 1961), by which time it was to reapportion its lower house. The legislature made it, with one hour and forty-five minutes to spare.

[17] Baker v. Carr, 369 U. S. 186 (1962). The case before the Court concerned Tennessee, whose legislature had not reapportioned the state since 1901. The result was a 19-1 disparity between the populations of the largest and smallest districts in the State. And Tennessee did not occupy first place in terms of the inequities that it tolerated.

[18] See Royce Hanson, "Courts in the Thicket: The Problem of Judicial Standards in Apportionment Cases," *American University Law Review*, XII (January, 1963), p. 51.

have near-revolutionary results. The passion with which Justice Frankfurter dissented from what he saw as the abandonment of his 1946 position indicated that he was fully cognizant of how sharp a break the Court had made with the past.

The case in which the Supreme Court acted involved *state* legislative districts rather than *congressional* districts. Congressional districting is a far more delicate matter. But the Court soon went on to apply the principles of the 1962 case to the malapportionment of congressional districts, too.[19] Even before it made that move, however, it was evident that the step it took regarding state legislative districts would have a profound, if only gradual, effect on the complexion of the House. For the end of the malapportionment of state legislative districts will result in the election of a greater number of urban-oriented members to the state legislatures. And it will be these reformed legislatures that will have the power to draw the lines of new congressional districts.

Sound and Fury

The Supreme Court made more enemies in Congress soon after its controversial decision on legislative districting when the same year and again in 1963 it invaded another sensitive area and held that both prayer and Bible reading in the public schools are unconstitutional. The uproar was deafening. "They put the Negroes in the schools—now they have put God out of the schools," fumed a southern congressman. Scarcely a day passed without a few brickbats hurled from the Capitol in the direction of the Supreme Court. Chief Justice Warren, author of the opinion in the 1954 school segregation cases,[20] became the principal target of an impeachment campaign. No one should be appointed to the Supreme Court

[19] Wesberry v. Sanders, 376 U. S. 1 (1964).
[20] Brown v. Board of Education, 347 U. S. 483; Bolling v. Sharpe, 347 U. S. 497.

without prior judicial experience, it was said. The Court should stop "coddling Communists." There should be an end to "judicial law making."[21]

This attack on the Supreme Court, like others in the past, has been prompted by congressional objections to specific judicial actions. Debate today tends to focus on these specifics, not—except for those belonging to a fringe on the far right— on the possibility of reconsidering the Court's role as supreme expositor and interpreter of the Constitution.[22] Responsible conservatives, although they are distressed by the decisions of the Warren Court, are prevented by their underlying ideology from trying to subvert the most conservative institution established by the Founding Fathers. The prospect, therefore, is that Congress will continue to inveigh against the Supreme Court for particular decisions, while at the same time casting no doubt on the Court's right to interpret authoritatively both the Constitution of the United States and the laws enacted under its authority.

[21] One congressman resorted to rhyme to register his protest against judicial law making:

> Of the United States we are the Supreme Court.
> Remaking the Constitution is our forte.
> Our present Constitution is but a relic of a former day,
> And we have dedicated ourselves to putting it safely
> away. . . .
> In the segregation cases we dealt a heavy blow,
> As out of the window the Constitution we did throw. . . .
> Congressional legislation we have remolded to meet
> our will,
> The congressional intention we have not hesitated to kill.

Congressional Record, September 21, 1962, pp. 19139-41 (daily edition).
[22] See Marbury v. Madison, 1 Cranch 137 (1803).

15

Congressional Ethics

CONGRESS IS ALMOST PURITANICAL in enforcing the highest possible standards of ethical conduct on members of the Executive Branch. Both virtue and the appearance of virtue are demanded. It is taken for granted, for example, that no official will hold stock in any company whose fortunes might be affected by his actions, or accept any gifts from people who might expect him to reciprocate. But Congress applies very different standards of behavior to its own members. It permits payrolls to be padded with relatives; it allows pleasure jaunts to be disguised as trips made for official business; and it also tolerates the existence of spectacular conflicts of interest.

A Washington columnist has listed some of the most obvious conflicts of interest with which Congress is riddled:

> Members . . . are engaged in the oil business, and they vote legislation giving special tax provisions to the oil industry. They are engaged in farming, and they vote on farm subsidies. They take legal fees from the railroads, and legislate on railroads. They are publishers, and they vote on second-class postal rates for their publications. They are lecturers, and they take lecture fees from groups who are affected by their legislation.

They are lawyers, and they make money from a wide range of clients who have a stake in legislation.[1]

One example will suffice. The late Senator Robert S. Kerr (D., Okla.) was a multimillionaire who made his money in oil and uranium. Yet he always voted on oil and uranium legislation, and two of his committee assignments were closely related to his financial interests. As a powerful member of the Finance Committee, which writes tax bills, he was in a position to protect the $27\frac{1}{2}$ per cent oil depletion allowance, a key factor behind the fabulous profits in the oil industry. And as chairman of the Space Committee he was ideally situated to press for those space ventures that would enhance the value of his uranium holdings.

Both the House and Senate have rules intended to preclude situations such as these. A House rule says that representatives shall vote on every question except if they have "a direct personal or pecuniary interest in the event of such question."[2] The Senate, too, permits a member to ask that he be excused from voting.[3] These rules were obviously derived from Jefferson's *Manual of Parliamentary Practice,* which provides categorically: "Where the private interests of a member are concerned in a bill or question, he is to withdraw." Since no man should be "a judge in his own cause," explained Jefferson, "it is for the honor of the House that this rule of immemorial observance should be strictly adhered to."[4] Yet in practice the two rules are seldom even mentioned and hardly ever observed.

In the typical conflict-of-interest situation, Federal law is

[1] Roscoe Drummond, *Oregon Journal,* June 11, 1958, reprinted in *Congressional Record,* June 24, 1958 (daily edition).

[2] Rule VIII.

[3] Rule XII.

[4] Section 17, Jefferson's *Manual of Parliamentary Practice,* published in House Document No. 619, 87th Congress, 2d Session, p. 115 (1963).

no more helpful than congressional rules. For the law makes it possible to charge a congressman with having committed a criminal offense only if he has taken money to cast his vote a certain way or to render any services in proceedings before a governmental agency. But it is extremely difficult to prove the existence of a connection between money paid to a congressman and services that he renders to the donor, and of course a member does not have to be bribed to vote against a project that would have unfavorable consequences on his personal financial situation.[5]

Because existing procedures have proved so inadequate in dealing with the problem of conflict of interest, a reform has been recommended. It has been proposed that congressmen be compelled to file annual statements of their outside income, on the theory that the voters at least have a right to know about any personal involvements of their congressmen that might affect performance of their public duties. Congress, however, seems unwilling to give a hearing to this recommendation. Members do not even readily admit that a problem exists. Senator Goldwater, for instance, said this to a critic who had expressed concern at conflicts that might arise for congressmen who also hold military reserve commissions: "By applying your logic, it would be impossible to find a person in the United States, short of a bum, who would not conceivably have a conflict of interest."[6] Several congressmen, fearing that disclosure legislation will never be enacted, have

[5] Convictions, though infrequent, are not nonexistent. In 1962, two members of the House were indicted for trying to influence the handling of a criminal case by the Department of Justice. The Government charged that money and real estate totalling almost $4 million changed hands. Both men, Thomas F. Johnson (D., Md.) and Frank W. Boykin (D., Ala.) were convicted and fined. In addition, Johnson received a six-month jail sentence.

[6] Letter to Dean Earl H. DeLong, School of Government and Public Administration, The American University, July 16, 1963.

instituted the practice of voluntarily making known the facts about their financial condition each year. Their action, however, has not set off a stampede.

Nepotism vies for first place with conflict of interest among the unethical practices of which congressmen are most often accused. An impressive number of members seem to find in their own family just the talent they need for their staff. Some of them increase their government salary 50 per cent or more by putting their wives on the payroll. Even first-term congressmen seem to learn the ropes quickly. In 1959, for example, at least 6 of the 82 new members of the House put their wives on the payroll within days after taking their oaths as members of Congress. Interestingly, the jobs for which close relatives are favored seldom seem to necessitate putting in an appearance at the office.

Newsmen who try to collect information on "relativism" in Congress have a most difficult task. It is not easy to uncover the facts, for example, when the wife of a congressman uses her maiden name or when his daughter uses her married name. There was a time, however, when reporters wished that they had only this sort of problem to contend with. In 1947 and 1948 the Senate kept from public view even the barest facts on salaries of employees in the offices of individual members and on the staffs of committees. It then relented, and for the next ten years a lump sum amount was disclosed for each office and each committee, but it was impossible to tell from this how the money was being divided among the various employees. Continuous needling by the press convinced the Senate in 1959 that as long as it practiced concealment it would be widely suspected of having something to conceal. In the 1960 fiscal year, therefore, it began to publish detailed quarterly and annual salary reports.

Few congressmen are willing to admit that relatives may

be placed on payrolls for reasons that have nothing to do with their competence. One of the exceptions, the late Senator Kefauver, candidly admitted when he was a member of the House that nepotism was practiced, but he insisted it was "the only way for some members to avoid bankruptcy" as long as congressional salaries remained low.[7] Salaries have since been raised to the respectable sum of $22,500, but nepotism is as widespread as ever—and once again there is serious talk about another increase in the pay of congressmen. Such an increase would doubtless be justified. A congressman has to maintain one home in his constituency and one in Washington, and his social, political, and travel expenses quickly eat up both his salary and his allowances.[8] But no matter how much congressmen are paid, there will always doubtless be some who covet even more and will use the device of nepotism to get it. Others will continue to seek additional funds by doing work for their old law firms, by lecturing for money, and by accepting subsidies from wealthy supporters. And each of these practices, too, poses acute ethical problems.

Although the argument can be made that low salaries help account for some unethical practices in Congress, no such defense can be made for one of the most unscrupulous wastes of the taxpayers' money—junketing. Legitimate travel on congressional business can, of course, be of great value to the institution of which the congressman is a member and the Nation which he serves. Since the interests of the United States Government today encompass the globe, there is nothing automatically suspect about a trip abroad at public expense. But:

[7] Estes Kefauver and Jack Levin, *A 20th-Century Congress* (New York: Duell, 1947), p. 216.

[8] Donald R. Matthews, *U. S. Senators and Their World* (Chapel Hill: University of North Carolina Press, 1960), pp. 87-89.

—The "number of statesmen who have found it necessary to inspect American facilities in Paris and Rome is amazing. . . ."[9]

—A committee chairman had the State Department plan a trip for him that included theatre tickets in London, reservations at the Lido night club in Paris, and a six-day boating excursion through the Greek islands.[10]

—Congressmen who have been defeated for re-election have often managed to spend their remaining weeks in office traveling abroad—at government expense, of course. After the 1962 election, for example, at least ten "lame ducks" went on junkets. Since they had already been turned out of office, there was some question as to whether the public would be able to benefit from all that they may have learned during their trips.[11]

—Congressmen have been reimbursed without challenge for "bar bills altered to appear as 'food,' chits for lengthy excursions to resort areas, and excessive charges categorized as 'tips.' "[12]

—A southern senator applies himself assiduously to realizing his announced ambition to visit every country in the world while he is in the Senate. In a remarkable number of the countries he has visited, his statements—including racist comments made while he was in Africa—created serious embarrassment for the United States Government.[13]

[9] *Ibid.*, p. 80.

[10] *The New York Times,* September 6, 1962, p. 18, col. 3 (late city edition). The congressman was Adam Clayton Powell, Jr. (D., N. Y.), chairman of the House Committee on Education and Labor.

[11] *Ibid.,* November 20, 1962, p. 32, col. 2 (city edition).

[12] Douglass Cater, "Who Checks the Congressional Expense Account?" *Reporter,* October 11, 1962, p. 33, based on material published by Don Oberdorfer and Walter Pincus in the *Chicago Daily News* and other Knight newspapers in 1960.

[13] See, for example, *The New York Times,* December 2, 1962, p. 50, col. 4 (late city edition). The senator is Allen J. Ellender (D., La.).

Stung by press criticism of junketeering, the House in 1963 took a step toward meeting at least one aspect of the problem. Before it acted, representatives had been helping themselves freely to "counterpart funds," which are foreign currencies deposited to the credit of the United States by recipients of its aid programs but available for spending only in the particular country that has supplied them. The House decided to prohibit members from drawing on counterpart funds for more than the standard travel allowances established for Government employees. In addition, only the members of five committees with overseas responsibilities[14] could travel abroad on authorized funds without the specific approval of the House.

It seems that only the pressure of publicity is effective in persuading congressmen that honesty is the best policy. Some staff members, too, need a little adverse publicity to convince them that they should not emulate congressmen. In 1963, for instance, a Washington newspaper revealed that the Clerk of the House—the chief administrative officer of that body—was using his government-furnished Cadillac for trips to out-of-town race tracks. The Clerk defended himself by saying that he also used the car for trips to church, but the press exposé persuaded Speaker McCormack to announce that the Clerk would no longer use the vehicle at all except "for official purposes." In the same year, the secretary to the Senate majority resigned under fire after unsavory facts about his outside business interests had been exposed in a private lawsuit.

It was Juvenal who asked the question, *"Quis custodiet ipsos custodes?"* Congressmen, who so zealously guard the public treasury from officials of the Executive Branch, are still not prepared to reply and tell us "who will guard the guards themselves."

[14] Armed Services, Foreign Affairs, Government Operations, Interior and Insular Affairs, and Science and Astronautics.

Conclusion: The Limits of
Congressional Reform

CONGRESS IS TODAY UNDER HEAVY ATTACK along a broad front. It is accused of being slow, inefficient, and haphazard, and shot through with conflicts of interest. Its procedures are stigmatized as undemocratic, irrational, and obstructionist. Its representative character is thrown into serious question and criticism is levelled too at the extent to which its leaders exercise power without commensurate responsibility and accountability. The demand for reform is widespread.

At various other times in the Nation's history, defects in the operation of Congress have been recognized and attempts made to eliminate them through reform. But the unpleasant truth is that reform has seldom accomplished its intended purpose and occasionally has created new and even more serious problems.

In 1910, for example, the House underwent drastic reform after a revolt against the dictatorial power of Speaker Cannon. The revolt was designed to force the democratization of procedure and the diffusion of power. Both aims were achieved, but in the process even greater problems were created. Before 1910, it had been possible for an irate electorate to punish the party of the Speaker for what it had done or failed to do. The party could not defend itself by insisting that it had lacked authority to fulfill its campaign promises. Members of the opposition party and even members of the majority party might resent the inconsequential role into which they had been shunted by the Speaker's pre-eminence, but this was of scant importance to the voter, who was more concerned with being able to hold somebody accountable for what government was doing than with enhancing the self-esteem of representatives.[1]

Just as the 1910 reform was not an unmitigated success, the optimism that attended passage of the 1946 Legislative Reorganization Act soon proved to have been excessive. Although the new law was designed to strengthen Congress by streamlining its procedures and providing professional assistance in the discharge of its legislative duties, these goals have not been realized. Duplication and inefficiency are as rife today as ever before, and congressmen continue to wait hand and foot on their constituents instead of giving priority to their work as members of the National Legislature.

The reforms of 1910 and 1946 left untouched two fundamental problems that must be faced if Congress is to achieve its true potential in the American governmental system.

[1] Somewhat similarly, the binding caucus that operated among the Democrats during the first Wilson Administration made congressmen little more than cogs in a machine once their party had taken a decision. Abandonment of the binding caucus, however, meant that even when the Democrats were nominally the majority party they could seldom count on majority support for their program unless they could attract votes from some Republicans. Government by a majority party on which the people could pass judgment at the polls yielded to government by coalitions that could never be brought to book.

Neither problem can be solved through mere institutional tinkering, for each one goes to the heart of American politics.

The first problem relates to the operation of the two-party system. Every four years, each party assembles in a national convention and produces a statement of principles on which its candidates are presumed to stand. The party's representatives in Congress, however, almost invariably pay little attention to this platform. Thus the voter only deludes himself if he casts his vote for a congressional candidate on the assumption that the man will give his support to the program of the party whose emblem he wears.

The irrationality does not stop here. Every aspect of the organization of Congress rests on the unspoken assumption that party lines really mean something. The Speakership, the committee chairmanships, and a majority of the seats on each committee go to representatives of the party whose candidates hold the most seats in the house in question. But such an organizational scheme makes sense only if the two parties stand for different programs and each candidate identifies himself with the program of his party. These conditions are not being met, and serious frustration is the inevitable consequence. Because of the seniority system, for example, a voter who supports a candidate for his stand on a particular issue may actually be helping to give a chairmanship to a congressman who is on the opposite side of that very issue.

A second fundamental problem regarding Congress is the local orientation of its members. Representatives, who are chosen from single-member constituencies, and senators, who are chosen from dual-member constituencies, need only satisfy their individual electorates in order to assure themselves of continuation in office. Because there is no penalty for one who is faithless to party principles, the member can be pardoned if he concentrates on trying to curry favor with his constituents through crass methods such as promoting the establishment of Federal projects in the locality and playing the part of an errand boy whenever a petty favor is asked of him. Instead of being concerned with how best to represent his constituency, he concentrates rather on how best to manipulate it. The voters are often looked on as nothing but troublesome creatures who must be placated so that they will let him stay in Congress where he can continue to seek personal power—not for its own sake, he insists, but for the good it will enable him to do.

At a time when problems such as localism and party irresponsibility fairly cry out for solution, more and more senators and representatives are becoming interested in the subject of congressional reform. There is increasing talk about establishing a joint committee, modeled after the LaFollette-Monroney Committee of 1945, to recommend a new Legislative Reorganization Act. The bleak prospect, however, is that if such a committee is created at all it will almost surely be foreclosed from dealing with the fundamental problems. Like the 1945 committee, it will probably not even be allowed to examine the cloture rule and the seniority system.

Without any doubt, the reforms that are really needed will not emanate from a willing Congress. The situation will change only if an aroused public makes it clear to representatives and senators that Congress is the property of the American people as a whole, not the private preserve of the 535 men elected to serve in it. Not until then can Congress be expected to begin laying the groundwork for the kind of restructuring that is needed if representative democracy is to regain the respect it enjoyed when there was a true appreciation of its meaning and its worth.

Books on Congress

Acheson, Dean G. *A Citizen Looks at Congress*. New York: Harper, 1957.

American Political Science Association, Committee on Political Parties. *Toward a More Responsible Two-Party System*. New York: Rinehart, 1950 (also published as a supplement to Volume XLIV of the *American Political Science Review*, 1950).

Association of the Bar of the City of New York. *Conflict of Interest and Federal Service*. Cambridge: Harvard University Press, 1960.

Atkinson, C. R. *The Committee on Rules and the Overthrow of Speaker Cannon*. New York: Columbia University Press, 1911.

Bailey, Stephen K. *Congress Makes a Law: The Story behind the Employment Act of 1946*. New York: Columbia University Press, 1950.

———— and Samuel, Howard D. *Congress at Work*. New York: Holt, 1952.

Barth, Alan. *Government by Investigation*. New York: Viking, 1955.

Beck, Carl. *Contempt of Congress*. New Orleans: Hauser, 1959.

Berman, Daniel M. *A Bill Becomes a Law: The Civil Rights Act of 1960*. New York: Macmillan, 1962.

Binkley, Wilfred. *President and Congress*. New York: Vintage, 1962.

Bone, Hugh A. *Party Committees and National Politics*. Seattle: University of Washington Press, 1958.

Buckley, William F., ed. *The Committee and Its Critics*. New York: Putnam, 1962 (on the House Committee on Un-American Activities).

Burdette, Franklin L. *Filibustering in the Senate*. Princeton, N.J.: Princeton University Press, 1940.

Burkhead, Jesse. *Government Budgeting*. New York: Wiley, 1956.

Burnham, James. *Congress and the American Tradition*. Chicago: Regnery, 1959.

Burns, James M. *Congress on Trial: The Legislative Process and the Administrative State*. New York: Harper, 1949.

――――. *The Deadlock of Democracy: Four-Party Politics in America*. Englewood Cliffs, N.J.: Prentice-Hall, 1963.

Byrd, Elbert M. *Treaties and Executive Agreements in the United States: Their Separate Roles and Limitations*. The Hague: Nijhoff, 1960.

Cannon, Clarence. *Cannon's Procedure in the House of Representatives*. Washington: Government Printing Office, 1944.

Carr, Robert K. *The House Committee on Un-American Activities, 1945-1950*. Ithaca, N.Y.: Cornell University Press, 1952.

Carroll, Holbert N. *The House of Representatives and Foreign Affairs*. Pittsburgh: University of Pittsburgh Press, 1958.

Ch'iu, Ch'ang-wei. *The Speaker of the House of Representatives since 1896*. New York: Columbia University Press, 1928.

Clapp, Charles E. *The Congressman: His Work as He Sees It*. Washington, D.C.: The Brookings Institution, 1963.

Clark, Joseph S. *Congress: The Sapless Branch*. New York: Harper & Row, 1964.

――――. *The Senate Establishment*. New York: Hill and Wang, 1963.

Colegrove, Kenneth. *The American Senate and World Peace*. New York: Vanguard, 1944.

Dahl, Robert A. *Congress and Foreign Policy*. New Haven, Conn.: Yale Institute of International Studies, 1949.

Dangerfield, Royden J. *In Defense of the Senate: A Study in Treatymaking*. Norman: University of Oklahoma Press, 1933.

Deakin, James. *Pressure on the Potomac*. New York: Holt, 1964.

De Grazia, Alfred. *Apportionment and Representative Government*. New York: Praeger, 1963.

Dimock, Marshall E. *Congressional Investigating Committees*. Baltimore: Johns Hopkins Press, 1929.

Eberling, Ernest J. *Congressional Investigations: A Study of the Origin and Development of the Power of Congress to Investigate and Punish for Contempt*. New York: Columbia University Press, 1928.

Egger, Rowland and Harris, Joseph P. *The President and Congress*. New York: McGraw-Hill, 1963.

Evins, Joe L. *Understanding Congress*. New York: Potter, 1963.

Farnsworth, David N. *The Senate Committee on Foreign Relations*. Urbana: University of Illinois Press, 1961.

Follett, M. P. *The Speaker of the House of Representatives*. New York: Longmans, Green, 1896.

Freeman, J. Leiper. *The Political Process: Executive Bureau-Legislative Committee Relations*. New York: Random House, 1955.

Froman, Lewis A., Jr. *Congressmen and their Constituencies*. Chicago: Rand McNally, 1963.

Fuller, Hubert Bruce. *The Speakers of the House*. Boston: Little, Brown, 1909.

Galloway, George B. *Congress at the Crossroads*. New York: Crowell, 1946.

———. *History of the House of Representatives*. New York: Crowell, 1962 (also published in a shorter version by the Government Printing Office).

———. *The Legislative Process in Congress*. New York: Crowell, 1953.

Grassmuck, George L. *Sectional Biases in Congress on Foreign Policy*. Baltimore: Johns Hopkins Press, 1951.

Green, Harold P. and Rosenthal, Alan. *Government of the Atom: The Integration of Powers*. New York: Atherton, 1963.

Griffith, Ernest. *Congress: Its Contemporary Role*. New York: New York University Press, 1961.

Gross, Bertram. *The Legislative Struggle: A Study in Social Combat*. New York: McGraw-Hill, 1953.

Hacker, Andrew W. *Congressional Districting: The Issue of Equal Representation*. Washington, D.C.: The Brookings Institution, 1963.

Harris, Joseph P. *The Advice and Consent of the Senate: A Study of the Confirmation of Appointments by the United States Senate*. Berkeley: University of California Press, 1953.

Hasbrouck, Paul DeWitt. *Party Government in the House of Representatives*. New York: Macmillan, 1927.

Haynes, George H. *The Senate of the United States*. Boston: Houghton Mifflin, 1938.

Heller, Robert. *Strengthening the Congress*. Washington: National Planning Association, 1945.

Herring, E. Pendleton. *Group Representation before Congress*. Baltimore: Johns Hopkins Press, 1929.

————. *Presidential Leadership: The Political Relations of Congress and the Chief Executive*. New York: Rinehart, 1940.

Hinds, Asher C. and Cannon, Clarence. *Precedents of the House of Representatives of the United States*. Washington: Government Printing Office, 1907 and 1936.

Horn, Stephen. *The Cabinet and Congress*. New York: Columbia University Press, 1960.

Huntington, Samuel P. *The Common Defense: Strategic Programs in National Politics*. New York: Columbia University Press, 1961.

Huzar, Elias. *The Purse and the Sword: Control of the Army by Congress through Military Appropriations*. Ithaca, N.Y.: Cornell University Press, 1950.

Hyneman, Charles S. *Bureaucracy in a Democracy*. New York: Harper, 1950.

Jewell, Malcolm E., ed. *The Politics of Reapportionment*. New York: Atherton, 1962.

Johnsen, Julia E., ed. *The Investigating Powers of Congress*. New York: Wilson, 1951.

Kefauver, Estes and Levin, Jack. *A 20th-Century Congress*. New York: Duell, 1947.

Key, V. O., Jr. *Politics, Parties, and Pressure Groups*. New York: Crowell, 1958.

Kofmehl, Kenneth. *Professional Staffs of Congress*. West Lafayette, Ind.: Purdue University [Studies: Humanities Series], 1962.

Luce, Robert, *Congress: An Explanation*. Cambridge: Harvard University Press, 1926.

———. *Legislative Assemblies*. Boston: Houghton Mifflin, 1924.

———. *Legislative Problems*. Boston: Houghton Mifflin, 1935.

———. *Legislative Procedure*. Boston: Houghton Mifflin, 1922.

Maass, Arthur A. *Muddy Waters: The Army Engineers and the Nation's Rivers*. Cambridge: Harvard University Press, 1951.

MacNeil, Neil. *Forge of Democracy: The House of Representatives*. New York: McKay, 1963.

Martin, Joe (as told to Robert J. Donovan). *My First Fifty Years in Politics*. New York: McGraw-Hill, 1960.

Mason, Edward Campbell. *The Veto Power: Its Origin, Development, and Function in the Government of the United States, 1789-1889*. Boston: Ginn, 1890.

Matthews, Donald R. *U. S. Senators and their World*. Chapel Hill: University of North Carolina Press, 1960.

McClure, Wallace. *International Executive Agreements: Democratic Procedure under the Constitution of the United States*. New York: Columbia University Press, 1941.

McConachie, L. G. *Congressional Committees: A Study of the*

Origin and Development of our National and Local Legislative Methods. New York: Crowell, 1898.

McCown, Ada C. *The Congressional Conference Committee.* New York: Columbia University Press, 1927.

McGeary, M. Nelson. *The Development of Congressional Investigative Power.* New York: Columbia University Press, 1940.

McPhee, William N. and Glaser, William A., eds. *Public Opinion and Congressional Elections.* New York: Free Press, 1962.

Miller, Clem. (John W. Baker, ed.) *Member of the House.* New York: Scribner, 1962.

Murphy, Walter F. *Congress and the Court: A Case Study in the American Political Process.* Chicago: University of Chicago Press, 1962.

Nelson, Harold L. *Libel in News of Congressional Investigating Committees.* Minneapolis: University of Minnesota Press, 1961.

Peabody, Robert L. and Polsby, Nelson W., eds. *New Prospectives on the House of Representatives.* Chicago: Rand McNally, 1963.

Pritchett, C. Herman. *Congress versus the Supreme Court, 1957-1960.* Minneapolis: University of Minnesota Press, 1961.

Rhode, William E. *Committee Clearance of Administrative Decisions.* East Lansing: Michigan State University Bureau of Social and Political Research, 1959.

Riddick, Floyd M. *The United States Congress: Organization and Procedure.* Manassas, Va.: National Capitol Publishers, 1949.

Robinson, James A. *Congress and Foreign Policy-Making: A Study in Legislative Influence and Initiative.* Homewood, Ill.: Dorsey, 1962.

———. The House Rules Committee. Indianapolis: Bobbs-Merrill, 1963.

Rogers, Lindsay. *The American Senate.* New York: Crofts, 1931.

Schattschneider, Elmer E. *Party Government*. New York: Rinehart, 1942.

————. *The Struggle for Party Government*. College Park: University of Maryland, Department of Government and Politics, 1948.

Smithies, Arthur. *The Budgetary Process in the United States*. New York: McGraw-Hill, 1955.

Steiner, Gilbert Y. *The Congressional Conference Committee. Seventieth to Eightieth Congresses*. Urbana: University of Illinois Press, 1951.

Taylor, Telford. *Grand Inquest*. New York: Simon and Schuster, 1954.

Thomas, Norman C. and Lamb, Karl A. *Congress: Politics and Practice*. New York: Random House, 1964.

Truman, David B. *The Congressional Party: A Case Study*. New York: Wiley, 1959.

Turner, Julius. *Party and Constituency: Pressures on Congress*. Baltimore: Johns Hopkins Press, 1951.

Wahlke, John C. and Eulau, Heinz. *Legislative Behavior*. Glencoe, Ill.: Free Press, 1959.

Walker, Harvey. *The Legislative Process: Lawmaking in the United States*. New York: Ronald, 1948.

Wallace, Robert Ash. *Congressional Control of Federal Spending*. Detroit: Wayne State University Press, 1960.

Westerfield, H. Bradford. *Foreign Policy and Party Politics: Pearl Harbor to Korea*. New Haven, Conn.: Yale University Press, 1955.

Westphal, Albert C. F. *The House Committee on Foreign Affairs*. New York: Columbia University Press, 1942.

White, William S. *Citadel: The Story of the U. S. Senate*. New York: Harper, 1956.

Wilmerding, Lucius, Jr. *The Spending Power: A History of the Efforts of Congress to Control Expenditures*. New Haven, Conn.: Yale University Press, 1943.

Wilson, H. H. *Congress: Corruption and Compromise.* New York: Rinehart, 1951.

Wilson, Woodrow. *Congressional Government.* New York: Meridian Books, 1959 (originally published in 1885).

————. *Constitutional Government in the United States.* New York: Columbia University Press, 1908.

Young, Roland. *The American Congress.* New York: Harper, 1958.

————. *This is Congress.* New York: Knopf, 1943.

INDEX

absentee voting
  in committee, *see* proxy
  on the floor, *see* pairs, "live"
absenteeism, 45n., 154, 219, 234f.,
    272, 275f., 278, 295
accountability, 49, 129
Acheson, Dean G., 94, 94n.
"across the board," 352
act, 302
Adams, John, 53 f., 73, 313
adjournment, 59, 62, 157n., 161,
    161n., 165, 165n., 211, 272,
    272n., 294, 294n., 300, 310
  sine die, 161n., 257, 295, 297,
    312n., 316
administration, supervision of,
    167n., 172, 357ff., 381
  by Appropriations Committees,
    see Appropriations Com-
    mittees, supervision of ad-
    ministration by
  by General Accounting office,
    see General Accounting Of-
    fice
  by Government Operations Com-
    mittees, *see* Government
    Operations Committees
  investigations, *see under* com-
    mittees, investigations by

administration—*Contd.*
  by legislative committees, *see un-
    der* committees, legislative
  legislative veto, 170ff., 170n.,
    358, 358n.
administrative assistant, *see under*
    staffs, personal
"advice and consent," 361, 369ff.
Africa, 398
agencies, executive, *see* executive
    agencies
Agency for International Devel-
    opment, *see* International
    Development, Agency for
agreements, executive, *see* execu-
    tive agreements
agriculture committees, 81, 103,
    149, 350
Agriculture, Department of, 58,
    81, 93, 201, 323, 348
Alabama, 38, 39n.
Alaska, 41n., 100n., 290
Albert, Carl, 135
All-Republican Conference, 242
"alphabet agencies," 83n.
ambassadors, 363f.
amendments
  in committee, 46, 157, 162, 166,
    207, 251, 303
  constitutional, 157n., 312n.,

413